P9-ARO-450

Secrets of the National Parks

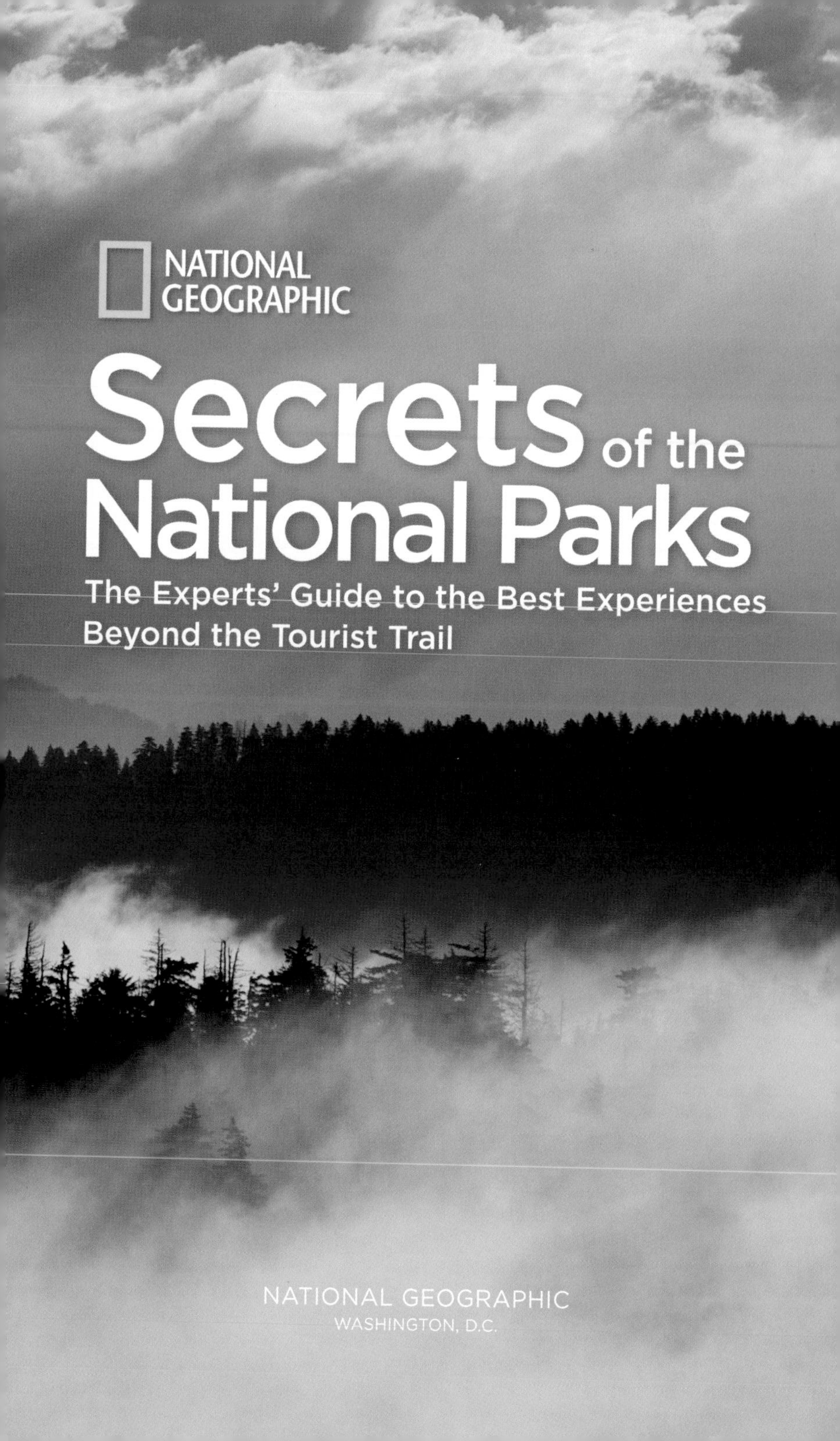

NATIONAL GEOGRAPHIC

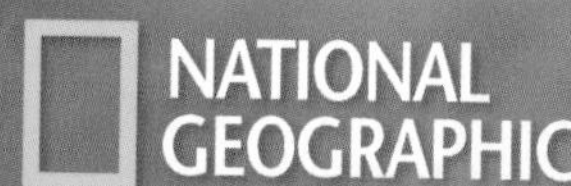

Secrets of the National Parks

The Experts' Guide to the Best Experiences Beyond the Tourist Trail

NATIONAL GEOGRAPHIC
WASHINGTON, D.C.

Contents

Pages 2-3 Newfound Gap, Great Smoky Mountains National Park
Page 4 Chisos Mountains, Big Bend National Park

INTRODUCTION

Our national parks are places of majesty that hold secrets large and small for those with a curious eye and adventurous spirit. Even our most traveled parks are constant sources of discovery, as I have found in my years working with the National Park Trust.

For 30 years, the Trust has worked to acquire privately held areas in our parks (including several of those mentioned below), to fulfill the vision of the National Park System's founding fathers to set aside lands "for the benefit and enjoyment of the people"—and, more recently, to educate future generations of conservationists in the preservation and protection of those critical areas. The pursuit of these missions has led me to look at our parks through a lens of discovery. Let me share a few secrets.

Here's the secret: We are drawn to the fact that, for the first time in human history, land—great sections of our beautiful natural landscape—was set aside, not for kings or noblemen or the very rich, but for everyone, for all time.

—KEN BURNS
Filmmaker
National Park Trust 2009 Recipient
American Park Experience Award

Lassen Volcanic National Park in northeastern California is a little-visited gem—a vast park dominated by a volcano and studded with lakes, with wonderful hiking and camping. A hike to the summit of Lassen Peak along a trail maintained in part by young conservationists is a memorable experience. It is brought to life, however, by the story of a trek made by three hikers in 1915 just after a volcanic eruption. Unfortunately for the hikers, as they neared the top there was a second explosion. Two members of the party escaped the peak; the third was left unconscious on the volcano. Miraculously, he survived and, when he awoke, saw an expanse of lava and miles of devastation spread below him. With a little effort, today one can stand on his spot and share his feeling of awe as he surveyed the devastated area.

In comparison to Lassen, Shenandoah National Park in Virginia is less dramatic, yet it is full of quiet corners and secrets of its own. One of my favorites is late spring along the Hughes River. A walk along the Hughes on the first hot weekend in June has been a wonderful time for our youngsters to play in its brimming pools and falls, and then dry in the sun. On one of our visits, a fat and lazy diamondback rattler shared the sun with us. And only a short drive away are the little-visited West Virginia homes of the George Washington family, another retreat from the heat of a Piedmont summer.

Our national parks include important aquatic resources. The rugged yet fragile ecosystem of the Virgin Islands National Park is best seen when you are in (and under) its waters. In the last century, the distance by boat around St. John was cut by using a narrow isthmus just outside the park to pull boats across the island. The "pull-over" is a little used entry for snorkelers not only to enjoy the underwater beauty of the park, but also to appreciate the interaction of water and land that makes the place so special.

Each national park has its secrets, whether it's walleyed pike spawning in a trickle in the middle of Voyageurs in Minnesota, or grizzlies viewed from the old school bus that runs deep into Alaska's Denali, or bugling elk at dusk in Wyoming's Grand Teton. In Mojave National Preserve, near Death Valley and Joshua Tree National Parks in the Southwest, the Trust co-sponsored a group of young students who, cameras in hand, explored the secrets of the endangered desert tortoise. Their book of photography, *Tortoises Through the Lens,* is a testament to the wonders of our parks when seen through fresh eyes. We hope this book and its secrets will encourage you, like these young people, to explore our parks and to share your secrets with family, friends, and the National Park Trust. And be sure to bring our mascot, Buddy Bison, along.

—F. WILLIAM BROWNELL
Chair, Board of Trustees
National Park Trust

Manzanita Lake, Lassen Volcanic National Park

ABOUT THIS BOOK

This is a book of secrets—hundreds of items of information designed to help you get the most out of exploring America's true treasures, our national parks.

For this guide, the editors of National Geographic called on some of the best nature writers and most experienced travelers to visit 32 of the most popular parks across the nation. Their mission? Tell us about the hidden gems in the places off the well-beaten tourist tracks, those lesser known experiences that can make a trip to a national park truly special, exciting, and memorable.

Yes, there are still secrets to be found in such long-traveled parks as the Grand Canyon, Death Valley, Petrified Forest, Haleakalā, and Wind Cave (to name only a few). Our writers-at-large talked to park rangers,

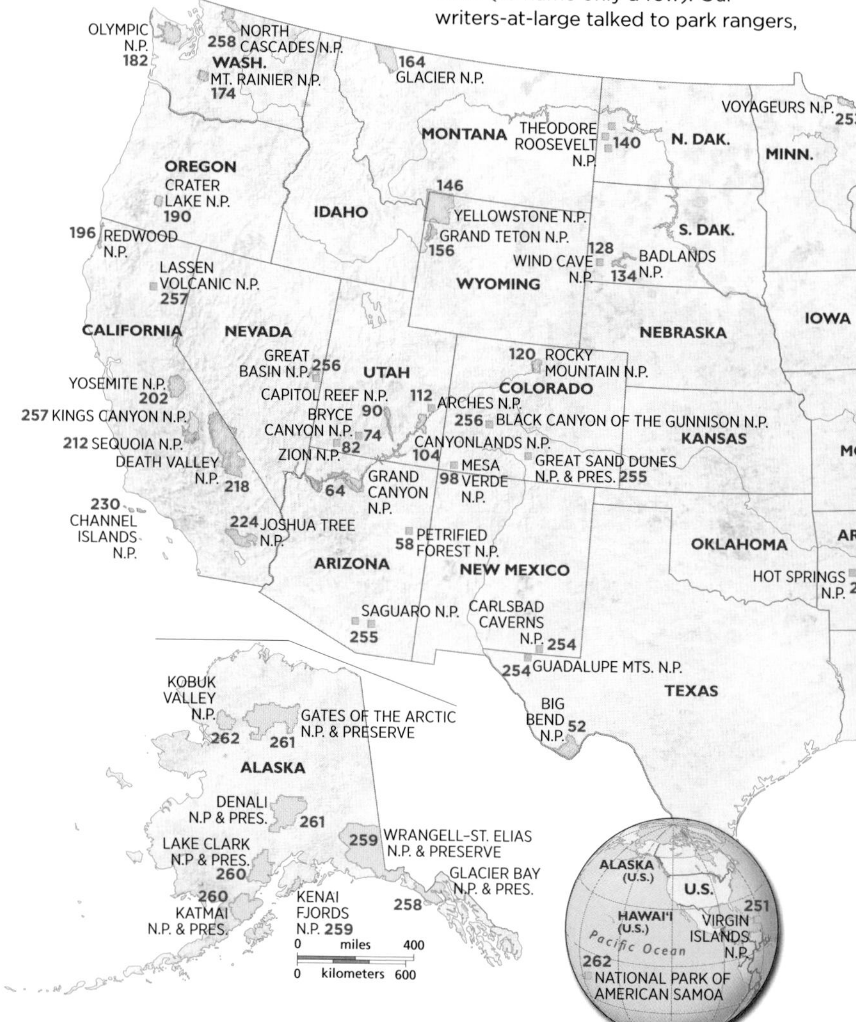

outfitters, and local guides, among others, to uncover the least crowded beaches, barely tramped trails, hard-to-find sights, and more. They then organized the secrets into easy-to-read narratives to help you plan and enjoy your national park adventures.

Each park description includes inspiring photos of the scenery and wildlife awaiting you on your visit, plus National Geographic maps to orient you to the areas, though you'll want to grab detailed park maps at visitor centers showing roads, trails, and other features before you set out to explore.

The book is broken down into three chapters, each organized geographically, making it easier to tackle the parks in small chunks or to focus on a specific destination. We arrange our secrets starting with the iconic spots and moving out from them to the less visited spots. In addition, members of the National Park Trust, local park staff, frequent visitors, and outfitters offer their thoughts on traveling in the national parks.

And, so as not to leave any park out, we've added a chapter of secrets from the rest of the national parks.

Sit back and learn about the secret side of our national parks, then head out on a trip to one or more. We hope soon you'll discover your *own* secrets in America's national parks.

NOTE: *Red numbers indicate the pages on which the parks are featured within this book.*

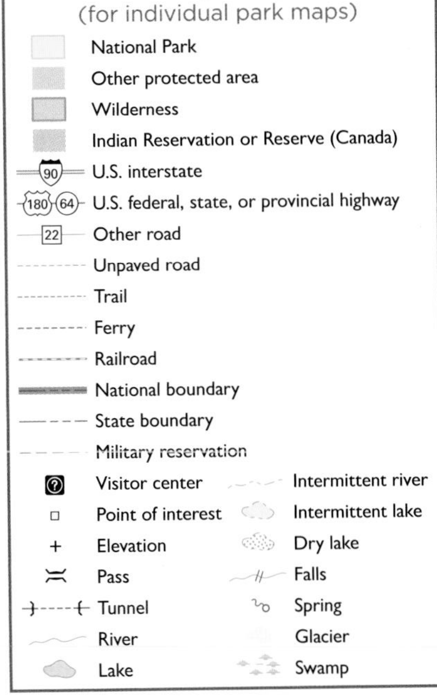

"Our national parks embody a conservation ethic that is inherently democratic, open to all. While Maine enjoys countless beauties, Acadia is a crown jewel. With Cadillac Mountain, miles of rocky coastline, and the carriage trails, it is easy to understand why."

—SENATOR SUSAN M. COLLINS, MAINE
NATIONAL PARK TRUST 2011 RECIPIENT
BRUCE F. VENTO PUBLIC SERVICE AWARD

[1]

THE EAST

Spruce Flats Falls in autumn, Great Smoky Mountains National Park

Sailing from Bar Harbor, off Mount Desert

ACADIA

Long before parts of it became a national monument in 1916 (and a national park three years later), Maine's Mount Desert Island was attracting visitors eager to savor its mountains, forests, lakes, and, especially, its stunning coastline. These included many of America's wealthiest families, who built opulent summer homes in the Bar Harbor area, as well as tourists who filled more than two dozen island hotels.

Some of Mount Desert's well-to-do residents, alarmed that the very scenic qualities they loved were threatened, pushed for the creation of a national park, donating land and money for that purpose. Over the years, Acadia National Park has grown to encompass more than 40 percent of the island, as well as areas on nearby Schoodic Peninsula and Isle au Haut.

Although more than two million visitors come to Acadia annually, there are still secret spots to be found if you know where to look.

Year-Round Visitor Center

- **Park Headquarters**
  On Maine 233, 2 miles west of Bar Harbor

Seasonal Visitor Centers

- **Hulls Cove Visitor Center**
  On Maine 3, north of Bar Harbor
- **Thompson Island Information Center**
  On Maine 3, north end Mount Desert Island

207-288-3338, *www.nps.gov/acad*

▶ The Eastern Park

If you encounter occasional road traffic or a crowded scenic spot, bear in mind that without the foresight of island lovers more than a century ago the first national park east of the Mississippi would never have existed, and Mount Desert would be far far less accessible to travelers than it is today.

The center of much island activity is the town of Bar Harbor, which sits on the northeastern shore.

❶ **Bar Island** There's a great view of town and the mountains of eastern Mount Desert Island from a high point on Bar Island, which sits less than 0.5 mile out from shore. Surprisingly enough, you can actually walk to the island, as long as you begin and end your hike during the period 1.5 hours on either side of low tide. (Check at a visitor center for tide schedule.)

You'll have plenty of company on your walk, so here's an alternative: Rent a canoe or kayak and paddle to Bar Island during the other nine hours of the tidal cycle. You may not be alone on the island, but you'll enjoy its view in far greater solitude.

Although this is a short trip on a fairly protected part of the bay, you'll still be on the ocean, so know your abilities, such as swimming, and check the weather forecast before setting out.

❷ **Park Loop Road** This 27-mile road was designed in part by landscape architect Frederick Law Olmsted, Jr., who wanted to showcase scenery that he described as having "a certain bigness of sweep."

The route provides access to many of Acadia's most scenic spots, including **Sand Beach, Otter Cliff, Jordan Pond,** and **Cadillac Mountain.** As such, it often suffers from traffic congestion and crowded parking lots along the shore section called **Ocean Drive.**

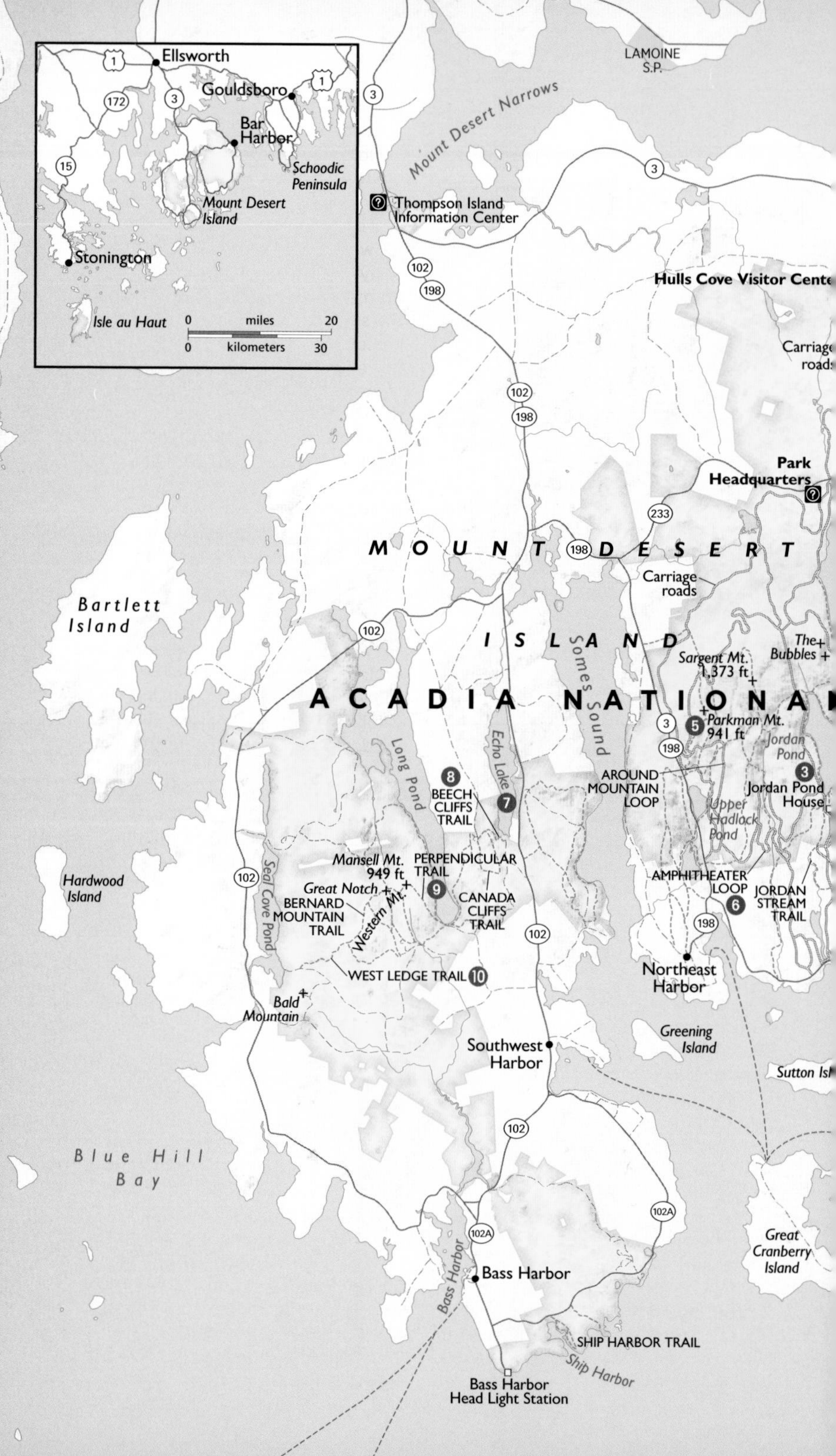

Ellsworth
Gouldsboro
Bar Harbor
Schoodic Peninsula
Mount Desert Island
Stonington
Isle au Haut
0 miles 20
0 kilometers 30
LAMOINE S.P.
Mount Desert Narrows
Thompson Island Information Center
Hulls Cove Visitor Cente
Carriage roads
Park Headquarters
MOUNT DESERT ISLAND
ACADIA NATIONA
Carriage roads
The Bubbles
Sargent Mt. 1,373 ft
Parkman Mt. 941 ft
Jordan Pond
Jordan Pond House
AROUND MOUNTAIN LOOP
Upper Hadlock Pond
AMPHITHEATER LOOP
JORDAN STREAM TRAIL
Somes Sound
Bartlett Island
Long Pond
Echo Lake
BEECH CLIFFS TRAIL
Mansell Mt. 949 ft
PERPENDICULAR TRAIL
Great Notch
Western Mt.
BERNARD MOUNTAIN TRAIL
CANADA CLIFFS TRAIL
Hardwood Island
Seal Cove Pond
WEST LEDGE TRAIL
Bald Mountain
Northeast Harbor
Greening Island
Southwest Harbor
Sutton Is
Blue Hill Bay
Great Cranberry Island
Bass Harbor
SHIP HARBOR TRAIL
Ship Harbor
Bass Harbor Head Light Station

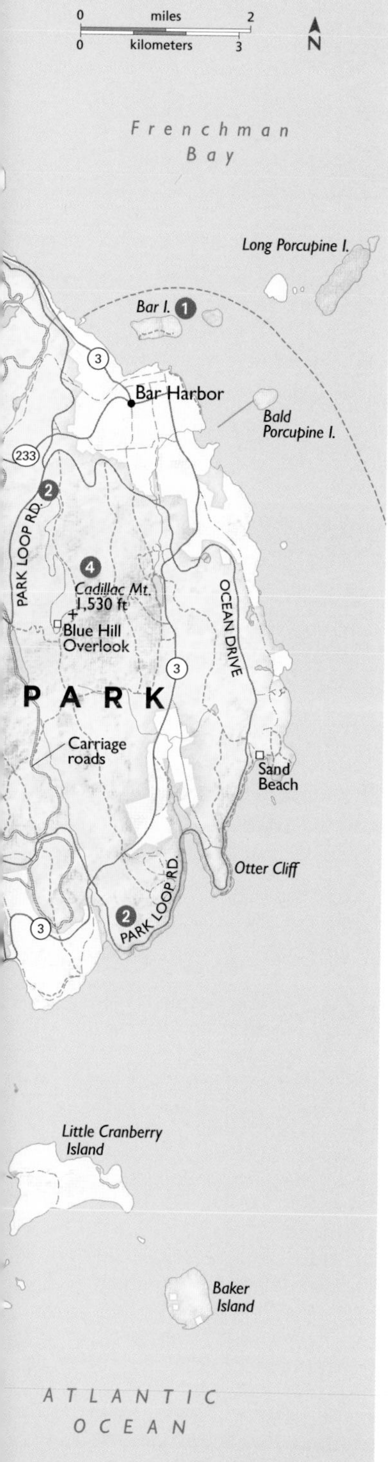

0 miles 2
0 kilometers 3
N
Frenchman Bay
Long Porcupine I.
Bar I. 1
3
Bar Harbor
Bald Porcupine I.
233
2
PARK LOOP RD.
4
Cadillac Mt. 1,530 ft
Blue Hill Overlook
OCEAN DRIVE
3
PARK
Carriage roads
Sand Beach
Otter Cliff
2
PARK LOOP RD.
3
Little Cranberry Island
Baker Island
ATLANTIC OCEAN

Nonetheless, here's the secret of beating the crowds: "People forget that there are really beautiful views and interesting things to do at night between sunset and sunrise," says Sonya Berger, park interpreter. "One of my favorite places to go after the sun sets is to one of the busiest places during the day, which is Ocean Drive. You can find your own private piece of rock and sit down and watch the stars come out.

"On a clear night along the coast you'll have an uninterrupted view of the swath of stars dipping down into the ocean. It's a fantastic view." It helps that in 2008, Bar Harbor initiated light-control rules to help protect the island's night skies.

3 Jordan Pond Despite the crowds, Jordan Pond is a must for all park visitors, for two main reasons: the view of the twin hills called **The Bubbles** and the popovers at the **Jordan Pond House** restaurant. These baked delights make a nice reward for a completed hike or bike ride.

A favorite walk for some park interpreters is the easy **Jordan Stream Trail,** which heads south along the outlet creek of Jordan Pond. It ranks among the park's prettiest locations,

Deer encounter

Bass Harbor dock, Mount Desert Island

and as a bonus, after 0.6 mile you reach the first, and perhaps most famous, of the carriage road bridges (see below). This bridge is the only one in the park faced with cobblestones instead of cut rock.

Wherever you walk in Acadia, check the possibility of using the free **Island Explorer** buses (summer only) to do one-way hikes and avoid full trailhead parking lots.

4 Cadillac Mountain A side road off the Park Loop leads to the top of 1,530-foot Cadillac Mountain. Heading south along the Atlantic shore trail, you'll find no higher mountain spot until Rio de Janeiro.

Watching the sunrise from the pastel pink granite summit has become a Mount Desert Island rite, attracting big crowds. For a slightly less congested alternative, drive up the mountain before dusk and find a seat near the **Blue Hill Overlook,** less than 0.25 mile back down the road from the summit parking lot.

If the clouds and the light align properly, you'll be treated to one of the best sunset views of your life.

▶ Carriage Roads

Acadia is justly famed for its carriage roads: wide, unpaved paths on which motor vehicles are banned and walkers, bicyclists, horseback riders, skiers, and, yes, carriages rule.

Forty-five miles of these roads wind through the national park, with another few located on private land outside the park. (Bicycles are prohibited on carriage roads outside the park.) Seventeen bridges, each with its own design and faced in native stone, decorate the park routes.

The busiest carriage roads are those between Bar Harbor and Jordan Pond, such as the loop around **Eagle Lake.**

For a less congested (and more strenuous) hike or ride, park along Maine 3 north of **Upper Hadlock Pond** and travel the route climbing northwest of **Sargent Mountain.** It's steep in places, but offers some fine western vistas. (Think of the popovers waiting.)

For a real workout, you can continue to make the full **Around Mountain Loop** of 11.1 miles. Otherwise, retrace your path back to Maine 3.

5 Parkman Mountain Though no carriage road goes all the way to the summit, while you're in this area consider a hike to the top of 941-foot Parkman Mountain.

Even if it's not one of the park's most famous summits, this peak's rocky top provides views westward over glacier-carved **Somes Sound.**

6 Amphitheater Loop To see two of the famed stone bridges in a little more than 5 miles, start near the southern end of Jordan Pond and follow the carriage-road route called Amphitheater Loop, which hugs hillsides between two ridges to form a natural amphitheater.

▶ The Quiet Side

The area of Acadia west of Somes Sound is often called the park's "quiet side"—though **Bass Harbor Head Light Station** and **Echo Lake** certainly get their share of visitors.

Nonetheless, this section is generally calmer than the hubs of Jordan Pond and Cadillac Mountain.

7 Echo Lake Moderately challenging trails (leading from the parking lot for the swimming area) ascend to fine views of Echo Lake and surrounding areas of the island as well as

> *Because of Acadia's location, it's one of the few places along the East Coast where you can actually see the Milky Way and other nighttime sights that are being lost to light pollution in other spots.*
>
> —SONIA BERGER
> *Acadia National Park interpreter*

Local Intelligence

A different sort of wildlife can be found along the rocky shore of Mount Desert Island—a type that many visitors overlook. The **Ship Harbor Trail,** a 1.3-mile loop just east of the **Bass Harbor Head Light Station,** provides easy access at low tide to the island's intertidal zone, a fascinating ecosystem with a surprising number of species including fish, reptiles, amphibians, and invertebrates.

Find a tide pool and a place to sit amid the pink granite ledges, and spend some time just looking down into the clear water. Creatures such as barnacles and mussels will be obvious, but by watching closely you'll likely spot crabs, periwinkles, whelks, limpets, sea stars, sea urchins, and many other animals. (Please do not disturb.) Sure, it's fun to see large wildlife such as white-tailed deer or Bald Eagles elsewhere, but the teeming life of a tide pool is in its own way just as rewarding to observe—not to mention a solitary escape from the island's crowded roads and towns.

Morning fog above an autumn forest

of the **Cranberry Isles** off the southern coast.

8 Beech Cliffs Trail This trail includes some very steep sections where ladders are used, while the **Canada Cliffs Trail** is less precipitous. Depending on the challenge you want to face, you can ascend or descend either path and walk loops atop the cliffs for a round-trip of about 2 miles.

9 Perpendicular Trail If the steepness of the Beech Cliffs Trail doesn't faze you, consider climbing the Perpendicular Trail, a strenuous ascent of **Mansell Mountain** that begins at the southern end of **Long Pond.** The climb is short, leading to rewarding views of Long Pond.

"The Perpendicular Trail was built by the Civilian Conservation Corps [CCC] in the 1930s," says Charlie Jacobi, park recreation specialist. "It was beautifully constructed. You won't find a prettier set of stonework and steps. Once you get up the trail you've got three or four options to come down, depending on how far you want to walk: Mansell Mountain, **Razorback, Great Notch, Sluiceway,** even the **Bernard Mountain Trail,** which goes all the way around what's called the **Western Mountain.** You can make the trek as long or as short as you want it. This area is mostly forested, with occasional rock outcrops with views, and it's not very traveled."

10 West Ledge Trail The 3-mile West Ledge Trail, a spur off the Bernard Mountain Trail leading to Bald Mountain, offers views of the western coast of Mount Desert Island. It can also be reached from the unpaved road leading to **Seal Cove Pond,** a site for canoeists and kayakers looking for relaxing paddling opportunities. With its mixture of wooded shoreline and marsh, Seal Cove Pond often offers the chance to spot birds and other wildlife.

▶ Isle au Haut

High Island was the name given to this 12-square-mile island by Frenchman Samuel Champlain in 1604. Lying southwest of Mount Desert Island, Isle au Haut offers scenery and solitude to visitors who make advance arrangements to visit. The only access is by private ferry, operating from the mainland town of **Stonington** and providing space on a first-come, first-served basis.

About half the island is under National Park Service administration; a small campground is available (reservations needed). Even on a day visit, though, you're likely to find yourself alone on the 18-mile trail system, enjoying forest, bogs, rocky shoreline, and a freshwater lake.

A hike along portions of the **Goat, Cliff,** and **Western Head trails** is an ideal way to experience the island's highlights: listening to bird songs, smelling the ferns and conifers, and watching the fishermen on lobster boats checking their traps.

▶ Schoodic Peninsula

The only part of Acadia National Park located on the mainland, Schoodic Peninsula encompasses 2,266 acres of strikingly rugged granite landscape across **Frenchman Bay** from Bar Harbor. A one-way scenic drive leads to **Schoodic Point,** which, as a park guidebook accurately states, "provides an outstanding vantage point for witnessing the power of the sea."

Bill Weidner, an Acadia ranger, recommends taking the ferry (summer only) from Bar Harbor to Winter Harbor ("You could see Osprey for sure, and maybe an eagle or some harbor porpoises") and then hopping on an Island Explorer bus to make the Schoodic Loop.

"Bring a picnic lunch or have lunch in Winter Harbor," Weidner says. "It's really convenient if you don't mind doing a little planning about where the bus is going to be at a particular time."

Many visitors walk to the top of 440-foot **Schoodic Head** for a sweeping view of the coastline. You can walk up the dirt road and down one of several hiking trails. "What you don't want to miss is Schoodic Point," Weidner says. "If there's any wind driving the surf, the wave action is spectacular." At any time, the granite shore with its "dikes" of solidified magma provides endless opportunities for photos or contemplation.

Surf-pounded boulders at Schoodic Point

Shenandoah's fall landscape

SHENANDOAH

As the closest national park to Washington, D.C., Shenandoah is an oasis straddling 300 square miles of southern Appalachian ridgeline for metro residents and other visitors.

To the east is the Appalachian Piedmont, to the west the Shenandoah Valley, and in the corridor between expansive mountain vistas, abundant black bears and deer, and secluded waterfalls and swimming holes.

Homesteaders first settled these mountains in the 1750s, and their descendants were displaced in the 1920s and 1930s when the Commonwealth of Virginia acquired the land to create the park.

Some were allowed to stay in their homes (the last resident died in 1979), and some worked with contractors to help build Skyline Drive and other park facilities. Family cemeteries and ruins serve as enduring reminders of the farm families who once lived here.

Seasonal Visitor Centers

- **Dickey Ridge Visitor Center**
  At milepost 4.6 on Skyline Drive
- **Harry F. Byrd, Sr. Visitor Center**
  At milepost 51 on Skyline Drive

540-999-3500, *www.nps.gov/shen*

▶ North District: Skyline Drive From Front Royal to Byrd Visitor Center

The park's 105-mile long spine is Skyline Drive, a scenic roadway (speed limit 35 mph) built in part along trails blazed by Indians, fur traders, and pioneers.

Mileposts begin at zero at the northernmost point—Front Royal, Virginia (US 340)—and count up as you drive south. The drive and the park end at milepost 105, **Rockfish Gap** (I-64), where Skyline Drive connects to the **Blue Ridge Parkway.**

Viewing the park in three leisurely driving chunks—North, Central, and South—makes it more likely you'll take the time to explore the side trails off Skyline Drive and stop at the scenic overlooks.

While the 75 overlooks along the ridge-crest route (the high point is 3,680 feet) make the Appalachian mountain vistas accessible to all, appreciating the park requires approaching it as more than a drive-through destination, says Andy Nichols, director of programs for a local guide company. "Shenandoah has more than 500 miles of trails, most of which lead to stunning places, but few people ever get out from behind the wheel. There are some often overlooked trails that are true gems."

❶ **Fox Hollow Trail** The first stop for most people who enter the park via Front Royal is the **Dickey Ridge Visitor Center,** where clean restrooms and an information center are the main draws.

Few people venture across Skyline Drive from the center to the Fox Hollow trailhead. The 1.2-mile loop doesn't offer any of Shenandoah's sweeping panoramas, but it does provide a window into the history of the people who lived here before the park was created.

The trail is named for the Fox family, tenant farmers here from the early 1800s through 1936. Thomas Fox eventually bought this site from owner Marcus Buck and built a seven-room log house in this area. The forest has reclaimed their cornfields and pastures, but the family's cemetery and homesite remain.

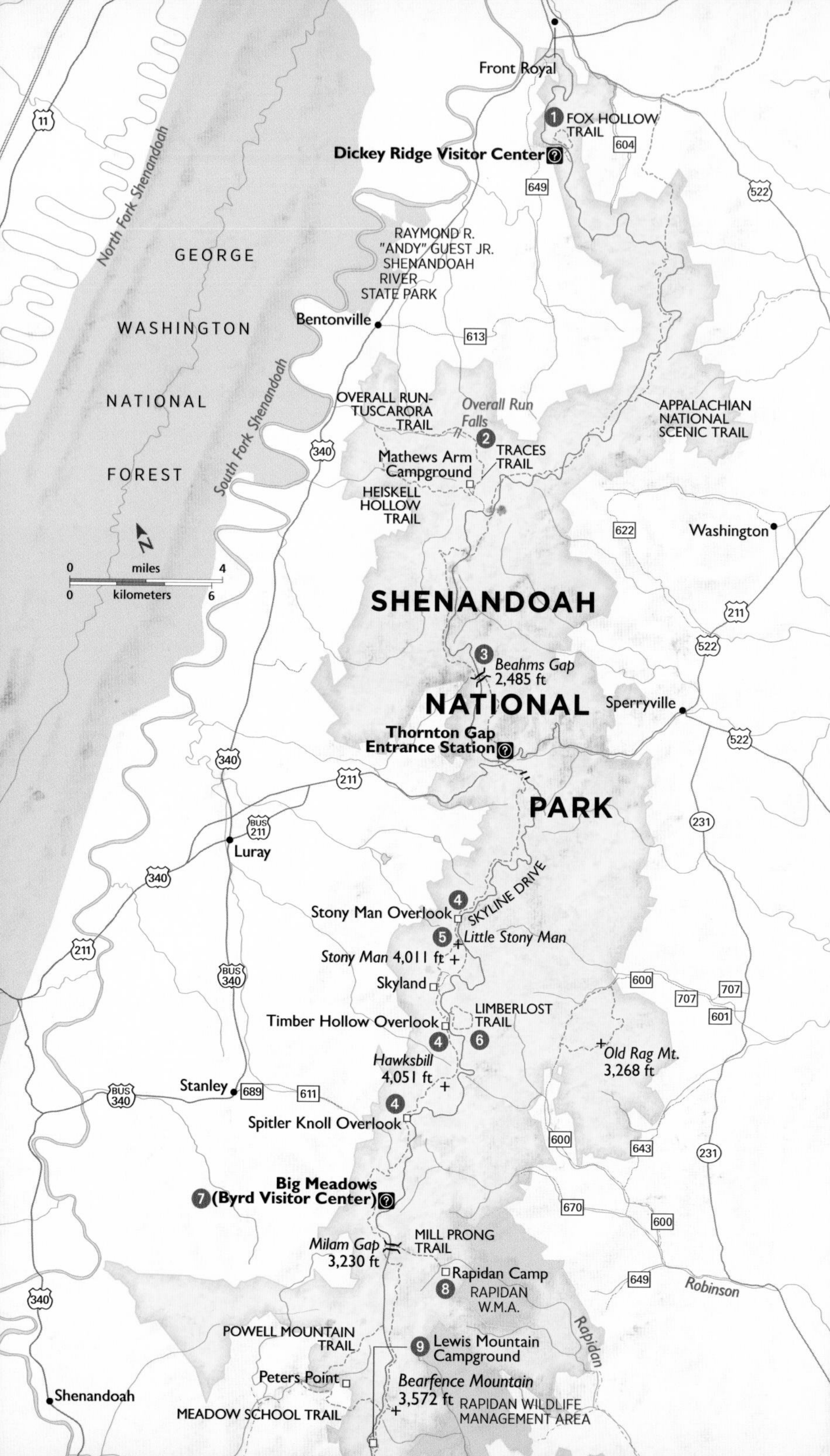

Front Royal
FOX HOLLOW TRAIL
Dickey Ridge Visitor Center
604
649
522
11
North Fork Shenandoah
GEORGE
WASHINGTON
NATIONAL
FOREST
RAYMOND R. "ANDY" GUEST JR. SHENANDOAH RIVER STATE PARK
Bentonville
613
South Fork Shenandoah
OVERALL RUN-TUSCARORA TRAIL
Overall Run Falls
TRACES TRAIL
APPALACHIAN NATIONAL SCENIC TRAIL
340
Mathews Arm Campground
HEISKELL HOLLOW TRAIL
622
Washington
0 miles 4
0 kilometers 6
SHENANDOAH
211
522
Beahms Gap 2,485 ft
NATIONAL
Sperryville
Thornton Gap Entrance Station
522
340
211
PARK
BUS 211
Luray
231
340
SKYLINE DRIVE
Stony Man Overlook
Little Stony Man
211
Stony Man 4,011 ft
BUS 340
Skyland
600
707
707
LIMBERLOST TRAIL
601
Timber Hollow Overlook
Old Rag Mt. 3,268 ft
Hawksbill 4,051 ft
Stanley
689
611
BUS 340
Spitler Knoll Overlook
600
643
231
Big Meadows (Byrd Visitor Center)
670
600
MILL PRONG TRAIL
Milam Gap 3,230 ft
Rapidan Camp
649
Robinson
RAPIDAN W.M.A.
340
Rapidan
POWELL MOUNTAIN TRAIL
Lewis Mountain Campground
Peters Point
Bearfence Mountain 3,572 ft
Shenandoah
MEADOW SCHOOL TRAIL
RAPIDAN WILDLIFE MANAGEMENT AREA

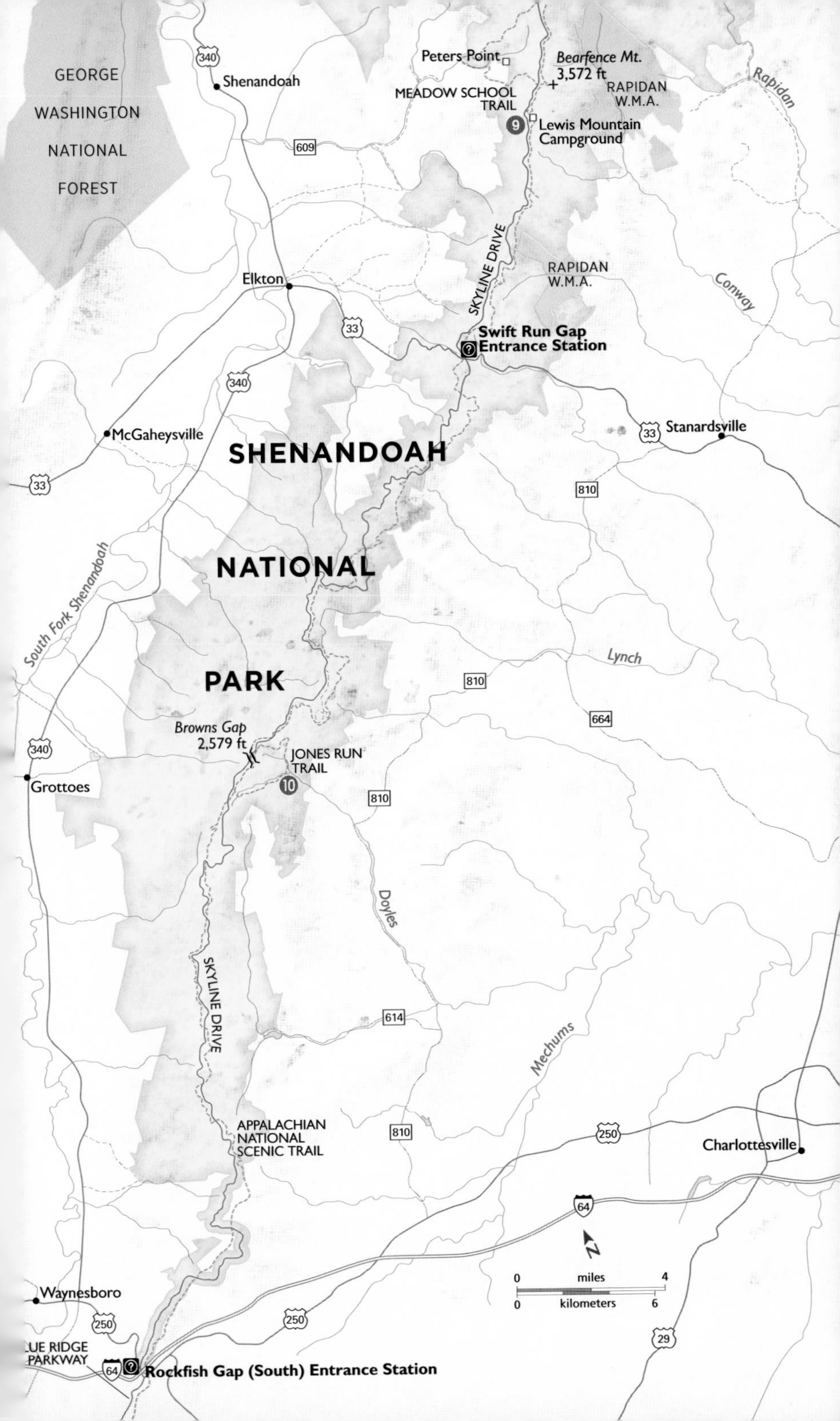

GEORGE WASHINGTON NATIONAL FOREST
Shenandoah
Peters Point
Bearfence Mt. 3,572 ft
MEADOW SCHOOL TRAIL
RAPIDAN W.M.A.
Lewis Mountain Campground
Rapidan
SKYLINE DRIVE
RAPIDAN W.M.A.
Conway
Elkton
Swift Run Gap Entrance Station
Stanardsville
McGaheysville
SHENANDOAH
NATIONAL
PARK
South Fork Shenandoah
Lynch
Browns Gap 2,579 ft
JONES RUN TRAIL
Grottoes
Doyles
SKYLINE DRIVE
Mechums
APPALACHIAN NATIONAL SCENIC TRAIL
Charlottesville
Waynesboro
LUE RIDGE PARKWAY
Rockfish Gap (South) Entrance Station
miles
kilometers

2 Overall Run/Heiskell Hollow Trail If you're physically up to a challenging circuit hike (about 12.5 miles, half that if you only go to the falls and back), this one delivers Shenandoah's best in microcosm.

"There are beautiful falls [including the park's tallest, 93-foot **Overall Run Falls**], great views, and swimming holes near the bottom," says Nichols. "In summer the swimming is amazing, and in winter the upper falls are magnificent." Freezing temps can turn the cascades into icicles.

From Skyline Drive, park at the Matthews Arm Campground amphitheater and follow **Traces Trail** to the **Overall Run–Tuscarora Trail,** connecting with Heiskell Hollow to complete the circuit.

3 Beahms Gap With 101 miles of the Appalachian Trail (AT) paralleling much of Skyline Drive through the park, it's easy to hike a short section. White blazes on trees mark the AT. Blue signifies park trails, and yellow, horse trails (hiking allowed).

The AT crossing near Beahms Gap is only a few hundred yards from the parking area and is a favorite birding spot of biologists Ann Simpson and her husband Rob, co-owners of a local photography business.

Eastern tiger swallowtail

"More than 200 species of birds are found in the park," says Ann. "In summer, look for Scarlet Tanagers, Indigo Buntings, and Rose-breasted Grosbeaks. In fall, sparrows, Eastern Towhees, and migrating warblers love the scrubby, insect-filled cover here."

Shenandoah is a place where you can slow down. Amid the gentle forested hills, sparkling waterfalls, and softly flowing streams you can find solitude and reconnect with life.

—ANN AND ROB SIMPSON
Virginia biologists and nature photographers

▶ Central District: Thornton Gap to Swift Run Gap

To meet Shenandoah in the middle, enter the park through Thornton Gap or Swift Run Gap, and drive between the two. This is the highest section of the park, and it includes its highest peak, at **Hawksbill** (4,051 feet), and second highest point, 4,011-foot **Stony Man.**

4 Stony Man to Spitler Knoll Overlooks With 75 Skyline Drive vista overlooks, it can be difficult to pick the perfect spot to pull off and watch the sun go down. "Most of the overlooks are oriented with a westward view into the Allegheny Mountains, so there are many that are nice for sunset pictures," says Rob Simpson.

Red hues on the fall fields in Big Meadows

To snap the quintessential Shenandoah sunset vista, the Simpsons suggest staking out an unobstructed view at one of their favorite photo stops along this stretch of Skyline Drive: Stony Man, **Timber Hollow,** or Spitler Knoll.

5 Stony Man The popular loop hike to the top and back is steep (about 340 feet upward) and rocky (it's called Stony Man for a reason) in spots.

At only 1.6 miles, however, it's a short way for some long views west over wave after wave of forested Appalachian Mountain ridges. Park at historic **Skyland Resort** early in the day to make the climb before the crowds arrive.

For a shorter option with similar views, hike the trail to **Little Stony Man,** a 0.9-mile round-trip.

6 Limberlost Trail The easy Limberlost Trail (named for an early 1900s novel) is Shenandoah's most accessible woodlands, wetlands, and wildlife trail.

The 5-foot-wide crushed green-stone walkway loops through 1.3 miles of forest. Mountain laurels bloom in June and white-tailed deer are regularly spotted here throughout the year.

The gentle grades make it possible to push a stroller or wheelchair, but ruts can form and wooden bridge surfaces can get slick when wet. If you're a wheelchair hiker, invite a friend to join you (always a good idea for any hiker on any trail).

7 Big Meadows The **Byrd Visitor Center** is a popular rest stop since it sits roughly at the halfway point along Skyline Drive.

Take some time here to stretch your legs and walk across Skyline Drive to Big Meadows, the park's largest open vista, suggests Mary Craig, summer park teacher.

The meadowlands' low-bush blueberry, maleberry, and deerberry bushes; two nutrient-rich wetlands; and native grasses attract abundant wildlife and insects, including some species found nowhere else in Shenandoah.

"Early morning or just before sunset are the best times to wander Big Meadows," says Craig. "It's a quieter period with fewer visitors and more opportunities to see white-tailed deer and black bears."

While any of the bigger mammals are fairly obvious, spotting the four-toed salamanders, eastern gray tree frogs, upland chorus frogs, and other critters that live here requires walking softly and listening closely.

Adds Craig, "Unplug from your electronics and have your kids do the same. When you get engaged in the outdoors, you see and hear so much more."

8 Rapidan Camp Before President Franklin Roosevelt established the USS Shangri-La retreat (renamed Camp David) as the presidential country residence, President Herbert Hoover built this fishing camp on the **Rapidan River.**

"The Hoovers enjoyed 'Camp Hoover' during the summer months to escape the heat of Washington and to entertain government officials and international guests," explains Ann Simpson. "On a pleasant 4-mile

Jones Run Falls

Local Intelligence

Experience the park like a local by choosing the trail less traveled. In Shenandoah, that means avoiding **Old Rag,** the park's most popular and most dangerous trail. "Old Rag Mountain is being overrun with visitors, to the tune of 2,000 to 3,000 on any weekend day," says Andy Nichols, director of programs for a local guide company. "The negative impact is overpowering, and the numbers of rescues required for novice hikers is staggering." As an alternative, Nichols suggests the **Peters Point** area. "Follow either **Powell Mountain Trail** or **Meadow School Trail** for a drop down into one of the locals' favorite areas: deep woods and solitude."

Note: Due to scheduled 2012–13 overlook construction, check trail access at www.nps.gov/shen/planyourvisit/hiking-alerts.htm *for these and other trails in the park.*

round-trip hike along **Mill Prong Trail** from the **Milam Gap** parking area, you can reach Rapidan Camp, explore the area, and enjoy the same inspiring mountain trout stream that soothed the souls of many famous national and world leaders."

To fish here, bring your gear and purchase a five-day nonresident fishing license at the Big Meadows Wayside or a local sporting goods store.

9 Lewis Mountain Campground The campground is the park's smallest, making it a quiet, somewhat secret retreat. When visiting with children, this also is an ideal setting for an impromptu discussion about the civil rights movement, say Ann and Rob Simpson.

"The Lewis Mountain facilities opened in 1940 as a segregated campground," says Ann Simpson. "Later, that segregation ended and the campground was freely shared by everyone."

The site is close to the Appalachian Trail, so through-hikers often camp here to shower, wash clothes, and stock up on supplies.

Near the campground facilities, hike to the summit of **Bearfence Mountain,** suggests Rob Simpson. "The name comes from the palisade-like rocks resembling a fence that surround the summit. The hike is a fairly easy 1.2-mile circuit to a 360-degree vista."

▶ South District: Rockfish Gap and North

"The southern edge of Shenandoah is much less populated, but there's still plenty to see and do," says Craig. Approach the park through the southernmost **Rockfish Gap Entrance** at US 64 for a different perspective.

Heading north up Skyline Drive from here, there's generally less traffic, and in early morning and early evening, adds Craig, more chance you'll spot black bears, deer, or Wild Turkeys walking or feeding near the road.

10 Jones Run/Doyles River In summer, pack a picnic and towel and spend a day cooling off in the swimming holes along this 6.6-mile loop trail, suggests hiking guide Andy Nichols. Park at **Browns Gap** (milepost 83) lot, cross Skyline Drive, and follow the AT along the ridge for 1.4 miles to the **Jones Run Trail.** "This is a fun and rewarding hike on a hot day," says Nichols. "There's not quite as much solitude as some of my other 'secret' hikes, but it's great for waterfalls and pools."

Dawn from Clingmans Dome

GREAT SMOKY MOUNTAINS

Its location within a day's drive for tens of millions of Americans helps make Great Smoky Mountains the most popular national park in the United States. The 800-square-mile international biosphere reserve is split about evenly between Tennessee and North Carolina, and it protects some of the oldest mountains on Earth. More than 1,500 species of flowering plants and 60 species of native mammals, including deer, black bears, and elk, live within these often mist-shrouded mountains. The 384 miles of park roads and more than 800 miles of hiking trails make it easy to stroll along a rushing stream without straying far from your car. Join a ranger-led program to discover a few of the park's 30 species of salamanders, the world's most diverse population for an area this size.

Year-Round Visitor Centers

- **Cades Cove Visitor Center**
  On Cades Cove Loop Road, near the midpoint
- **Oconaluftee Visitor Center**
  On US 441, north of Cherokee, N.C.
- **Sugarlands Visitor Center**
  On US 441, 2 miles south of Gatlinburg, Tenn.

Seasonal Visitor Centers

- **Clingmans Dome Visitor Contact Station**
  At the Clingmans Dome trailhead, 7 miles off US 441

Visitor Centers Outside the Park

- **Gatlinburg Welcome Center**
  Off US 441, Gatlinburg, Tenn.
- **Sevierville Visitor Center**
  On Tenn. 66, Sevierville, Tenn.
- **Townsend Visitor Center**
  On US 321, Townsend, Tenn.

865-436-1200, *www.nps.gov/grsm*

▶ Cades Cove

The paved, 11-mile, one-way driving loop through Cades Cove, in the park's southwest corner, offers a glimpse of pre-park Smokies life. Farm families who sold their land to create the park left behind homes, churches, and barns. These open-air museums—plus wildflowers and wildlife—make this an extremely popular tourist route. Pick up an auto tour pamphlet (donation suggested) at the orientation shelter for descriptions of the 18 numbered stops.

Traffic is heaviest on warm-weather weekends, and traffic jams occur any time a bear is spotted. Avoid the noise and congestion by walking or biking the loop when it opens at sunrise, on a weekday, or when it's closed to motorized vehicles Wednesday and Saturday mornings (sunrise until 10 a.m.), early May to late September.

❶ Rich Mountain Loop Trail

Driving through Cades Cove can take two to three hours when traffic is heavy, providing even more incentive to park and walk. Motorists rarely notice the Rich Mountain Loop trailhead because it's on the right near the start of the one-way loop where horses typically graze on the left-hand side of the road. Follow the trail through the lowland woods about 1.3 miles to the early 19th-century **John Oliver Cabin,** the

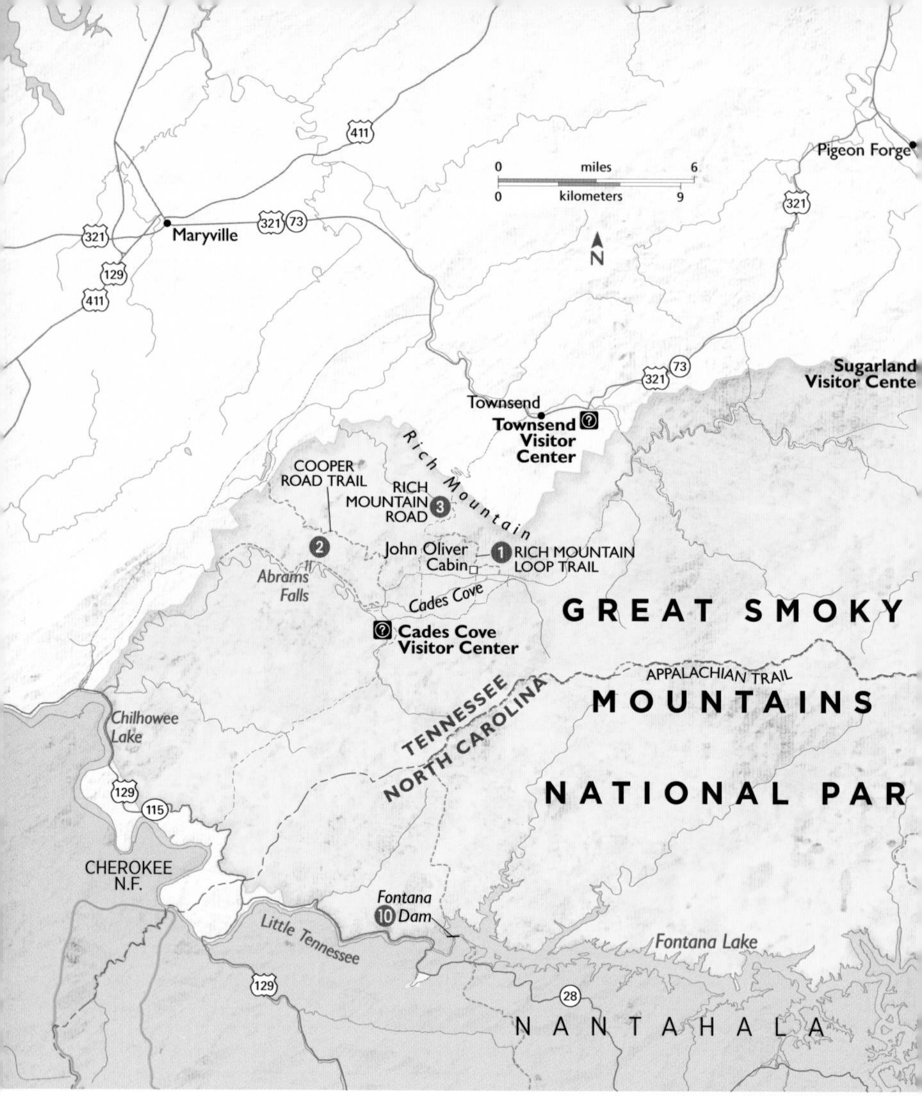

cove's oldest log home.

"It's an easy, pleasant path meandering up and down along the base of Rich Mountain," says Liz Domingue, local naturalist, guide, and tour operator. "You are in the forest but you are walking along the edge of the cleared fields so it's a great way to see Wild Turkeys, as well as deer in the fields, in the woods, and sharing the path with you." The trail is closed in winter.

2 Cooper Road Trail Abrams Falls (trailhead between stops 10 and 11 on the auto tour) is the most popular hike in Cades Cove and one of the most heavily traveled trails in the park. Nearby Cooper Road (stop 9) isn't as dramatic (no roaring water flowing over a bluff), but it's guaranteed to be less crowded.

The former Native American trail once was the main wagon route connecting the cove to the city of **Maryville.** Named for Joe Cooper, who widened the path for wagons, it extends 10.5 miles, so walk as far as you'd like across several creeks and small ridges.

3 Rich Mountain Road The brown sign at the base of Rich Mountain Road is enough to make most motorists pass by: "Unimproved, primitive access, one way (no re-entry)."

That's true, and it's also what makes the narrow, gravel route up and over Rich Mountain worth taking. Before you do, however, make sure you've seen everything you want to see in Cades Cove. It's 12 miles and about 90 minutes to **Townsend** (and civilization) from where the road begins, and there's no turning back.

Except for the occasional hikers and hard-core mountain bikers, you are likely to have the potholed route to yourself. With solitude comes several perks, including better odds of seeing black bears (from the safety of your car), and of hearing the distinctive trilling sound of the Eastern Screech-owl.

As with everywhere in the Smokies, the views through the red maples, chestnut and scarlet oaks, magnolias, and black gums change with the seasons. In spring, trailing arbutus, galax, and dogwoods bloom pink and white. Come fall, the crest of the road is the best place to pull off and take in the blazing red and soft yellow Cades Cove foliage panorama below.

▶ Greenbrier Cove

Off the beaten tourist path yet easily accessible from the main road, the Greenbrier Cove section of the park is a local favorite.

The single brown sign marking the park border is easy to miss. From Gatlinburg, head out 6 miles on US 321 and turn right onto Greenbrier Road at the Little Pigeon River Bridge.

The transition from highway to deep woods is immediate: big trees, bountiful wildflowers, and (spring through early fall) dozens of butterflies leading the way through one of the park's prettiest and most discreet side entrances. The narrow, partially paved road hugs the rushing **Middle Prong Little Pigeon River,** and there are plenty of pull offs to park and picnic, or (carefully) climb on to the boulders to view the cascades.

Turk's cap lily

4 Porters Creek Trail Greenbrier's biggest draw is the **Ramsey Cascades Trail,** a strenuous 8-mile round-trip hike leading to the park's tallest (100-foot) waterfall.

The views from Porters Creek aren't as dramatic, but it's an easy trail through eastern hemlocks and Frasier magnolias with roaring cascades, 30 to 40 species of wildflowers, and remnants of the thriving farming community that once stood here (stone walls, homesites, and the Ownby Cemetery)—most visible within the first mile.

Park at the one-way traffic loop at mile 4.1 and walk to the gate at the end of the lot to start the hike. It's 3.6 miles from here to 40-foot **Fern Branch Falls** and back, yet you don't have to venture that far to safely get "lost" in the woods.

▶ Roaring Fork Motor Nature Trail

Meandering at 10 miles per hour along this 6-mile, one-way motor loop is like hiking in your car. For people with limited mobility, driving the winding trail is the best way to get up close views of rushing mountain streams, historic log cabins, and old-growth forest.

If mobility isn't an issue, Roaring Fork puts some of the park's prettiest waterfalls and premier destinations (including **Mount Le Conte)** within somewhat easier reach.

5 Trillium Gap Trail A moderate 2.6-mile round-trip hike on the **Trillium Gap Trail** brings you to **Grotto Falls,** the only waterfall in the park that you can walk behind. Note black bears are sometimes seen along this trail.

Even if you don't want to hike, the

Local Intelligence

Those students and tourists you see catching, tagging, and releasing monarch butterflies in a meadow or mapping fungi locations with a handheld GPS likely are "citizen scientists." With a little advance planning, you can be one, too.

"Citizen scientists are nonscientists who help with seasonal research projects in the Smokies," says Ken Voorhis, executive director of the Great Smoky Mountains Institute at Tremont (GSMIT). "Check out our website *(www.gsmit.org)* to see if there is a program—like bird-banding or monitoring the streams for salamander populations—that you can participate in during your visit."

Data you collect could become part of the All-Taxa Biodiversity Inventory (ATBI), the long-term effort to identify and map all of the park's 50,000 to 100,000 estimated species.

Trillium Gap trailhead is worth a visit on Monday, Wednesday, or Friday mornings mid-March through mid-November, when the llama train arrives to gear up for the climb to Le Conte Lodge. No roads lead to the lodge (which, sitting near the summit at 6,360 feet, is the highest resort east of the Mississippi), so pack llamas are used to carry in supplies. Of all the trails to Le Conte, the 6.5-mile route up Trillium Gap is the easiest for the llamas to navigate. The llamas usually hit the trail by 8 a.m., so if you're planning a hike, walk ahead of the pack part of the way (behind, or downwind, is less pleasant).

▶ Newfound Gap Road (US 441)

If you only have a day in the park, this 30-mile (one way) scenic drive is the one to take. Connecting the park's major visitor centers **Sugarlands** (near Gatlinburg, Tennessee) and **Oconaluftee** (near Cherokee, North Carolina), the road climbs to 5,046 feet at its midpoint, Newfound Gap.

A wooden sign in the middle of the parking lot here marks the border between the states. If you see any hitchhikers with serious backcountry gear up here, chances are they are Appalachian Trail (AT) through-hikers looking for rides down to **Gatlinburg** to restock supplies and get a hot meal and shower. The AT diagonally crosses the Newfound Gap parking lot. Walk past the restrooms (just beyond the stone **Rockefeller Memorial** where President Franklin Roosevelt dedicated the park on September 2, 1940) to meander along the AT for a bit.

It's frequently misty and foggy up here, so don't count on seeing much from the overlook. Your best bets for scenic views are on the drive back down to Gatlinburg. All the bends and switchbacks on Newfound Gap Road make it easier to see the cascades and overlooks heading south to north.

6 Cove Hardwood Nature Trail The **Chimneys Picnic** area is extremely popular in summer, and for good reason: picnic tables tucked under the trees, big river rocks that some walk on in the clear stream (although the park discourages it), and lots of shade. What's less obvious—and often overlooked—is the Cove Hardwood Nature Trail located up the wood planks on the right side of the parking area.

"One of the great features of this short walk (0.75 mile) is it goes through our most diverse forest community, one of the few remaining stands of old growth in the park," says Domingue.

Pick up a pamphlet at the trailhead to follow the self-guided trail. There are sugar maple and yellow buckeye trees here more than 100 feet tall and at least 150 years old.

Signpost 15 marks the logging line. Above this point, spared from the sawmill, are the largest cove hardwoods. The white basswood, yellow birch, beech, and silverbell trees stretch so high in the sky that it's tough to see the leaves, but the colors, during spring wildflower season and fall leaf turning, rival other spots in the park.

Understanding the Smokies requires paying attention to what's at your feet. There's an amazing diversity—from the wildflowers to the hardwoods, and from the salamanders to the black bears. The secrets here are found in the small stuff if you look, listen, and move through the forest slowly.

—LIZ DOMINGUE
naturalist, guide, and tour operator

▶ Clingmans Dome

Reaching the highest point in the park, 6,643-foot Clingmans Dome, is fairly easy since it's only a 0.5-mile climb from the parking area to the summit. The path is steep, but it's paved and there are benches along the way.

The real challenge is in seeing anything from the observation platform up top. On the Smokies' rare, brilliant blue sky days, the mountain, forest, and foothill views can extend nearly 100 miles north into Tennessee and south into North Carolina.

When clouds or the park's smoky blue haze hangs over the ridgeline, however, it can be tough to see beyond your own outstretched arms. If possible, choose a sunny day to make the 7-mile drive up Clingmans Dome Road (closed in winter) from Newfound Gap.

7 Clingmans Dome Bypass Trail Grab a pair of trekking poles to hike this less traveled trail to the top, suggests Vesna Plakanis, a Smokies guide and tour operator.

Reach the bypass by turning left at the **Forney Ridge Trail** sign (just before the paved path) and then right on the AT. This short, twisting route leads past exposed metamorphosed sandstone rocks more than 570 million years old.

"While these rocks were forming, there was almost no multicelled life on Earth, and the rocks are devoid of fossils. You are truly walking across the spine of time," says Plakanis.

8 Andrews Bald Unobstructed views and colorful shrubbery make the Smokies' treeless, grassy "balds" some of the best places to hike in the park. One of the easiest to reach is Andrews Bald, a 3.6-mile round-trip hike from the Clingmans Dome parking lot via the Forney Ridge Trail. The trailhead is located at the far end of the parking lot.

"A bald is a natural clearing. This means great visibility when the sun goes down and turns those rolling hills into purple mountain majesty," says Paul Hassell, local adventure photographer and guide. "Remember to bring a couple flashlights. The walk home is much easier if you can see."

▶ Eastern Side

The park's more than half million acres are divided pretty evenly between western North Carolina and eastern Tennessee, yet most day visitors gravitate toward the Tennessee side. Some of the North Carolina sections are more remote, but there are plenty within easy driving distance where you won't have much company.

9 Cataloochee Valley Neither route into this former farming community is easy. The 45-minute curvy crawl along Route 32 from North Carolina to Cosby, Tennessee, is legendary for inducing motion sickness, and the serpentine mountain road from I-40 (NC exit 20, Cove Creek Road) doesn't have guardrails.

On a clear day with a picnic and a full tank of gas, however, there's no better place in the park to view elk and Wild Turkeys, and walk a trail with few in sight. The remote location also is popular with local equestrians (there's a horse camp here).

This isn't a drive you want to make in the dark, so arrive early in the day (the elk tend to congregate in the meadows early in the morning).

10 Fontana Dam Fontana Lake forms the park's southwestern border, and 480-foot Fontana Dam formed the lake. It's the tallest concrete dam east of the Rocky Mountains, and one of two Tennessee Valley Authority (TVA) dams with Appalachian Trail crossings on top (the other is Watauga Dam near Elizabethton, Tennessee).

Take the short AT walk over the top to look down (very carefully) at the powerhouse on one side and across pristine **Fontana Lake** on the other. The view offers a rare peek into the park's remote southwestern reaches.

Clear day atop Clingmans Dome

Red mangrove, Boca Chita Key

BISCAYNE

Ninety-five percent of Biscayne National Park's surface area is composed of the sparkling blue waters of Biscayne Bay and the Atlantic Ocean off Florida's southeastern coast. Combining that geographic fact with another—the park's northern boundary is only a few miles from Miami's Rickenbacker Causeway—means that a lot of people visit Biscayne simply to cruise in their power boats, or to anchor for a sunset view of the metropolitan skyline.

That's too bad, because they're missing many of the secrets of a place unique in our National Park System. Foremost among the park's attractions are the colorful inhabitants of the world's third largest coral reef system, though Biscayne's bounty ranges from flocks of wading birds to the silent undersea travels of sharks to shipwrecks that evoke the always-fickle temperament of the sea.

Year-Round Visitor Center

- **Dante Fascell Visitor Center**
  At Convoy Point—9700 SW 328 Street, Homestead

  305-230-7275, *www.nps.gov/bisc*

▶ Boat Tours

Except for local residents who own boats, most visits to Biscayne National Park begin at the **Dante Fascell Visitor Center,** located on the mainland south of Miami at a site called **Convoy Point.** There's a short interpretive trail here that's best visited on weekdays; on weekends the area can be crowded with anglers and picnickers.

Getting off the beaten path at this national park is more difficult than at most others; you can't just lace up your boots, sling on a day pack, and head down a hiking trail. The essential fact regarding Biscayne is this: You have to get out on the water to truly appreciate the park.

Choosing the way to do that depends on your interests, physical abilities, time you have, and season. For some of the best experiences, advance schedule planning is vital. Luckily, as Matt Johnson, park ranger, says, "We offer different ways for people to get out on the water."

A park concessionaire operates paid boat tours to both the northernmost of the **Florida Keys** and the coral reefs beyond those islands. One popular trip is a three-hour glass-bottom boat ride, crossing **Biscayne Bay** to the reefs.

On days with good water visibility (more common in summer) you can see many species of fish and other reef life, sometimes including sharks or sea turtles; dolphins might even accompany the boat.

Vast beds of turtle grass and water only 4 to 10 feet deep make Biscayne Bay a nursery for a host of young marine animals—look for shrimp, spiny lobsters, sponges, and crabs.

Scan the sky for Brown Pelicans, cormorants, and herons.

Snorkel trips offer better views of the reef habitat. Snorkeling equipment is available, and a park ranger presents an introductory briefing before the trip leaves the harbor.

With their in-water viewpoint, snorkelers may see sea cucumbers, Christmas tree worms, sponges, and fish including such spectacular species as butterflyfish, parrotfish, damselfish, wrasses, angelfish, and gobies. All told, more than 500 types of fish ply park waters.

1 Elliott Key The concessionaire offers tours to **Boca Chita Key,** a popular camping and picnicking spot with a 65-foot-high ornamental lighthouse, and sometimes to Elliott Key.

The latter is of greater interest to nature lovers; a 6-mile trail runs the length of the island through a subtropical forest full of birds, butterflies, and distinctive plants. (Known as the "Spite Highway," the trail was originally a six-lane road bulldozed in the 1960s by developers trying to prevent the establishment of a national monument.)

Elliott Key has primitive campsites, restrooms, a nature trail, a swimming area, and a ranger station.

The schedule for some of these trips varies seasonally, so checking first with the concessionaire *(www.biscayneunderwater.com)* is always wise.

▶ Kayak/Canoe/Private Boat Trips

All in all, it pays to plan ahead and check with park personnel and the concessionaire for options at the time of your visit in terms of renting nonmotorized boats or bringing your own craft.

The same is true for other seasonal park tours. Both the ranger-led **Jones Lagoon** and wreck-snorkeling trips operate on limited schedules. Other paddling trips are offered more frequently in the park's winter season. (Mosquitoes, heat, and humidity make many activities unpleasant in hotter months.)

2 Jones Lagoon There is a secret world within the park—quieter and more solitary—among the keys south

Coral reef

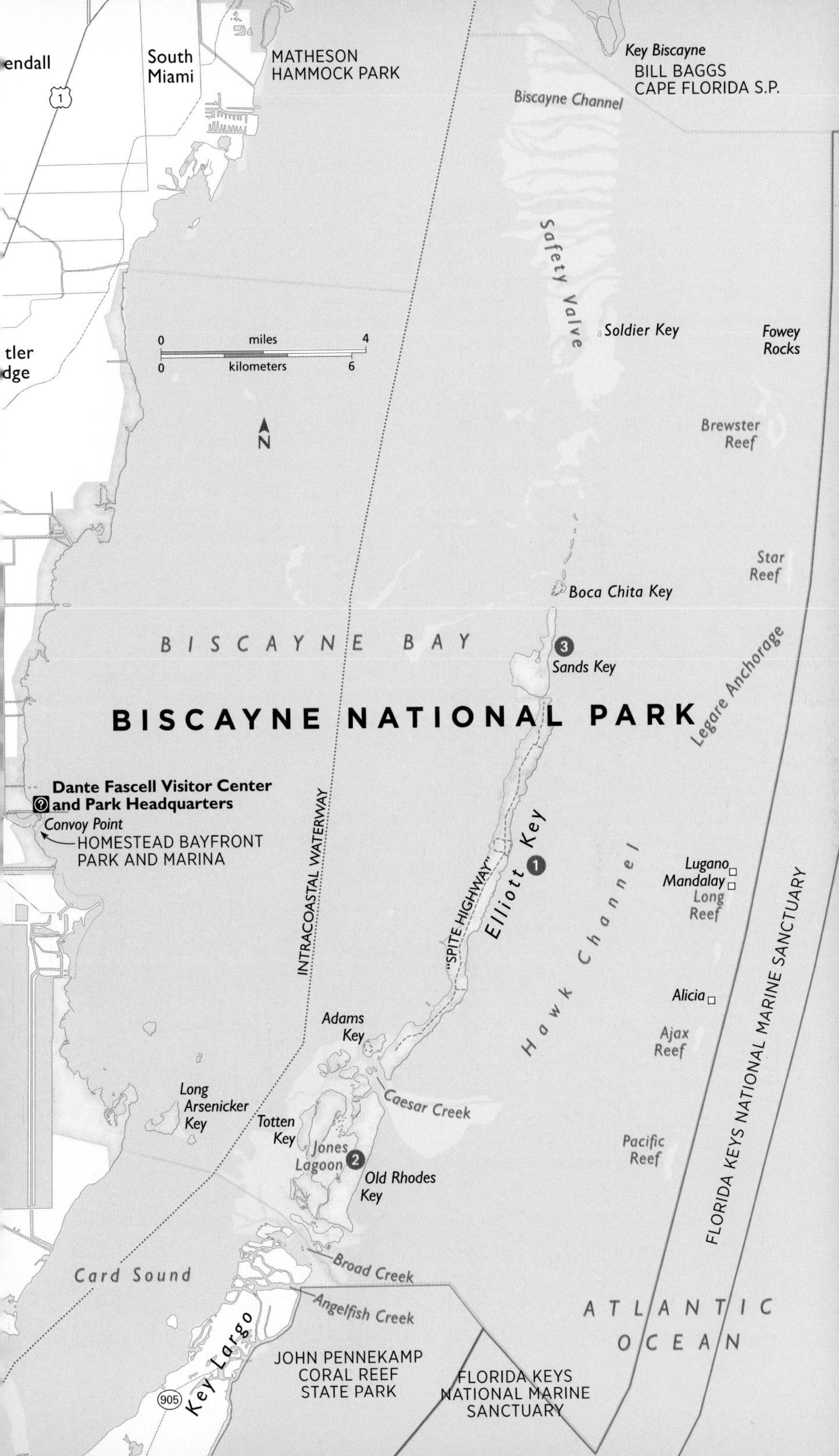

endall
South Miami
MATHESON HAMMOCK PARK
Key Biscayne
BILL BAGGS CAPE FLORIDA S.P.
Biscayne Channel
Safety Valve
Soldier Key
Fowey Rocks
0 miles 4
0 kilometers 6
N
tler
dge
Brewster Reef
Star Reef
Boca Chita Key
BISCAYNE BAY
3
Sands Key
Legare Anchorage
BISCAYNE NATIONAL PARK
Dante Fascell Visitor Center and Park Headquarters
Convoy Point
HOMESTEAD BAYFRONT PARK AND MARINA
INTRACOASTAL WATERWAY
"SPITE HIGHWAY"
Elliott Key
1
Hawk Channel
Lugano
Mandalay
Long Reef
FLORIDA KEYS NATIONAL MARINE SANCTUARY
Alicia
Adams Key
Ajax Reef
Caesar Creek
Long Arsenicker Key
Totten Key
Jones Lagoon
2
Old Rhodes Key
Pacific Reef
Card Sound
Broad Creek
Angelfish Creek
ATLANTIC OCEAN
Key Largo
905
JOHN PENNEKAMP CORAL REEF STATE PARK
FLORIDA KEYS NATIONAL MARINE SANCTUARY

of **Caesar Creek,** the water gap at the southern end of Elliott Key.

The park offers a kayak and canoe trip to Jones Lagoon. Johnson notes: "You spend the day with a park ranger. The trip is offered only in winter to a limited number of people, and it depends on the weather.

"You enter a different world, even though when you leave you're within sight of downtown Miami. I've worked at eight parks across the country, including Yellowstone and Grand Canyon, and it amazes me each time I go to Jones Lagoon, there's so much life. You might see Cassiopeia jellyfish, also known as upside-down jellyfish. There's a rookery of Roseate Spoonbills, and Magnificent Frigatebirds soar overhead."

Roseate Spoonbills

Sharks and rays are often seen on these guided paddling trips, along with smaller but equally intriguing creatures such as sea stars, spiny lobsters, and the primitive animals called tunicates. Because there is a shuttle from Adams Key to Jones Lagoon, this is the only park-operated canoe/kayak trip that requires paying a fee.

While it's possible to visit Jones Lagoon and the surrounding channels on your own, the logistics are difficult. Kayaks and canoes can be rented at Convoy Point, but private watercraft can only be taken to Jones Lagoon by concessionaires; sometimes a concessionaire will ferry private canoes or kayaks to the keys if space is available on their boats. (They may charge a fee.)

3 Sands Key Gary Bremen, long-time park ranger, has another off-the-beaten-path suggestion for people with their own boats.

"There's a little hole in the middle of Sands Key, which is an area that most people don't visit. It almost became a marina in the 1960s when the whole area was threatened with development. Skilled boaters who know where it is can sneak in there and have this private lagoon in the mangroves to themselves."

▶ Maritime Heritage Trail

"People know about the reef, but they often forget about our shipwrecks,"

Local Intelligence

One paddling trip offered more frequently in the park's winter season is a near-shore ranger-led canoe trip among the mangroves. One of the four ecosystems represented in the national park, mangroves may not be as immediately attractive as Biscayne Bay, the keys, or the reef, but these trees harbor a diversity of life. Along with wading birds, fish, and crabs, visitors might see a manatee (the large, harmless marine mammal that feeds on aquatic vegetation and can weigh a ton or more) or even a crocodile.

Prop roots of mangroves

says Bremen. "For a different experience, I'd suggest a ranger-led snorkel tour on one of the sites of the Maritime Heritage Trail."

Among the dozens of wrecks in the park are six sites on the Maritime Heritage Trail.

"I would focus on *Mandalay,* which ran aground on Long Reef on New Year's Day, 1966," Bremen says. "The wreck has been there long enough that there's fire coral and other things growing on it, and there are lots of fish associated with the site. It usually has very clear water."

Other wrecks on the Maritime Heritage Trail include *Alicia,* which sank in 1905, and *Lugano,* which at the time of its grounding in 1913 was the largest vessel ever to founder in the Florida Keys.

Note that because of the depth at which they landed, shipwrecks other than *Mandalay* are more suited for exploration by scuba divers than by snorkelers. Contact the park for schedules and required reservations. All tours are weather dependent.

One wonderful trip that we offer is to a little-known area called Jones Lagoon. It's not very accessible because it's very shallow, but kayaks and canoes can get in there easily.

—MATT JOHNSON
Biscayne National Park ranger

White egret near the Anhinga Trail

EVERGLADES

Beyond the theme parks and hotel-lined beaches of South Florida, beyond the golf courses and city skyscrapers, Everglades National Park protects more than 2,400 square miles of Florida's primeval past.

Comprising most of the southern tip of the state's peninsula, the park has as its heart a "river of grass" where water flows seasonally north to south across a flat sawgrass prairie, fueling an ecosystem known for abundant wildlife, from alligators to flocks of colorful wading birds.

Agriculture and urban development have seriously altered natural habitats in the Everglades ecosystem, yet this place endures as a must-see destination for environmentally minded travelers. Nothing like it exists anywhere else on the planet—reason enough for its designation as a World Heritage site, an international biosphere reserve, and a wetland of international importance. It's an otherworldly place of secrets.

Year-Round Visitor Centers

- **Ernest F. Coe Visitor Center**
  At 40001 Fla. 9336/SW 344 St. in Homestead
- **Flamingo Visitor Center**
  On Main Park Road, 38 miles south of the park entrance
- **Shark Valley Visitor Center**
  Off Tamiami Trail, 25 miles west of Florida Turnpike
- **Gulf Coast Visitor Center**
  On Fla. 29, 5 miles south of Tamiami Trail, Everglades City

305-242-7700, *www.nps.gov/ever*

▶ Main Park Road

Getting off the tourist trail is a little more difficult at Everglades than in many parks. Around 86 percent of the park is federally designated wilderness (the largest east of the Rockies), composed of freshwater and coastal prairie, marsh, pine and cypress woods, mangroves, and the waters and islands of **Florida Bay.**

Much of the wet-prairie and slough area seems fairly inaccessible to the average visitor; the nature of the landscape limits hiking trails. Most backcountry campsites are reached by boat, and a canoe or kayak along the 44-mile wilderness waterway or out into Florida Bay is often the best way to enjoy the park in solitude.

Visiting in the off season (the rainy summer, from May through November) cuts the crowds, but brings discouraging issues: heat, humidity, curtailed park activities, and, worst of all, abundant mosquitoes. Wildlife is dispersed through sprawling wetlands and harder to observe. The ideal time to see Everglades is usually mid-March through April.

The main park road runs 38 miles from the **Ernest F. Coe Visitor Center** on the eastern edge of the park to the Flamingo area on Florida Bay. Driving out and back along this route and stopping along the way to hike, bike, canoe, or take a boat or tram tour are the park's most popular activities.

1 Gumbo Limbo Trail The 0.5-mile **Anhinga Trail** at the **Royal Palm** area is definitely on the tourist itinerary, but the chance to see and photograph gators, turtles, and birds is too good to pass up. The best advice: Be here just after dawn. Far fewer people take the time to walk the short Gumbo Limbo Trail nearby; if you do, you'll have a good chance to see songbirds and some of the park's fantastic array of butterflies.

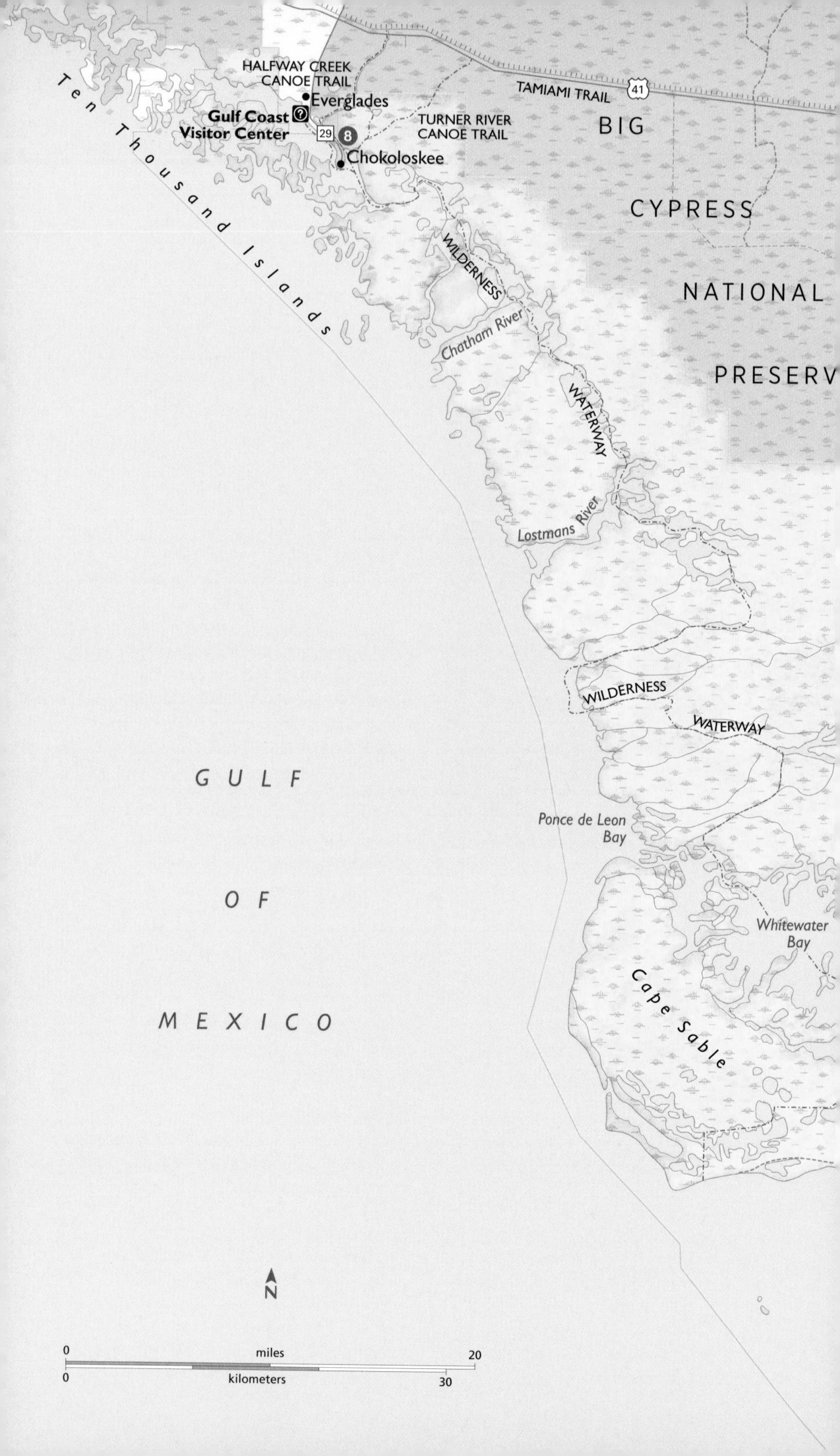

HALFWAY CREEK CANOE TRAIL

Everglades

Gulf Coast Visitor Center

29

8

Chokoloskee

TURNER RIVER CANOE TRAIL

TAMIAMI TRAIL

41

BIG CYPRESS NATIONAL PRESERV

Ten Thousand Islands

WILDERNESS

Chatham River

WATERWAY

Lostmans River

WILDERNESS

WATERWAY

Ponce de Leon Bay

Whitewater Bay

Cape Sable

GULF OF MEXICO

N

0 miles 20

0 kilometers 30

THE EVERGLADES
EVERGLADES NATIONAL PARK
Shark Valley Visitor Center
BOBCAT BOARDWALK
OTTER CAVE HAMMOCK TRAIL
7
6
TRAM TOUR
Observation Tower
TAMIAMI TRAIL
FLORIDA'S TURNPIKE HOMESTEAD EXTENSION
94
41
997
836
826
821
874
1
9336
905
Pa-hay-okee
Double Dome
PINELANDS TRAIL
3
MAIN PARK ROAD
RESEARCH ROAD
2
Nike Missile Site HM 69
Royal Palm
1 ANHINGA TRAIL
GUMBO LIMBO TRAIL
Ernest F. Coe Visitor Center and Park Headquarters
Homestead
Florida City
BISCAYNE NATIONAL PARK
Mahogany Hammock
5 NINE MILE POND CANOE TRAIL
4 SNAKE BIGHT TRAIL
Snake Bight
Flamingo Visitor Center
CROCODILE LAKE N.W.R.
Key Largo
JOHN PENNEKAMP CORAL REEF STATE PARK
Key Largo
OVERSEAS HIGHWAY
FLORIDA BAY
FLORIDA KEYS NATIONAL MARINE SANCTUARY
Plantation Key

Palmetto plants in the Pinelands area

② Research Road Nearby Research Road is a place to experience what Lori Oberhofer, wildlife biologist, calls the Everglades soundscape. "I love the concert of peeps and croaks from frogs and toads after a late afternoon thunderstorm," she says. "There's an amazing chorus of green tree frogs, cricket frogs, chorus frogs, oak toads, and southern toads, among others. I'm impressed at how an area so quiet during the heat of the day comes alive with a symphony of sound after a cooling rainstorm."

③ Pinelands Trail The main park road passes through pine forest habitat (the short Pinelands Trail on the north side is a good introduction to this ecosystem), then reaches an area where bald cypresses are the dominant tree.

Note the circular stands of cypress locally called "domes." These are favorite destinations for naturalists who enjoy "slough-slogging," walking through shallow water that forms the "river of grass." Sturdy shoes and clothes you don't mind getting wet are essential, of course.

"I have gone into the slough since I was little, but each and every time it's a new adventure and I become like a child again, giddy about exploring," Yvette Cano, park ranger, says. "I love to discover the magic under the water. At first people are overwhelmed with fear and apprehension, but as soon as they set foot in the slough it transforms them, and they see the beauty and mystery."

Double Dome, near the Pa-hay-okee overlook, is a favorite destination for slough sloggers. If you're unsure of your abilities, check with a ranger for advice. Ranger-guided slough walks are offered regularly.

④ Snake Bight Trail All the interpretive trails along the park road, such as **Mahogany Hammock,** are worth trying, but for a bit of solitude,

Nicholas Aumen of the park's science staff recommends this 1.8-mile (one way) hike from the road to a "bight" (small bay) on Florida Bay. "Walk to the platform at the end of the trail," he says. "Take along binoculars for bird-watching."

For a different perspective on the same scene, Aumen says visitors should continue to the ranger station and marina at **Flamingo,** rent a kayak, and paddle to Snake Bight: "You'll have almost guaranteed viewings of Roseate Spoonbills, eagles, Reddish Egrets, sharks, crocodiles, porpoises, and a wide variety of wading birds, especially on exposed mudflats at low tide—and the occasional flamingo."

You don't have to paddle all the way to Snake Bight to enjoy park bird life. "I like watching birds silhouetted across the setting sun as they fly by off Flamingo," Oberhofer says. "You can sit out there in a boat or kayak and watch flocks of ibises, egrets, herons, and pelicans flying from the mainland to their night roosts on the islands in the bay. It's a beautiful and peaceful experience, and it reminds me of how diverse the wildlife is in this park and how accessible it is if you simply take a moment to really look and listen."

On the mangrove Tunnel Tour [that departs from Everglades City], discover a different ecosystem. That's the area of alligators, river otters, wading birds, turtles, and other reptiles.

—CHARLES WRIGHT
local tour guide

5 Nine Mile Pond Consider taking a canoe trip on one of the trails near Flamingo. The best for beginners is probably the 5-mile loop at Nine Mile Pond, which has numbered markers for guidance. (An optional shortcut makes the loop 3.5 miles.)

You'll likely see alligators and a wide variety of birds. Rangers tell paddlers not to be discouraged if the beginning of the trip, across the open water of Nine Mile Pond, is made strenuous by wind. Paddling gets easier once you're in the marsh. The trip takes four to five hours.

(Free guided canoe trips are offered during the December to March season, but you must make reservations well in advance.)

▶ Shark Valley

A smaller percentage of visitors travel to Shark Valley in the northern part of the park, reached off US 41 **(Tamiami Trail)** west of Miami.

6 Tram Tour There's one main attraction here: an old oil exploration route now a 15-mile scenic loop, which offers a look at the freshwater slough that makes up the heart of the park. The ranger-guided tram tour illuminates this ecosystem.

To get really close to the slough, rent a bicycle and use pedal power to travel the loop. The trip takes two or three hours, and, of course, the landscape is as flat as the proverbial pancake.

In the midst of this vast scene of seasonally flooded sawgrass, you'll appreciate the uniqueness of the water-powered natural world of the Everglades. Stop at the observation tower at the southern end of the loop for an elevated panorama of the terrain. (Bring plenty of water, as there are no facilities on the route.)

7 Shark Valley Walks At the beginning of the loop (if you bike it in the recommended counterclockwise direction) are two short walks designed to showcase specialized Everglades habitats. The **Bobcat Boardwalk** passes through a bayhead, an isolated hardwood grove with a specialized group of species including red bay. The 0.25-mile **Otter Cave Hammock Trail** winds through a hammock, a dense stand of hardwoods growing just slightly higher than a bayhead, with trees such as live oak, maple, mahogany, gumbo limbo, and cocoplum.

Anywhere along the loop, watch for the Snail Kite, a tropical raptor

Local Intelligence

"**Everglades National Park** may bring thoughts of alligators, wading birds, and wilderness, but it also holds mysteries that stretch back to the Cold War," says Ryan Meyer, park ranger. "Deep within the river of grass lies a former U.S. Army missile site that operated for fifteen years protecting Miami from threat of aerial attack."

Established in 1964 near the town of Homestead, the once fiercely guarded, now long-abandoned **Nike Missile Site HM-69,** located off Research Road, was opened to the public for tours in 2009. Designed to defend against attacks from Cuba, the site once included missiles carrying nuclear weapons. Tours offered in season visit missile locations as well as guard-dog kennels, barracks, control centers, and other buildings. Check with the park headquarters to make reservations for these popular guided tours.

Aerial view of the Ten Thousand Islands

found in the United States only in southern Florida. As its name implies, it feeds mostly on large freshwater snails. Seeing one of these rare birds is a unique Everglades thrill.

▶ Gulf Coast

Continuing west from Shark Valley on the Tamiami Trail brings you to the turn south for **Everglades City** and the **Gulf Coast Visitor Center** in the Ten Thousand Islands.

8 Ten Thousand Islands Accurately described as a maze, this coastal region comprises mangrove islands separated by narrow channels, and stretches southeast more than 60 miles to Flamingo. The issue here, as Charles Wright, commercial tour guide, says, is that "the only access to it is by water."

The road reaches a dead end at **Chokoloskee,** and hiking trails are almost nonexistent. Luckily, options are available for exploring the area. A park concessionaire offers cruises through both saltwater and brackish water areas. Others operate tours that take visitors to various destinations, such as a barrier island, by motorboat, then switch to kayaks for access to small channels and close-up looks at the environment.

"The big critters folks would normally see would be manatees, dolphins, various types of sea turtles, various raptors including eagles and hawks, lots of shorebirds, and wading birds," Wright says. But on the Tunnel Tour more inland creatures are seen—alligators, river otters, wading birds, turtles.

Travelers who want to explore the park's Gulf Coast area on their own can bring or rent canoes or kayaks for routes ranging from a few hours to several days (the latter only for well-prepared and experienced paddlers).

The **Halfway Creek and Turner River Loop,** for example, takes about four hours and passes through tunnels of mangroves for much of the way.

Talk to rangers about where to go, and take maps, a compass, proper clothing, sun protection, and water.

"In 1976, my brother and I climbed the Diamond Face of Longs Peak [in Rocky Mountain National Park]. After a night tethered to a 3-foot-wide perch at 13,800 feet, we awoke to a spectacular sunrise."

—SENATOR MARK UDALL, COLORADO
NATIONAL PARK TRUST 2010 RECIPIENT
BRUCE F. VENTO PUBLIC SERVICE AWARD

[2] SOUTHWEST AND THE ROCKIES

The Watchman near the south entrance of Zion National Park

Rio Grande near hot springs

BIG BEND

Set in remote southwestern Texas, far from major cities and interstate highways, Big Bend National Park isn't a place travelers visit on a whim. It lies just across the Rio Grande from Mexico, at the end of a long road that doesn't go much of anyplace else. Most of the park is Chihuahuan Desert; in the center, the Chisos Mountains rise to 7,832 feet.

There are those who simply cruise the park's paved roads by car, ascending to the stunning Basin and descending to Santa Elena Canyon, and then move on. Perhaps they're a little bit intimidated by Big Bend's jagged terrain and immense distances; by plants armed with spines and points; by the black bears, mountain lions, and rattlesnakes that find homes here. That's a shame, because the park offers a great many relatively easy ways to experience its secrets, including striking rock formations, spectacular vistas, and awesome river canyons.

Year-Round Visitor Centers

- **Panther Junction Visitor Center**
  3 miles east of Chisos Mountain Basin Junction, 26 miles south of North Entrance
- **Chisos Basin Visitor Center**
  On Chisos Basin Road, 6 miles south of main park road
- **Persimmon Gap Visitor Center**
  On US 385, at North Entrance

Seasonal Visitor Centers

- **Castolon Visitor Center**
  On Ross Maxwell Scenic Drive, 22 miles south of Santa Elena Junction
- **Rio Grande Village Visitor Center**
  20 miles east of Panther Junction, Tex.

432-477-2251, *www.nps.gov/bibe*

▶ The Basin

Heading up Green Gulch on Chisos Basin Road, a first-time visitor will likely be in a hurry to reach the Basin, where the massive rock formation called **Casa Grande** looms enticingly ahead.

❶ **Lost Mine Trail** At 5.1 miles from Basin Junction is the trailhead for one of the best short hikes in the park. The Lost Mine Trail is a 2.4-mile out-and-back hike, ending in a wonderful panoramic view after an elevation gain of more than 1,000 feet.

An alternative is to walk just the first mile, stopping at a saddle where the vista is almost as good, taking in Casa Grande, **Juniper Canyon,** and a long-distance view south into **Mexico.**

❷ **Boot Canyon** Chisos Basin Road continues to the Basin itself, with its campground, ranger station, and Chisos Mountains Lodge (the only noncamping accommodations in the park). A variety of hikes are possible here, from strenuous multi-day backpacking trips around the Chisos Mountains to the 0.3-mile, accessible **Window Trail.** The latter provides a look through the Window, a low place in the Basin wall where all the rainfall in the area drains via Oak Creek.

Trails in the Basin area are well traveled, so it's difficult to get off the beaten path. Nonetheless, if you're going to do only one hike here, consider the fairly strenuous 9-mile round-trip to Boot Canyon (bring plenty of water). It's a steep climb up switchbacks on the **Pinnacles Trail** (3.5 miles) to a pass with wonderful views of Big Bend country, where

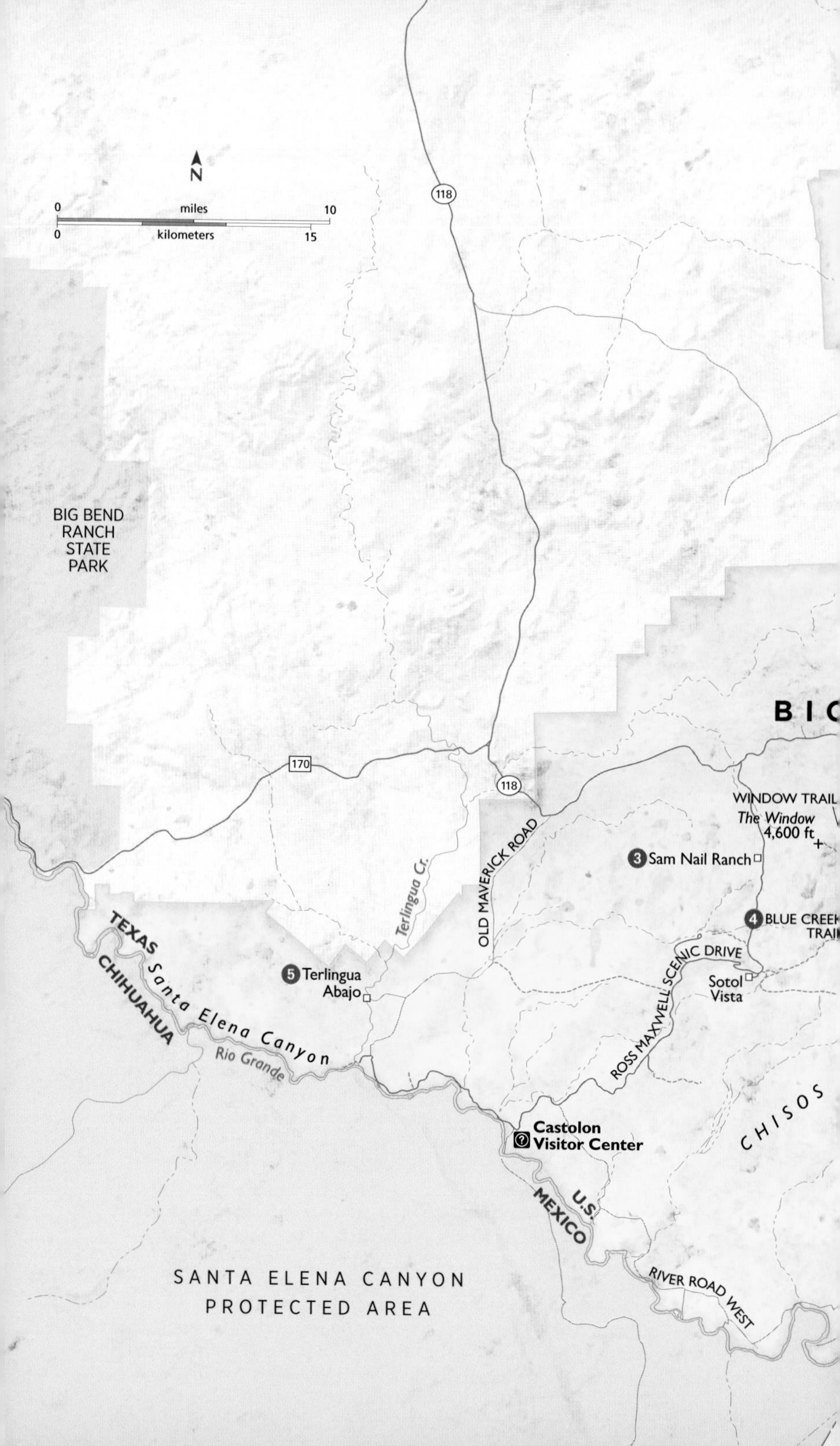

N
0
miles
10
0
kilometers
15
118
BIG BEND
RANCH
STATE
PARK
170
118
BIG
WINDOW TRAIL
The Window
4,600 ft
OLD MAVERICK ROAD
3 Sam Nail Ranch
4 BLUE CREEK
TRAIL
Terlingua Cr.
ROSS MAXWELL SCENIC DRIVE
Sotol
Vista
TEXAS
CHIHUAHUA
Santa Elena Canyon
Rio Grande
5 Terlingua
Abajo
Castolon
Visitor Center
CHISOS
U.S.
MEXICO
RIVER ROAD WEST
SANTA ELENA CANYON
PROTECTED AREA

385
Persimmon Gap
Visitor Center
2627
BLACK GAP
WILDLIFE MANAGEMENT AREA
ROSILLOS
RANCH
BEND NATIONAL PARK
Rio Grande
TEXAS
COAHUILA
MADERAS
DEL CARMEN
PROTECTED
AREA
Panther Junction
Visitor Center and
Park Headquarters
BASIN ROAD
LOST MINE TRAIL 1
Casa Grande
7,325 ft
Boot Canyon 2
Emory
Peak
MOUNTAINS
Boquillas
Canyon
Overlook
8
Boquillas Canyon
Rio Grande
Village
Visitor
Center
7 Hot Springs
RIVER ROAD EAST
6 Mariscal
Mine
Rio Grande

you're surrounded by spires of volcanic rhyolite. From there it's a comparatively easy walk to get a view of **The Boot,** an odd rock column that does look like an upside-down cowboy boot.

▶ Ross Maxwell Scenic Drive

This 30-mile (one way) paved road leads from the main east-west park highway southwest to **Santa Elena Canyon** on the **Rio Grande.** Along the way it offers views of the **Chisos Mountains** to the east, and several opportunities for exploration.

3 Old Sam Nail Ranch A few miles along the route, stop at the Sam Nail ranch to see the remains of a homestead dating from 1916.

"This is our favorite site on the west side of the park for a quiet, cool birding experience," say Ron and Jane Payne, park volunteers. "You can sit on a bench, beneath the pecan trees planted by Sam and Nena Nail in the early 20th century, and enjoy a dozen or more bird species and perhaps even a javelina or gray fox that has come to water beneath the creaky cranking of the windmill. It is a lovely way to spend a morning or evening in the park."

4 Blue Creek Trail Less than 5 miles farther, stop at the Blue Creek Ranch overlook, the start of a moderately strenuous hike with fine scenic rewards. Walk down to the buildings below the road, built for a ranching operation in the 1940s.

Terlingua Abajo has a grave site and old homesteads. Families still go back because they have folks buried out there.

—GLEN HENINGTON
local guide

Then hike the first 2 miles or so of the Blue Creek Trail. This route was established to move sheep from the hot lowlands into the cooler Chisos in summer. It's a hard climb all the way to the top, but you don't have to go that far to enjoy **Red Rocks Canyon,** where you'll be surrounded by a variety of spires and "balanced" rocks in a multitude of delightful forms.

5 Terlingua Abajo Past the historic community of **Castolon,** Ross Maxwell Scenic Drive parallels the Rio Grande to magnificent **Santa Elena Canyon,** where the river has cut a deep canyon with claustrophobia-inducing

Local Intelligence

Along the Ross Maxwell Scenic Drive, Sotol Vista, named for an abundant plant with dagger-like leaves and a tall flowering spike, is one of the park's major attractions, but for a special experience, visit in the evening. "I chose this spot for an evening program so I could enjoy magnificent sunsets and watch the craggy mountains and deep canyons disappear into the shadow of twilight," says Gail Abend, park interpreter. "The silence on Sotol Vista enhances the celestial display as the stars appear one by one, unaffected by any man-made light."

walls. A walk into the canyon is a must-do at Big Bend.

Far less visited is the abandoned community of Terlingua Abajo, located about 3 miles north and reached via the unpaved **Old Maverick Road.** The site is a favorite of local guide Glen Henington, who finds it evocative of a time when Mexican farmers, Anglo ranchers, and mining companies were scattered across this harsh landscape, before the national park was established.

"A hundred years ago this was amazingly inhabited for the middle of nowhere," Henington says.

▶ West and East River Road

Another of Henington's favorite Big Bend spots requires some planning to visit. The River Road runs 51 miles across the southern part of the park, from near Castolon to the vicinity of **Rio Grande Village** on the east. A high-clearance vehicle is needed for this primitive route (rentals are available from local outfitters), and weather sometimes makes the road impassable (check with a ranger).

6 Mariscal Mine About halfway along River Road lies Mariscal Mine, significant as Texas' best preserved historic site from the era of mercury mining. The Big Bend country once produced one-third of the country's output of "quicksilver."

"The Mariscal Mine brings in the human occupation of Big Bend, which started with the Native Americans," Henington says. "I like to walk up to the top of those ruins and just sit there and contemplate what life must have been like in the late 1800s and early 1900s, mining mercury by hand."

The site, a national historic district, includes houses, offices, kilns, furnaces, and a blacksmith shop.

Claret cup cactus

▶ The Eastern Park

A visitor center, store, picnic area, and very popular campground make the Rio Grande Village area a primary destination for many park visitors. A walk on the nature trail accessible from the campground is a must for wildlife-watchers (especially birders).

7 Hot Springs Here you can see the ruins of a bathhouse constructed in the early 20th century. Possibly the first tourist attraction in the area, it offered "healing" water to visitors for decades. Only the foundation of the bathhouse remains, but you can still soak tired muscles in the 105°F water flowing from the ground.

8 Boquillas Canyon While Santa Elena Canyon in the western part of Big Bend is justifiably famous, don't overlook Boquillas Canyon, at the end of a spur road 4 miles east of Rio Grande Village. A 1.4-mile round-trip walk here takes you to the top of a cliff overlooking the Rio Grande and then into the canyon itself.

Landscape littered with 225-million-year-old petrified trees

PETRIFIED FOREST

Of all our national parks, Petrified Forest surely ranks among the most susceptible to the dreaded drive-through visit. This situation results from the park's layout: A 28-mile road runs its length, with separate and convenient entrances and exits off I-40. It's easy for a visitor to cruise through, stopping to gaze over the Painted Desert and walk a short trail among the giant logs, before returning to the freeway, missing the secrets waiting in this 346-square-mile expanse of northern Arizona's Colorado Plateau region. Start with a fascinating geological past (which created the colors that inspired the name Painted Desert as well as the petrified logs) then add fossilized prehistoric creatures, archaeological sites of ancient peoples, and diverse animals and plants.

Year-Round Visitor Center

- **Painted Desert Visitor Center**
  North Entrance, off I-40

  928-524-6228, *www.nps.gov/pefo*

▶ Park Road, Northern Section

Just north of I-40, enter the **Painted Desert Visitor Center** to watch the film "Timeless Impressions," shown every half-hour. With this overview of the park you're ready to start your exploration—but first, take time for one more indoor activity.

Head north less than 2 miles to the **Painted Desert Inn,** built in 1924 on historic and legendary Route 66, and once home to the famed "Harvey Girls," waitresses who served travelers in the mid-20th century.

The former inn now functions as a bookstore and museum, which features historic murals by Hopi artist Fred Kabotie.

1 Black Forest Because of the nature of Petrified Forest's landscape and layout, getting off the tourist route often involves a bit of cross-country travel, and that means using basic backcountry equipment and skills. Wear good boots and a hat, take plenty of water and sunscreen, and carry a map and compass or GPS—and know how to use them. Even though some off-trail travel is fairly simple, it's always better to use too much caution than not enough. If in doubt, ask a park ranger for advice.

Your first chance to leave the beaten path begins at a trailhead behind the Painted Desert Inn. Seeing what Bill Parker, park paleontologist, calls "one of the most scenic places in the park" requires a 5-mile round-trip hike north into the **Painted Desert—**a small challenge with a big reward. It's about a mile to the usually dry **Lithodendron Wash,** and about 0.5 mile farther to the petrified logs of the **Angels Garden** area.

"The Black Forest is one of the largest accumulations of petrified wood in the park, but it's seen by only a small percentage of park visitors because of its remoteness," Parker says.

This moderately strenuous route requires an awareness of the weather, because Lithodendron Wash should not be crossed if it's raining or threatening rain; consult a ranger if you're unsure of conditions.

You'll be glad you made this hike when you're standing amid massive petrified tree trunks, surrounded by the deep reds and ochers of rugged landforms. A free permit is required for overnight camping.

PETRIFIED FOREST NATIONAL WILDERNESS AREA
PAINTED DESERT
PETRIFIED FOREST
Angels Garden
BLACK FOREST
1
Painted Desert Inn National Historic Landmark
HISTORIC ROUTE 66
40
Private Land
Lithodendron Wash
Painted Desert Visitor Center
BURLINGTON NORTH SANTE FE RAILROAD
Puerco
Private Land
40
NATIONAL
Puerco Pueblo
2
Newspaper Rock
Puerco
BLUE MESA TRAIL
3
Billings Gap Overlook
Blue Mesa
Dry Wash
Private Land
Jasper Forest
4
Jasper Forest Overlook
PARK
Crystal Forest
PETRIFIED FOREST NATIONAL WILDERNESS AREA
Martha's Butte
5
Walker's Stump
Rainbow Forest Museum
GIANT LOGS TRAIL
LONG LOGS TRAIL
6
Long Logs
N
0 miles 4
0 kilometers 6
180

❷ Puerco Pueblo and Newspaper Rock Back on the park road, cross old Route 66, I-40, and the Sante Fe railroad line, stopping often to admire the Painted Desert scenery. Stop, too, at popular Puerco Pueblo (the remains of a 100-room settlement of the Ancestral Puebloan people, abandoned in the 14th century) and Newspaper Rock (boulders covered in hundreds of petroglyphs).

❸ Billings Gap Overlook Take the side road to the **Blue Mesa Trail** (1 mile), an otherworldly landscape of conical, multilayered hills formed of clay and sandstone. The moderately strenuous trail is well worth walking. (The upper portion is flat and easy.)

To see a less visited area, park at the fourth pullout on the loop road and strike out east along the northern edge of steep-sided **Blue Mesa.** A hike of less than a mile leads to the Billings Gap Overlook, a favorite spot for Bill Reitze, park archaeologist.

"It's a great viewpoint of the badlands to the north and the broad grassy valleys to the south," Reitze says. "You may also see petrified wood flakes used as prehistoric tools in the dunes on the mesa top." (A gentle reminder to you and your children: All petrified wood and artifacts should, of course, be left in place for future visitors.)

On your return, head southwest from the overlook just about 0.4 mile for a view into a picturesque amphitheater, naturally created by the elements. This walk, though not difficult, is unmarked, so take normal backcountry precautions.

Striations on Blue Mesa

▶ Park Road—Southern Section

The Jasper Forest-to-Long Logs Trail section of the north-south park road contains the majority of the park's petrified wood. This ancient wood comes from trees that grew here more than 200 million years ago.

4 Jasper Forest Back on the main road, it's about 3 miles south from the Blue Mesa Trail side road to the Jasper Forest Overlook.

While most visitors simply stand and admire the view, there's a way to see what Parker calls "an incredible garden of petrified wood" much more closely.

Walk back to the main park road and then head to the north about 250 yards. On the west you'll see the traces of a 1930s road dropping down into Jasper Forest. Though the route has been abandoned for decades, it can still be followed with care; it heads northwest about 200 yards and then north.

This is an easy stroll, though it does require sturdy shoes, nimble feet, and a good sense of direction.

Jasper Forest was once called First Forest, because it was the first group of petrified logs encountered by visitors heading south by wagon from the rail station 6 miles away.

The deep blues, purples, and whites that color the badlands [of Blue Mesa] seem to shift throughout the day and with the season. You may also encounter remains of prehistoric structures.

—BILL REITZE
Petrified Forest National Park archaeologist

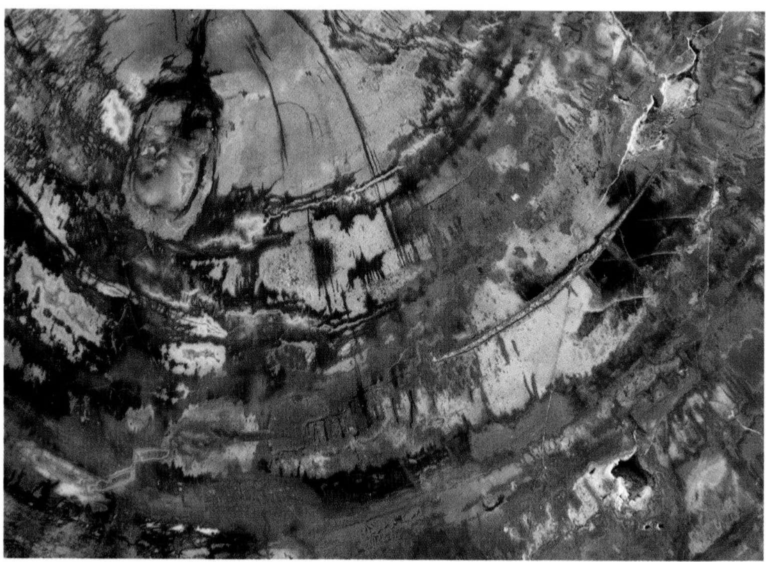

Petrified wood, cut and polished with intricate patterns and colors

Petrified logs along the Long Logs Trail

5 Martha's Butte About 1.8 miles south of the **Crystal Forest** parking area you'll find another opportunity for a solitary and rewarding walk through interesting terrain. Park at the bridge over Dry Wash and look northwest for Martha's Butte, prominent on the horizon 0.8 mile away as the crow flies. To reach it, walk the bed of the wash north about 0.7 mile, then strike out northwest another 0.5 mile.

You'll see petrified wood and maybe, if you are lucky, fossils. You might spot artifacts from historic and prehistoric times, as well.

Check about 100 yards southeast of Martha's Butte for **Walker's Stump:** not really a stump, but a petrified log that was buried upright by a flowing stream, then uncovered by erosion millions of years later.

6 Long Logs and Giant Logs Trails South on the park road you'll find must-see sites, including **Rainbow Forest Museum,** with exhibits including a diorama of some of the extinct reptiles that lived in this region tens of millions of years ago and examples of fossils found in the park. The museum sits in the **Rainbow Forest,** one of four major concentrations of petrified logs the park calls "forests."

Nearby are the Giant Logs and Long Logs Trails, both easy walks leading to some of the park's most impressive displays of large petrified trees. "Old Faithful," on the Giant Logs Trail, is nearly 10 feet in diameter. The great concentration of logs on the Long Logs Trail is thought to have resulted from a logjam in an ancient stream. Some of the logs seen here are more than 100 feet long.

An awe-inspiring view of sun on the canyon

GRAND CANYON

To understand the number of people who visit the Grand Canyon annually, picture all the passengers boarding airplanes for an entire year at a good-size airport—say, Kansas City International. In hard figures, that's close to five million yearly visitors.

The magnet for these journeys is what 19th-century explorer John Wesley Powell called the "most sublime spectacle on the earth": the iconic mile-deep gorge that ranks among the world's most beautiful and most renowned geological features.

The Grand Canyon's climate and topography mean that the great majority of visitors arrive during a seven-month warmer weather period and gather at a limited number of sites. The result is often crowding that degrades what should be an inspirational experience. The secret is to find alternatives to the most popular roadside viewpoints.

Year-Round Visitor Centers

- **Grand Canyon Visitor Center**
  South Rim by Mather Point, off of South Entrance Road
- **Backcountry Information Center**
  Village historic district, east of Maswik Lodge
- **Verkamp's Visitor Center**
  East of El Tovar Hotel and Hopi House
- **Desert View Visitor Center and Bookstore**
  25 miles east of Grand Canyon Village on South Rim

Seasonal Visitor Center

- **North Rim Visitor Center**
  Grand Canyon Lodge, adjacent to the parking lot on Bright Angel Point

928-638-7888, *www.nps.gov/grca*

▶ South Rim

It's simple to explain how to escape crowds at Grand Canyon: Descend into the canyon from the "rim"—the flattish plateau that surrounds the mammoth gorge—or travel to the North Rim.

The great majority of visitors enjoy the spectacular views down into the canyon without exploring its depths, and only about 10 percent of visitors leave the main tourist facilities on the South Rim to go to the north side of the park.

You shouldn't underestimate the physical effort and planning required to visit the inner canyon, however. Trails descend steeply, and in summer temperatures rise rapidly as elevation decreases. (The canyon floor at the Colorado River, at the bottom of the chasm, may be 25 degrees hotter than the rim.)

Every year park rangers have to rescue scores of people who hiked down a trail into the canyon without proper clothing or footwear, without enough food or (especially) water, or who didn't understand that *it takes at least twice as much time and energy* to ascend back to the rim as it takes to go down. The standard rule for a hike into the canyon is to turn around when you have drunk one-third of your water and/or spent one-third of the time you have available.

As for visiting the North Rim: Although you can see it from the South Rim's Grand Canyon Village—it's an average of about 10 miles away—the drive to the Grand Canyon Lodge area is 215 miles and requires

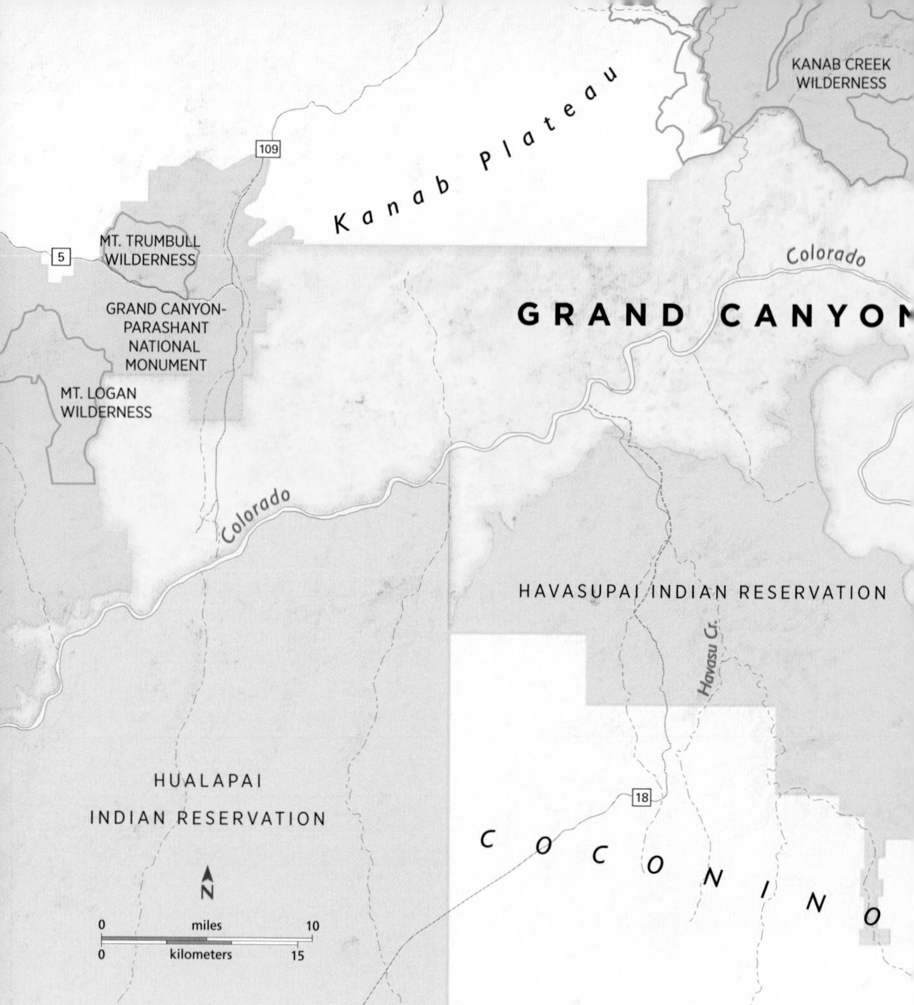

at least five hours. Hiking from the South Rim to the North Rim is only for extremely fit people who have made advance arrangements to spend one or, preferably, two nights in the inner canyon. Park rangers say that hiking down to the **Colorado River** and back up in one day is more difficult than running a marathon.

❶ East to South Kaibab Trailhead

Grand Canyon experts do know a few ways, though, to avoid the most concentrated of the South Rim crowds, ranging from simple strolls to strenuous hikes.

Take **Mather Point,** for example, the iconic spot where the **Grand Canyon Visitor Center** is located. Thousands of people enjoy the magnificent view here daily in summer; of those who walk part of the 13-mile **Rim Trail,** most head west toward the developments around Grand Canyon Village.

Instead, walk east along the easy paved trail toward the South Kaibab Trailhead. You won't be alone, but you'll have much less company along this path while you savor views into the canyon that are just as fine as elsewhere.

Options abound here: Walk 1.4 miles to the **Pipe Creek Vista** and catch the free shuttle bus back to Mather Point, or continue another

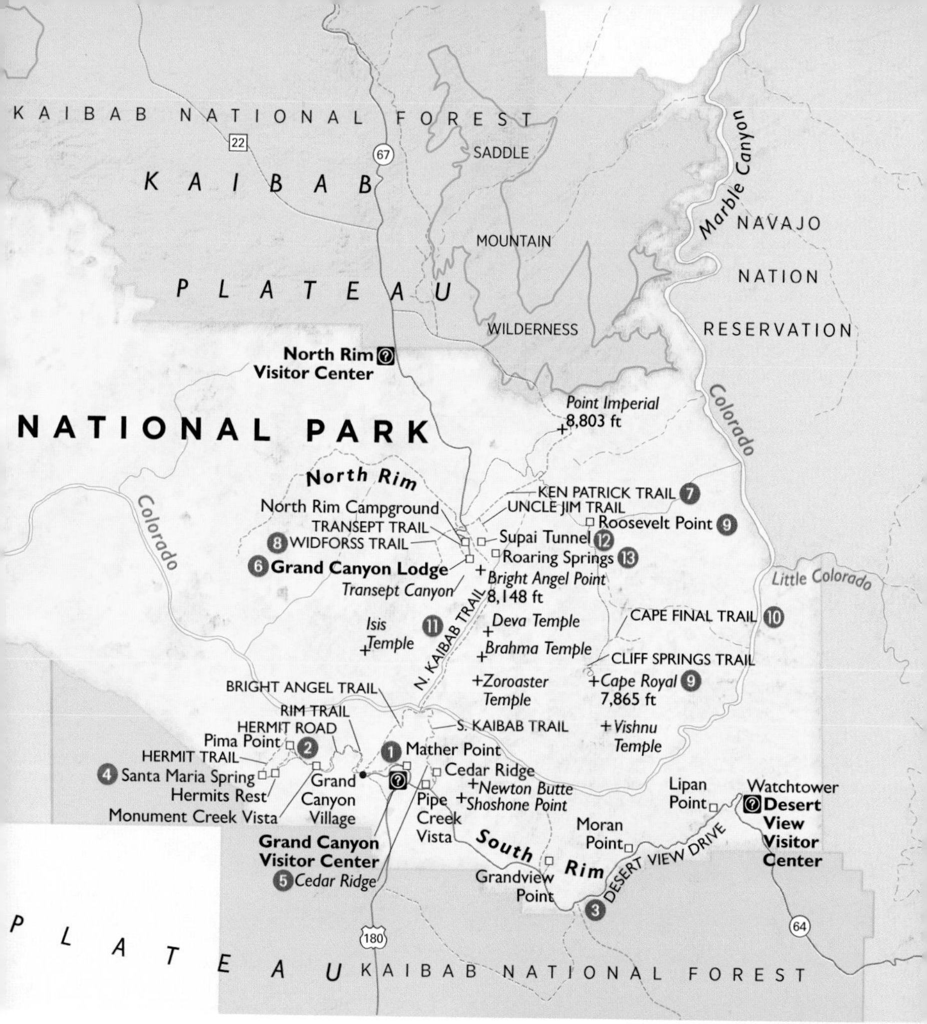

0.8 mile to the South Kaibab Trailhead and hop on the bus there. Of course, you can walk back to appreciate the vistas from another direction.

2 Trail From Monument Creek Vista to Pima Point Andy Pearce, a park education specialist, recommends another less traveled section of the Rim Trail. It's reached via **Hermit Road,** which is closed to private vehicles from March through November but is served by the shuttle bus.

"Out near the end of the road there's a segment of the trail that's really nice, and that receives quite

Elk in Grand Canyon

a bit less use than other parts of the Rim Trail," he says. "It's from Monument Creek Vista to Pima Point, and then on to **Hermits Rest.** If you do the whole thing it's about 2.8 miles, but Pima Point provides a midway shuttle-bus stop if you want to do half the hike."

Pearce points out that rising early is always a great way to avoid crowds. "The Hermits Rest shuttle bus starts running before sunrise," he says. "For anybody who's on it early in the morning, before 8:30 a.m. or so, it can be really quiet out there, even in the middle of the summer. Get up and take in the sunrise and have alone time on a trail that by ten or eleven o'clock is just packed."

3 Desert View Drive The 25-mile road that runs east from Grand Canyon Village to the famed **Watchtower** is known for popular overlooks such as **Grandview, Moran,** and **Lipan Points.** One sure way to beat the crowds while enjoying the fantastic views from this part of the South Rim is to visit **Shoshone Point,** a highlight for former park staff member Richard Ullmann.

"This overlook is not shown on some maps of the Grand Canyon," he says. "The views are spectacular and panoramic. You can clearly see the Colorado River and glimpse the Desert View Watchtower along the rim some 20 miles away. There are rarely more than a few folks out there at any given time."

Pausing along the Kaibab Trail on a hike into the canyon

The national park makes Shoshone Point available for weddings and other celebrations (Ullmann's own wedding took place there). When such events are taking place, other visitors should respect the privacy of those using the site.

The main reason for Shoshone Point's solitude, though, is access. To reach it, park along Desert View Drive at an unmarked side road with a locked gate 1.2 miles east of the Yaki Point Road. Then you must hike a mile along a dirt road to the point.

"The walk along the road is pleasant, winding through ponderosa pine forest," Ullmann says. "I often see deer and elk along the way."

At the point, **Newton Butte** is prominent right below, while in the distance such formations as **Zoroaster, Brahma,** and **Vishnu Temples** are visible.

Pearce adds a simple way to avoid the crowds along the rest of Desert View Drive's overlooks: Stop at some of the unnamed overlooks instead.

"It's funny," he says, "you put a sign with a name on it at a viewpoint and everybody thinks it's somehow going to be a lot more spectacular. In reality, a lot of those viewpoints without names are just as beautiful. Even in the busy part of the year, maybe a handful of other people stop there, but those places don't have the crowds of the marked viewpoints."

As you're traveling Desert View Drive, watch for "roving rangers":

Grand Canyon Lodge at sunset

park interpreters who station themselves at viewpoints. Stopping for informal chats with these helpful folks is a great chance to ask questions, learn about wildlife and geology, and generally get more out of your visit.

▶ Down Into the Canyon

The most popular paths down into the canyon are the **Bright Angel** (24.8 miles) and **South Kaibab Trails** (7 miles). If you have the physical ability to descend into (and ascend out of) the canyon and would like a less crowded experience, consider the **Hermit Trail** (7 miles round-trip). The trailhead is reached by a brief walk from Hermits Rest at the end of Hermit Road.

4 Santa Maria Spring The Hermit Trail is not an easy walk. It descends steeply from the rim as it makes switchbacks down the canyon wall. Developed a century ago to serve a tourist camp, it has not been maintained like the more trafficked trails and in places has eroded significantly.

Nonetheless, with proper gear and water, and by taking things slowly, moderately fit people can enjoy an inner-canyon day hike by walking to Santa Maria Spring, 2.2 miles one way. (Keep right at two trail intersections.)

There are notable views here, and sharp-eyed hikers may spot fossil reptile tracks in the rocks along the trail. Santa Maria Springs is 1,640 feet in elevation below the trailhead.

The top portion of the Hermit

There's a spot near Cape Royal that a lot of people miss. The Cliff Springs Trail is only a mile round-trip, but it's nice. There's an ancient Native American granary there, and a seep at the end. It's an easy trail for people with kids, and it shows another aspect of the canyon.

—ROBIN TELLIS
Grand Canyon interpretive ranger

Trail faces west, and so it is the first South Rim trail to be free of ice in springtime.

5 Cedar Ridge Hike For many people, the best way to get a taste of the inner canyon is the ranger-led Cedar Ridge Hike, conducted daily from spring through fall. Beginning around 8 a.m. (check at visitor center for exact time) at the South Kaibab Trailhead (take the free shuttle bus), this 3-mile round-trip hike takes three to four hours to descend and ascend 1,140 feet.

The ranger guide will check to make sure that all participants have proper footwear and at least two quarts of water. It goes without saying that the vistas along the trail are inspirational (one spot along the way is called **Ooh Aah Point**), and the guide will point out rock layers—Kaibab limestone, Toroweap formation, Coconino sandstone, and Hermit shale—on the descent.

Though more crowded than the Hermit Trail, this section is also an excellent day hike for prepared canyon newcomers to do on their own.

▶ North Rim

As noted above, simply by traveling to the North Rim of the Grand Canyon you're distancing yourself from 90 percent of the visitors to the national park. One thousand feet higher than the South Rim, the North Rim is closed to vehicles from around November to mid-May, depending on snowfall. (Intrepid hikers and cross-country skiers can enter in winter.) Lodging and other park facilities are also closed in winter.

Apart from less visitation, the North Rim offers other enticing aspects. It's cooler in summer than the South Rim and presents many more opportunities for relatively doable day hikes. Because of the general slant of the plateaus surrounding Grand Canyon and the resulting erosion, many of the most beautiful and iconic buttes (the "temples" of fanciful historical nomenclature) are closer to the North Rim than to the South.

Cactus in bloom

Local Intelligence

In 2011, Grand Canyon National Park experimented with renting bicycles at the South and North Rims. The effort went well enough that the park contracted with a concessionaire to continue the business. This offers visitors a new way to see the park, traveling, for example, at the South Rim along the paved **Greenway Trail** (2.8 miles) as well as **Hermit Road** (7 miles), which is closed to private vehicles for most of the year. On a bike, you can cover more ground and see more sights than by hiking.

6 Grand Canyon Lodge A must first stop is the 1937 Grand Canyon Lodge, perched on the canyon edge and designed to offer visitors a "surprise view" through large windows in the Sun Room. Then, crowds or no crowds, it's time for the 0.25-mile walk on a paved trail to **Bright Angel Point.** Located on a narrow point between **Roaring Springs** and **Transept Canyon,** Bright Angel combines accessibility with one of the most awe-inspiring panoramas of the entire park.

Don't hurry hiking to the point; there are views into both side canyons and visible fossils along the way. Although the Colorado River can't be seen from here, look for Brahma, **Deva,** and Zoroaster Temples, listen for the sound of Roaring Springs 3,000 feet below, and peer across the canyon to the distant **San Francisco Peaks,** including the highest point in Arizona.

7 Ken Patrick Trail The **Transept Trail** provides a lot of scenery for little effort. Running just 1.5 miles between Grand Canyon Lodge and the main North Rim Campground, it looks down into the canyon for which it's named.

A similar but longer walk overlooking Roaring Springs Canyon is the 5-mile round-trip that begins on the Ken Patrick Trail and then branches off on the **Uncle Jim Trail** loop, leading to yet another canyon vista worth a few dozen photos.

8 Widforss Trail For a longer hike and more solitude, drive north from the lodge area a little more than a mile and turn west on a side road to the trailhead for the Widforss Trail.

This is an out-and-back trail that makes for a 10-mile round-trip if you go all the way to a point on the canyon rim about 2 miles west of Bright Angel Point. There are nice views into Transept Canyon during the first couple of miles, so it's rewarding to hike even part of this path. In fall, the aspens can be colorful here.

9 Roosevelt Point and Cape Royal Of course, if you've made the effort to reach the North Rim, you're going to want to drive to **Point Imperial** and Cape Royal, two famed viewpoints reached by road east of the lodge-campground area.

Point Imperial is the highest spot on either rim of the Grand Canyon (8,803 feet), and is renowned as a place at which to watch sunrise.

You probably won't be alone here even at dawn, but the experience is worth it. The Roosevelt Point and Cape Royal Trails are short, easy, popular, and inspiring.

10 Cape Final Trail To escape the crowds at the major viewpoints, hike the 4-mile round-trip Cape Final Trail (an abandoned but easy-to-walk road).

"Cape Final is a really good example of what a ponderosa pine forest should look like," Tellis says. "These days, with people keeping fires tamed, ponderosa forests have changed. A true ponderosa forest has a lot of space and few trees. Going down the Cape Final Trail you can see big open areas with large ponderosas. And the views at Cape Final are truly some of the best."

Many longtime Grand Canyon travelers, in fact, consider this their favorite of the North Rim viewpoints.

⓫ **North Kaibab Trail** The only maintained trail down to the inner canyon from the North Rim is the North Kaibab Trail, and cautions apply concerning strenuousness and thorough preparation. The route starts out at a heady elevation of 8,250 feet.

⓬ **Supai Tunnel** For a taste of the north side of the canyon below the rim, you can make the 1.5-mile round-trip hike to **Coconino Overlook,** which descends only 800 feet from the trailhead.

Tellis says that continuing to Supai Tunnel (4 miles round-trip, 650 feet in elevation change) takes you under trees, so it's shaded. Once you go through the Supai Tunnel, the scenery changes: The trees go away to reveal a great view. The Supai formation of red rock can be seen from the trail above or at this spot.

⓭ **Roaring Springs** Physically fit hikers who begin the trip very early in the morning might consider a trek to the cascades at Roaring Springs. A 9.4-mile round-trip with an elevation loss and gain of 3,050 feet, this is a journey only for the fit, prepared, and experienced.

Autumn aspens on the North Rim

View from Sunrise Point

BRYCE CANYON

Angka-ku-wass-a-wits ("red painted faces") is one of several names for Bryce Canyon attributed to the Paiute people, who believed the ruddy pillars of the area were their human ancestors turned to stone.

It is said that pioneer Ebenezer Bryce, for whom the canyon is named, gazed down into the rocky maze and quipped that it was "one heck of a place to lose a cow."

The canyon's great secret is that it's not a canyon at all; rather, it's a series of 14 limestone amphitheaters cut into the eastern edge of the Paunsaugunt Plateau in southern Utah. The domes and pillars (collectively called "hoodoos") were formed over millions of years by snow, frost, and rainwater weathering the weak Claron formation limestone. While red is the predominant hue, Bryce's palette features more than 60 distinct colors.

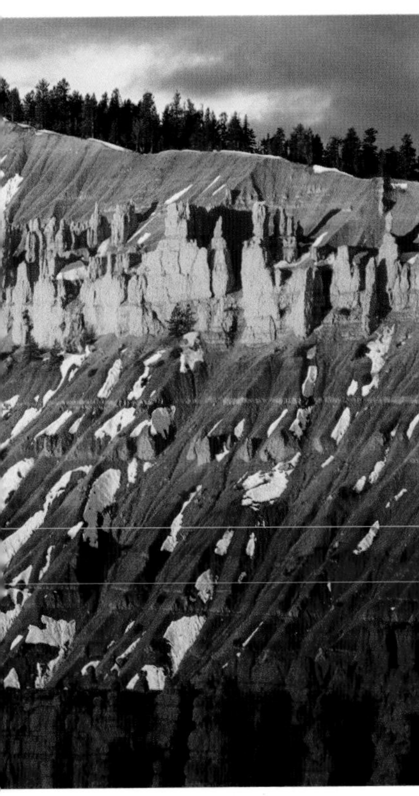

▶ Bryce Amphitheater

This amphitheater is the largest and most popular one in the park, but it shouldn't be skipped, as the park's central features are located along it.

❶ Fairyland Point On their rush into the heart of Bryce Canyon, visitors often overlook a turnoff to the left just beyond the park entry sign.

One mile down a side road flanked by ponderosa pines is Fairyland Point, which looks out across chromatic **Boat Mesa** and **Fairyland Canyon,** just a hint of what's to come farther into the park. Those who can't wait to see hoodoos can follow the Fairyland Loop to formations such as **Tower Bridge** and the **China Wall.**

Year-Round Visitor Center

- **Bryce Canyon Visitor Center**
  On Utah 63, 1.5 miles inside North Entrance

  435-834-5322, *www.nps.gov/brca*

❷ Dave's Hollow Meadow Another mile down the main road is **Bryce Canyon Visitor Center** with its displays on park natural and human history, an orientation film, and plenty of advice on where to go and what to do during your sojourn at the park.

Ask about the various interpretive programs and ranger-led activities that take place daily, especially during the summer season.

Directly west of the visitor center is Dave's Hollow Meadow, which flows down into **Dixie National Forest.** Sarah Haas, park biologist, says this is the "very best place in the park to see prairie dogs. If you look toward the west, there are a couple of colonies that are very easy to see from the parking lot or the road."

❸ Rim Trail East of the visitor center, Bryce Amphitheater's Rim Trail provides an opportunity to see the depression from above.

Among its much photographed landmarks are **Thor's Hammer, Queen Victoria,** and **Wall Street.** Four spectacular overlooks along the edge can be reached by foot, private vehicle, or the free park shuttle.

Linking these viewpoints is the popular 5.5-mile (one way) Rim Trail, which gains height as it moves from north to south, peaking at 8,296-foot **Bryce Point.**

Tom Hart, assistant general manager of the Lodge at Bryce Canyon and a veteran Utah rock climber, recommends that visitors explore the same overlook or trail at three or four different times during a given day

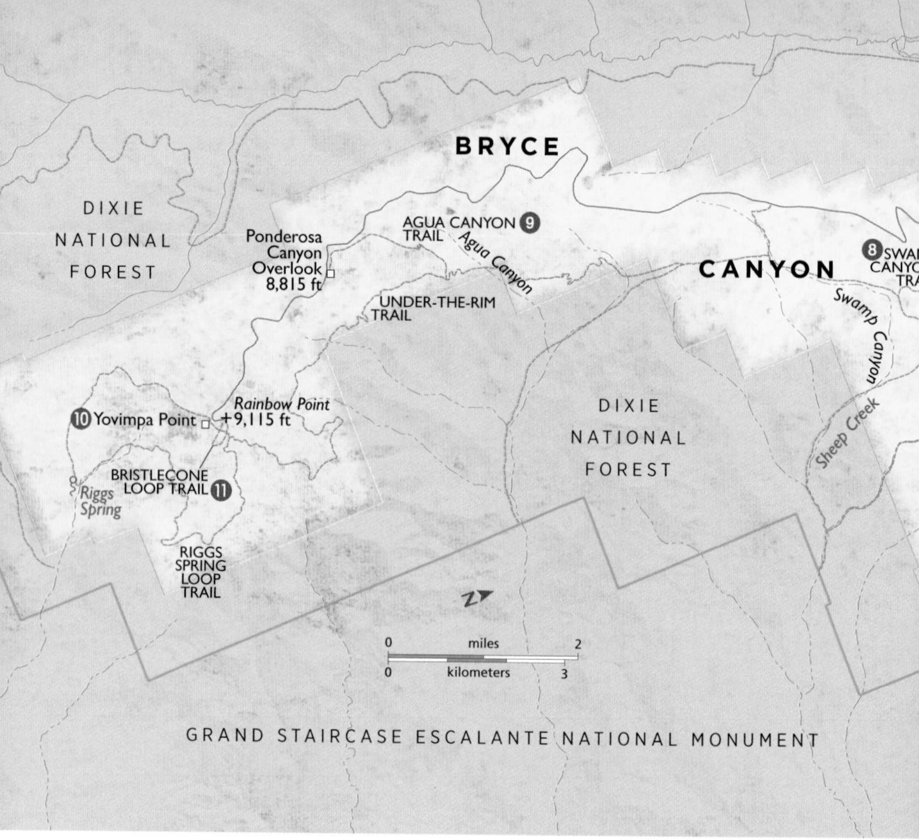

and to take special notice of how the landscape changes.

"The trails have a varied look and feel depending on the time of day," says Hart. "It's not just such a visually majestic park because of the nature of the formations and the sandstone cliffs, but also because it looks completely different at dusk, or at sunrise, or in the bright sunshine in the middle of the day as the reds, the oranges, and the browns pick up the sunlight."

If you walk all the way [on the Tropic Trail] from the rim to the town of Tropic, it takes about 2.5 to 3 hours.

—SARAH HAAS
Bryce Canyon National Park biologist

4 Peek-a-boo Loop Trail You can descend into the main amphitheater at six different points along the rim (one of them is reserved for equestrian tours).

Don't expect to have the hoodoos to yourself on popular trails such as the **Queens Garden** and **Navajo Loops.** But you can get long periods of solitude along some of the tougher walks.

From Bryce Point, the Peek-a-boo Loop circles the southern part of the amphitheater, passing the **Wall of Windows,** the **Three Wise Men,** and other remarkable geology. Given the steep grade coming back up, allocate three to four hours for this 5.5-mile (one way) hike.

5 Tropic Trail The least traveled route in the main amphitheater area

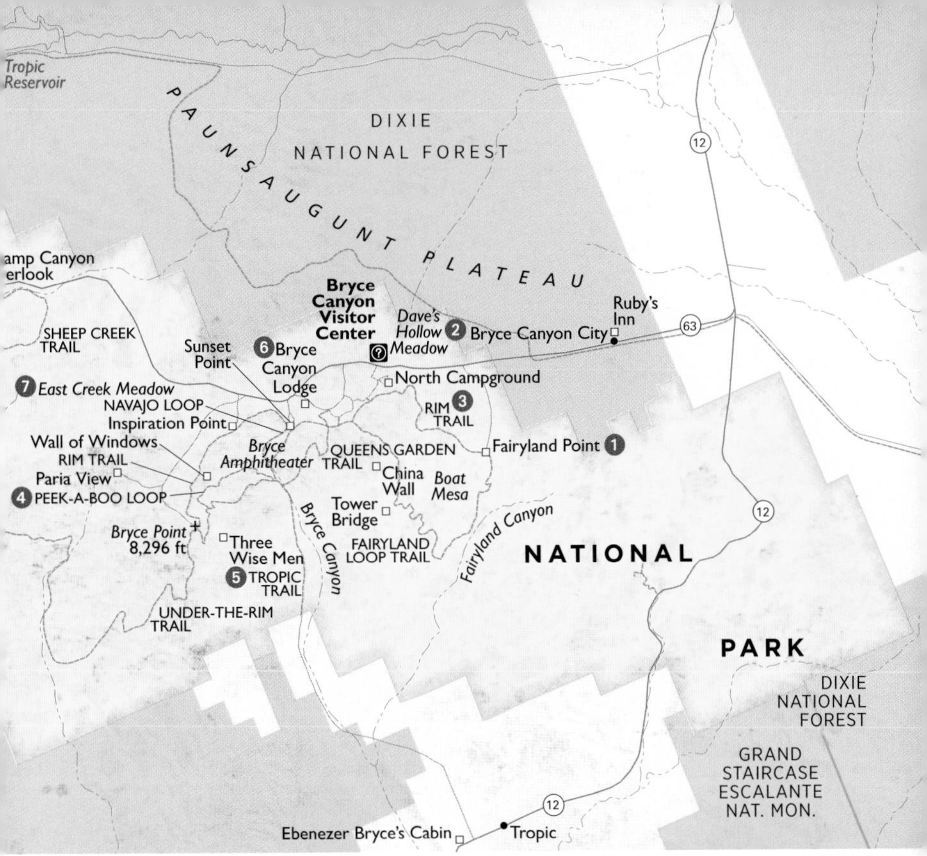

Tropic Reservoir
PAUNSAUGUNT PLATEAU
DIXIE NATIONAL FOREST
12
amp Canyon erlook
Bryce Canyon Visitor Center
Dave's Hollow 2 Meadow
Bryce Canyon City
Ruby's Inn
63
SHEEP CREEK TRAIL
Sunset Point
6 Bryce Canyon Lodge
North Campground
7 East Creek Meadow
NAVAJO LOOP
RIM 3 TRAIL
Inspiration Point
Wall of Windows
Bryce Amphitheater
QUEENS GARDEN TRAIL
Fairyland Point 1
RIM TRAIL
Paria View
China Wall
Boat Mesa
4 PEEK-A-BOO LOOP
Tower Bridge
Fairyland Canyon
12
Bryce Point 8,296 ft
Three Wise Men
Bryce Canyon
FAIRYLAND LOOP TRAIL
NATIONAL
5 TROPIC TRAIL
UNDER-THE-RIM TRAIL
PARK
DIXIE NATIONAL FOREST
GRAND STAIRCASE ESCALANTE NAT. MON.
12
Ebenezer Bryce's Cabin
Tropic

is the Tropic Trail that runs across the middle of the park to **Bryce Canyon.** This can be done as a round-trip to the park boundary and back, or as a one-way (mostly downhill) walk to the pioneer town of **Tropic,** which requires prearranged transport back into the park.

Ebenezer Bryce's log cabin (built circa 1881) sits near the south end of Main Street in Tropic. "This is the trail I probably walk the most because I live in Tropic," says Haas. "On most days when I walk it—even during the summer high season—I don't see anyone else. It still has wilderness character and it's a great birding area. As you descend, the landscape transitions from ponderosa pine into Gambel oak and a manzanita understory."

6 Bryce Canyon Lodge The Bryce Canyon Lodge is also worth a look. This masterpiece of American national park architecture was built in the

Prairie dog

Bryce landscape in winter

1920s and is now a national historic landmark. Although it's been renovated several times since, the lodge retains its rustic ambience. It consists of a large main building with a distinctive green roof and log cabins set along the canyon edge. Constructed by the Union Pacific Railroad to lure visitors to Bryce, the lodge was designed by Gilbert Stanley Underwood, one of the mavens of the national park style.

"It's been modernized over the years, but it's also been kept to its historical grandeur," says Hart, who works in the main building. "This is the only lodge from that period that hasn't burned to the ground and been rebuilt. This is the only one in its original state. But these are very hard buildings to maintain. Eighty percent of the windows in the lodge are hand-blown glass and there's only one place left in the world that makes them anymore. So it's a big deal when we have to replace one. When I go to work, I feel like I'm a steward of a piece of history."

▶ 18-Mile Scenic Drive and Rainbow Point

Beyond Bryce Amphitheater, the park thins into a narrow wedge atop part of the **Paunsaugunt Plateau,** a scenic tableland that runs roughly north-south at an altitude between 7,000 and 9,100 feet within the park. Meandering along the top of this ridge is an 18-mile scenic drive that ends at Rainbow Point in the deep south. Most people drive the route—flanked by red-rock chasms on one side, woodland, and meadows on the other—but a free shuttle also plies the route twice a day in summer season.

7 East Creek Meadow One of the first things you come across on the scenic drive is East Creek Meadow, which sprawls along the road just south of the turnoff to Bryce Point.

"This is the park's largest meadow," says Haas, "and a good place to see wildlife. It's pretty rare if you don't spot a pronghorn, deer, wild turkey, or raptor. We're also trying to get prairie dogs back into the meadow. Stop in the Civilian Conservation Corps [CCC] picnic area. It's kind of back in the trees, but it still borders the meadow, which you are able to walk in."

8 Swamp Canyon Trail While the overlooks can get crowded at times, the trails that descend into the canyons seldom do. Swamp Canyon Trail is probably the most rewarding hike

Local Intelligence

While it may seem counterintuitive—given its iconic desertlike landscapes—Bryce Canyon transforms into a frozen wonderland between November and April, when the plateau is often shrouded in snow. "It's like *The Shining* in the wintertime," says Tom Hart. "There are years where you can't see 8-foot-tall trees because they're covered with snow."

The park service plows the main road to just beyond **Sunset Point** turnoff and also keeps the main parking lots snow-free so that visitors can access **Bryce Amphitheater.** "You can still get on the trails," says Hart. "So if you want to get on your boots and go down into the canyon itself, you can. When they're covered in snow, the hoodoos look like some crazy dessert or ice cream cone."

Snowshoers can follow the **Rim Trail** to **Inspiration Point** and **Paria View,** or tramp along the main road south of the winter closure point to meadows and woodland along the park's western edge. Cross-country skiing is forbidden inside the national park. But right outside the entrance gate is a Nordic ski area with more than 20 miles of groomed trails maintained by **Dixie National Forest.** Snowshoes and cross-country gear can be rented at **Ruby's Inn Winter Activities Center** (1.4 miles north of the park entrance), which also offers sleigh rides, ice skating, and snowmobiling in the national forest.

Hart also recommends a winter visit for avid stargazers. "With the altitude, the coldness of the night air, and the lack of pollution, this is one of the best places in the United States to view the night sky. You can be amazed on no-moon nights, especially in the wintertime, looking up into the heavens and seeing the entire Milky Way."

The **Lodge at Bryce Canyon** is closed from November to April. The only accommodation inside the park that remains open during winter is the **North Campground.**

Mule deer in the woods

given its diverse habitats and terrain. It winds down through a maze of hoodoos to a lush canyon fed by creeks and springs. It's not a swamp per se, but there is enough moisture for willows, reeds, and the toxic western iris, which contains a poisonous chemical. Keep an eye out for tiger salamanders in the wetter areas.

"In the bottom of Swamp Canyon is a huge wetland meadow," says Haas. "It's the only place in the park like that. The willows are pretty thick. We have bears in that area and lots of deer down there. Some of our rare bird species will be down there too."

Swamp Canyon Trail eventually tumbles into the 22.9-mile **Under-the-Rim Trail,** the park's major back-country route. Hang a left and walk about a mile to the **Sheep Creek Trail,** which leads back up the wall to the **Swamp Canyon Overlook.**

"The whole loop is about 4.5 miles," says Haas. "It takes two or three hours depending on how fast you hike."

9 Agua Canyon Trail Another good hike off the scenic road is the Agua Canyon connecting trail, which starts near the **Ponderosa Canyon Overlook** and runs through woodland before plunging into another hoodoo-filled chasm.

Rock formations called **The Hunter** and **The Rabbit** dominate the foreground, but your eyes soon migrate to that massive geological feature dominating the eastern horizon—the **Grand Staircase.**

Don't expect a lush oasis at Agua Canyon, though. "The name is a bit of a misnomer," explains Haas. "The area does have some springs, but there's no perennial water source."

10 Yovimpa Point At the bottom end of the road is aptly named **Rainbow Point,** where nature's colors run a spectrum from sky blue and cloud white to pink, orange, beige, and vermilion stone and the dark green trees of the plateau top.

Soaring to more than 9,100 feet, this is the park's highest point and one of its most dramatic.

A short trail leads to Yovimpa Point, with its panoramic views of the Grand Staircase. Squint your eyes and imagine you're standing at the prow of a great ship like the *Titanic*, sailing southward toward Zion National Park and the Grand Canyon, because the view—sometimes approaching 200 miles—truly makes you feel like you're the king of the world.

⓫ **Bristlecone Loop Trail** Also starting from the Rainbow Point parking lot is the short Bristlecone Loop Trail, which ambles through a mixed forest of spruce, firs, and bristlecone pines; some of the latter are more than 1,800 years old and without doubt the oldest living things in the Bryce Canyon area.

If you haven't eaten lunch, chow down at the Rainbow Point picnic area with its expansive views.

Reenergized, have a jaunt down part of the **Riggs Spring** or Under-the-Rim Trails. The 8.8-mile Riggs Springs Loop dives into one of the park's most remote corners. It can be tackled as a long (and very rewarding) day hike or a two-day walk with overnight at one of four primitive campsites along the route.

Sooth your walk-weary muscles at Riggs's namesake spring near the halfway point, an oasis-like patch of water, grass, wildflowers, and ponderosa pine.

The Under-the-Rim Trail features eight campsites. Both it and Riggs are considered backcountry hiking and suitable only for the experienced and physically fit; the air gets thinner as you climb through elevations ranging from 6,800 feet to 9,115 feet. Note that permits are required for overnight stays; pick them up at the visitor center.

Weathered Claron formation

The Virgin River flowing through sandstone walls in autumn

ZION

While other great canyons awe with sheer size, Zion, a relatively small national park, wows in a much more subtle manner, with artistry rather than magnitude, rock canvases and stone sculptures that seem crafted by some ancient Michelangelo rather than the whim and fancy of nature.

The Mormon settlers who pioneered southern Utah from the 1850s to the 1860s thought the canyon was heaven sent. They named it after a biblical place of peace and endowed many of its natural features with spiritual appellations—Great White Throne, Angels Landing, and Altar of Sacrifice.

The forces of nature—in particular floods—kept the canyon from being heavily settled and retained its atmosphere of secrecy. President Theodore Roosevelt gave it federal protection in 1909 and ten years later Zion became Utah's first national park.

▶ Zion Canyon

Located in the town of Springdale, the **Zion Canyon Visitor Center** should be the first stop for anyone visiting the park. In addition to maps and brochures, the information desk has the latest weather reports and road conditions for anyone contemplating the main canyon hikes or planning a trip to the park's extensive wilderness.

Right outside the visitor center you can hop a free shuttle that runs the length of Zion Canyon. The shuttle stops at various well-known canyon landmarks, including **Emerald Pools, Zion Lodge, The Grotto,** and **Weeping Rock.**

At the first stop, the **Human History Museum,** watch a park film providing a good introduction to the area. The last stop lets visitors off at the start of the popular **Riverside Walk,** which snakes around the towering **Temple of Sinawava** to the lower end of **The Narrows.**

Year-Round Visitor Centers

- **Zion Canyon Visitor Center and Backcountry Desk**
  South Entrance, Zion-Mount Carmel Highway
- **Kolob Canyons Visitor Center**
  I-15, exit 40, East Kolob Canyon

435-772-3256, *www.nps.gov/zion*

❶ **Hidden Canyon Trail** Don't expect peace and solitude along the canyon floor trails, especially during the summer months. There are, though, a few paths that don't attract the crowds, in particular the Hidden Canyon Trail, a three-hour, 2.4-mile round-trip that starts from the **Weeping Rock Shuttle** stop.

"You get up into a narrow canyon," says Adrienne Fitzgerald, the park's chief of interpretation. "Not a slot canyon, but a fracture control canyon with straight walls. It's a little cooler and vegetated. You can't really go far before it turns into a very difficult scramble. It's a good morning hike because it's still in the shade."

But the hike comes with a caveat. "It has sheer drop-offs and a narrow trail, so it's not suitable for everyone," Fitzgerald adds. "In a couple sections, the path is only a couple feet wide with a 300-foot drop-off and chains to hold on to. And places where people can't pass—it's that narrow."

Rock slides are also a concern; in 2012, 11 hikers were briefly trapped on the trail by falling stones.

❷ **Watchman Trail** Fitzgerald also recommends the Watchman Trail, a two-hour round-trip that commences at the campground of the same name near the canyon visitor center. "It's got really nice views," she says. "You hit a few different vegetation zones along the way, but you start out with the more low-desert stuff. There is a little spring that you come to. It's incredibly hot in summer, and you can only really hike it in the early morning because it does get baked. But in the spring you get some nice wildflowers. And it's a great winter hike. When a lot of the other trails are icy, this one can be in good shape."

Bighorn sheep

3 The Narrows Located at the upper (north) end of Zion Canyon, this remains the holy grail for hikers. The thrill is double-edged: walking, wading, and sometimes swimming in the **Virgin River** and peering up through a rock chasm that reaches

15
Taylor Cr.
11 MIDDLE FORK TAYLOR CREEK
Kolob Canyons Visitor Center
Double Arch Alcove
Middle Fk.
Kolob Canyons Overlook
KOLOB CANYONS
10 TIMBER CREEK TRAIL
12 LA VERKIN CREEK TRAIL
Kolob Arch
La Verkin Creek
North Creek
Crater Hi
5,192
9
Virgin
Virgin
N
0 miles 4
0 kilometers 6

Kolob Reservoir
Blue Springs Reservoir
Lava Point
Deep Creek
Chamberlain's Ranch
North Fork Virgin
KOLOB TERRACE ROAD
WEST RIM TRAIL
The Narrows
Wildcat Canyon Trailhead
NORTHGATE PEAKS TRAIL
Wall Street
ZION NATIONAL PARK
N. Guardian Angel 7,395 ft
Orderville Canyon
The Narrows
S. Guardian Angel 7,140 ft
RIVERSIDE WALK
Observation Point 6,508 ft
Temple of Sinawava
Weeping Rock
Echo Canyon
Cable Mountain
Angels Landing 5,785 ft
HIDDEN CANYON TRAIL
The Grotto
EAST RIM TRAIL
Emerald Pools
Great White Throne 6,744 ft
Zion Lodge
ZION CANYON
Altar of Sacrifice 7,505 ft
ZION-MOUNT CARMEL HWY.
Checkerboard Mesa 6,670 ft
Pine Cr.
Zion Human History Museum
Quilt Mesa
PARUNUWEAP CANYON TRAIL
WATCHMAN TRAIL
Zion Canyon Visitor Center
CANYON OVERLOOK TRAIL
Watchman Campground
Coalpits Wash
Springdale
N. Fk. Virgin
Parunuweap Canyon
Grafton (Ghost town)
East Fork Virgin
9

2,000 feet in height and that narrows to 20 feet wide in some places.

"People are drawn there for the unique environment and the grandeur," says Amelia Gull, a native of southwestern Utah and outfitting manager for a local tour operator in Springdale. "There really is no other place like it in the Southwest. It provides quite a few people with a sense of awe and solitude in a relatively quick and accessible way. You feel very big and very small at the same time. It's a humbling experience."

You can walk The Narrows on your own or as part of a group tour offered by locally based private outfitters. Ranger-guided hikes up the watercourse are no longer offered by the Park Service. The lower part of The Narrows—up to **Orderville Canyon** and **Wall Street**—is fairly easy to negotiate, but often teeming with hikers during the summer season.

Avoid the rush by moving upstream from the Orderville junction into a part of The Narrows where few people tread.

Time your hike out according to how long you want your total walk to be. It normally takes two hours to reach Orderville Canyon, so a total round-trip time of six hours should be enough to give you a few hours of sublime solitude.

Gull recommends setting off early in the morning—say 8 a.m. "If you go farther than about 2.5 miles in, you hardly see any people," she says. "You're really getting past the crowds, which you won't hit until your way back."

❹ **Chamberlain's Ranch** Another option is a long day hike all the way down The Narrows from Chamberlain's Ranch. Several local outfitters run one-way shuttles from Springdale to the ranch trailhead. The downstream hike takes 10 to 12 hours

Local Intelligence

Visitors who crave an intimate encounter with Zion should check out the in-depth workshops offered by the **Zion Canyon Field Institute (ZCFI).** Founded in 2002, it offers a wide variety of classes in geology, flora, archaeology, photography, painting, and even poetry, many of them taught by PhDs in those fields. Some of them are quite specialized—like the Thomas Moran painting workshops and native plant seed propagation.

"The park service asked the Zion Natural History Association to start the field institute because they wanted to be able to offer the visitor an interpretive experience that was more intense and of longer duration then the usual ranger-guided hikes, campfire programs, or evening talks," says ZCFI director Michael Plyler, a trained geologist, archaeologist, and photographer. "For example, you can take an all-day class on geology, birds, or botany."

Workshops are offered year-round, but there are more in the spring and autumn. Most are available on a walk-up basis, but check ahead of time with the park for popular choices.

The field institute also offers private interpretive experiences. "You can hire a field institute naturalist either on a half-day or full-day basis," says Plyler. "Specify the topic or otherwise we do a general program that covers geology, botany, biology, ecosystems, and human history so you get a broad overview of the park."

Hikers on Angels Landing

and can also be done as a two-day trip with an overnight at a primitive campsite in the canyon.

No matter how you decide to tackle The Narrows, special equipment is highly recommended, in particular waterproof boots or hiking shoes, neoprene socks, and a walking stick to aid balance on the slippery river rocks.

▶ East Side

Most visitors are content with staring up at the **Great White Throne** and the **Temple of Sinawava** formations on the park's east side. With a little effort, however, you can also get stunning horizontal views of Zion's geological icons. Blazed in the early 1920s, the trails to **Angels Landing** and **Observation Point** have long been popular day hikes from the canyon floor. But there are others much less trodden.

Little-visited eastern Zion is also the best part of the park for wildlife viewing. In addition to mule deer and seldom seen mountain lions, desert bighorn sheep call this area home.

"The sheep seem to like to pose for pictures on top of rocks and cause traffic jams along the Mount Carmel Highway," says Gull. "Look for them anywhere from the east entrance to the first tunnel. Early morning and later evening they'll be out a little more, especially during the summer."

5 Canyon Overlook Trail On the east side of the park, the Canyon Overlook Trail is short but sweet. It is a 1-mile walk from a small parking lot off the **Zion–Mount Carmel Highway.** It features some pretty steep drop-offs along the way, so be cautious. The view at the end is straight down **Pine Creek Canyon** to lower **Zion Canyon.**

"It's a wonderful view, a really cool little trail on slickrock," says Fitzgerald. "It's a fantastic short hike for a big view. The problem is that parking is really limited up there. So it's self-limiting in that sense—that is the reason you won't find a lot of people along that trail."

❻ **East Rim Trail** Much more challenging (and rewarding) is the East Rim Trail, which starts just inside the park's east entrance. The walk starts with a panoramic view of **Checkerboard Mesa** and ends with close-up views of **Echo Canyon, Cable Mountain,** and **Observation Point.** Most hikers approach the East Rim Trail (10.6 miles) as a one-way hike taking six hours that ends on the canyon floor.

Get to the Parunuweap, and you've got one serious canyon. You can hear the East Fork Virgin River, but you need to be nimble to get down into it.

—RON STENFORS
Zion Lodge manager

---

❼ **Parunuweap Canyon Trail** Ron Stenfors, a former submariner who's now the front desk manager at Zion Lodge, recommends walking the little-used, challenging, and long Parunuweap Canyon Trail on the east side.

The trailhead lies on the southern side of the Zion–Mount Carmel Highway between Checkerboard and **Quilt** Mesas. From there it runs almost straight south to the edge of the Parunuweap, a spectacular slot canyon once explored by Maj. John Wesley Powell.

"Boy, you can get back into some country out there that's just so beautiful and so stark," observes Stenfors. "For example, the Parunuweap is one serious canyon.

▶ Kolob Terrace

The west rim is equally empty and also ripe for exploration by those who want to experience a side of Zion that few visitors ever see.

The best access is on **Kolob Terrace Road (KTR)** from **Virgin,** 15 miles west of Springdale on Utah 9. The paved route meanders 24 miles through the Zion wilderness to **Lava Point** and **Kolob Reservoir,** with trailheads and pullouts along the way.

"That road literally takes you on top of Zion National Park," says lead park ranger Mike Ball. "It's a steep mountain road with some steep grades, but it is paved. It certainly is a great half-day or full-day adventure.

"You gain more than 4,000 feet until you're up at 8,000 feet above sea level. So you're in the high country."

❽ **Northgate Peaks Trail** Among half a dozen easy day hikes in the area, Ball recommends the Northgate Peaks Trail, which starts at the **Wildcat Canyon** pullout and winds through ponderosa pine forest and ridgelines to a view of the white sandstone **Guardian Angel** summits.

"That's about a two-hour hike round-trip. It's mostly level through the forest," Ball says. "You see parts of Zion that you wouldn't otherwise. For example, you look down on temples and towers that you would normally see from the canyon floor."

❾ **West Rim Trail** Farther up the road is a turnoff to **Lava Point** and the West Rim Trail, another special walk into the main canyon that can be accomplished in a single day.

Michael Plyler, Zion Canyon Field Institute director, highlights this as his favorite hike in the entire park: "The vistas off the trail are amazing in both directions. And if you start at the top it's downhill. It takes seven to nine hours—about 14 miles—and it's easily doable in a day if you're a relatively avid hiker."

▶ Kolob Canyons

Spanish Franciscan monks Silvestre Vélez de Escalante and Francisco Atanasio Domínguez Escalante explored the Kolob Canyons in 1776 and in the process became the first Europeans to visit what is now Zion National Park.

After 19 years as a national monument, Kolob was added to the park in 1956, essentially doubling Zion's size. Despite its proximity to I-15, it remains the park's least used region.

"The Kolob Canyons area is a great hidden treasure of Zion," says Gull.

⑩ Timber Creek Trail Just off I-15 at East Kolob Canyon Road, exit 40, is the **Kolob Canyons Visitor Center**. A paved road leads about 5 miles to the splendid Kolob Canyons Overlook with its views across the park's wild west end.

Trek the short Timber Creek Trail to a bluff with a spectacular view across southwest Utah.

"You see the whole region from up there," says Fitzgerald.

⑪ Middle Fork Taylor Creek For something a little more ambitious, hike up the Middle Fork Taylor Creek, a 5.4-mile round-trip that takes three to four hours.

A moderate day hike that's not going up a cliff, it takes you into a canyon drainage and up through an alcove with a double arch. In the spring there's often a waterfall coming off the top.

A warning to hikers, especially with children: This trail is known for having rattlesnakes. Ask a ranger for more information.

⑫ La Verkin Creek Trail For a unique reward, take the La Verkin Creek Trail to **Kolob Arch.** At the end of this 7-mile jaunt is the second longest natural arch in the United States (287.4 feet) after Arches National Park's Landscape Arch.

"For most people it's really tough getting there in one day, especially in summer," Fitzgerald warns. "This is my favorite place to go backpacking. You feel like you have the place to yourself. Even some of the rangers don't know what's out there."

Ponderosa pine at base of Checkerboard Mesa

Waterpocket Fold at Panorama Point

CAPITOL REEF

Capitol Reef may be one of the most secret and underappreciated national parks in the country—and the lack of crowds translates into a real sense of discovery for those who spend the time to get to know it. But you better hurry, as word is spreading: This 378-square-mile park in Utah offers similar geologic wonders to Zion or Arches, but is larger than either, and it occupies an even more isolated and varied setting.

The park may stretch for 100 miles north to south, but like the "Reef" itself—a name given to impassable geologic barriers by the early explorers—it's quite narrow. Its defining feature is the Waterpocket Fold, a 100-mile-long monocline thrust up 6,800 feet from the Earth's surface some 65 million years ago before it was eroded to its current 1,500 feet, a real wrinkle in time through which visitors seeking secrets can escape into untouched wilderness.

▶ Fruita Historic District

On the main road through the park, vestiges of a 200-acre settlement offer a taste of Mormon pioneer life in more ways than one. The pioneer remnants here include a one-room schoolhouse, a toolshed and blacksmith shop, a refurbished homestead, and rusting farm machinery. The standout feature is 18 orchards totaling more than 3,000 trees, many still watered by the original gravity-fed ditches and pipes the pioneers used.

Some of the trees are antique varieties producing rare fruits you've never tasted: Flemish Beauty pears, Yellow Egg plums, or Red Astrachan apples. Something is always fruiting, beginning in mid-June (cherries) until

Year-Round Visitor Center

- **Visitor Center**
  Utah 24, Fruita District, 10 miles east of Torrey
  435-425-3791, *www.nps.gov/care*

mid-October (apples). Each orchard has a self-pay station with scales and price list. You can climb a ladder and harvest fruit to take home—or eat your fill on-site for free.

❶ **Cohab Canyon Trail** Just beyond the historic Fruita district near the main campground, this one-way 1.75-mile-long trail is a more intimate alternative to often-crowded **Grand Wash.** You'll see far fewer people—if any—on this trail, underscoring its clandestine history. (According to local legend, Mormon polygamists or "cohabitationists" would hide up here to escape raids by the Feds intent on enforcing antipolygamy laws.)

"You're seeing the escarpment of the monocline here, a beautiful rock sequence," says Lori Rome, chief of interpretation. "You pass through three mini-slot canyons, then you go through a gorgeous water-pocketed canyon, and up to two really awesome viewpoints that put you right above Fruita, the orchards, and the river. It's visually stunning."

▶ Scenic Drive

While most of the park is free to visit, the 8.3-mile Scenic Drive costs $5 per vehicle at a self-pay station, which gives access to two of the park's most popular hiking trails.

Tip: Stop at the visitor center to pick up a free *Guide to the Scenic Drive*, a geological tutorial to the rock formations you will pass.

❷ **Grand Wash** A shorter version of the Zion Narrows, this easy

Sunflowers and buttes

2.5-mile-long canyon trail is a proverbial walk in the park—unless there's a heavy rain, when flash floods can turn it into a death trap.

For 0.5 mile, the 300-foot-high sandstone walls narrow to within 16 feet of each other, an eerie sensation of being enveloped within the stony heart of the **Waterpocket Fold.**

Instead of following the crowd, break off on the 1.75-mile side route, marked by signs, up to one of the park's largest arches, **Cassidy Arch,** named after Butch, who allegedly used Grand Wash on his way back and forth from nearby **Robber's Roost.** As the trail comes out above Cassidy Arch, it's easy to overlook: You have to gaze below where you are standing to spot this span. While you are at it, keep an eye out for desert bighorn sheep, especially in the early morning or evening when they're active and easier to spot.

❸ **Capitol Gorge** Five miles beyond Grand Wash, this gorge was a historic thoroughfare, as seen by its two main attractions. You'll pass numerous but faint Fremont petroglyphs (A.D. 600 to 1300) carved into the north side of the wash.

Just 0.25 mile beyond that is the **Pioneer Register,** where those passing would stop to carve their names into the canyon wall, each trying to outdo the other. Some even tried to write their names with gunshot, but other inscriptions are a tad more elegant, like that of prospector, occasional outlaw, and former member of Quantrill's Civil War Raiders Cass Hite (for whom Hite Crossing at Lake Powell is named).

Just beyond the Pioneer Register are **The Tanks,** another name for the many potholes prevalent in the fold, each teeming with its own mini-ecosystem of water striders, algae, and snails.

If you're looking for more exercise than scrambling up to the Tanks, or find the gorge views too confining, try climbing the 1.2-mile-long **Golden**

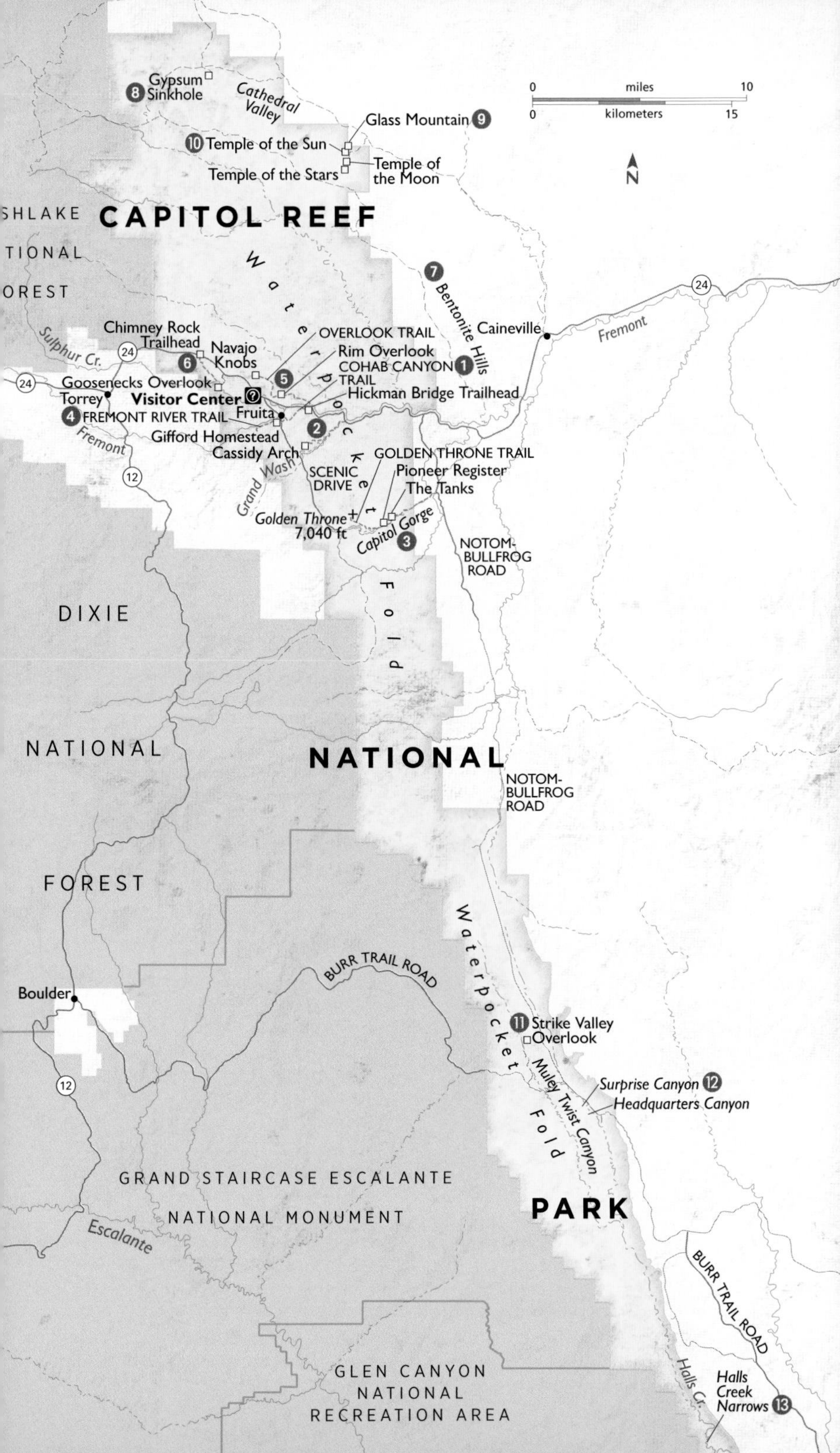

CAPITOL REEF
NATIONAL
PARK
0 miles 10
0 kilometers 15
N
8 Gypsum Sinkhole
Cathedral Valley
Glass Mountain 9
10 Temple of the Sun
Temple of the Stars
Temple of the Moon
SHLAKE
TIONAL
OREST
Waterpocket Fold
7 Bentonite Hills
Caineville
24
Fremont
Chimney Rock Trailhead
Sulphur Cr.
6
Navajo Knobs
OVERLOOK TRAIL
Rim Overlook
5
COHAB CANYON TRAIL 1
Goosenecks Overlook
Torrey
Visitor Center
Hickman Bridge Trailhead
4 FREMONT RIVER TRAIL
Fruita
Gifford Homestead
2
Cassidy Arch
12
Grand Wash
SCENIC DRIVE
GOLDEN THRONE TRAIL
Pioneer Register
The Tanks
Golden Throne 7,040 ft
Capitol Gorge 3
NOTOM-BULLFROG ROAD
DIXIE
NATIONAL
FOREST
BURR TRAIL ROAD
Boulder
11 Strike Valley Overlook
Muley Twist Canyon
Surprise Canyon 12
Headquarters Canyon
GRAND STAIRCASE ESCALANTE
NATIONAL MONUMENT
Escalante
GLEN CANYON
NATIONAL
RECREATION AREA
Halls Cr.
Halls Creek Narrows 13

Throne Trail (it begins at the parking lot), which puts you on top of Capitol Reef, at the base of monolithic **Golden Throne,** one of the prominent points in the park.

▶ Utah 24

The park, founded as a national monument in 1937, gained dramatically in visitation after Utah 24 was built in 1962 through the Fremont River Canyon to replace the old Capitol Gorge wagon road.

It made parts of the park readily accessible to the passing public, yet despite the added pressure, it doesn't take much effort to shake the crowds and be immersed in nature's serenity.

4 Fremont River Trail This footpath, just over a mile long, begins with an easy stroll through an orchard (snatch an apple for the climb), but after 0.5 mile, the crowd thins as the trail steeply ascends 480 feet for some great river views.

On the way back, scan for prolific bird life along the river: warblers, Bullock's Orioles, Black-headed and Evening Grosbeaks, and the elusive Yellow-breasted Chat (it's heard at all hours, but rarely seen). Keep an eye out for rare Golden Eagles soaring high above (not to be confused with the more common Turkey Vulture, which has a V-shape).

5 Rim Overlook and the Navajo Knobs Start from the **Hickman Bridge Trailhead,** where a popular self-guided 1-mile trek to a natural bridge begins. You'll pass vegetation such as squawbush, four-wing saltbush, and dwarf yucca, known for its many uses (rope, needles, sandals, baskets, and even shampoo).

After 0.25 mile of switchbacks, break off on the **Overlook Trail,** leaving behind the international tourist brigade, as you contour through the ledgelike Kayenta formation and past strange black lava boulders to an overlook of **Hickman Bridge.**

Keep going to Rim Overlook (2.3 miles from the trailhead), which serves up another panorama of the visitor center and the Fremont River flowing through Fruita below. It's another 2 miles to the Navajo Knobs following cairns across the slickrock.

"I've worked in a lot of national parks in 15 years, and this has got to be one of the best hikes I've been on," says Rome. "You are on top of the world, you really feel the solitude, and there are stunning 360-degree views all the way across the fold to the mountains beyond."

This park is an intimate look at the Colorado Plateau and the processes that created it. Unlike the Grand Canyon, where you can't even see the river unless you hike down 10 miles, here you get to see the sculptor of this place up close and personal.

—LORI ROME
Capitol Reef National Park chief of interpretation

6 Sulphur Creek Most visitors head to **Goosenecks Overlook** off Utah 24 for views of Sulphur Creek without realizing there's a better way to experience this meandering stream. In fact, the most refreshing route in the park is the 5.8-mile-long trail that follows Sulphur Creek on its way downstream from the trailhead at **Chimney Rock** on Utah 24.

The trail passes through the **Goosenecks,** down three waterfalls, through various strata of rock (including Kaibab limestone, the park's oldest layer, as well as the youngest layer of the Grand Canyon), before emerging conveniently at the visitor center.

"It's a great route, and very pretty once you're in the canyon. There are stretches where you walk right in the water," says Rick Stinchfield, volunteer ranger and guidebook author. "And you've got a good light in there, even in the middle of the day, so it's great for photographers."

Of course, keep an eye out for flash floods. "It's not the place to be when there is any threat of thunderstorms," says Stinchfield, who advises checking the weather at the visitor center before setting off.

▶ Cathedral Valley

Empty, desolate, and rich in looming silence, this northern reach of the park is certainly cathedral-like for the awe it evokes. (Even the monolithic towers are referred to as "temples.")

As in any good pilgrimage, to get here involves a bit of challenge in the form of a 58-mile dirt road loop that demands high-clearance vehicles and the fording of a river 12 miles east of the visitor center.

"To do the full loop, you have to drive through the Fremont River. That's 10 to 18 inches of flowing water, something most people aren't used to doing," says Rome. Forget about it during spring runoff or during rains, she warns. (Access to Cathedral Valley is possible from the other end of the loop without crossing River Ford, 19 miles east of the

One-hundred-thirty-three-foot Hickman Bridge

Temple of the Sun monolith

visitor center, but you'll miss the **Bentonite Hills,** plus you'll have to drive back the way you came or exit the park through United States Forest Service lands.)

7 Bentonite Hills While not actually within the park, these barren badlands should be. The surreal, softly molded hills of Morrison formation shale are unique to the Southwest.

"The mounds are absolutely barren, denuded of vegetation," says Stinchfield, "and there are a lot of colors besides gray at work: There are mauves and pinks and blues, and in a good light—holy cow—it's just incredibly photogenic."

Some believe the Navajo name for the Capitol Reef region is Land of the Sleeping Rainbow, and nowhere is it better illustrated than here.

The crinkly clay, which looks like a Berber carpet and is crunchy when dry, swells in the rain, turning into a sticky mud trap—not a good place to be mired. "Even during our busiest time, you might only see three or four vehicles during the entire day," says Stinchfield.

8 Gypsum Sinkhole As this big plug of gypsum (similar to Glass Mountain) dissolves underground, it has created a true desert curiosity: a 200-foot-deep sinkhole.

As the process is ongoing, it is prohibited for visitors to get close to the edge, and for good reason: The area is quite unstable.

9 Glass Mountain This large 15-foot-high mound of selenite crystals glints like glass, and it looks like a sparkly geological platform for the nearby Temple of the Sun. Alas, this plug of gypsum is probably destined to end up someday as a sinkhole.

⑩ **Temple of the Sun** A monolithic sentinel of eroding Entrada sandstone rises 400 feet from the valley floor in a show of sheer physical prowess. If you're lucky enough to be here at sunset, the sight of its pink and reddish colors igniting in vibrant hues above the darkening valley floor is an unforgettable image, especially with **Temple of the Moon** and **Temple of the Stars** brightening the background. If there is a secret icon of the American Southwest still to be discovered, this is it.

▶ Notom-Bullfrog Road

This 45-mile-long road runs parallel to the Waterpocket Fold on its eastern side, connecting Utah 24 to the **Burr Trail Road** (5.3 miles within Capitol Reef) and the **Bullfrog Marina** on Lake Powell. This well-maintained road—it has both dirt and paved sections—dips into the southern half of the park, offering access to some of its rarely visited treasures.

⑪ **Upper Muley Twist Canyon** Considered by local experts to be the best day hike in the park, this 9-mile loop (15 miles if you lack the high-clearance vehicle needed to make it to the **Strike Valley Overlook** trailhead) serves up beautifully exposed Wingate and Navajo sandstone layers eroded into scenic shapes, including some big arches.

"Half of it is on a high skyline taking in the most stunning geologic scenery you've ever seen in your life, then you drop down in the Muleys, a narrow, winding, long canyon rimmed with water pockets," says Rome.

This is a route, not a maintained trail, so watch for cairns. While you're at it, keep an eye (and ear) out for the local bird life: Ash-throated Flycatchers, warblers, Western Kingbirds, and that feisty icon of the Colorado Plateau, the Canyon Wren.

⑫ **Headquarters and Surprise Canyons** These two family-friendly spots offer a taste of canyoneering in slotlike canyons (no equipment needed); each is a moderate 2-mile round-trip hike; and the two are often combined into a half-day adventure.

Kids like to scramble, squeeze, and scurry through the narrow clefts of the Waterpocket Fold, which allows you to go as far as your canyoneering skills take you.

⑬ **Halls Creek Narrows** If Headquarters Canyon is for families, *this remote narrows is for expert hikers only,* as it requires a 22-mile, two-to-four-day trek to experience its 3-mile-long, tunnel-like slot, which often means wading in spots. Needless to say, thorough preparation is necessary.

Local Intelligence

The 1908 Gifford Homestead is a museum-like still-life of early Mormon pioneer days, but it's frequently overlooked by visitors, who miss out on the homemade pie sold in the old kitchen, not to mention the locally made scones, fresh ice cream, jellies, and dried fruit. But don't wait for the afternoon.

"The best time for pie is 8 a.m.," advises Lori Rome, chief of interpretation. "That's when it arrives fresh and hot from the oven."

One-hundred-fifty-room Cliff Palace

MESA VERDE

Around the same time the Roman Empire was on its last legs and western Europe was sliding into the Dark Ages, an entirely different civilization was moving onto a broad, flat mountain that would later be called Mesa Verde. Soaring more than 8,500 feet above sea level, the tableland *(cuesta)* provided an ideal perch for the Ancestral Puebloan—a source of abundant food, shelter, and spiritual inspiration that would evolve into the richest archaeological cache of the American Southwest.

Mesa Verde National Park harbors nearly 5,000 ancient sites, including some of the nation's biggest and most impressive cliff dwellings—multistory adobe villages where hundreds of people once lived, worked, and worshipped in underground kivas. For reasons still secret, residents left Mesa Verde by 1300. In 1906, President Theodore Roosevelt named the area the first national park protecting human, not just natural, treasures.

Year-Round Visitor Center

- **Visitor and Research Center**
  Off US 160, Park Entrance Station

  970-529-4465, *www.nps.gov/meve*

▶ North Rim

Although all visitors must pass through the park's northern frontier to reach the renowned archaeological sites, the North Rim has long been overlooked and underused.

That changed in fall 2012 with the opening of the **Mesa Verde Visitor and Research Center,** just off US 160 near the entrance station. The new complex is a must stop for park maps, brochures, and information. It's also the only place in Mesa Verde to sign up for popular ranger-guided tours of **Cliff Palace, Balcony House,** and **Long House.**

Beyond the new visitor center, the main road (built in 1914) crawls up the sheer face of the North Rim past the popular **Mancos Valley** and **Montezuma Valley** overlooks, as well as **Morefield Campground,** the only camping facility in the park.

But the rest of the North Rim remains refreshingly vacant. There are no major archaeological remains in the area, just sublime nature and the park's best animal viewing.

1 Point Lookout Trail "The Point Lookout Trail offers a terrific view as you walk up to the tallest point in the park," says Carol Sperling, chief of interpretation and visitor services. "The main attraction is nature. But you've also got culture in the sense that there are nice views of the **Mancos** and **Montezuma Valleys,** which were inhabited by Ancestral Pueblo people at the same time as Mesa Verde." The 2.2-mile path starts at the north end of the amphitheater parking area.

2 Prater Ridge Trail Sperling says the North Rim is also the best place for wildlife. "Driving between Morefield Campground and Montezuma Valley Overlook, I've seen more big mammals than anywhere else in the park." The chance of spotting critters is better away from the main road, especially along the 7.8-mile Prater Ridge Trail, which loops through the woodlands west of the campground.

▶ Far View

At Far View, the main road through the park branches into forks that lead due south to **Chapin Mesa** and west toward **Wetherill Mesa.** Across the road is Far View Lodge, the park's

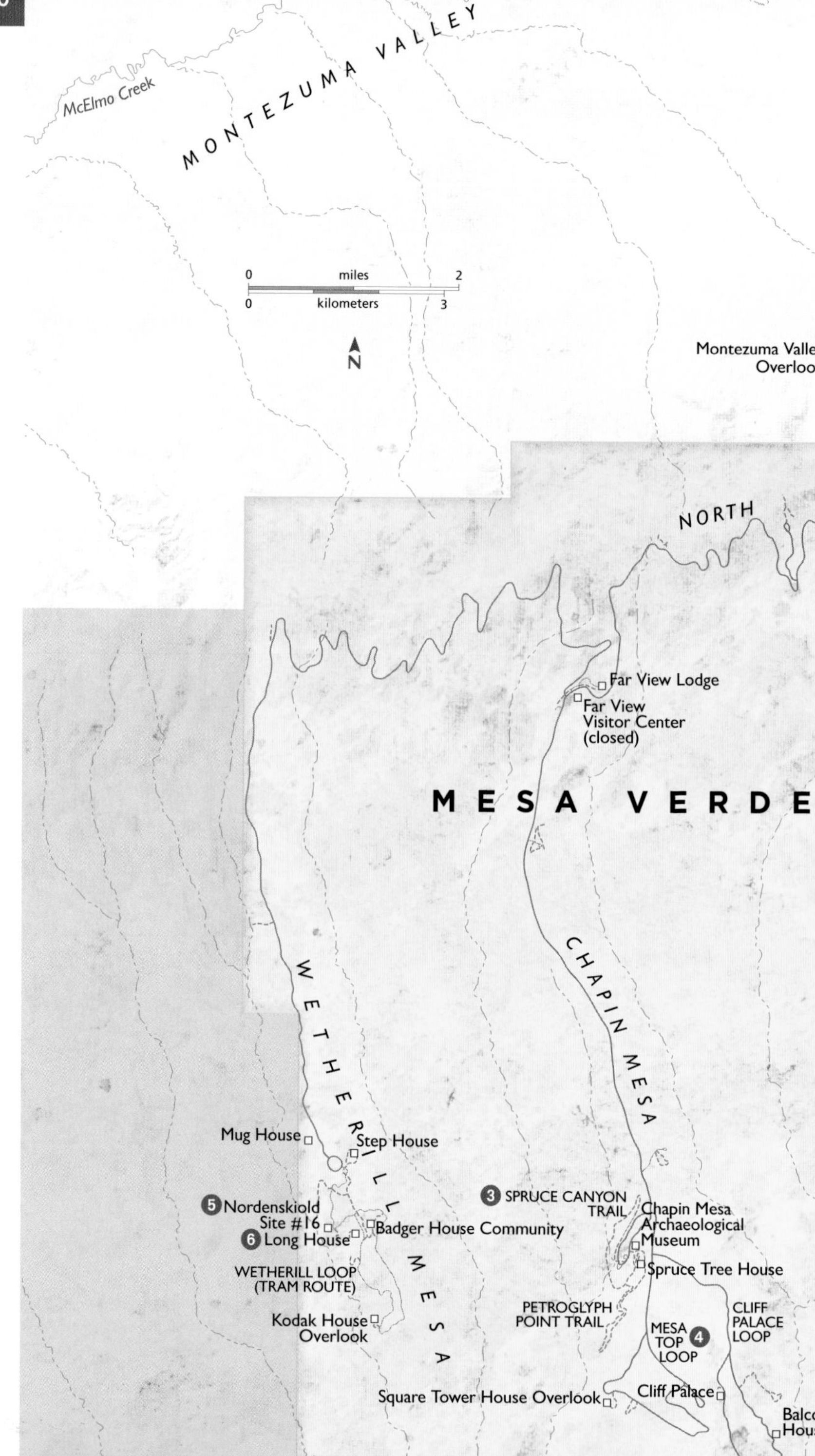
MONTEZUMA VALLEY
McElmo Creek
0 miles 2
0 kilometers 3
N
Montezuma Valley Overlook
NORTH
Far View Lodge
Far View Visitor Center (closed)
MESA VERDE
CHAPIN MESA
WETHERILL MESA
Mug House
Step House
3 SPRUCE CANYON TRAIL
5 Nordenskiold Site #16
6 Long House
Badger House Community
Chapin Mesa Archaeological Museum
Spruce Tree House
WETHERILL LOOP (TRAM ROUTE)
PETROGLYPH POINT TRAIL
CLIFF PALACE LOOP
MESA TOP LOOP 4
Kodak House Overlook
Cliff Palace
Square Tower House Overlook
Balcony House

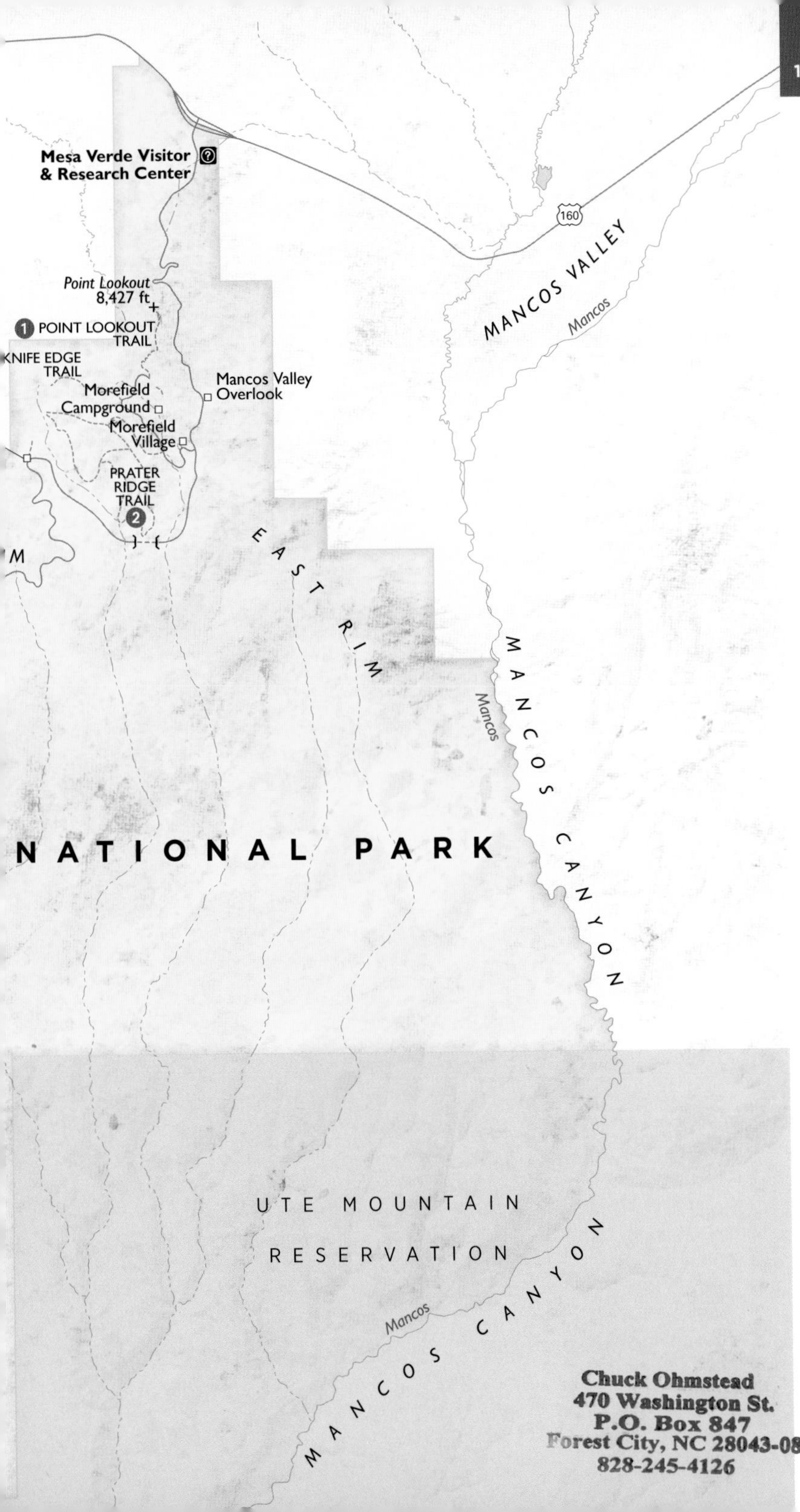
Mesa Verde Visitor & Research Center
Point Lookout
8,427 ft
1 POINT LOOKOUT TRAIL
KNIFE EDGE TRAIL
Morefield Campground
Morefield Village
Mancos Valley Overlook
PRATER RIDGE TRAIL
2
160
MANCOS VALLEY
Mancos
EAST RIM
MANCOS CANYON
Mancos
NATIONAL PARK
UTE MOUNTAIN RESERVATION
Mancos
MANCOS CANYON

only hotel. Even if you're not staying overnight, the lodge terrace is the place to check out the daytime view reaching four states or the night sky.

"I remember being there as a child and watching thunderstorms off the lodge balcony," says Sperling. If you haven't eaten, pop into **Metate Room** for dishes like *poblano relleno* and *masa* chicken *asadero* that include ingredients that would have been used by the Ancestral Puebloan.

▶ Chapin Mesa

Chapin Mesa has long been the park's focal point, both for its grand views over the **Four Corners** region and its renowned archaeological sites. Hundreds of artifacts from these sites are on display in the **Chapin Mesa Archaeological Museum,** built in 1924 and a historic structure in its own right. From just behind the museum, a 0.5-mile trail leads down to **Spruce Tree House,** one of the most notable cliff dwellings, tucked beneath a rock overhang.

3 Spruce Canyon Trail Most visitors head straight back up the cliff via the main trail. An alternative route back to the museum parking lot is the Spruce Canyon Trail, which can be combined with **Petroglyph Point Trail** into a nearly 6-mile jaunt through gorgeous mesa country.

4 Cliff Palace and Mesa Top Loops South of the museum are scenic roads that lead to more rewarding overlooks and ancient high-rise dwellings.

Both Cliff Palace and **Balcony House**—which can only be visited on pre-ticketed, ranger-guided tours—are situated along the 6-mile Cliff Palace Loop. Mesa Top Loop (6 miles) meanders through the piñon-juniper woodland to 12 pullouts with viewpoints of the landscape or archaeological sites.

One of these looks down on **Square Tower House,** part of a new Park Service "Backcountry Hikes" program launched in 2010 to open a few of Mesa Verde's more fragile archaeological sites on a rotating basis to small, guided groups of ten people or less. Some of these ruins have not been accessible to the general public since the 1930s. Another site, open in 2012, is **Mug House** on Wetherill Mesa. Check the park's website for what ruins are open when you travel.

Square Tower is Sperling's favorite site: "It's intimate and beautiful—a

Local Intelligence

Mesa Verde's ancient inhabitants were part of a much larger cultural zone that now includes nearby sites in southwestern Colorado like **Hovenweep National Monument,** the **Canyon of the Ancients National Monument,** and **Ute Mountain Tribal Park** on the Indian reservation of the same name. "I would recommend all of these for people interested in Ancestral Puebloan culture," says Carol Sperling, chief of interpretation and visitor services.

Bordering Mesa Verde to the west and south, Ute Mountain Tribal Park is a rich store of ancient sites rarely visited because of their remoteness and rugged terrain. Starting from the visitor center in **Towaoc,** Colorado, tribal guides take visitors on half- and full-day tours to secluded cliff dwellings like **Eagle Nest House** in **Lion Canyon** as well as on once-a-year hikes to almost inaccessible cliff dwellings like **Casa Blanca** and **Casa Colorado.**

touching setting, a gorgeous little spot, but not easy to reach." The trail, which descends 100 feet into the canyon, requires clambering over boulders, scaling three ladders, and slipping past steep drop-offs. The reward at the other end is a cliff dwelling that includes a four-story **Crow's Nest** (the "square tower" of the name) and an original, intact kiva roof.

▶ Wetherill Mesa

Open to the public since 1973, the Wetherill Mesa area embraces some of the park's most impressive cliff dwellings yet is visited by only about a quarter of the people who enter Mesa Verde each year.

"Oh gosh, it's amazing," says Sperling. "It's a much different experience than Chapin Mesa. Much quieter, more wide open and less congested."

The Ute Mountain and Mesa Verde sites were built by the same people in the same time period. People today should see them as the same culture.

—JACOB DANCE, JR.
Tribal park spokesman

Open only between late May and early September, Wetherill Mesa Road rambles from Far View to the Wetherill Mesa information kiosk parking lot and picnic area.

From there, visitors can take a tram tour of the **Wetherill Loop**—including a look down at secluded **Kodak House**—or strike off on several self-guided tours. The more popular of these options are the short hike to **Step House** and the wandering path to the **Badger House Community** mesa-top sites.

Spruce Tree House reconstructed kiva

5 Nordenskiold Site No. 16 It's the lesser used trails that reveal the richness of Wetherill. Named after a Swedish aristocrat turned archaeologist who undertook the first extensive survey of Mesa Verde in 1891, this 1-mile round-trip is an elongated cliff dwelling with around 50 rooms that includes both stone structures and rooms carved into the sandstone face.

6 Long House The mesa's star attraction is Long House, least visited of the park's five major cliff dwellings and another Sperling favorite. "Long House was thought to be a kind of a community center," she says.

With more than 150 rooms spread across three levels, Long House is the second largest of the park's cliff dwellings. While it is open daily during the summer season, it can only be visited on ranger-guided hikes.

Canyon walls above the Colorado River

CANYONLANDS

This is the Great American Outback, a vast park containing the rawest, most rugged land in the lower 48, an untrammeled wilderness that looks no different than when Maj. John Wesley Powell first traveled through it on his Colorado River exploration in 1869. The 527-square-mile park has been neatly carved into three districts—Island in the Sky, The Maze, and The Needles—by its primary engineers, the Green and Colorado Rivers, which join forces at the Confluence, the park's arterial heart.

Each district is of distinct character. Motorists prefer Island in the Sky for its easily accessible yet far-reaching overlooks where views of 100 miles are not uncommon. The Needles district appeals to hikers seeking to lose themselves amid the secrets of its surreal spires and wandering canyons. The Maze tests the limits of the most intrepid adventurer, and requires a GPS unit, compass, topographic maps, and nerve to explore.

Year-Round Visitor Centers

- **Island in the Sky Visitor Center**
  On Utah 313, 23 miles southwest of US 191
- **Needles Visitor Center**
  35 miles west of US 191
- **Hans Flat Ranger Station**
  46 miles west of Utah 24

435-719-2313, *www.nps.gov/cany*

▶ Island in the Sky

This high desert mesa (6,080 feet) towers 2,200 feet above the **Green** and **Colorado Rivers** below, and it is crossed by 20 miles of paved road that winds through rice grass and juniper trees while stopping at the park's most popular sights: **Mesa Arch, Grand View Point,** and the **Green River Overlook.** If you're seeking to steer clear of the car-bound crowds, a little sweat equity put into hiking pays huge dividends.

❶ **White Rim Overlook** This gentle trail leads a mile to the end of a narrow promontory offering an even wider panoramic spectacle than the more popular Grand View Point Overlook—and you're likely to have it all to yourself. (There are only four parking slots at the trailhead.)

"I call it the O. Henry trail for its sudden ending," says Kathryn Burke, seasonal ranger. "You're walking though piñon-juniper scrubland and bam, the end hits you and you can hardly breathe. Your jaw just drops at the sudden appearance of the canyons below." (Watch your step, though; unlike at Grand View Point, there are *no* guardrails.)

The 300-degree views are of a geologic layer cake of chocolate-colored canyons frosted with White Rim sandstone, while the **La Sal** and **Abajo Mountains** ride on the horizon under a big western sky.

❷ **Murphy Point** This may be the best sunset-watching site in the whole Island in the Sky area (if not in the entire park), but ever since the dirt road was turned into a 1.8-mile-long foot trail, it gets far fewer visitors than the other overlooks.

From the promontory's ramparts, the far-reaching views of **Candlestick Tower, Turks Head, Soda Spring Basin,** and the distant Maze can occupy you for hours. This is also the only place atop the Island in the Sky mesa where you can pitch camp, apart from the 12-site **Willow Flat** campground, though you'll need to snag a backcountry permit. (Since only one permit at a time is issued for Murphy Point, you'll have the place to yourself.)

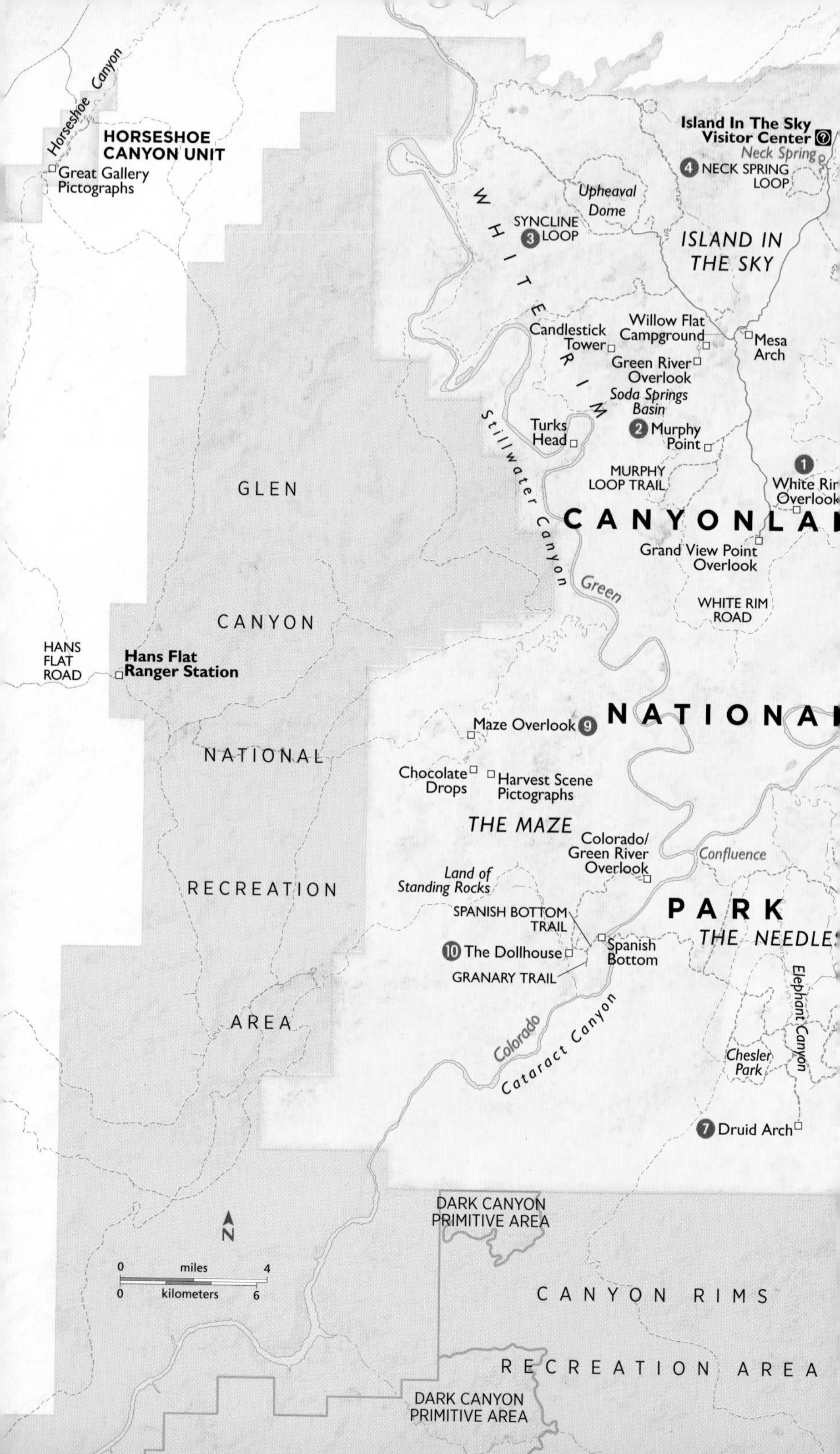

Horseshoe Canyon
HORSESHOE
CANYON UNIT
Great Gallery
Pictographs
Island In The Sky
Visitor Center
Neck Spring
4 NECK SPRING
LOOP
Upheaval
Dome
SYNCLINE
3 LOOP
W H I T E R I M
ISLAND IN
THE SKY
Willow Flat
Campground
Candlestick
Tower
Mesa
Arch
Green River
Overlook
Soda Springs
Basin
Stillwater Canyon
Turks
Head
2 Murphy
Point
1
MURPHY
LOOP TRAIL
White Ri
Overlook
GLEN
CANYONLA
Grand View Point
Overlook
Green
WHITE RIM
ROAD
CANYON
HANS
FLAT
ROAD
Hans Flat
Ranger Station
Maze Overlook 9
NATIONA
NATIONAL
Chocolate
Drops
Harvest Scene
Pictographs
THE MAZE
Colorado/
Green River
Overlook
Confluence
Land of
Standing Rocks
RECREATION
SPANISH BOTTOM
TRAIL
PARK
THE NEEDLE
10 The Dollhouse
Spanish
Bottom
GRANARY TRAIL
Elephant Canyon
AREA
Colorado
Cataract Canyon
Chesler
Park
7 Druid Arch
DARK CANYON
PRIMITIVE AREA
N
0
miles
4
0
kilometers
6
CANYON RIMS
RECREATION AREA
DARK CANYON
PRIMITIVE AREA

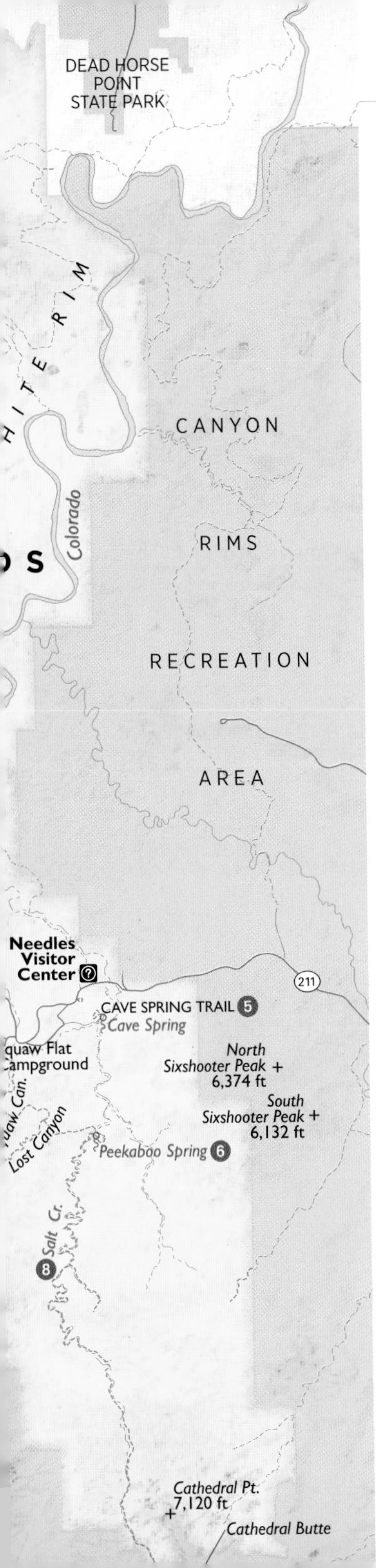

DEAD HORSE POINT STATE PARK

WHITE RIM

CANYON RIMS RECREATION AREA

Colorado

Needles Visitor Center

211

CAVE SPRING TRAIL 5

Cave Spring

quaw Flat ampground

North Sixshooter Peak + 6,374 ft

South Sixshooter Peak + 6,132 ft

uaw Can.

Lost Canyon

Peekaboo Spring 6

Salt Cr.

8

Cathedral Pt. 7,120 ft

Cathedral Butte

If you're feeling even more adventurous, take the nearby 10.8-mile **Murphy Loop Trail,** which descends 1,400 feet of switchbacks down cliffs of Wingate sandstone, then follows an exhilarating hogback all the way to the **White Rim Road** before looping back up.

3 Syncline Loop Those who complete the 8.3-mile trail around the rim of **Upheaval Dome** earn plenty of bragging rights.

"It beats me up every time I do it," says Burke. "But I keep going back for more because it is so brutally beautiful. It's mostly cairned, and the terrain is rocky and varied, so you really have to keep an eye out. Most of our rescues take place here."

A 3-mile spur trail takes hikers into enigmatic Upheaval Dome, an inexplicable mile-wide bull's-eye of a crater. Scientists still argue whether it is a collapsed salt dome or the remains of an ancient meteor strike. "I think a

Canyonlands-resident lizard

Chesler Park in the Needles District

good mystery makes every park better," says Burke. "This one is ours."

The six- to eight-hour trek gives plenty of time for hikers to puzzle over the green, purple, and brown geologic formations at the core of the crater.

4 Neck Spring Loop Probably the most secret trail in the park, this 5.8-mile-long, three- to four-hour loop is the only moderate-length hike on the Island that doesn't mimic a StairMaster workout on the return leg. It also offers more of a chance to see wildlife than anywhere else, so bring binoculars.

The presence of year-round water attracts animals such as mule deer, coyotes, desert bighorns, and many smaller mammals. A sharp eye will also reveal flint-knapping chips from the Ancestral Puebloan and weathered ranching gear left over from the park's cattle days.

"You aren't on top of the mesa, but underneath it," says Cindy Donaldson, park guide. "You follow in and out of these little drainages where you'll find some really neat things, like maidenhair ferns underneath the Navajo sandstone cap."

▶ The Needles

Named after the red and buttery-white striped towers of Cedar Mesa sandstone that dominate the district, this is a backpackers paradise, offering more trails than either The Maze or Island in the Sky.

While most visitors will make a deserved beeline for the spire-fringed meadows of **Chesler Park,** those seeking a less traveled trail will love a more than 60-mile network of narrow interconnected routes that allow for plenty of improvisation when exploring the region's many canyons, joints (splits in the rock), graben valleys, and arches.

This area also has far more ruins, pictographs, and petroglyphs than elsewhere in the park, which adds a haunting human dimension to an already mind-bending landscape.

5 Cave Spring Trail Often overlooked for being too short and easy, this 0.6-mile loop is a CliffsNotes version of the park, summing up all of its aspects in a 45-minute loop.

Due to the year-round springs, you'll come across a historic cowboy line camp in one alcove. Just beyond is evidence of an earlier occupation.

"There are two sets of pictographs, one by the spring and the other one in the next alcove over on the ceiling. It's where the Ancestral Puebloan lived, and if you keep your eyes open you'll spot lots of archaeological stuff," says Cindy Donaldson.

More apparent are the signs identifying many of the park's plants: Utah serviceberry, four-wing saltbush, and squawbush, for example. Two ladders hoist you up to the slickrock, where, reports Donaldson, "you'll get amazing views of The Needles."

6 Peekaboo Spring This 10-mile round-trip, which leaves the Squaw Flat campground and crosses both **Squaw** and **Lost Canyons,** is one of the few trails here that is mostly on slickrock, especially the last 2.5 miles to Peekaboo.

"You walk on top of these headwalls that are pretty tall, which give you dramatic views of the **La Sal Mountains** and **Six-Shooter Peak,**" says Brad Donaldson, backcountry ranger, who counts this as his favorite hike. "There's some exposure. It's scary, but not risky," he adds.

Two well-placed ladders help with the scrambling as you navigate atop a labyrinth of mostly inaccessible canyons and drainages. The payoff?

"You come to a brilliant rock art site, with the oldest art at least 1,000 years old, with more recent—say 700-year-old—art painted right over it," says Brad.

7 Druid Arch This trail shares the same path with popular **Chesler Park** for the first 2.1 miles, but as soon as it drops down into **Elephant Canyon,** it departs from the more trodden route and strikes up a scenic canyon for another 3.3 miles, passing narrow-leaf yucca, Mormon tea, Indian paintbrush, and seasonal pools of water. (Don't expect much shade on this hike.)

Local Intelligence

Island in the Sky is "home to the only native herd of desert bighorn sheep remaining in Utah, about 300 to 400 animals," says Chris Dyas, seasonal park ranger. "Typically all the literature says that they stay below the White Rim, but we are getting more sightings of them atop the mesa. You'll have the best chance of spotting wildlife at places with water, such as **Upheaval Dome,** and close to the visitor center at **Neck Spring."** Look for their telltale white behinds on rocky slopes of 45 degrees. In hot summer, they stay close to water sources, and in late November, you might hear the resounding crack of the rams' head-butting contests. "They'll slam into each other about five times an hour," says Dyas, "which is when those big horns and double craniums come in handy."

The same type of banded spires populating Chesler Park guard the canyon walls here. The last third of a mile is a scramble, helped with the aid of a ladder, before reaching the impressive Druid Arch, named after the creators of Stonehenge, due to its angular look.

Photographers should get here early—locals say the morning light brings Druid Arch to life.

An increasing number of people are taking the jet boat from Moab down the Colorado River to Spanish Bottom, where a trail gets you up into The Maze. It's cheaper than renting a 4WD vehicle, takes less time, and isn't as arduous.

—GARY COX
Canyonlands National Park ranger

---

8 Salt Creek Now that four-wheel-drive vehicles are banned, prolific amounts of wildlife are returning to this riparian corridor.

"You don't expect black bears in the desert, but there's a real possibility of running into one here," says Brad Donaldson.

Obtain a backcountry permit, and take three or four days to hike this convoluted 23-mile-long cultural adventure, allowing time to explore the many cliff dwellings and granaries *(warning: Entry is against the law),* petroglyphs and pictographs, and other evidence of the Ancestral Puebloan's centuries-long tenure. For example, the squash plants they introduced still grow wild in places.

Because backcountry permits are regulated, you won't run into many people. While shorter trips can be accomplished starting from the northern trailhead, most hikers prefer to begin at **Cathedral Point—**at 7,120 feet, the park's highest spot—where the trail drops into the upper end of Salt Creek.

▶ The Maze

The Maze can make parts of The Needles or Island in the Sky appear as civilized as Central Park. It's virtually trail-less, with routes usually marked by cairns—if at all. This is about as remote an area as there is in the American West, and any visit should entail a serious amount of planning, gear, and fortitude.

"People out here get in touch with their mortality sometimes," warns Joyce Evans, park ranger.

Just to reach most trailheads requires a high-clearance four-wheel-drive vehicle and three hours of rough-terrain driving from the **Hans Flat Ranger Station** (itself reached only after 46 miles of rough two-wheel-drive dirt road from Utah 24).

Your reward? The same sense of satisfaction in self-reliant exploration shared with the early explorers to this region—only about 3,000 people a year make the trek.

9 Maze Overlook The views across this curving labyrinth of interconnected canyons are worth every bump along the 30 miles of pretty rough four-wheel-drive road it takes to reach them (leaving from the Hans Flat Ranger Station).

From the overlook, you can see

a frozen maelstrom of sandstone crested by the **Chocolate Drops**—350-million-year-old Organ shale formations. If the view isn't enough, take the cairned trail that drops down into this maze, the portal for multiday backpacking adventures.

"It's not for the faint of heart or people who aren't comfortable scrambling over steep rocky areas," says Gary Cox, park ranger. "You have to lower yourself down to narrow ledges with steep drop-offs, worm yourself through very narrow cracks, and step down footholds carved into the rock."

If you don't have several days, a relatively short 2.3-mile, two-hour scramble down from the overlook brings you to the unforgettable 2,000- to 8,000-year-old **Harvest Scene pictographs.**

"They're very detailed and intricate," says Cox, "and best seen in the late afternoon light."

⑩ The Dollhouse One of the more remote, yet popular, campsites in The Maze (reached via 42 miles of tough four-wheel-drive road), the Dollhouse is named for the dreamlike rockscape.

"Hoodoos [rock formations] in variegated colors surround the campground. It looks like a procession of rock marching off into the desert," says Evans.

It also is the trailhead to three very different day hikes: the **Colorado/Green River Overlook** (9 miles), the **Granary Trail** (2 miles to Ancestral Puebloan granaries), and the **Spanish Bottom Trail,** which drops 3 miles down to the Colorado River.

The mysterious ancient stonework along parts of the Spanish Bottom Trail is historically significant. "The best information from oral history suggests the stone steps were built by French Basque sheepherders in the 1880s—they had lots of time on their hands—though there is romantic folklore that claims it's a branch of the Old Spanish Trail," says Cox.

The Colorado River near Spanish Bottom

▶ Floating the Green and Colorado Rivers

While hiking has its rewards, take a page from Major Wesley Powell's journal and spend four or five days drifting 54 miles through the heart of the park, an option most visitors never consider—other than a few ripples, it's all flat water.

Start at **Mineral Bottom** on the Green River just north of the park, and glide through aptly named **Stillwater Canyon** to the confluence with the Colorado, then travel on another 4 miles to **Spanish Bottom.** (Don't go farther; that thundering is **Cataract Canyon,** home to some of North America's biggest rapids.)

Permits cost $30 a person; fire pans and portable toilets required. Choose any date; there are no daily launch limits. Rent rafts, inflatable kayaks, or canoes in **Moab.** Schedule a pickup by jet boat.

North Window and Turret Arches

ARCHES

The 119 square miles of Arches National Park hold the world's greatest collection of natural stone arches—more than 2,300 of them—along with a supporting cast of fins, spires, hoodoos, domes, and towers. This is the real Jurassic Park, a 300-million-year-old story written in stone of a time when coastal dunes and a primeval inland sea deposited sediments that have since been uplifted, carved, eroded, and scoured by the forces of nature.

A single 18-mile paved road with two short spurs threads it all together, offering easy access to the iconic arches and rock formations for which this park is famous. In fact, visitors can see a lot without leaving their cars, but doing so would mean missing the park's many secrets.

"Arches may be a small and famous park," explains Karen Henker, the park's lead interpreter, "but it still has a lot of hidden corners waiting for folks to explore."

Year-Round Visitor Center

- **Arches Visitor Center**
  On US 191, north of Moab

  435-719-2299, *www.nps.gov/arch*

▶ Arches Scenic Drive

From the visitor center, the main road makes a pulse-pounding entrance as it switchbacks up steep cliffs of white Navajo sandstone and into the salmon-hued Entrada slickrock. Every curve in the road reveals new and surreal vistas of monolithic formations, arches, and sweeping panoramas—**Balanced Rock,** the **Windows,** and **Fiery Furnace,** for example—before the road ends in a giant roundabout at **Devil's Garden.**

❶ **Park Avenue** Those who want to see the park's famous arches are likely to miss this impressive mile-long hike down a corridor of sandstone skyscrapers with names like **Queen Nefertiti** (instantly recognizable) opposite **Queen Victoria** (not so much; the formation looks more like Whistler's mother).

While strolling though the gently descending sandy wash, listen for the warble of Canyon Wrens and keep an eye out for White-throated Swifts flitting around the cliffs.

The trail ends back on the main road at **The Organ,** where you can catch a shuttle ride (check the schedule). Otherwise, it's a slightly more aerobic hike back to the trailhead.

❷ **Courthouse Wash** Though it is not a maintained trail, this flat and sandy route along a gurgling stream is certainly among the most refreshing in the park.

From the parking lot by the bridge, head upstream via the dry wash bed, or better yet, go downstream into a narrowing canyon shaded by tall cottonwood trees and flowering with sand verbena and evening primrose. Keep an eye out for birds such as Spotted Towhees, dippers, and Great Blue Herons.

At the numerous stream crossings, scan for animal prints in the sand—beaver, coyote, mule deer, bighorn sheep, and if you're lucky, the pad marks of a rare mountain lion.

Plan on four hours to meander down **Lower Courthouse Wash,** which comes out 1 mile southeast of the park entrance, on US 191. (Leave a vehicle at the parking lot here beforehand for a ride back.)

Don't depart before checking out the haunting 3,000-year-old **Archaic-era rock paintings** of life-size spectral figures at trail's end—a sign will point you in the right direction.

3 Windows Primitive Trail You can escape the crowds viewing the park's most visited arches in the Windows Section while enjoying a better view of them by taking this short trail at the base of **South Window Arch.**

The narrow 1-mile path bends around the backside of these towering spans, revealing not only a dramatic panorama overlooking **Salt Wash,** but, from this perspective, showing that the two separate **North** and **South Arches** are actually cut from the same Entrada sandstone fin. They combine into a single feature resembling a pair of sky blue eyes with a big rock nose in the middle, what locals traditionally call "**The Spectacles.**" (It's a favorite early morning photo op.)

Ute petroglyphs at Wolfe Ranch

4 Wolfe Ranch and Ute Petroglyphs Going to Arches without visiting **Delicate Arch** is like going to the Louvre without seeing the *Mona Lisa.* Don't get caught up in the daily "march to the arch" without taking the time to view **Wolfe Ranch,** a roughshod cabin in which Civil War veteran John Wesley Wolfe and his family lived at the turn of the 20th century. It's the park's only evidence

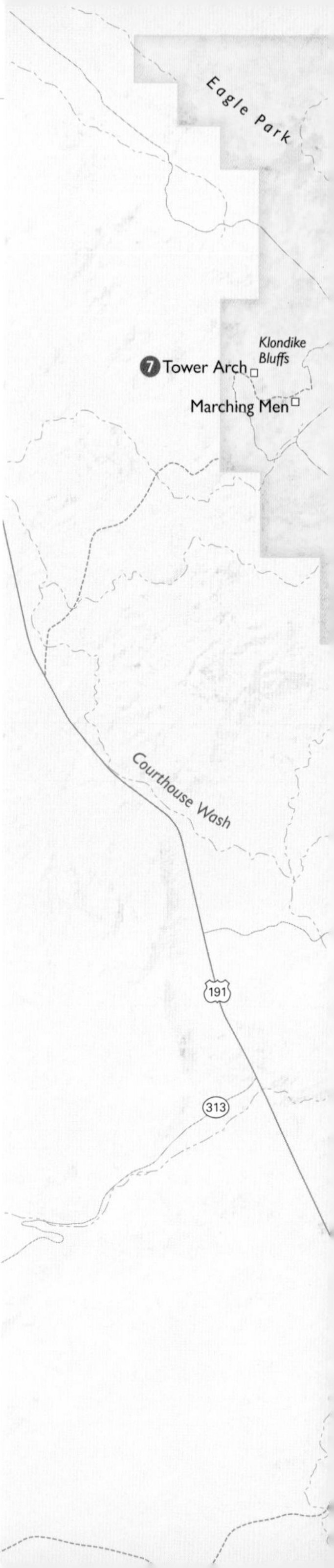

Eagle Park
Klondike Bluffs
7 Tower Arch
Marching Men
Courthouse Wash
191
313

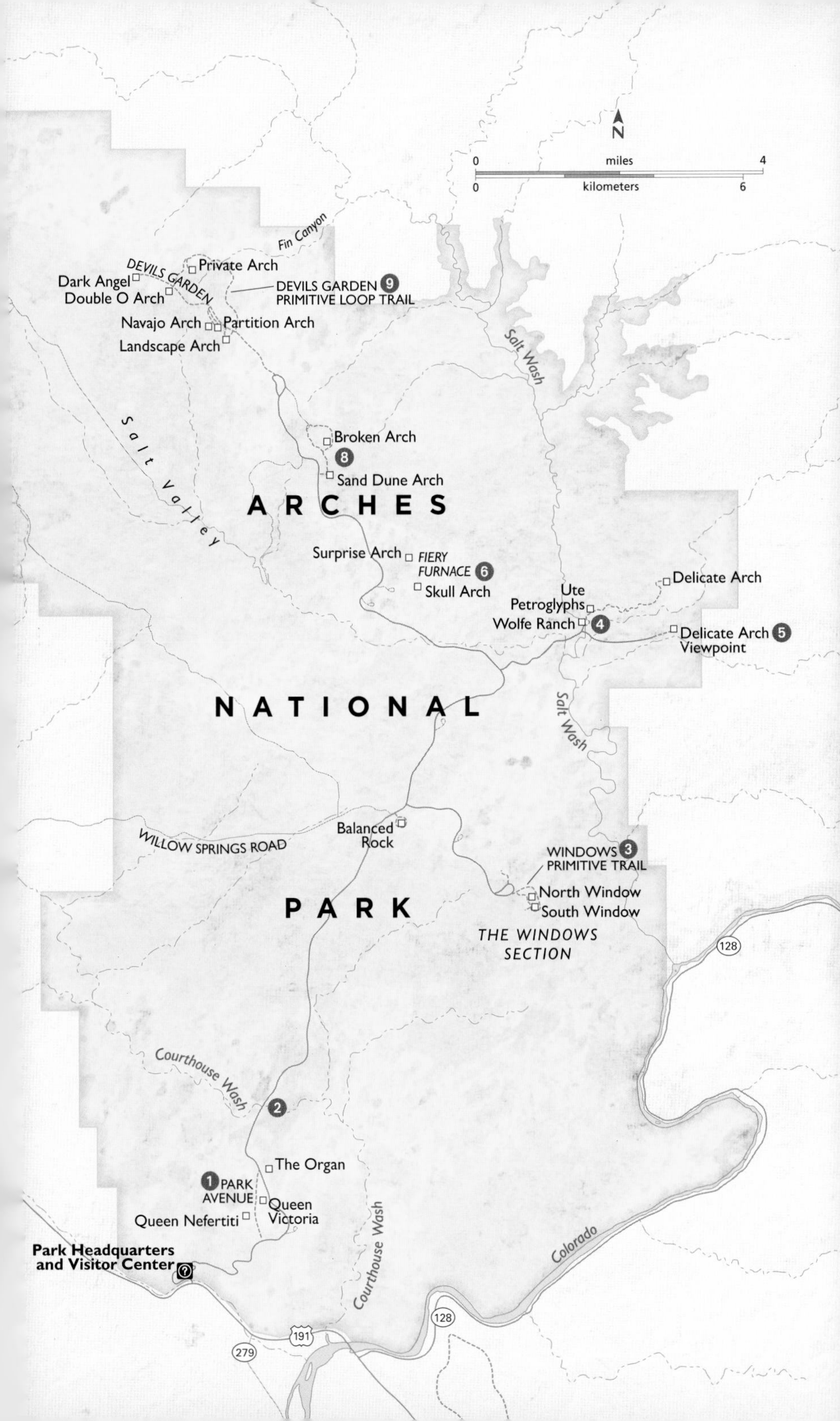
N
0
miles
4
0
kilometers
6
Fin Canyon
Private Arch
DEVILS GARDEN
Dark Angel
Double O Arch
DEVILS GARDEN 9
PRIMITIVE LOOP TRAIL
Navajo Arch
Partition Arch
Landscape Arch
Salt Wash
Salt Valley
Broken Arch
8
Sand Dune Arch
ARCHES
Surprise Arch
FIERY
FURNACE 6
Skull Arch
Delicate Arch
Ute
Petroglyphs
Wolfe Ranch
4
Delicate Arch 5
Viewpoint
NATIONAL
Salt Wash
Balanced
Rock
WILLOW SPRINGS ROAD
WINDOWS 3
PRIMITIVE TRAIL
North Window
South Window
PARK
THE WINDOWS
SECTION
128
Courthouse Wash
2
The Organ
1 PARK
AVENUE
Queen
Victoria
Queen Nefertiti
Courthouse Wash
Colorado
Park Headquarters
and Visitor Center
128
191
279

Delicate Arch landscape

of permanent habitation, a stark reminder of how unaccommodating this land is to humans.

The native Fremont, Ancestral Puebloan, and Ute knew better than to actually live here, though they left evidence of their passing. Walk up 600 feet from the cabin to ponder a Ute petroglyph panel, one of the few to depict horses (and dogs), which dates them to after the mid-1700s Spanish incursion.

5 Delicate Arch Viewpoint If the day is a scorcher, or if hiking 3 miles over steep slickrock is beyond your ability, you can still see the state's iconic arch on something other than Utah's license plates.

Drive 1 mile past the Delicate Arch trailhead to where the road ends. The 300-foot-long handicapped accessible "lower" trail and the 0.5-mile-long "upper" trail will not get you as close to the arch (it's still 0.5 mile away), but you'll see the big picture that people hiking to the arch miss—the arch itself is actually

Fiery Furnace is pure wilderness in a little pocket in the park. It's all about exploration, with no destination other than what you find.

—KAREN HENKER
Arches National Park interpreter

perched on the precipitous edge of a monumental cliff. (While Delicate Arch glows in the sunset, from here the best viewing is in the early morning light.)

6 Fiery Furnace This confusing maze of sandstone fins makes up the park's most rugged terrain. Topological maps and GPS coordinates are useless, and leaving behind cairns or trail markers to find your way out is forbidden.

"This is pure wilderness in a little pocket in the park. It's all about exploration, with no destination other than what you find," says Henker.

The only safe way to navigate this labyrinth is by joining a scheduled three-hour tour led by park rangers (you can reserve six months in advance at *www.recreation.gov*).

How tough a hike is it? "You'll definitely have a chance to channel your own inner Spiderman," says Henker. "There are some fun little moves."

Resourceful hikers are allowed in unescorted after paying for a $4 permit and watching a mandatory video explaining the rules of environmental protection—stay on slickrock, walk in washes, and don't build cairns, for example.

The reward?

Skull and **Surprise Arches,** the possibility of stumbling upon **Abbey Arch** (discovered by Edward Abbey himself), potholes teeming with micro-life, and an up close look at the Arches biscuitroot, a plant that only grows in sandy soil between fins of Entrada sandstone.

With not a lot of room to navigate between the fins—in some places you may squeeze through sideways—this is a good place to keep an eye out for the park's only venomous snake, the midget faded rattlesnake.

Don't let the name Fiery Furnace scare you. Come summer, this is one of the shadier spots in the park.

A blooming prickly pear cactus

Local Intelligence

Edward Abbey wrote much of his book *Desert Solitaire* while working in Arches as a seasonal park ranger. "The trailer he lived in is no longer there, but it was located right by the picnic tables on the **Willow Springs** road, close to **Balanced Rock,"** says Lee Ferguson, park ranger. One of only three picnic sites in the park, this unmarked location makes the perfect lunch stop to pay homage to the author while savoring the same far-reaching views—**Fiery Furnace,** Balanced Rock, the snow-speckled **La Sal Mountains—**that inspired his environmental masterpiece.

Tower Arch in the Klondike Bluffs section

7 Tower Arch To experience a truly monumental arch in sublime solitude, this is your best bet, thanks to the 8.3 miles of dirt-pack washboard that keeps the general public at bay.

"It's my favorite arch, and you just might have it to yourself," says park ranger Kathryn Burke. "It's the first place I heard my own heartbeat."

It may take a little heart-thumping to scramble over the rocky ridge marked by cairns before descending on a sandy single track through a valley full of juniper trees, claret cup cactus (one of the few cacti found at these higher elevations), and leafless clumps of Mormon tea. Three pinnacles, called the **Marching Men,** point you in the right direction.

The 2.5-mile-long trail ends at the park's fifth largest arch, backed by a minaret-like tower, which inspired the inscription carved into its northern base by its purported discoverer: MINARET BRIDGE H.S. BELL 1927.

The name never stuck, as the park's founding father, Alex Ringhoffer, had actually discovered the arch five years earlier. (His name—mysteriously misspelled—is inscribed on the arch's southern base.) In fact, this grand arch motivated Ringhoffer to lobby for help making Arches a national monument in 1929, and, in that sense, Tower Arch can be considered the park's founding arch.

8 Sand Dune and Broken Arches A short trail connects kid-friendly Sand Dune Arch, tucked up in a sandbox fin marking the northern boundary of Fiery Furnace, with Broken Arch on the southern edge of **Devils Garden** via a wide grassy meadow bright with wildflowers and tweeting birds. (Listen for the melodious call of the Western Meadowlark.)

"It's not a very popular hike, and every time I do it, I'm grateful for that fact, because I never run into anybody. It is a nice easy loop, under a mile round-trip, and it explores in between the fins," says Henker. "It doesn't have famous arches, but a lot of them are hiding in here."

The level open terrain makes this trail especially appealing for a full moon hike, though Henker warns: "A lot of the desert's wildlife is out at night, including scorpions and our one-and-only rattlesnake species, the midget faded. So folks who want to take night hikes should wear close-toed shoes and keep their fingers and toes out of little dark holes, because that's where the dangerous stuff is hanging out."

9 Devils Garden Primitive Loop Trail The paved road ends at Devils Garden trailhead, which is filled with cars and RVs in season, but the crowd thins once you trek beyond the trail's first attraction, **Landscape Arch,** the world's longest arch.

There's a reason for this. "Past Landscape, the primitive trail takes it up the next notch as far as the height of exposure and difficulty of scrambling. You definitely need to have flexible hips and good observation skills to see the trail markers," says Henker. "Since this is the longest trail in the park—7.2 miles round-trip—you should plan on spending at least half a day."

The payoff? The largest concentration of natural arches in the world, including **Partition, Navajo, Private,** and **Double O.**

Before returning along the backside of the primitive loop, which offers jaw-dropping views of **Fin Canyon,** take a side trip out to **Dark Angel,** a 0.5-mile hike to the northwest from Double O Arch. This brooding 150-foot-high sandstone spire was used as a historic landmark by ancient travelers, and you might stumble across petroglyphs and the signatures of Ancient Puebloan or early sheepherders who used this area as a natural campsite. (Denis Julien, a French-American trapper, was the first white man to record his presence in the park in 1844.)

Beyond Dark Angel lies the most remote part of Arches, the trailless **Eagle Park district,** where the sandstone fins of Devil's Garden open to empty wide-open spaces. "In the three years I've been here, I've never issued a backcountry permit for Eagle Park," says Chris Stefanides, seasonal ranger—proof that there's still a lot of exploring to be done in Arches.

Wandering atop Devils Garden

Fall aspens in Rocky Mountain

ROCKY MOUNTAIN

The highest elevation national park in the United States, Rocky Mountain protects more than 415 square miles of some of the most spectacular scenery in Colorado. Almost a third of the park lies above the tree line, a harsh alpine environment reaching its summit on 14,259-foot Longs Peak. Rugged mountains dominate vistas from anywhere in the park, which encompasses more than 70 peaks above 12,000 feet in elevation.

The lure of the high country is understandably irresistible, and nearly all visitors feel the urge to immerse themselves in the alpine scenery. The park makes it easy to do just that. Famed Trail Ridge Road crosses the park from east to west, climbing up and over the Continental Divide at a maximum elevation of 12,183 feet. Bear Lake Road, to the south, offers access to many popular destinations, while the western side of the park sees far fewer visitors. Search for secrets at this park high in the sky.

Year-Round Visitor Centers

- **Beaver Meadows Visitor Center**
  On US 36 at East Entrance
- **Kawuneeche Visitor Center**
  On US 34, 1 mile north of Grand Lake Entrance

Seasonal Visitor Centers

- **Alpine Visitor Center**
  At Fall River Pass, junction of Trail Ridge and Old Fall River Roads
- **Fall River Visitor Center**
  On US 34, 5 miles west of Estes Park
- **Moraine Park Visitor Center**
  On Bear Lake Road, 1.5 miles from Beaver Meadows
- **Holzwarth Historic Site**
  Bear Lake Road, 7 miles north of Grand Lake Entrance

970-586-1206, *www.nps.gov/romo*

▶ Trail Ridge Road

This route (US 34) is the highest continuous paved road in the United States, and quite literally every turn along its 48 miles brings a new and awe-inspiring panorama.

Open from about late May to late October (depending on snow cover), Trail Ridge Road is heavily traveled, yet most people drive straight through, stopping only at one or two scenic overlooks and the **Alpine Visitor Center.** It's far more rewarding to leave your vehicle and experience the environment up close.

1 Beaver Ponds Eager to reach those postcard mountain views, nearly all visitors pass by the Beaver Ponds along **Hidden Valley Creek,** between **Deer Ridge Junction** and **Hidden Valley.** An accessible boardwalk makes for fine wildlife viewing. Watch for birds such as Mountain Chickadee and MacGillivray's Warbler.

2 Tundra Communities Trail Once above the tree line on Trail Ridge Road, where severe weather means trees can't grow, the landscape looks barren at first glance. Yet gorgeous wildflowers, delicate grasses, and colorful lichens abound in summer.

An excellent place to enjoy the alpine habitat is the 0.5-mile Tundra Communities Trail at **Rock Cut,** a parking area west of the **Forest Canyon Overlook.**

Alpine sunflowers, snow buttercups, and alpine avens bloom, and a lucky hiker might spot the elusive White-tailed Ptarmigan, a chicken-like bird that camouflages itself by

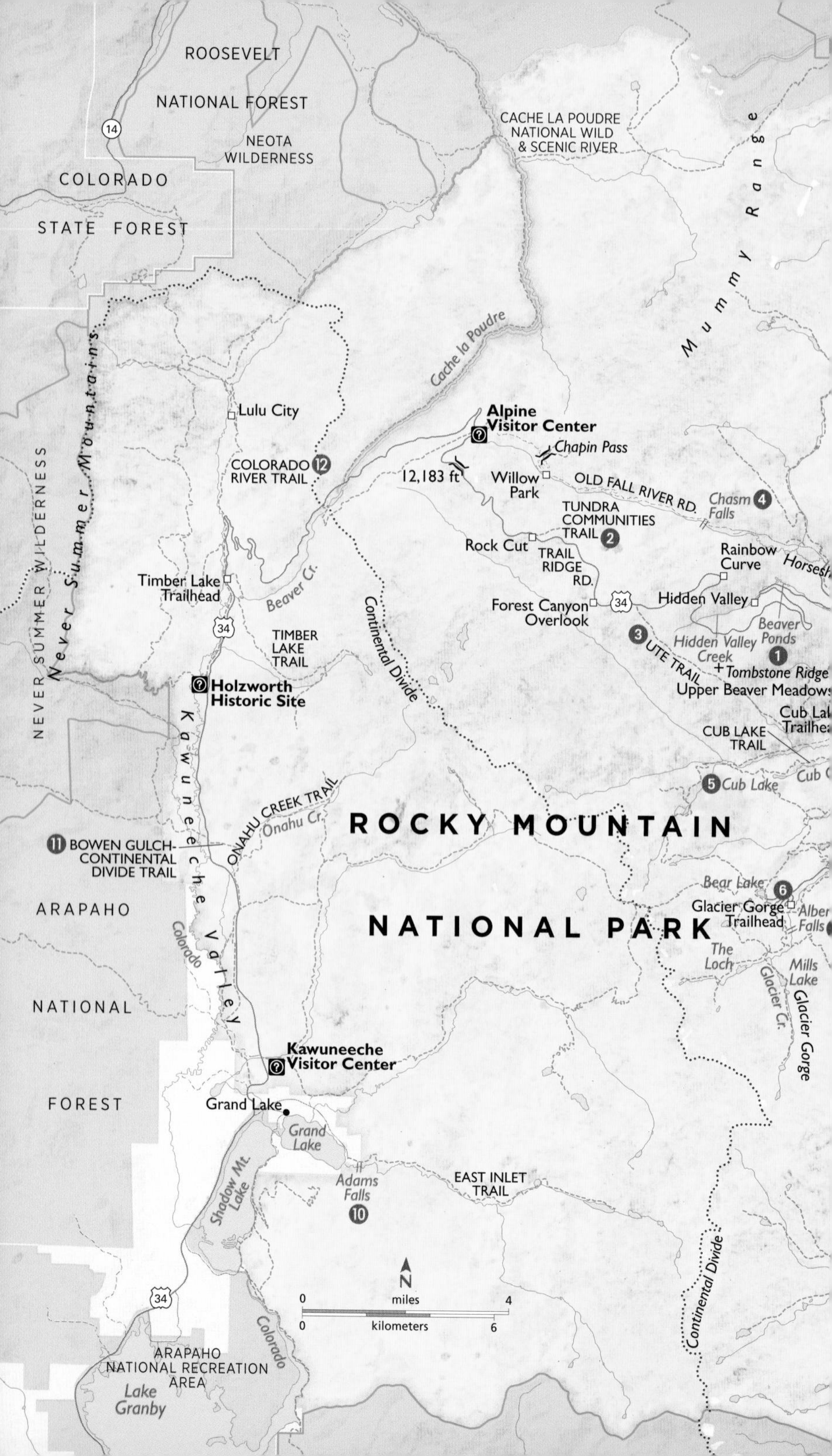

ROOSEVELT
NATIONAL FOREST
NEOTA
WILDERNESS
CACHE LA POUDRE
NATIONAL WILD
& SCENIC RIVER
COLORADO
STATE FOREST
Mummy Range
Never Summer Mountains
NEVER SUMMER WILDERNESS
Cache la Poudre
Lulu City
Alpine
Visitor Center
Chapin Pass
COLORADO
RIVER TRAIL
12
12,183 ft
Willow
Park
OLD FALL RIVER RD.
Chasm
Falls
4
TUNDRA
COMMUNITIES
TRAIL
2
Rock Cut
TRAIL
RIDGE
RD.
Rainbow
Curve
Timber Lake
Trailhead
Beaver Cr.
Continental Divide
Forest Canyon
Overlook
34
Hidden Valley
Beaver
Ponds
3
UTE TRAIL
Hidden Valley
Creek
1
Tombstone Ridge
Upper Beaver Meadows
TIMBER
LAKE
TRAIL
Holzworth
Historic Site
Kawuneeche Valley
CUB LAKE
TRAIL
5
Cub Lake
ONAHU CREEK TRAIL
Onahu Cr.
ROCKY MOUNTAIN
NATIONAL PARK
11
BOWEN GULCH-
CONTINENTAL
DIVIDE TRAIL
ARAPAHO
NATIONAL
FOREST
Colorado
Bear Lake
6
Glacier Gorge
Trailhead
The
Loch
Mills
Lake
Glacier Cr.
Glacier Gorge
Kawuneeche
Visitor Center
Grand Lake
Grand
Lake
Shadow Mt.
Lake
Adams
Falls
10
EAST INLET
TRAIL
N
0
miles
4
0
kilometers
6
ARAPAHO
NATIONAL RECREATION
AREA
Lake
Granby
Colorado

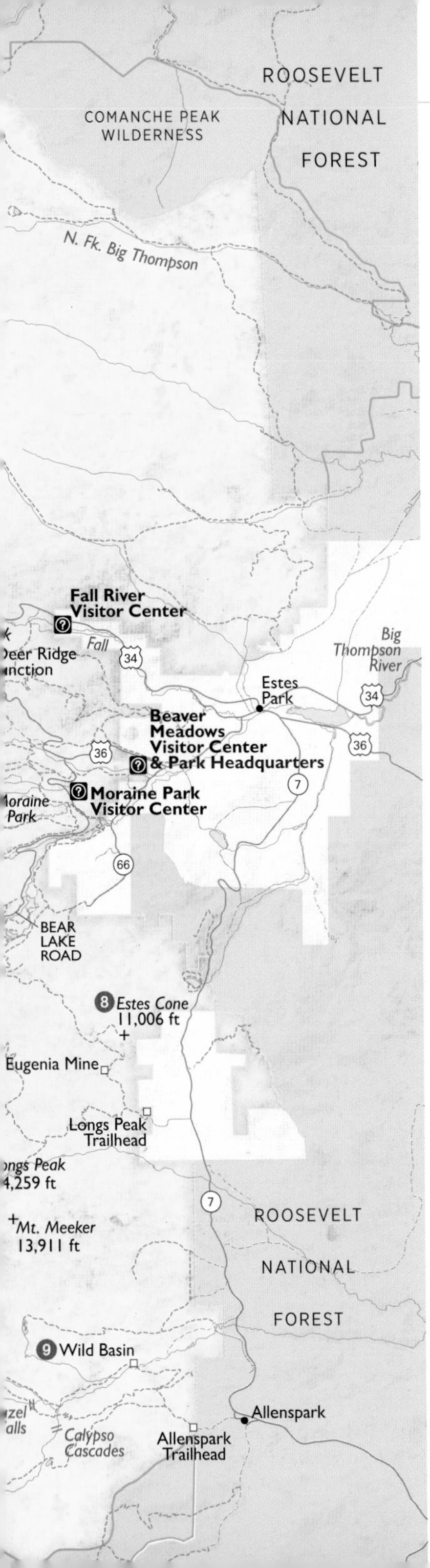

changing color from winter white to summer brown.

This path ascends only moderately, although people with heart or breathing problems should use caution at this lung-straining altitude.

3 Ute Trail To experience the tundra with far greater solitude, walk the section of the Ute Trail that leaves Trail Ridge Road between **Rainbow Curve** and Forest Canyon Overlook.

Remaining fairly flat as it passes below the striking rocks called **Tombstone Ridge,** the Ute Trail quickly makes hikers feel far removed from civilization. The route descends 6 miles to **Upper Beaver Meadows,** but unless you've arranged for a shuttle, it's best to walk the first mile or two and retrace your steps back to Trail Ridge Road.

Named for the Ute Indians who used the path to cross the mountains centuries ago, the route was later followed by other tribes and early European explorers. Imagining the long heritage of travelers here makes a walk more meaningful to modern hikers, who have access to equipment and resources unimaginable to ancient peoples.

Yellow-bellied marmot

Local Intelligence

Here and there in Rocky Mountain National Park (at **Moraine Park,** for example) you'll notice tall fencing around areas such as willow or aspen groves. These "exclosures" keep elk and moose out of places suffering from overgrazing, allowing natural vegetation to recover.

As Michele Simmons, park interpreter, points out, "Many visitors don't know that they're allowed to enter these fenced areas, as long as they close gates behind them. They can be excellent places for bird- and butterfly-watchers." Wildflower enthusiasts and photographers, too, will be pleased to see the substantial difference in flora in habitats where grazing is limited.

Though alpine plants must be tough to survive, they're highly vulnerable to careless hikers. With the short growing season at this elevation, many small plants are actually years or even decades old—yet they can be destroyed with one wrong step of a boot.

On the tundra, even more than other parts of the park, it's vital to stay on the trail. Look for moss campion, a low-growing "cushion" plant that colonizes disturbed soil and displays beautiful pink flowers. With luck, you might spot bighorn sheep, in a location far removed from the often crowded viewing area at **Horseshoe Park.**

▶ Old Fall River Road

A less traveled and more adventurous drive to the tundra is Old Fall River Road, an 11-mile unpaved route that in places is twice as steep as Trail Ridge Road. Following Indian paths and built in part by convict labor, this route has been making drivers nervous since its completion in 1920. Lacking guardrails, with many tight switchbacks, it is nonetheless safe for drivers who obey the 15-mile-per-hour speed limit and keep their eyes on the road, rather than the scenery.

4 Chasm Falls Open for a relatively short summer season, the Old Fall River Road is one-way ascending only: Once you start, you can't turn around and must continue to the Alpine Visitor Center on Trail Ridge Road.

Stop often at overlooks, beginning at striking Chasm Falls, where **Fall River** roars through a chute in the rocks. Watch for elk at **Willow Park,** just before a series of switchbacks up to **Chapin Pass.** Beyond is a fine example of an alpine cirque, or glacier-carved bowl, at the head of the valley.

The primitive nature of Old Fall River Road sends most motorists to more sedate Trail Ridge Road, with the result that the former seems a trip to an earlier era of park exploration.

▶ Bear Lake Road

Driving Bear Lake Road to beautiful **Bear Lake** ranks among the most popular activities at Rocky Mountain National Park—so much so that traffic can often be dismaying. The large parking lot at Bear Lake fills up early on summer mornings, and the park encourages visitors to take a shuttle bus. The attraction: a gorgeous high-elevation lake that can be reached by a paved road, and trailheads to many other scenic sites.

5 Cub Lake In a hurry to get to Bear Lake, many people pass by a trail that offers a fine natural experience for minimal effort.

A short side road in **Moraine Park** leads to the Cub Lake trailhead, starting point for an easy 2.3-mile one-way hike that goes through meadows, wetlands, and woods of ponderosa pine and aspen where wildlife and wildflowers abound. Passing through willow thickets along the **Big Thompson River,** the flat trail rounds large rock outcrops to the pretty valley where Cub Creek flows.

Mule deer are seen often, beaver and ducks may swim in shallow pools, and elk sometimes come down from the forests at dusk to feed. (Muddy edges of ponds are good places to look for animal footprints.) Broad-tailed Hummingbirds sip nectar from trailside flowers, making a distinctive buzzing noise as they zip from bloom to bloom.

The Cub Lake Trail showcases some of the park's geological features, as well. In the distant past, glaciers slowly flowed down this valley, pushing rocks to the side as they moved. The upland to the south is a moraine: a long hill formed by glacial debris. The large boulders along the trail are called "glacial erratics." Picked up and shaped by moving ice, they were carried down the valley and left in new positions when the glacier finally melted.

6 Glacier Gorge Trailhead It pays to heed the words of Kent Dannen, author of several excellent guides to the park: "The easy and spectacular hikes from **Glacier Gorge Trailhead** or Bear Lake are, of course, very popular. Nonetheless, by exploiting the philosophy of, 'No pain, no gain,' hikers can experience beyond-normal benefits on these trails in relative seclusion. The pain comes from rising early to be on the trail by 6 a.m. in summer. Yes, kids and adults hate early rising, but the gain is the peace, joy, and beauty of dawn on the trail, which are beyond description."

7 Alberta Falls At Glacier Gorge trailhead, near the end of Bear Lake Road, another short trail leads to one of the park's most welcoming waterfalls. From the trailhead it's a walk of less than a mile, with just a mild elevation gain, to Alberta Falls, a thunderous cascade on **Glacier Creek.**

The sight of Alberta Falls, combined with its easy access, makes this a very popular hike; this is another place to heed Dannen's advice about a dawn start.

From the falls, consider continuing to either **Mills Lake** or **The Loch,**

Bear Lake autumn reflection

both in rugged alpine settings, and both among the park's most majestic mountain lakes.

▶ Southeastern Corner

If you'd like to climb to the summit of a national park mountain without hours of approach hiking and strenuous elevation gain, consider heading to Estes Cone or, for flatter alternatives, try the hikes of Wild Basin.

❽ **Estes Cone** Located on the east side of the park, the nicely symmetrical Estes Cone provides plenty of reward at the end of a 3.3-mile hike.

With a height of 11,006 feet, Estes Cone is a bit of a runt compared to its towering neighbors, but thanks to its isolated location it offers clear vistas of the park's giants.

The route begins at the **Longs Peak** trailhead, and along the way passes **Eugenia Mine,** the tumbledown remains of a failed mining operation from the 19th century. Traversing forest and open areas, the trail ascends Estes Cone and requires a small amount of rock scrambling at the end, though it's nothing a moderately fit person can't handle.

The summit of Estes Cone is a place to relax, enjoy a snack, and take in the view of Longs Peak and **Mount Meeker** to the southwest.

❾ **Wild Basin** The Wild Basin area, in the southern part of the park, once was a relatively untrafficked destination. No more: The park now warns that parking lots fill up early in summer, despite having been enlarged lately.

One of the closest and most popular Wild Basin sites is **Calypso Cascades,** a long and lovely waterfall named for an equally lovely orchid species blooming in July. Rangers suggest getting there from the **Allenspark Trailhead,** a mile longer hike than from the Wild Basin Trailhead.

"Lacking the streamside views of the **Wild Basin Trail,**" Dannen says, "the **Allenspark Trail** offers spectacular vistas of high peaks due to a 1978 wildfire that cleared much forest and created more habitat for elk and deer. Hikers with two vehicles can park one at each trailhead and enjoy a one-way hike with both mountain and white-water views."

Once you're at Calypso Cascades, you might as well continue to roaring **Ouzel Falls,** just 0.9 mile farther.

Calypso Cascades is reached via Wild Basin Trailhead, but it's also served by much less used Allenspark Trailhead, 1.2 miles longer.

—KENT DANNEN
guidebook author

▶ West Side

Park areas west of the Continental Divide see many fewer visitors than do sites to the east. That's just fine with many experienced travelers who prefer this area, enjoying greater solitude on trails as well as excellent wildlife-viewing opportunities.

❿ **Adams Falls** One spot where you won't be alone, though, is Adams Falls, reached by an easy walk along the **East Inlet Trail** near the town of **Grand Lake.** This roaring waterfall is less than 0.5 mile from the trailhead.

"Most people go to the falls, turn around, and go right back to their car," Michele Simmons, district interpreter, observes. "But if folks go

Headwaters of the Colorado River, Kawuneeche Valley

about another 0.25 mile, they get to a meadow with views up into the high mountain peaks. It's fairly level, it's a beautiful walk, and it leads to this gorgeous viewpoint. And if they're willing to go one more mile, they get to a second meadow, which again opens up into some beautiful views."

Wildflowers can be abundant along the **East Inlet Trail,** and if you didn't see a moose along the main park road north of Grand Lake, you may be able to spot one here.

⓫ Bowen Gulch–Continental Divide Trail Farther north, take the **Onahu Creek Trail** 0.3 mile to reach a connector path to the Bowen Gulch–Continental Divide Trail (30 miles). A short walk here leads to a bridge over **Onahu Creek** and a meadow that Simmons calls "a little gem of a spot."

At the head of the **Kawuneeche Valley,** a similar hike on the **Timber Lake Trail** (4.8 miles) leads to a bridge over **Beaver Creek** and a rocky cascade—nothing approaching the splendor of Adams Falls, but a fulfilling reward for a small amount of effort.

⓬ Colorado River Trail As another alternative to the bighorn-viewing site at **Horseshoe Park,** take a walk up the 3.1-mile Colorado River Trail, which begins near the **Timber Lake Trailhead** and heads north toward **Lulu City.** While sheep sightings aren't guaranteed on the cliffs above, there's a good chance of one in early summer.

Sunset on giant thunder cloud over Wind Cave's open prairie

WIND CAVE

Rangers at Wind Cave encourage visitors to experience the "two worlds" of the park—that is, secrets above and below. One realm lies beneath the surface, while a far different, yet equally rewarding, environment awaits those who explore the national park's aboveground 44 square miles of prairie and pine forest. See only one of these two worlds and you will have missed half of this park in southwestern South Dakota.

Wind Cave is famed among geologists and serious spelunkers as the world's fifth longest cave system, and it is known for formations rare in other underground locations, especially the gratelike structure called "boxwork." Above its picturesque passageways lies a diverse terrain that's among the country's most underrated natural areas. As Mike Laycock, park ranger, says, "This is a great wildlife park. I've been in only two areas that are comparable—one's Yellowstone and one's Alaska."

Year-Round Visitor Center

- **Wind Cave Visitor Center**
  Off US 385, 11 miles north of Hot Springs

605-745-4600, *www.nps.gov/wica*

▶ Wind Cave

There's no getting off the tourist trail while experiencing the underground world of the park, because all visits are made on ranger-guided tours.

They range from the easy **Garden of Eden Tour** to the strenuous, crawling-required **Wild Cave Tour.** Advance reservations are needed for the latter, and strongly recommended for the **Candlelight Tour,** on which participants see the cave without electric lights, the way tourists did when it was a commercial attraction in the late 19th century. (For other tours, reservations are not accepted.)

Nevertheless, park staff members have a few hints for more enjoyable cave visits. In summer vacation season, the busiest days are not weekends but Tuesday through Thursday. If you arrive at midday on one of those days, the chances are good you'll have to wait a while for an open spot on a cave tour.

You'll increase the odds of getting in quickly if you arrive early in the morning or on weekends. If you do find tours booked when you get to the visitor center, you can purchase tickets for a tour later the same day and go for a hike or scenic drive.

Ranger Mike Laycock's favorite cave tour is the 0.5-mile, moderately strenuous **Natural Entrance Tour,** which gives visitors a chance to see the park's only known natural cave opening. (You'll actually enter through a nearby man-made entrance.)

Wind Cave got its name because a difference in air pressure between the surface and cave causes strong air currents in the natural entry.

"You see great examples of boxwork, which is the main decoration that Wind Cave is known for," Laycock says. "This tour has 300 stairs, but 289 of them go down. Then you get on an elevator to come out."

Bear in mind that the temperature in the cave is 53 degrees year-round, so a jacket or sweater will feel good.

▶ The Aboveground Park

With its combination of grassland (a blend of tallgrass and short-grass prairie), ponderosa pine forest, and riparian habitat, Wind Cave National

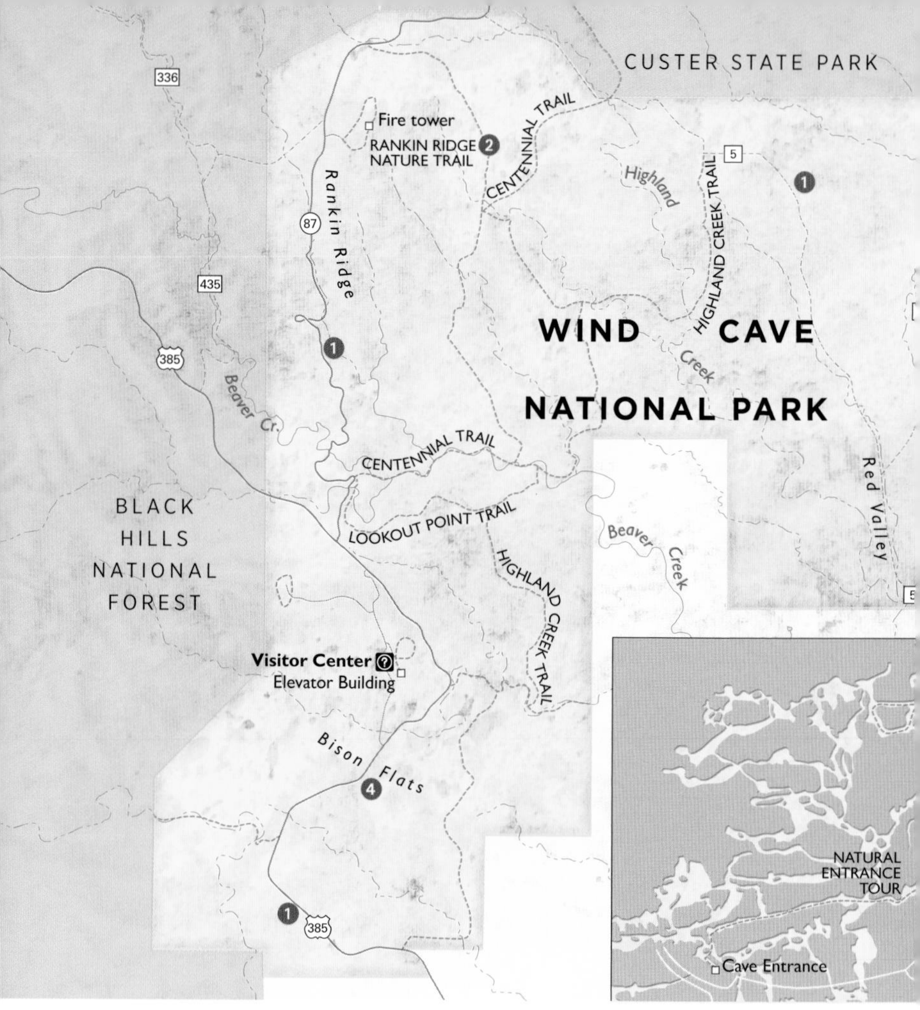

Park supports a wide array of animals. The generally open, rolling landscape means wildlife can often be seen well from roads, including US 385 and S. Dak. 87, both of which wind through the western part of the park.

1 Park Loop Staff members highly recommend an early morning or late afternoon drive on a 35-mile loop that comprises both paved and gravel roads.

From the park visitor center, drive north on US 385 a short distance and turn right on S. Dak. 87. Continue north about 6 miles and turn right onto unpaved Park Road 5. Follow this route east and south about 10 miles to 7-11 Road, also known as County Road 101. Turn west here and return to US 385. If you have time, a detour north on Park Road 6, which intersects Park Road 5, is often productive for animal watching.

"I've seen people in the visitor center who have just driven the loop, and they come in and their eyes are really big," Vidal Davila, park superintendent, says. "They say, 'Hey, I just saw my first bison.' It's really a great wildlife-viewing road."

In addition to bison (also known as buffalo), Wind Cave's loop road can bring sightings of pronghorn, prairie dogs, mule and white-tailed deer, and coyotes. Disappointingly, elk are seen less commonly, most often at dawn and dusk.

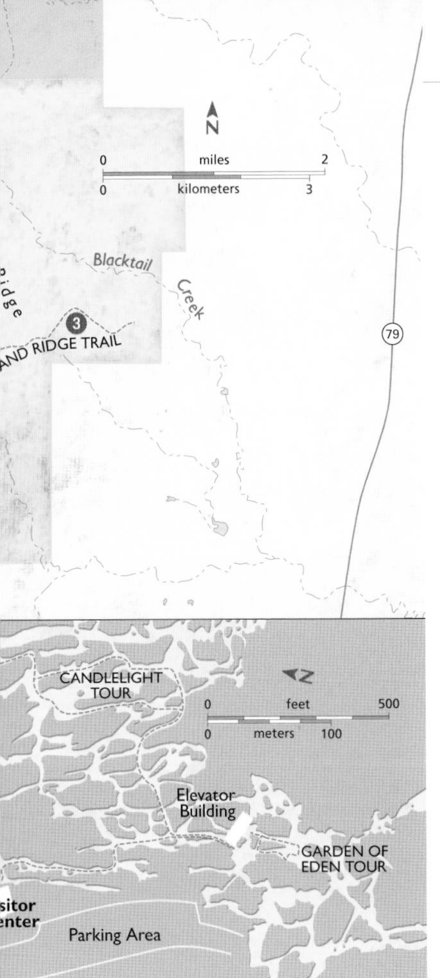

❷ Rankin Ridge Nature Trail

Seeing the park's environment on more intimate terms is made easy by a variety of hiking trails, including fairly easy nature trails, each about a mile long.

The 1-mile Rankin Ridge Nature Trail in the northern part of the park is a favorite of Laycock's, and one he often recommends to visitors.

"The loop goes up to our fire tower, through ponderosa pine forest," he explains. "It's one of the highest places in our park, so the view is excellent. And it's also pretty much above the prairie areas, so people usually don't have to worry about encountering bison."

The park features a relatively large herd of bison. Though these beasts often look sluggish, they can run much faster than humans. Eschew the temptation to get close for photos and stay at least 100 yards from these dangerous animals. The bison in the park are descendants of 14 animals reintroduced to the park in 1913 by the New York Zoological Society.

Wind Cave offers other trails, including a doable 4.5-mile loop that combines parts of the **Centennial, Highland Creek,** and **Lookout Point Trails** off S. Dak. 87.

Coyote with summer coat

Rolling prairies of Wind Cave

3 Boland Ridge Trail On the east side of the park, the Boland Ridge Trail, a strenuous 2.6-mile (one way) hike, provides an opportunity to experience the solitude and panoramic vistas that greeted the pioneers crossing the American prairies. The Boland Ridge trailhead is located on Park Road 6 about a mile north of the junction with Park Road 5. This challenging trail climbs the ridge to panoramic views of Wind Cave National Park, the Black Hills, Red Valley, and Battle Mountain.

Boland Ridge also gives hikers one of the best chances to catch sight of elk.

4 Bison Flats Travelers can go for a walk anywhere they would like to. "That's good for people to be aware of," Laycock says. "They can hike

Local Intelligence

Before or after a visit to Wind Cave, take a tour through **Custer State Park,** just to the north. A drive along the 18-mile **Wildlife Loop Road** brings almost certain sightings of bison, as well as the chance of spotting deer, pronghorn, bighorn sheep, and feral burros. Fine hiking trails abound in the park, and some are open to mountain biking.

out a hundred yards, or half a mile—whatever they desire. And that's a little bit easier in Wind Cave than in most parks, because the terrain usually isn't bad. There are a lot of rolling hills."

A favorite site for cross-country exploration is Bison Flats, stretching across US 385 just south of the road to the visitor center.

"I've gone out there and seen Burrowing Owls and badgers, and ventured a little farther and seen elk, all in the same easy stroll," Laycock says. "And I wasn't 300 yards from my car."

From this area there are panoramic views of the park, Buffalo Gap, and the Black Hills. Hike west across Bison Flats less than a mile from the highway for a superb sunset-viewing opportunity.

We have 30 miles of hiking trails in the park, but people can hike wherever they want to. They can park at one of the pulloffs along the road and just walk out into the prairie.

—MIKE LAYCOCK
Wind Cave National Park ranger

Mud buttes off Badlands Loop Road

BADLANDS

Reports from early explorers crossing the Great Plains led many to call the region the "Great American Desert." Ironically, parts of it now make up one of the world's most productive agricultural areas. In much the same way, places once dismissed as "bad" lands often rank with our most spectacular and fascinating natural areas. One good example: Badlands National Park in southwestern South Dakota—a forbidding place of secrets.

Shaped by erosion into countless bluffs, spires, and other striking formations, the landscape here presented difficult barriers to travelers, from the Arikara and Lakota tribes to French trappers to 19th-century pioneers. Today, visitors are awed by the infinite variations of this colorful terrain, as well as the rolling expanse of one of the largest remaining tracts of mixed-grass prairie in the United States. Diverse wildlife and abundant fossils provide additional good reasons to spend time here.

Year-Round Visitor Center

- **Ben Reifel Visitor Center**
  Cedar Pass off S. Dak. 240, Badlands Loop Road

Seasonal Visitor Center

- **White River Visitor Center**
  Junction of BIA 2 and 27

605-433-5361, *www.nps.gov/badl*

▶ North Unit

Most development is in the eastern **(Cedar Pass)** part of the park, reached from the Cactus Flats exit off I-90. Stop at the **Big Badlands Overlook** to see this region's most famous geological feature: **The Wall.** This eroded cliff separates the higher-elevation prairie to the north from the lower prairie of the White River drainage to the south. A half million years of sculpting by water created the bizarre formations. A 30-mile paved loop road (S. Dak. 240) follows the Wall through the park.

❶ Cliff Shell Trail "If you don't stop for anything, you can drive the whole loop road in an hour," Paul Ogren, park volunteer, says. "And unfortunately, that's what the majority of visitors do."

A far more satisfying experience awaits those who take the time to explore places such as the Cliff Shelf Trail, a 0.5-mile loop passing through an area where part of the Wall has "slumped" downward, creating a forested environment good for wildlife-watching, especially birding.

❷ Ben Reifel Visitor Center Stop at the visitor center to watch a fine introductory video and to get advice on enjoying Badlands from park rangers. For an easy, off-the-map hike recommended by Julie Johndreau, park education specialist, look for a prairie wash just across the road from the visitor center and head cross-country along this natural path (be sure to seek advice from a staff member if you are unsure where to go).

On the unmarked walk, "you can find lots of things like animal tracks, interesting rocks, and blooming flowers," Johndreau reports. "It's a really great walk to do with kids. Our Junior Ranger book has a scavenger hunt; you can bring it along and look for things on the bingo card. The walk is very open, through the grasslands. It's maybe 0.75 mile if you want to go all the way to the Badlands Wall.

"Badlands National Park is very accessible by car, but if you park and do that short hike, it's even more like you feel you're in the middle of nowhere. It's a lovely area, and you get a different perspective."

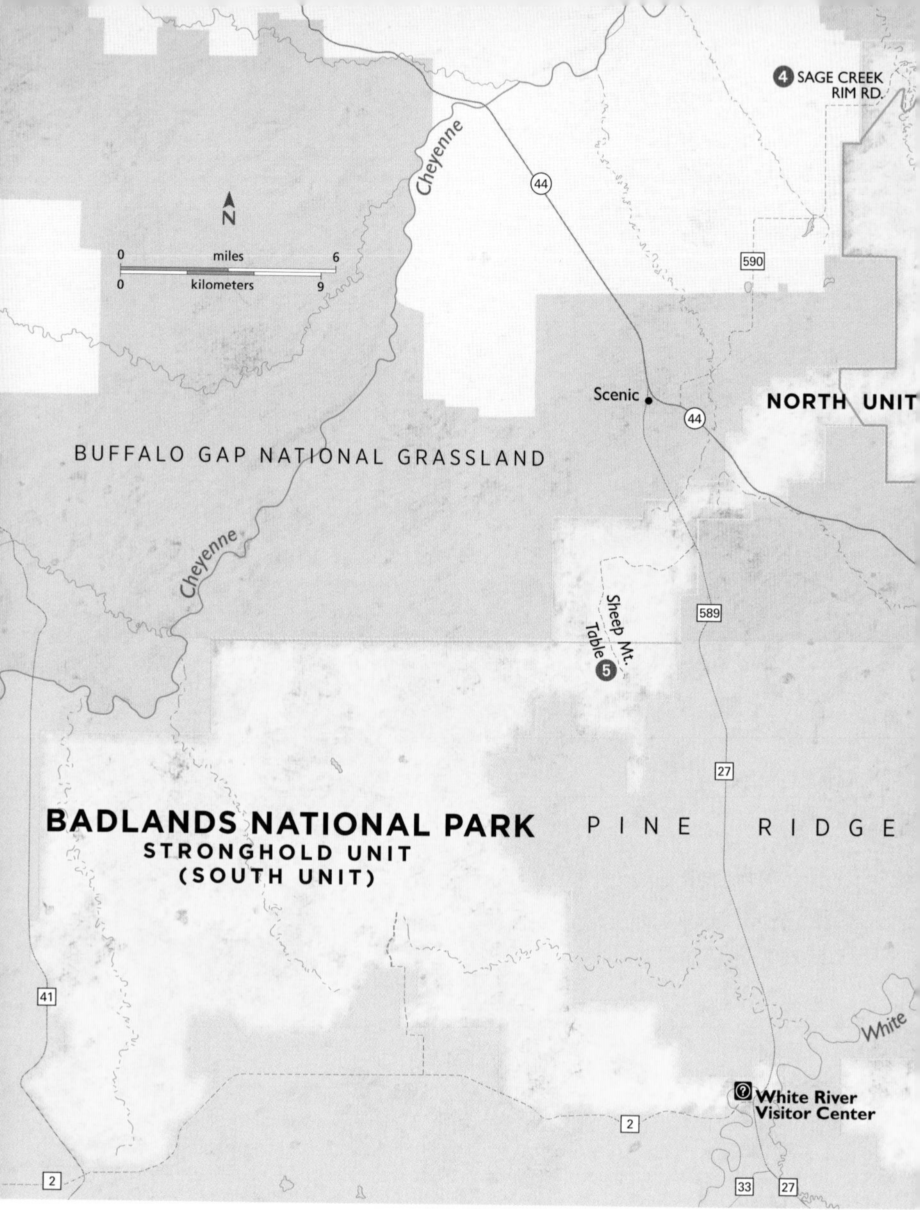

3 Deer Haven Continuing west on the loop road, the **Fossil Exhibit Trail** is a must-see. You'll have learned about the park's abundant fossils at the visitor center, and on this 0.25-mile trail you'll see reproductions of now extinct animals.

Just west of the **Yellow Mounds Overlook** near **Dillon Pass,** turn south on **Conata Road** to reach a relatively little-used trail that Aaron Kaye, park ranger, calls a personal favorite. Drive through the **Conata** picnic area to a gravel cul-de-sac at the rear, and look for the backcountry trail register. From here, it's a 3-mile round-trip to explore Deer Haven.

"The hike combines walking in the prairie, along the edge of the Badlands Wall, and then a scramble

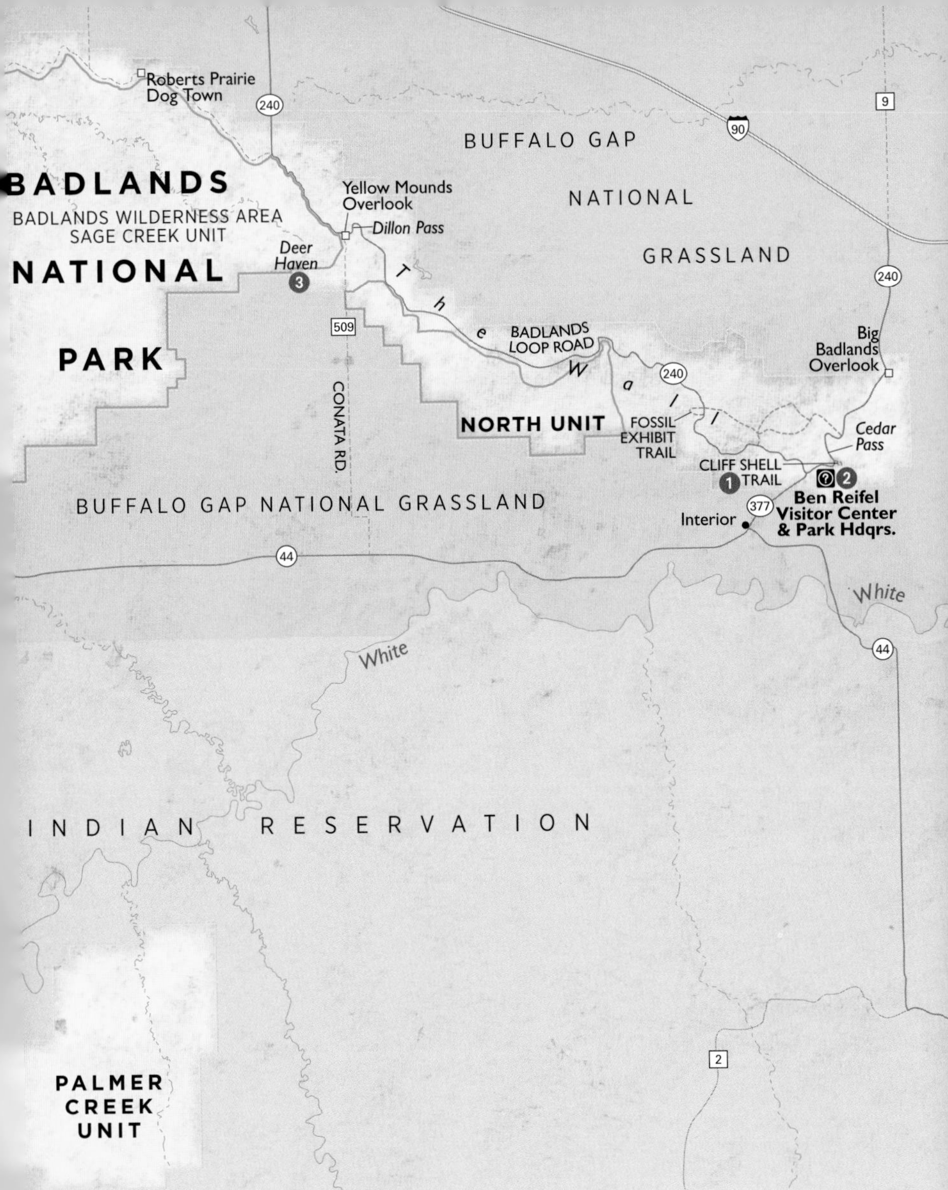

up onto a timbered shelf, which is actually a slump covered with juniper trees," Kaye says. "The timbered area is a unique perch because you've got the badlands surrounding you like a cirque [a hollow on a mountainside]."

Kaye says that the hike "is not too challenging, because most of it is on relatively flat ground," but recommends the usual preparations and precautions, such as proper footwear (most injuries at Badlands National Park result from falls on rugged terrain), plenty of water, a topographic map, and watching for bad weather or the occasional rattlesnake.

"It's a trip that's a little bit off the beaten path," Kaye says. "You're getting the best of both worlds that the park has to offer."

4 Sage Creek Rim Road When travelers reach the point where **Badlands Loop Road** (S. Dak. 240) turns north toward the town of Wall, most visitors follow the paved road out of the park. In so doing, they miss a beautifully scenic drive along the unpaved Sage Creek Rim Road on the northern edge of the park's 64,000-acre wilderness area.

Mule deer

The road passes by the large **Roberts Prairie Dog Town** (watch for the Burrowing Owls that share the tunnels with the rodents), and a side road reaches a primitive campground that is Ogren's favorite park location. "I encourage properly prepared people to walk away from the campground and find a canyon in the backcountry and just wander through it," Ogren says. "You never know what you might see. There's a lot of wildlife around there: coyotes and bobcats, Golden Eagles and Ferruginous Hawks.

"The wilderness area is also where we have our herd of 700 to 800 bison. Many times people wake up in the morning and there are anywhere from 10 to 200 bison right in the campground, which is pretty exciting for people who haven't seen them before."

(Ogren points out that visitors should keep a safe distance from these huge animals, which can run far faster than people.)

▶ South Unit

The South Unit of Badlands lies within the **Pine Ridge Reservation** of the Oglala Lakota Nation, and much of it comprises private land with limited access. Travelers are encouraged to stop at the **White River Visitor Center** (summer only), operated by Oglala Sioux Parks and Recreation Authority staff, for information.

5 Sheep Mountain Table One site on the South Unit that's always open for public access is Sheep Mountain Table, reached by an unpaved road heading west from BIA 27, a few miles south of the town of **Scenic.**

"It's a place that people driving through the main Badlands road might not know about," Sara Feldt, park ranger, says. "There's a 7-mile

Local Intelligence

Badlands National Park is famed for its fossils, especially of prehistoric mammals. Hikers who come across fossils should not touch them, but instead, tell a ranger. The first fossils were reported from this region in 1846, yet even today more and more are discovered. In 2010, a seven-year-old girl on a Junior Ranger program found a well-preserved skull of a saber-toothed cat more than 30 million years old, leading to the opening of a new dig area, called the Saber Site, located near the **Ben Reifel Visitor Center.**

Storm clouds over Sheep Mountain Table, South Unit

dirt road that starts out really flat, and then you get up on top and there are amazing views of the whole **White River Badlands Valley.** On a clear day you can see all the way to the **Black Hills.**

"After 5 miles the road turns into a really rutted two-track. You need high clearance or four-wheel drive, so we don't recommend driving the road after rain. If you are properly equipped you can keep driving or you can hike the last 2 miles. You'll come to areas with lots of junipers and ponderosa pines, and when you get to the end of the road, you see geologic features that look slightly different from the rest of the park. A lot of people compare it to Bryce Canyon National Park."

Because Sheep Mountain Table is sacred to the Oglala, camping is not allowed. "People go there for vision quests, and they leave offerings," Feldt says. "We ask visitors to be respectful of that."

In general the South Unit is probably my favorite part of Badlands. For a visitor who wants to find hidden places, the South Unit is great—plus, the history is fascinating.

—SARA FELDT
Badlands National Park ranger

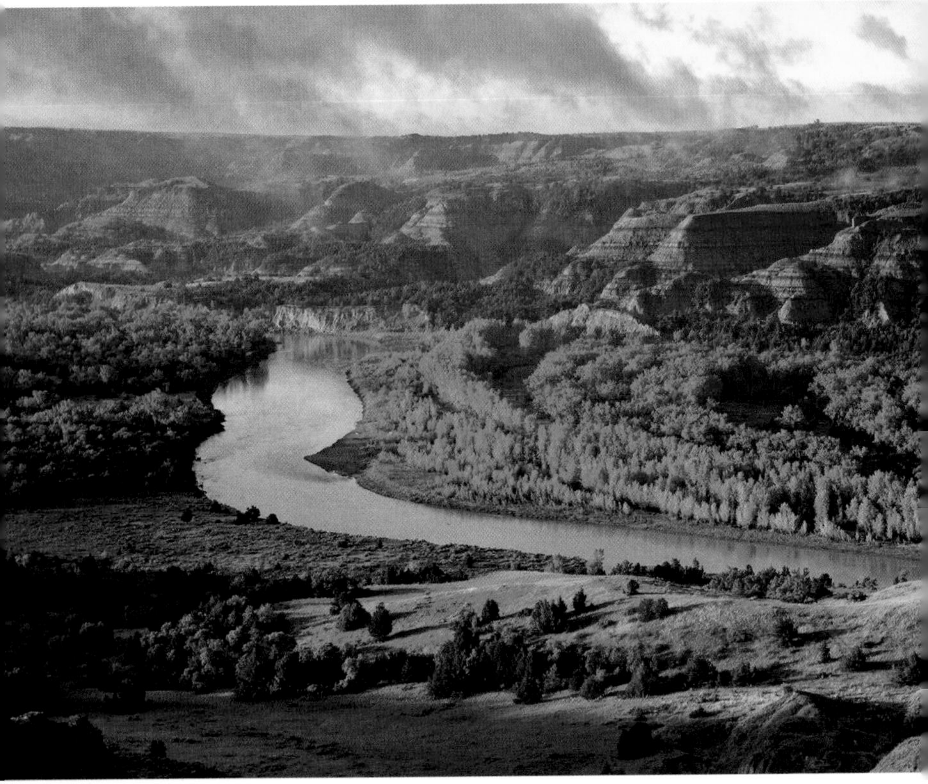

River Bend Overlook, North Unit

THEODORE ROOSEVELT

Few other parks besides Theodore Roosevelt in North Dakota offer such a combination of epic scenery, wildlife, and history—yet remain so secret to the average American.

The park would be even less visited if it weren't for the interstate highway running through it. (You can exit I-94 in southwestern North Dakota and be at the visitor center in less than five minutes.) Like Petrified Forest, this park has an easily accessible scenic drive that lets visitors cruise through, stop at a couple of overlooks, and be on their way again. That's a nice attribute for people in a hurry, but why rush? Take time to see the complete park—and to explore a landscape that inspired the nation's greatest conservationist President.

▶ South Unit

Theodore Roosevelt National Park is composed of three units; the great majority of visitors see only the South Unit, located just north of the town of **Medora.** Here you'll find a 36-mile scenic loop road, an assortment of trails, several miles of the Little Missouri River, and seasonal horseback riding (with guided trips offered by a concessionaire).

The park is named for the 26th President, who arrived in this region in 1883 to hunt bison and experience the West. He was so fond of the landscape that he became a partner in a cattle ranch and bought another on his own, living here sporadically for many years.

Year-Round Visitor Centers

- **Medora Visitor Center**
  In Medora, off Pacific Avenue
- **North Unit Visitor Center**
  On US 85, 10 miles south of Watford City

Seasonal Visitor Centers

- **Painted Canyon**
  South Unit, 7 miles east of Medora off I-94

701-623-4466, *www.nps.gov/thro*

"I enjoyed the life to the full," he later wrote of his ranching career. Near the visitor center you can see the **Maltese Cross Cabin,** where he lived for a time. It was moved here from the original site 7 miles south.

1 Wind Canyon Trail Take the quarter-mile loop road to enjoy fine panoramas of the badlands landscape, a rugged terrain created by stream deposition of sediments, volcanic action, and erosion.

Roosevelt described the cliffs and buttes as "so fantastically broken in form and so bizarre in color as to seem hardly properly to belong to this earth."

Don't miss following the Wind Canyon Trail to an overlook of the **Little Missouri River.** It's a favorite of local resident Dylan Edwards, who observes: "It's a beautiful overlook with great scenery and interesting geological features that you can't see from the road."

Park rangers recommend the spot for superb sunset viewing.

2 Jones Creek–Lower Talkington–Lower Paddock Trail Loop For those who want a moderately strenuous hike, Edwards suggests the Jones Creek–Lower Talkington–Lower Paddock Trail Loop, an 11-mile route that makes a circle mostly within the loop road.

"You can see a good variety of the terrain in the park," he says. "There's just a little bit of up and down. You pass through prairie-dog towns, and I've seen groups of bison, elk, and wild horses."

Indeed, Theodore Roosevelt National Park is known for wildlife, including bison, elk, wild horses, mule and white-tailed deer, pronghorn, bighorn sheep, badgers, coyotes, and porcupines, as well as abundant bird life. Many people, though, don't get much chance to enjoy this diversity.

Timing a visit is important. Park Superintendent Valerie Naylor notes, "The bison are usually cooperative, and the prairie dogs, but beyond that you don't see animals. People need to go out in the early morning or late in the evening. It's hard to make yourself get up, but once you do there's definitely a reward."

"The badlands hold a fantastic array of native plants in four distinct habitats," says Laura Thomas, park ranger. "The diversity of life here is rivaled only by the diversity of a rain forest. To experience these wonders firsthand, visitors can borrow a free family fun pack that includes field guides to plants and birds of the badlands, hand lenses, and binoculars. In a given day, one can find easily

Adult bison and calves graze on grasslands.

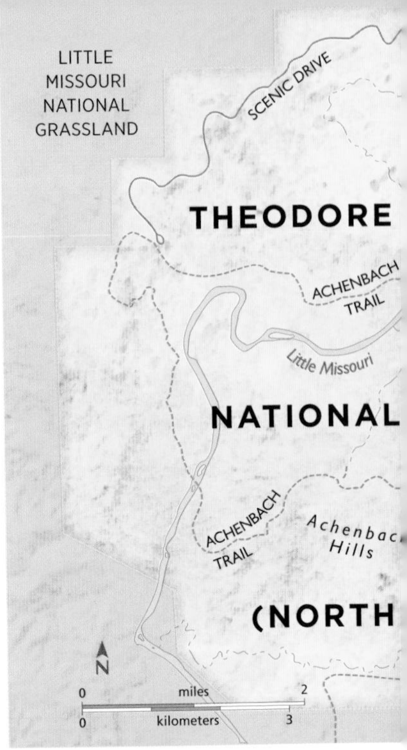

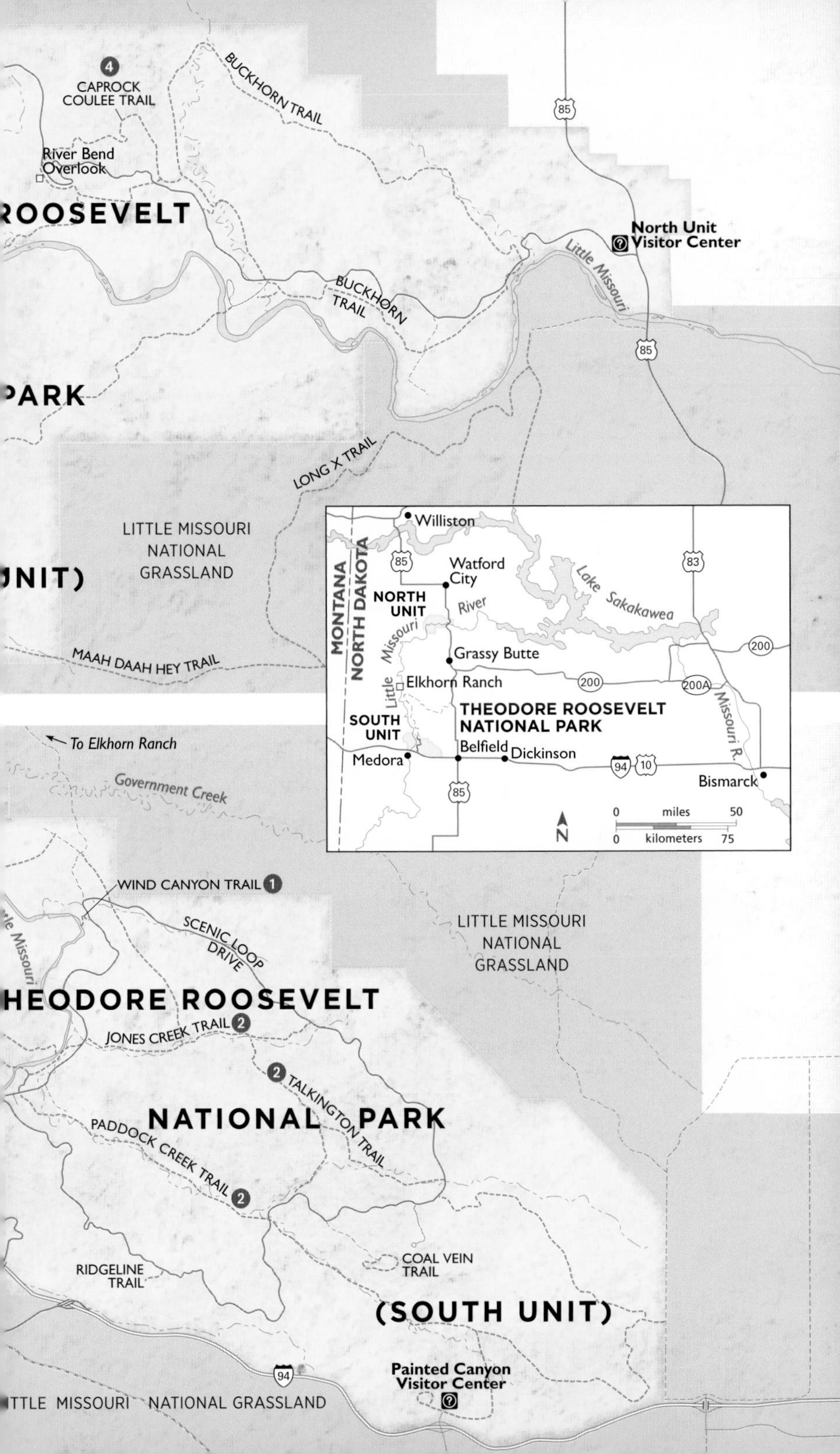

4
CAPROCK COULEE TRAIL
BUCKHORN TRAIL
River Bend Overlook
ROOSEVELT
North Unit Visitor Center
Little Missouri
BUCKHORN TRAIL
85
PARK
LONG X TRAIL
LITTLE MISSOURI NATIONAL GRASSLAND
NIT)
MAAH DAAH HEY TRAIL
Williston
MONTANA
NORTH DAKOTA
85
Watford City
83
NORTH UNIT
River
Lake Sakakawea
Missouri
200
Grassy Butte
Little
Elkhorn Ranch
200
200A
Missouri R.
THEODORE ROOSEVELT NATIONAL PARK
SOUTH UNIT
Medora
Belfield
Dickinson
94
10
Bismarck
85
N
0 miles 50
0 kilometers 75
To Elkhorn Ranch
Government Creek
WIND CANYON TRAIL 1
SCENIC LOOP DRIVE
LITTLE MISSOURI NATIONAL GRASSLAND
HEODORE ROOSEVELT
JONES CREEK TRAIL 2
2 TALKINGTON TRAIL
NATIONAL PARK
PADDOCK CREEK TRAIL 2
COAL VEIN TRAIL
RIDGELINE TRAIL
(SOUTH UNIT)
94
Painted Canyon Visitor Center
TTLE MISSOURI NATIONAL GRASSLAND

30 species of plants and as many, if not more, birds."

3 Petrified Forest Loop A significant portion of the park is designated wilderness, and Naylor recommends the Petrified Forest Loop "for those who have an interest in going a little bit into the wilderness without being too far away. People need to get a map at the visitor center and make sure they end up in the right place and that they have everything they need."

> *When it comes to wildlife viewing, the biggest issue is that 90 percent of visitors are here between 10 and 5, when you're not going to see much.*
>
> —VALERIE NAYLOR
> *Superintendent, Theodore Roosevelt National Park*

The reward for proper preparation for this 10-mile hike is a chance to explore the third most important collection of petrified wood in North America. Stumps have eroded out of colorful hillsides here, allowing visitors to imagine ancient times when this was a swampy plain where forests of magnolia, sequoia, and bald cypress grew.

There's an easier way to see the petrified forest. Take the West River Road exit off I-94 and follow dirt roads to the western edge of the park. From here, it's just a 3-mile hike to the petrified trees. Get a map and directions at the visitor center and check the weather forecast before setting out.

Note that a high-clearance vehicle may be needed.

▶ North Unit

With its access from I-94, the South Unit attracts far more visitors than the North Unit, though the latter can be reached by an easy drive 52 miles north of the interstate on US 85.

Cannonball concretions in North Unit badlands

Local Intelligence

Taking a canoe or kayak trip along the **Little Missouri River** can be a wonderful way to experience the Theodore Roosevelt National Park's scenery and wildlife. May and June are usually the best months suitable for floating, but that can change depending on rainfall. Check at the visitor center for current water level in the river and for other advice on paddling. Many people bring their own boats, but rentals are usually available in **Medora.**

"The North Unit is very different from the South, where people tend to drive around the loop road and maybe walk to the overlooks," Naylor says. "The North Unit is worth the extra drive. It's incredibly scenic, and quieter than the South."

The 14-mile scenic road here (out and back) passes trailheads for both easy walks near the **Little Missouri River** and longer hikes into the backcountry. Watch for longhorn cattle; this is a herd maintained to commemorate the historic Long-X Trail, a 19th-century cattle-drive route.

❹ **Caprock Coulee Trail** For the best introduction to the North Unit—in fact a microcosm of the badlands—Naylor urges visitors to hike the Caprock Coulee Trail, a 5.7-mile loop.

"It showcases everything the North Unit has to offer," she says. "It goes through prairie, it goes through woodland, it goes through some of the starkest badlands terrain, and it has an incredible view of the river, all in that one short hike. You can start at any one of about four places."

One part of the route is the **Caprock Coulee Trail,** a self-guided 1.5-mile loop that's only mildly strenuous; the rest of the longer trail is steeper and more rugged in places.

As you walk this or any trail in the park, keep in mind this advice from Thomas: "If you do a thorough job of seeing, you can find more in one small area than you'll be able to see in 10 miles of strenuous walking. So slow down. Distance does not equal discovery. Discovery is a matter of seeing, not seeking."

▶ Elkhorn Ranch

"For people willing to drive for about 60 miles or so round-trip on gravel roads, our Elkhorn Ranch is a great place to go," Naylor says. "It's the park's third unit, which not many people get to see. Once you get there, it's an amazing place, because it's where Theodore Roosevelt's home ranch was when he was here in the badlands."

Later in his life, Roosevelt famously wrote, "I never would have been President if it had not been for my experiences in North Dakota."

It was at his Elkhorn Ranch on the Little Missouri that he developed much of the appreciation of nature that led him to establish the United States Forest Service and create important nature preserves, national parks, and national monuments.

Though nothing is left of the actual ranch buildings here, the Elkhorn Ranch Unit remains "our most historically significant part of the park," Naylor says. "It's very much the way that it was when Roosevelt found it in 1884. Once you get there, you take a short 1.5-mile round-trip walk out to the **homesite.** There are exhibits that explain the history."

Roosevelt described the "sheer cliffs and grassy plateaus" and "weird-looking buttes" that he gazed upon from the veranda of his ranch house. For visitors who take the time to travel here, taking in these same vistas serves as a secret link to the President who arguably did more for conservation than any other American.

Hot springs along the Firehole River

YELLOWSTONE

Arguably the world's most famous national park, Yellowstone would appear to hold few secrets. Every year, millions of visitors pour through the park's entrances. Surely they must cover it all? Nope. They do not. The park's 3,400 square miles are filled with places rarely visited and sights seldom seen.

It is said that 99 percent of visitors see only 1 percent of the park. This is true in essence, if not a precise statistical fact. Most travelers stay close to the paved roads and gather at major sights—Old Faithful, Yellowstone Lake, and the Grand Canyon of the Yellowstone River. There's also a time factor. Most visitors tour the park in midday, and in midsummer. They miss the magic of dawn, dusk, and even the dark of night. Nor do they experience the pleasures of spring and autumn, to say nothing of winter, which is perfect for anyone seeking solitude.

Year-Round Visitor Centers

- **Albright Visitor Center**
  Mammoth Hot Springs
- **West Yellowstone Visitor Information Center**
  West Yellowstone Chamber of Commerce

Seasonal Visitor Centers

- **Canyon Visitor Education Center**
  Canyon Village complex
- **Fishing Bridge Visitor Center**
  East Entrance Road
- **Grant Visitor Center**
  1 mile off main park road at Grant Village Junction
- **Junior Ranger Station and the Madison Information Station**
  Madison Junction, Madison Picnic Area
- **Norris Geyser Basin Museum and Information Station**
  East of Norris Junction, off Grand Loop Road
- **Old Faithful Visitor Education Center**
  Near geyser

307-344-7381, *www.nps.gov/yell*

▶ Geyser Basins

Thoughts of geysers lead naturally to **Old Faithful.** The park's number one attraction, it draws upward of 30,000 people a day during the summer. Yet Old Faithful is not alone. It stands surrounded by hundreds of other geysers and hot springs, large and small, spread across the Upper Geyser Basin. There are many other such concentrations of thermal activity—some along the road, dozens in the backcountry, many with no official names. There is much to see beyond the main sites.

❶ **Upper Geyser Basin** Crowds at midday are no reason to avoid the Upper Geyser Basin. Privacy is possible, especially at dawn, before the park wakes up. The nearest campground is 16 miles away at Madison Junction and most campers are happily snoozing at first light.

"Crowds don't start pouring in until 10:30 a.m. or so," says Orville Bach, park ranger. "Hardly anyone is out at seven or eight in the morning."

Even guests at hotels beside the geysers tend to sleep late. They are missing the best time of day.

In the cool morning air, steam from geysers and hot springs looks more dense, lending a sense of primeval mystery to the valley. Large animals are more likely to be seen. Vegetation

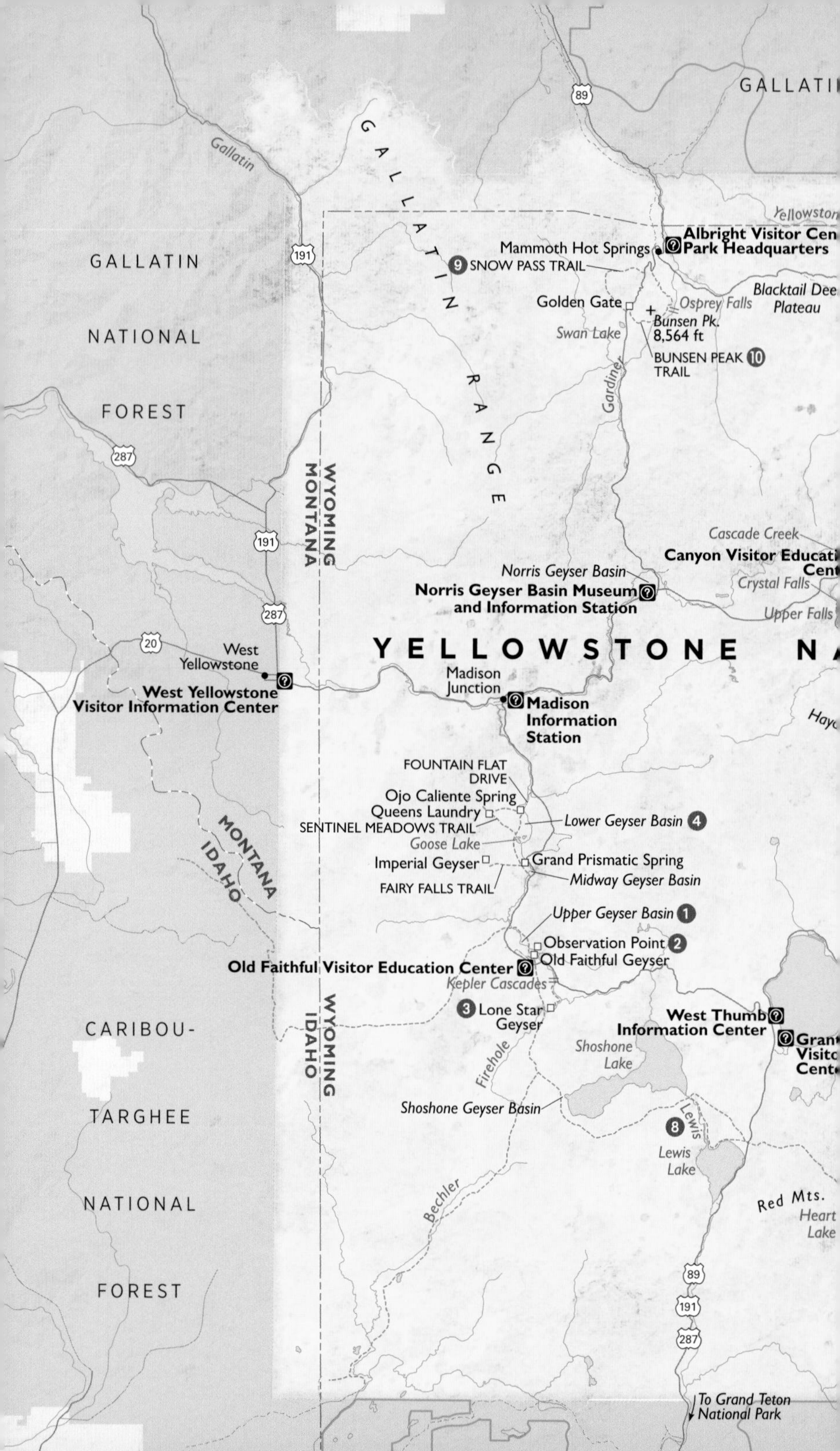

GALLATIN
NATIONAL
FOREST
GALLATIN RANGE
Gallatin
Yellowstone
Albright Visitor Center
Park Headquarters
Mammoth Hot Springs
9 SNOW PASS TRAIL
Golden Gate
Osprey Falls
Blacktail Deer Plateau
Bunsen Pk. 8,564 ft
Swan Lake
BUNSEN PEAK TRAIL 10
Gardiner
WYOMING
MONTANA
Cascade Creek
Canyon Visitor Education Center
Norris Geyser Basin
Norris Geyser Basin Museum and Information Station
Crystal Falls
Upper Falls
YELLOWSTONE NA
West Yellowstone
West Yellowstone Visitor Information Center
Madison Junction
Madison Information Station
FOUNTAIN FLAT DRIVE
Ojo Caliente Spring
Queens Laundry
SENTINEL MEADOWS TRAIL
Goose Lake
Lower Geyser Basin 4
Imperial Geyser
Grand Prismatic Spring
FAIRY FALLS TRAIL
Midway Geyser Basin
MONTANA
IDAHO
Upper Geyser Basin 1
Observation Point 2
Old Faithful Geyser
Old Faithful Visitor Education Center
Kepler Cascades
3 Lone Star Geyser
West Thumb Information Center
Grant Visitor Center
CARIBOU-
TARGHEE
NATIONAL
FOREST
WYOMING
IDAHO
Shoshone Lake
Firehole
Shoshone Geyser Basin
8
Lewis
Lewis Lake
Bechler
Red Mts.
Heart Lake
89
191
287
20
To Grand Teton National Park

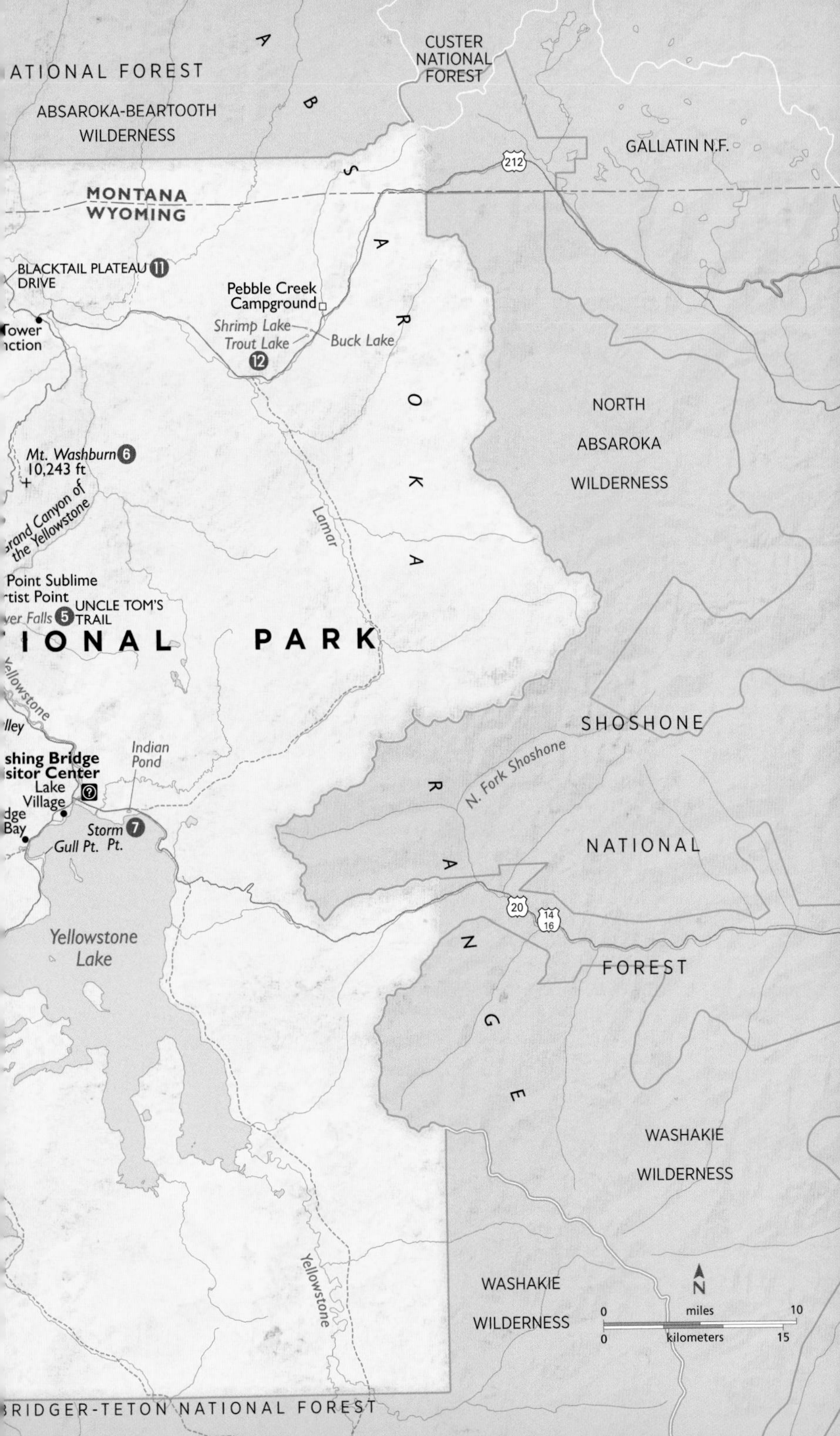

ATIONAL FOREST
ABSAROKA-BEARTOOTH
WILDERNESS
CUSTER
NATIONAL
FOREST
GALLATIN N.F.
212
MONTANA
WYOMING
BLACKTAIL PLATEAU 11
DRIVE
Pebble Creek
Campground
Shrimp Lake
Trout Lake
Buck Lake
12
Tower
nction
Mt. Washburn 6
10,243 ft
Grand Canyon of
the Yellowstone
Lamar
NORTH
ABSAROKA
WILDERNESS
Point Sublime
rtist Point
UNCLE TOM'S
TRAIL
ver Falls 5
IONAL PARK
Yellowstone
lley
shing Bridge
isitor Center
Lake
Village
Indian
Pond
dge
Bay
Storm 7
Pt.
Gull Pt.
SHOSHONE
N. Fork Shoshone
NATIONAL
FOREST
20
14
16
A B S A R O K A R A N G E
Yellowstone
Lake
WASHAKIE
WILDERNESS
WASHAKIE
WILDERNESS
Yellowstone
N
0 miles 10
0 kilometers 15
BRIDGER-TETON NATIONAL FOREST

Chromatic Spring, a hot spring in the Upper Geyser Basin

is touched by dew, and in spring and fall, delicate frost shapes appear during the night, then quickly melt away as day breaks.

Bach also recommends the "neglected parts of the basin, just off the main track." This includes the trail past **Daisy Geyser** to **Punch Bowl Spring** and **Black Sand Pool.** Also **Artemisia Geyser:** "It's just past Morning Glory Pool, where most people turn around. Artemisia is beautiful, but almost no one knows it's there. With a little imagination, I think you can always have a quality time in the basin."

❷ Observation Point This is another example of a side trail. It turns off the paved trail close to **Geyser Hill** and climbs about 200 vertical feet to a viewing platform standing atop the volcanic bluff, from where you can watch an eruption.

The trail continues through the woods, whose trees are scarred by bison rubbing against them (look for scraps of their wool), to **Solitary Geyser.** Alone in the forest, it is more pool than geyser, and it erupts frequently a few feet high.

Once a nonerupting hot spring, it changed its character after being tapped for hot water to supply a hot swimming pool near the hotel. That pool was removed long ago when the park realized that exploiting thermal features damaged them, but Solitary still erupts.

❸ Lone Star Geyser To see a truly wild geyser in its natural setting, walk the easy, partly paved trail to Lone Star Geyser, a 5-mile round-trip from the trailhead near **Kepler Cascades.**

An old service road, also open to bicycles, the trail follows a placid stretch of the **Firehole River** (watch for trout in the clear water) through a section of forest that did not burn in the great fires of 1988.

If you want a classic Yellowstone walk in the woods, it's 6 miles farther to **Shoshone Geyser Basin;** this is best done as an overnight hike.

4 Lower Geyser Basin The old road through Lower Geyser Basin and **Midway Geyser Basin,** once the main route, is now a quiet foot-and-bicycle path.

Fountain Flat Drive leads to a trailhead at the north end; there's another parking area at the south end. Between the two is an easy 4-mile walk through open meadows dotted with trees and numerous thermal features.

The trail passes **Ojo Caliente Spring, Goose Lake,** and the back side of **Grand Prismatic Hot Spring,** the largest in the park. Even less traveled is the **Sentinel Meadows Trail,** which loops 2.2 miles through a large thermal-studded meadow past a hot spring called **Queens Laundry** and the ruins of a simple bathhouse begun in 1881 but never completed, which is now a historic structure.

Another good hike is **Fairy Falls Trail,** a 6.5-mile loop leading to a misty 200-foot-high waterfall.

Beyond lies **Imperial Geyser,** which erupts frequently and feeds an unusual warm stream.

Young bear cubs amid wildflowers

▶ Canyon

At Canyon, Yellowstone's two grand waterfalls plunge into a spectacular yellow-rock gorge, attracting almost as many visitors as Old Faithful.

Popular overlooks are jammed at midday, yet even here, there are options, says Bach: "Park at Brink of the Upper Falls and walk to **Crystal Falls** on **Cascade Creek.** Almost no one goes there."

5 Uncle Tom's Trail In 1898, "Uncle" Tom Richardson built a rough trail to the base of the Lower Falls, and he sold guided trips that involved clinging to ropes in the steep places.

Local Intelligence

Every morning, a ranger at Old Faithful makes rounds of the Upper Geyser Basin to check the status of geysers and predict when the big ones might erupt. If you're on the boardwalks early, keep an eye out for the ranger uniform; ask for the first estimates of the day, among other tips. Also, a squad of volunteers known as "geyser gazers" monitor nearly every aspect of every thermal feature in the place. Most of them work at the general stores or hotels; some have spent summers here for decades and know the basin better than anyone. They do it because they love geysers, and they like to share knowledge with anyone who shows interest. Recognize them by their bicycles, calculators, and notepads, and be prepared for encyclopedic answers.

Later, the park built a more substantial path with paved switchbacks and steel stairways (500 feet down from the rim) to a superb viewpoint with a face-on view of the falls.

Above, the green river tips over the brink; below, all is white mist and churning froth. It's a strenuous, more than 0.5-mile climb both down and back, which means relatively few people make the trip.

6 Mount Washburn For another chance to trade sweat equity for a splendid uncrowded viewpoint, hike to the fire lookout on top of Mount Washburn.

The road goes partway; then it's a walk through alpine meadows strewn with wildflowers and frequented by bighorn sheep.

Two trails provide access to the lookout tower, either from **Dunraven Pass** picnic area 3 miles away (one way) or from **Chittenden** parking area 2.25 miles away (one way). The latter is an old roadbed on which cars once drove all the way to the summit, sometimes having to do it backward because of the better reverse gear ratio.

Washburn marks the rim of the Yellowstone caldera. On a clear day you can see the **Red Mountains** 40 miles south marking the far rim; the mountains were once continuous, until the great volcano blew everything within that 40-mile distance sky high.

The trail from Artist Point to Point Sublime starts at about the busiest place at the canyon, but everyone's looking the other way, at the falls. A few hundred yards down the trail, you get solitude.

—ORVILLE BACH
Yellowstone National Park ranger

Grand Canyon Yellowstone waterfall

▶ Yellowstone Lake

Located in the southeastern part of the park, this is the largest alpine lake in North America above 7,000 feet, and with 110 miles of shoreline it could be a park in its own right. Roads running along the north and west shores burrow through old-growth forest, past cobbled beaches and small wetlands where streams pour into the lake. In the remote southeastern part of the lake, several fjordlike arms extend deep into wilderness country, reachable

Lone Geyser, Yellowstone Lake

only on foot or by boat.

At **Gull Point,** near **Bridge Bay,** the highway cuts inland a short distance, but the original road stays close to shore, offering one of many chances to find a private spot by the lake.

Bison gather at the meadow near Bridge Bay, while moose like the ponds along the Gull Point Road.

7 Indian Pond and Storm Point Activity centers on the lake's outlet, where the Yellowstone River pours cold and smooth on its way to wildlife-rich **Hayden Valley.**

Hotels, campgrounds, general stores, and other services cluster at **Fishing Bridge** on one side of the river, and **Lake Village** on the other.

Three miles east, a stretch of secluded shoreline can be found at **Storm Point** near the deceptively ordinary-looking **Indian Pond.**

The 2.3-mile loop begins at the pond, which was created by a steam explosion near the end of the last ice age; the park has approximately a dozen such features. Reaching the lakeshore, the path turns west through deep forest to the point. It's also rewarding to wander the open meadows to the east.

8 Lewis River Channel Two neighboring lakes to the southwest of Yellowstone Lake—**Lewis** and **Shoshone**—are appealing in their own right, and receive less attention than their large cousin.

Shoshone is a wilderness lake, reachable on foot or by paddling a canoe upstream on Lewis River, which connects the two lakes. Anyone inclined toward canoe camping should put Shoshone at the top of his or her list. Day hiking is also good.

The channel is renowned among fishermen for the autumn spawning run of brown trout. One trail goes straight to Shoshone from the trailhead, while another closely follows the Lewis Lake shore and the river.

Local Intelligence

Yellowstone is a wildlife park as much as it is a geologic wonderland. A lot of animals can be seen simply by cruising the roads, especially early and late in the day. If there's something good to see, traffic piles up; cars stopped in the middle of the road are good indicators.

Skilled wildlife-watchers, however, don't rely on chance alone. They know that animals favor certain areas, varying with the season and the time of day. Food has a lot to do with it.

For example, elk go where the grazing is good, and wolves follow the elk. Terrain is also a factor. Bison take the easiest route from place to place. They avoid dense woods if possible; but of course forest creatures like pine martens shun the open meadows that bison prefer. Each species has its place and time. Those who learn where to look, and when, are soon able to mystify the uninitiated with their apparently uncanny ability to find critters.

▶ Mammoth and the North

The central and southern parts of the park were shaped by the great volcano and its aftermath, but the north is different. Landscapes here are more typical of the northern Rockies with glaciated valleys, high peaks, and limited thermal activity.

The terraces at **Mammoth Hot Springs** draw most visitors, and the crowd generally continues south. Smaller numbers head east, past **Tower Junction** to the mountain-rimmed valleys of the **Lamar River.**

Bison head-butting

9 Snow Pass For a hike that takes in a variety of sights, including hot spring terraces that few visitors see—and is downhill most of the way—start at the **Glen Creek** trailhead (you'll need a shuttle there) on the edge of **Swan Lake Flat.**

The trail skirts huge meadows before joining the 4.2-mile **Snow Pass Trail.** Cutting through a gap in the mountains, it drops back down to Mammoth through mixed forest. Until the current road was built through **Golden Gate,** horse-drawn coaches brought visitors on this route. It was a hard steep pull for horses.

In late summer and autumn, the woods ring with the sound of bugling elk. Before emerging at the **Upper Terrace Drive,** the trail passes several hot springs that might or might not be active; things change fast here.

10 Bunsen Peak Trail If you bring a bicycle, the Bunsen Peak Trail (4 miles) is a fine place to use it.

Another former road, this one starts across from the Glen Creek Trailhead, follows the base of Bunsen Peak to its east side, then drops through the canyon of **Gardiner River** back to the terraces.

A couple more strenuous hikes include one to the summit of **Bunsen Peak** and another to **Osprey Falls** in the canyon. Lacking a shuttle, or someone to drop you off at the start, you can still get the best of this trail by going out some distance and back the same way.

⓫ Blacktail Plateau Drive East of Mammoth, **Blacktail Deer Plateau** is mostly open country broken by strips of pine and aspen forest—the sort of place grazing animals prefer. The gravel road (one way, eastbound) meanders over it for 7 miles.

This is easy walking country, no trails needed. A short trip away from the car, perhaps to the top of a nearby hill, is bound to turn up something interesting.

Scan distant slopes with binoculars for elk, bison, wolves, and bears.

⓬ Trout Lake Perched 200 feet above US 212, out of sight but only 0.5 mile away, Trout Lake is a hidden gem with a reputation for good fishing and lovely mountain views.

Formerly called Fish Lake, it was a hatchery for cutthroat and rainbow trout until the 1950s, when fish-stocking operations were ended throughout the park. Otters are commonly seen here, catching fish and chasing each other playfully among the partially submerged tree trunks along the shore. You might see a moose in the shallows; bison and other wildlife roam the surrounding meadows.

The trailhead is not marked, but it's easy to find the vehicle turnout 1.2 miles south of **Pebble Creek Campground.** From there, it's less than 0.5 mile to the lake. You can walk around it, and also visit nearby **Buck Lake** and **Shrimp Lake.**

Aspens along Blacktail Plateau Drive

The largest herd of elk in the United States

GRAND TETON

The Teton Range demands immediate attention. From first sight, it's hard to tear your eyes from these towering crags. Pushed up along a sharp fault line, they rise in a single, audacious wall of granite 6,000 to 7,000 feet above Jackson Hole, the valley at their feet, which makes an ideal viewing platform. There are no foothills to speak of, nothing to block the view of coniferous forest, alpine meadows, bare granite, and light blue glaciers. No matter what you do—boating, hiking, bicycling, wildlife-watching, or simply gazing upward—the peaks are ever present and never far from your consciousness, hiding secrets in their shadows.

Their true magic lies in juxtaposition. Something small, a bird perhaps, or a cluster of wildflowers, captures your interest. For a moment, you forget the mountains, but then you lift your eyes and there they stand—high and distant but at the same time too close to be believed.

Year-Round Visitor Center

- **Craig Thomas Discovery and Visitor Center**
  Moose, 12 miles from Jackson on Teton Park Road

Seasonal Visitor Centers

- **Colter Bay Visitor Center**
  25 miles north of Moose
- **Flagg Ranch Information Station**
  2 miles south of Yellowstone's south boundary on the John D. Rockefeller, Jr. Memorial Parkway
- **Jenny Lake Visitor Center**
  South Jenny Lake, 8 miles north of Moose
- **Laurance S. Rockefeller Preserve Center**
  Moose-Wilson Road, 4 miles south of Moose

307-739-3300, *www.nps.gov/grte*

▶ US 89

The main road through the park is US 89, which leads north from the town of **Jackson** to Yellowstone National Park. Leaving town, it passes the **National Elk Refuge,** then climbs a small rise to emerge suddenly in full view of the Tetons.

For the next 30 miles to Moran Junction, the views are well worth stopping for and taking in, despite traffic that includes long-haul trucks headed east across Wyoming.

❶ **Kelly Road** Leave the highway at **Gros Ventre Junction** for a bucolic cruise through sagebrush-covered meadows on the east side of the park. The road follows cottonwood-lined **Gros Ventre River,** a spot to see Bald Eagles, moose, and waterfowl. On the open sagebrush flats, look for pronghorn, elk, and bison.

A mile beyond the hamlet of **Kelly,** the Gros Ventre Road climbs over aspen-covered hills toward **Lower Slide Lake,** outside of the park. The lake was created by a giant landslide in 1925 that blocked the Gros Ventre River. This road goes miles farther through untraveled country, but that is a separate excursion for those with time and an inclination to explore.

Return for now to Kelly Road, and continue north 2.5 miles to **Antelope Flats Road,** which leads back to US 89. On the way, it passes **Mormon Row,** the location of two historic barns built by pioneer settlers John and Thomas Moulton. Seen at dawn, with the peaks behind them, the barns are among the most photographed objects in the Tetons.

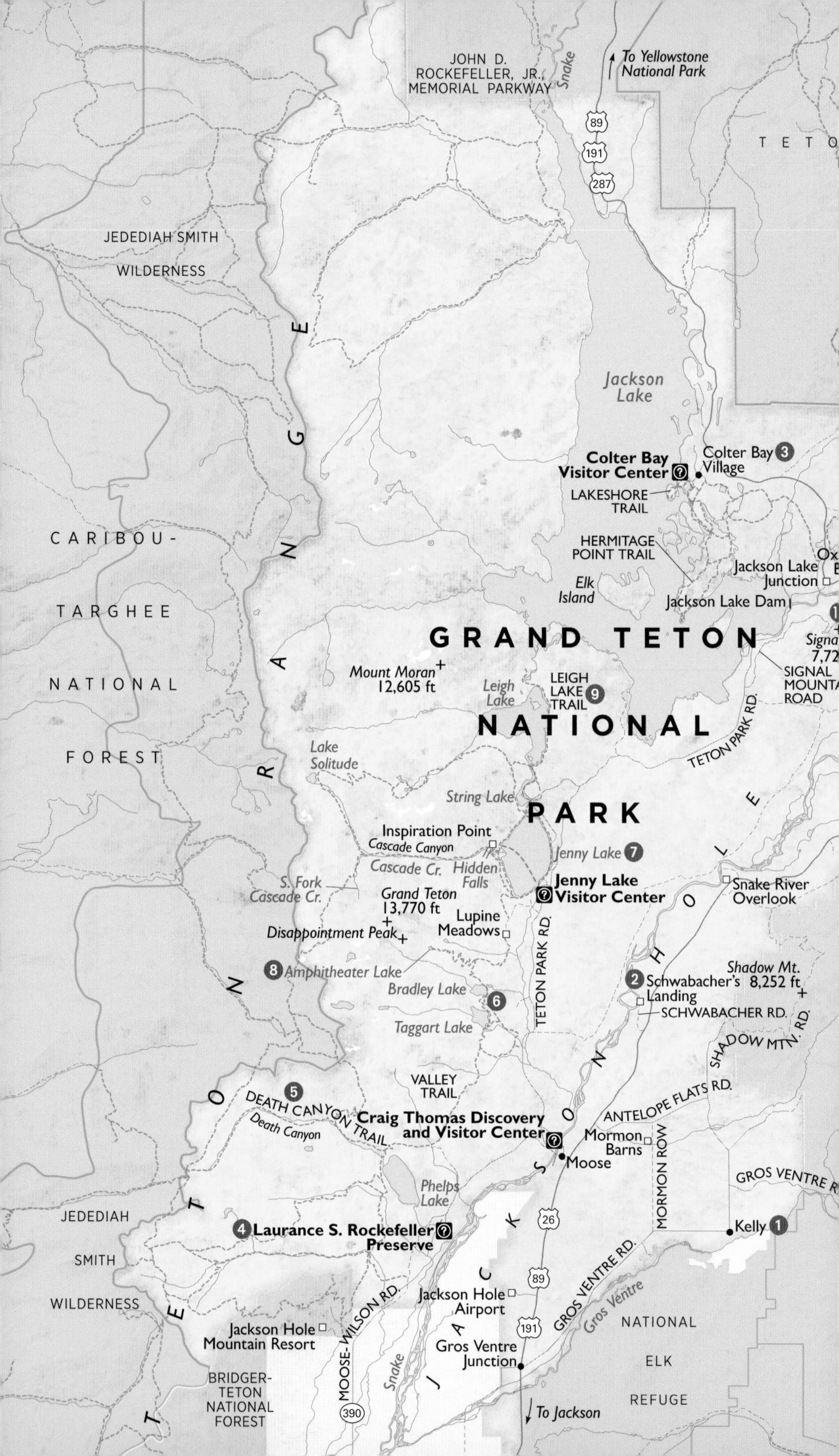

JOHN D. ROCKEFELLER, JR., MEMORIAL PARKWAY
Snake
To Yellowstone National Park
89
191
287
TETO
JEDEDIAH SMITH WILDERNESS
CARIBOU-TARGHEE NATIONAL FOREST
TETON RANGE
Jackson Lake
Colter Bay Visitor Center
Colter Bay Village 3
LAKESHORE TRAIL
HERMITAGE POINT TRAIL
Elk Island
Jackson Lake Junction
Jackson Lake Dam
GRAND TETON NATIONAL PARK
Mount Moran 12,605 ft
Leigh Lake
LEIGH LAKE TRAIL 9
SIGNAL MOUNTA ROAD
TETON PARK RD.
Lake Solitude
String Lake
Inspiration Point
Cascade Canyon
Cascade Cr.
Hidden Falls
Jenny Lake 7
Jenny Lake Visitor Center
S. Fork Cascade Cr.
Grand Teton 13,770 ft
Disappointment Peak
Lupine Meadows
Snake River Overlook
8 Amphitheater Lake
Bradley Lake
6
Taggart Lake
2 Schwabacher's Landing
Shadow Mt. 8,252 ft
SCHWABACHER RD.
SHADOW MTN. RD.
JACKSON HOLE
VALLEY TRAIL
5
DEATH CANYON TRAIL
Death Canyon
Craig Thomas Discovery and Visitor Center
ANTELOPE FLATS RD.
Mormon Barns
MORMON ROW
Moose
GROS VENTRE R
Phelps Lake
JEDEDIAH SMITH WILDERNESS
4 Laurance S. Rockefeller Preserve
26
Kelly 1
89
Jackson Hole Airport
GROS VENTRE RD.
Gros Ventre
MOOSE-WILSON RD.
Jackson Hole Mountain Resort
191
NATIONAL ELK REFUGE
Gros Ventre Junction
Snake
BRIDGER-TETON NATIONAL FOREST
390
To Jackson

A Moulton barn and the Tetons

2 Schwabacher's Landing For miles, US 89 stays above the braided, fast-moving **Snake River,** affording a fine view of cottonwood forest and sparkling water. For a closer look, take the short Schwabacher Road down to the river bottom *(four-wheel drive recommended),* where woods and shrubby meadows alternate with meandering streams, beaver ponds, and mirrored views of the mountains.

Those classic views of the Tetons at sunrise reflected warmly in dark waters? This is the place. Fishermen's trails lead in all directions. Otters, beavers, osprey, mergansers, and trout live here.

So do moose. Take care not to stumble upon a grazing moose; the animals appear placid but can be dangerous as they defend their territory.

3 Colter Bay Twenty-five miles farther north and home to an excellent visitor center, a marina, and other facilities, Colter Bay is a bustling place. Several trails, though, provide quick escape through pine forest to the smooth-cobbled beaches of

Jackson Lake with Grand Teton and Mount Moran

Jackson Lake. During midsummer and later, the water can be warm enough for swimming. Look for pelicans, gulls, and other waterfowl.

The **Lakeshore Trail** is an easy 2-mile jaunt around a small island—an ideal excursion for kids who want to skip stones on the water. For a longer, more secluded hike (9 miles), the **Hermitage Point Trail** leads to a treeless outlook with sweeping views.

▶ Moose-Wilson Road

For those not driving RVs or pulling trailers, the Moose-Wilson Road is the back way into the park. It starts near the town of **Wilson** as Wyo. 390 leading to **Jackson Hole Mountain Resort.**

Beyond the resort, it enters the park and becomes a winding, partly gravel and often bumpy byway for 8 miles to park headquarters at Moose. Because it snakes through forest much of the way, it offers few mountain views; rewards here go to those with keen eyesight.

"Moose-Wilson Road is one of the best areas in the park to view wildlife," says Jenny Anzelmo-Sarles of the Public Affairs Office at Grand Teton National Park. "Forests mixed with riparian (wetlands) boast prime habitats for moose, beavers, bears, elk, and owls."

❹ Laurance S. Rockefeller Preserve In the 1930s, John D. Rockefeller, Jr., purchased some 35,000 acres of Jackson Hole, which he donated to the nation in 1943 for the creation of the Jackson Hole National Monument. In 1950, the original 1929 Grand Teton National Park, which consisted only of the mountains and the glacial lakes at their base, was combined with the Jackson Hole National Monument to become the present-day park.

The family retained the **JY Ranch** at the south end of secluded **Phelps Lake** as a private retreat until Laurance S. Rockefeller transferred it to public ownership in 2007. Subsequently, cabins used by the Rockefellers were moved to other locations, a visitor center was built near the road, and once exclusive trails were opened to everyone. An invitation is no longer required to visit the lakeshore or walk the quiet forest paths, but it still feels like a privilege to be there.

Hundreds of people may be at the trail-head going south to Phelps Lake. If you go the other way, you're suddenly alone, all the way to Taggart Lake.

—JIM SPRINGER
Grand Teton National Park ranger

5 **Death Canyon Trail** A popular 1.7-mile trail leads from the Death Canyon Trailhead to a breezy view-point above **Phelps Lake.** Hikers stop here to enjoy the terrific view of the lake on one hand and Death Canyon on the other. Many continue to the canyon, which, belying its name, is a delight of cascading water and fra-grant woods.

Park ranger Jim Springer agrees that the canyon is okay, "but if you want a beautiful easy trail with no one else around, go north on the **Valley Trail** to **Taggart Lake**"—and truly stunning views of Grand Teton towering above. If you plan to go that far, arrange a shuttle to get back.

▶ Teton Park Road

The Teton Park Road begins at Moose and runs northward, as close to the mountains as you can go without hiking. It rejoins US 89 near the **Jackson Lake** dam, a distance of 20 miles.

Along the way, it takes in **Jenny**

Local Intelligence

Dawn is the best time to see the Tetons from almost any viewpoint, but particularly **Schwabacher's Landing** near **Moose** and **Oxbow Bend** near **Jackson Lake Junction.** Because the moun-tains face east, they catch the first light of day while the valley floor remains in misty shadow, and wildlife are more likely to be out in the open. The morning air is often calm, allowing mirrored reflections on the park's many lakes and ponds.

The trademark image is of a morning moose standing in that rose-colored reflection at the center of concentric ripples in the water. It's not a common sight, but it's possible almost any day. Also, pay attention to the lunar cycle. Once every month, a full moon sets behind the dawn-lit Tetons as the sun rises in the east—spectacular compensation for getting up early.

Reflection at sunrise in Jenny Lake

Lake, the most popular single place in the Tetons, along with numerous opportunities for mountain gazing and private excursions. Some trails scramble steeply upward; others stroll through gentle country on the valley floor. Four lakes—Jenny, **String, Leigh,** and Jackson—offer boating in addition to easy lakeside walking.

6 Bradley and Taggart Lakes When glaciers plowed down from the peaks, they not only carved the steep canyons between mountains, they also created piles of rock rubble—"moraines"—that today hold a string of alpine lakes at the base of the Tetons.

A few, including Jenny and Jackson, can be reached by road. Others, equally beautiful, lie beyond pavement. Bradley and Taggart are two such bodies of water, cupped in morainal hills, fringed by pines, and overshadowed by grand summits.

It's about 3 miles round-trip from the trailhead to Taggart, and double that if you include Bradley. Check the map for several options, all good.

7 Jenny Lake Almost everyone stops to appreciate Jenny Lake, and quite a few take the scenic boat ride to the western shore, where a 1.1-mile trail climbs through deep forest to **Hidden Falls** and beyond to **Inspiration Point.**

This is worthwhile any time, no matter the crowds, which at midday can fill the trail. For some privacy, carry on into **Cascade Canyon,** if only for a couple of miles. The trail ascends gradually along sparkling **Cascade Creek.** Crowds drop away as the mountains leap upward.

Seven and a half miles (via the shuttle boat) in, **Lake Solitude** offers stunning views of the central Tetons. It's not exactly crowded at the lake, but as Springer points out, for true solitude go another way. "Take a left at the forks," he advises, referring to the **South Fork Cascade Canyon.** "You'll hardly see a soul, and it's a spectacular place."

An easier way to find some privacy is to ride the boat only one way, then to walk back along the shore of Jenny Lake; either way is about 3 miles.

8 Amphitheater Lake The trail to Amphitheater Lake (10.1 miles round-trip) is a different beast from its more moderate cousin located in Cascade Canyon.

Beginning at **Lupine Meadows,** this one steams relentlessly up and up through steeply pitched meadows filled with the yellow flowers of balsamroot. Views of the valley become ever more expansive as altitude is gained—good diversion at breath-catching stops.

After climbing 3,150 more vertical feet, the trail tops out near timberline beside the icy lake.

Disappointment Peak towers overhead, and the valley below seems impossibly distant. There will be other hikers at the lake, but usually not many.

9 Leigh Lake Trail Not many walks in the Tetons can be called strolls, but this one qualifies. It begins along the shore of String Lake, a narrow channel popular for boating, because it's relatively sheltered, and swimming, because its shallow waters warm up earlier than the bigger lakes.

At 1.5 miles, the trail crosses a short divide where paddlers must portage their canoes, and it emerges on Leigh Lake.

Some locals say that the best thing is to come with a boat and paddle close beneath the stunning wall of **Mount Moran.** Others vote for walking the flat trail along the eastern shore, where sand beaches provide sweeping views of the peaks and pleasant picnic sites; the total distance from String Lake Trailhead to the far end of Leigh Lake is about 4 miles.

10 Signal Mountain Geology instructors know this place well, but most visitors pass it by. The best single place from which to view the physical structure of Jackson Hole and the Tetons is the summit of Signal Mountain.

A relatively humble peak, it stands away from the great mountains and near to Jackson Lake, offering a unique perspective on the park.

The short Signal Mountain Summit Road cruises smoothly to the top at 7,727 feet, no hiking boots needed. From here you can see that the valley floor tilts down toward the west as the mountain block rises. The two are going in opposite directions.

Along the Lupine Meadows Trail

View of the Lewis Range, where the Pacific Northwest Trail passes through Stoney Indian Pass

GLACIER

Sprawling across the Continental Divide in northern Montana, Glacier claims some 26 small alpine glaciers. But in fact, its name refers to the work of much larger glaciers during ice ages of the past. It was heroic business, judging by the monumental results. Attentive visitors soon learn to recognize formations secret to most: arêtes, horns, eskers, moraines, cirques, hanging valleys, U-shaped valleys, glacial plucking, and more.

The ice itself comes and goes. The great glaciers melted with the last ice age; the current ones occupy, in a sense, the footprints of their ancestors. Melting ice augments the water from melting snow each year to keep wildflower meadows lush, more than 700 sparkling lakes filled, and waterfalls cascading.

Naturalist John Muir called this area the "best care-killing scenery on the continent."

Year-Round Visitor Centers

- **Apgar Visitor Center**
  Apgar Village, 2 miles north of West Glacier near foot of Lake McDonald
- **Logan Pass Visitor Center**
  Logan Pass, midway along Going-to-the-Sun Road

Seasonal Visitor Center

- **Saint Mary Visitor Center**
  Off US 89, East Entrance

406-888-7800, *www.nps.gov/glac*

▶ Going-to-the-Sun Road

The central focus for most visitors to Glacier, and for good reason, is the 50-mile Going-to-the-Sun Road.

There's nowhere in the country quite like it—a two-lane road carved into a stunningly precipitous landscape, it transects the park through its scenic center. There are higher roads in the Rockies, but none better.

From the west side, it climbs out of deep-shadowed forest. Then, clinging to sheer cliffs above deep valleys, it arrives among wildflowers and snowfields at **Logan Pass.**

The east slope is equally spectacular, although being in the rain shadow of the **Continental Divide,** the climate is drier and the vegetation different. Go early in the morning to avoid the crush, but if the road is crowded, no matter. Take the drive, stop often, and revel in the scenery.

Better yet, take the park's free shuttle; it stops at trailheads and pullouts all along the road. This can be invaluable, especially at Logan Pass where the parking lot is often full at midday.

❶ **Logan Pass** The 1.5-mile hike to **Hidden Lake** overlook is the clear choice. You'll have plenty of company, but the surroundings make it all worthwhile.

On the other hand, if you wish to get away from crowds, there are options. The 7.6-mile **Highline Trail**—accessible from the Highline Trailhead located on the north side of the Going-to-the-Sun Road at Logan Pass—contours north from the pass, cutting across a near-vertical rock wall, so exposed that the park has strung a hand cable for nervous hikers to clutch. Some people turn around at the sight of it. Nonetheless, the Highline ranks among the finest high-altitude walks on the planet. **Haystack Pass,** 3.6 miles from the trailhead, offers a scenic climax for the trail.

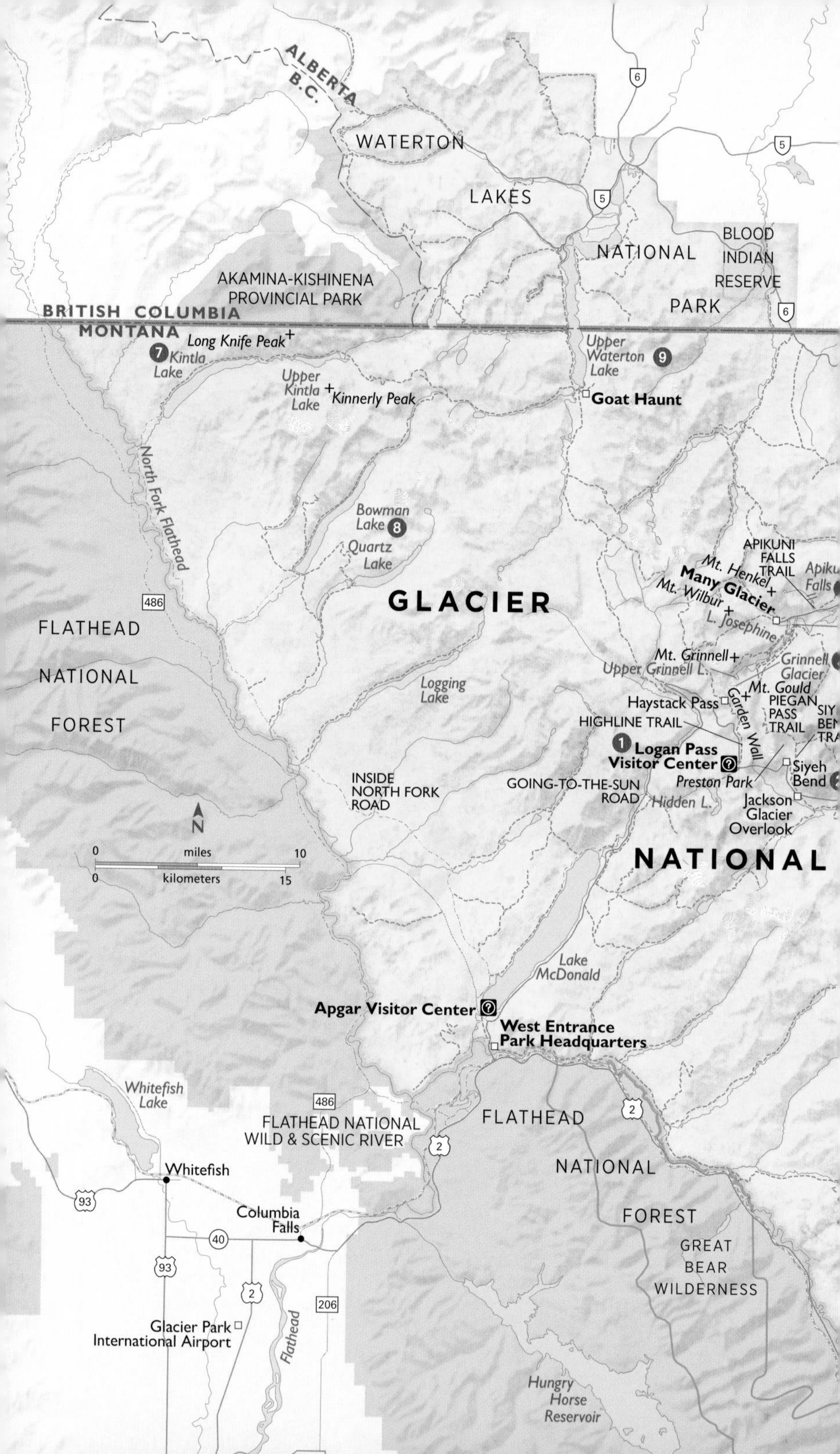

ALBERTA
B.C.
WATERTON
LAKES
NATIONAL
PARK
BLOOD
INDIAN
RESERVE
AKAMINA-KISHINENA
PROVINCIAL PARK
BRITISH COLUMBIA
MONTANA
Long Knife Peak
7 Kintla Lake
Upper Kintla Lake
Kinnerly Peak
Upper Waterton Lake
9
Goat Haunt
North Fork Flathead
Bowman Lake 8
Quartz Lake
GLACIER
NATIONAL
APIKUNI FALLS TRAIL
Apiku Falls
Mt. Henkel
Many Glacier
Mt. Wilbur
L. Josephine
Mt. Grinnell
Upper Grinnell L.
Grinnell Glacier
Mt. Gould
Haystack Pass
Garden Wall
PIEGAN PASS TRAIL
HIGHLINE TRAIL
1 Logan Pass Visitor Center
Preston Park
Siyeh Bend
GOING-TO-THE-SUN ROAD
Hidden L.
Jackson Glacier Overlook
Logging Lake
INSIDE NORTH FORK ROAD
FLATHEAD
NATIONAL
FOREST
486
N
0 miles 10
0 kilometers 15
Lake McDonald
Apgar Visitor Center
West Entrance
Park Headquarters
Whitefish Lake
486
FLATHEAD NATIONAL
WILD & SCENIC RIVER
FLATHEAD
NATIONAL
FOREST
GREAT
BEAR
WILDERNESS
Whitefish
93
Columbia Falls
40
93
2
206
Glacier Park
International Airport
Flathead
Hungry Horse Reservoir
6
5
5
6
2
2

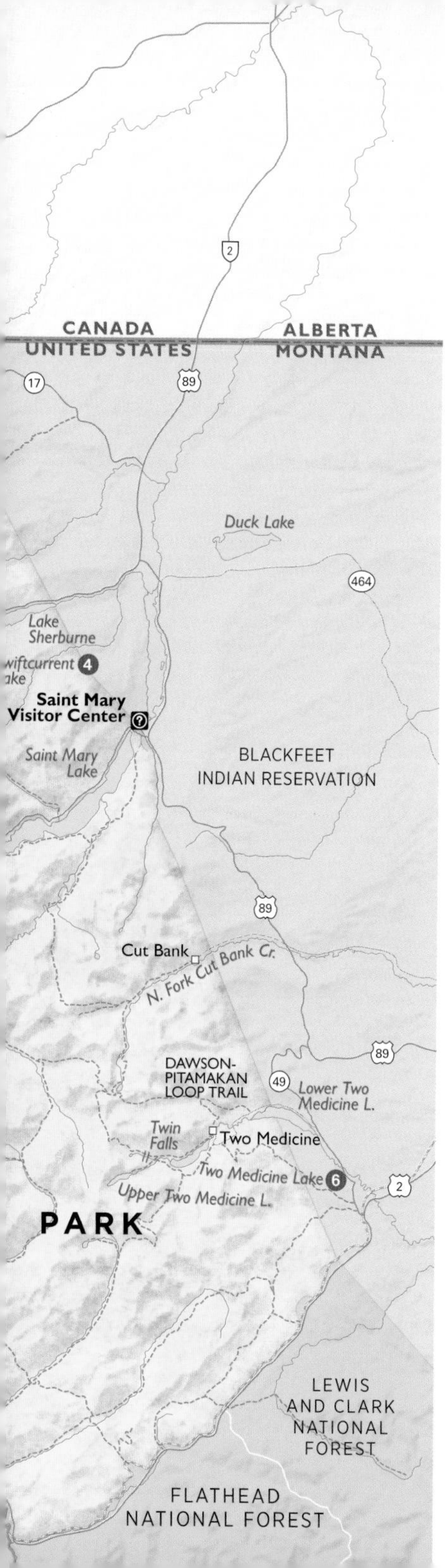

2 Siyeh Bend A less traveled option starts 2.2 miles east of Logan at Siyeh Bend (a shuttle stop). The Siyeh Bend Trail climbs for about a mile through forest, then joins the **Piegan Pass Trail.**

Turning right, you can return to the road at **Jackson Glacier Overlook—** making for a moderate and lovely hike of about 2.5 miles.

To the left, about 1.5 miles and some 800 feet higher, is **Preston Park,** featuring one of the park's best wildflower meadows.

▶ Many Glacier

Above all, Glacier is a hiker's park, and Many Glacier is the heart of it. Three magnificent valleys converge on **Swiftcurrent Lake.** A series of peaks—**Henkel, Wilbur, Grinnell,** and **Gould—**each one a model of glacial artistry, anchor the sharp ridge that connects the summits and carries the Continental Divide along its spine.

Streams pour into lakes and tumble over waterfalls in each valley. Wildflowers bloom most of the

A mountain goat and kids

Remnants of the vanishing Grinnell Glacier

summer. Distances are not long, and an excellent trail system provides access to it all. You can spend a week exploring here and still want more.

3 Grinnell Glacier Crowding is a relative term. The busiest trail at Many Glacier is a peaceful place compared to almost any park road. So, although Grinnell Glacier is a well-known and popular destination, it's a select group of visitors who make the trip on any given day.

It is worth the effort, not just because the scenery is spectacular, but also because the glacier, perhaps the most famous in the park, won't last much longer. If current warming trends continue, all the park's glaciers will have melted away by 2030.

Getting there involves a gentle 3-mile walk on Grinnell Glacier Trail to the head of **Lake Josephine,** and a steady climb of 1,600 feet to the glacier viewpoint at **Upper Grinnell Lake.** The trail passes through lush meadows filled with beargrass, Indian paintbrush, and, quite likely, a few mountain goats grazing. This is quintessential Glacier. Total distance to the glacier is 5.5 miles each way, or 3.8 if you ride the shuttle boat.

4 Swiftcurrent Lake At Glacier, trails may be busy, but the lakes usually aren't. Canoes and kayaks provide a simple way to escape into a zone of privacy.

It might be enough to drift along the shore of Swiftcurrent Lake, soaking up the scenery, but Lake Josephine beckons from the other side of a 400-yard portage. The Park Service and several concession companies offer guided tours that span the lakes or rent kayaks or canoes so you can do the route yourselves.

Going-to-the-Sun can open any time from the end of May to mid-July. We start plowing in April, but weather can happen any time.

—DENISE GERMANN
Glacier National Park ranger

Josephine is often empty of any boats except the sightseeing craft that runs from one end to the other. Rent a boat at **Apgar, Two Medicine,** or Many Glacier.

Note: To prevent introduction of invasive water pests (the New Zealand mussel, a primary concern), the park requires inspections for all watercraft.

❺ **Apikuni Falls** Short, steep (700 vertical feet in 1 mile), and often overlooked, the **Apikuni Falls Trail** offers a moderately strenuous route to a high, slender, multistaged waterfall. The trailhead is located 1.1 miles east of the Many Glacier Hotel.

For some hikers, the main reward for making the climb is the view that opens up as you go higher—**Mount Gould** and the **Garden Wall** framed by the smooth U-shaped valley.

▶ Southeast Corner

Two opposite corners of Glacier—the northwest and the southeast—are off the main track and extremely different in character.

The southeast, being on the rain-shadow side of the mountains and bordering the Great Plains, is drier, more open landscape. Like all of Glacier's eastern side, it can be a windy place. But it lacks nothing for scenery, and offers two relatively peaceful places to appreciate it.

One is **Cut Bank,** at the end of a 5-mile dirt road; it offers a primitive campground (bring your own drinking water), a historic ranger station, and little more than the natural surroundings. The other is Two Medicine.

❻ **Two Medicine Lake** A glance at Glacier's map shows why lakes are the focus of most activities. There are many, almost all of which occupy glacier-carved valleys.

The main ones are long and narrow,

Stunning sunset over Two Medicine Lake

Waterton Lakes in fall

and reach deep into the mountains like the ice rivers that made them. It's natural that visitors want to see what lies at their upper ends.

Two Medicine Lake is no exception. Overlooked by a ring of peaks, it was a busier place in early years, before construction of the Going-to-the-Sun Road shifted visitors' attention northward. Of course, nothing was lost except the crowds.

It's a fine place if you have a canoe or kayak and the wind is not blowing too hard. Rental boats are available, as is a boat tour that also serves as a hiker shuttle.

From the boat dock at the upper end, a gentle trail (2.2 miles each way) leads past **Twin Falls** to Upper Two Medicine Lake. Another option: the not-gentle 18-mile **Dawson-Pitamakan Loop Trail** from near Two Medicine.

▶ Northwest Corner

The northwest portion of Glacier is on the way to nowhere but itself. This is just fine with visitors looking to get away and seek serenity.

The **North Fork Flathead River** flows out of Canada to form the park boundary. Two roads flank the river. One road is outside the park, the other is inside—sensibly named the **Inside North Fork Road,** a rough and winding route not recommended for RVs or trailers.

The drive offers few mountain vistas. The theme here is deep, luxuriant forest, moist meadows, two magnificent fjordlike lakes—**Bowman** and **Kintla**—and solitude. Two additional lakes, also large and splendid, are even farther removed; **Logging Lake** and **Quartz Lake** are accessible only on foot.

7 Kintla Lake Although the road is rough and the driving slow, getting to Kintla Lake, the most remote vehicle-accessible place in Glacier, is worth the effort. It's possible to get there from **Lake McDonald** and back in a day, but the far better idea is to camp out a night or two.

This is no place to hurry. The campground is old-fashioned (with pit toilets and no hookups). It almost never fills up.

Take a paddleboat if you can. No motors are allowed on the water; the loudest sound could be the dip of your paddle.

Of course, the mountain views are excellent and only get better the farther up the lake you go. From Kintla's head, it's a 3-mile hike to Upper Kintla Lake, which lies in the embrace of **Kinnerly** and **Long Knife Peaks.**

8 Bowman Lake Bowman Lake is practically a twin to Kintla. Of similar size, also reached by a rough dirt road, and girded by mountains, Bowman is only a little less remote. Boat motors are allowed, but not larger than 10 horsepower.

9 Waterton Lakes Located in Canada, Waterton Lakes National Park adjoins Glacier, protecting an equally grand landscape; together they form **Waterton-Glacier International Peace Park,** the first such trans-border park in the world. **Upper Waterton Lake** extends across the border like a neighborly hand. Several times a day in summer, a sightseeing boat motors down to the remote American end, and U.S. and Canadian backpackers with identification are allowed to hike from there.

Local Intelligence

Visiting Glacier takes planning for a range of contingencies. **Going-to-the-Sun Road,** for example, is being rehabilitated in a project that will last until 2016. Delays and closures are likely to affect all traffic, depending on season and work schedules. The free shuttle is intended to reduce vehicle congestion during this period, but it might not continue to run after the work is done.

Going-to-the-Sun's schedule is driven by weather, and snow also complicates any attempt at trip planning. After the winter of 2010–11, the Going-to-the-Sun Road did not open until July 13. The park starts to plow the route in April; beware, however, that cold weather can strike even in the summer months. Keep up with bulletins posted on the park's website.

Trails are also affected. Steep, slippery snowfields can be a deadly hazard for the unskilled or unprepared. Says park ranger Denise Germann: "People need to evaluate their own skills, and sometimes it means not doing something you want to do."

She adds that while snow might block the pass or make hiking difficult, "the valley bottoms can be 60 or 70 degrees and beautiful, warm and green. Even without **Logan Pass** there are plenty of opportunities to enjoy the park in peaceful, scenic places."

She advises contacting the park in advance by calling or checking the official website, where the "Plan Your Visit" section is loaded with information on conditions, and webcams provide live images. Glacier also has a presence on social media sites.

"These are beautiful places and historic sites that have been passed on to us by past generations, and now we have a responsibility to pass on these treasures and their many secrets to our children and grandchildren."

—SECRETARY KEN SALAZAR, U.S. DEPARTMENT OF THE INTERIOR
NATIONAL PARK TRUST 2010 RECIPIENT
AMERICAN PARK EXPERIENCE AWARD

[3]

PACIFIC RIM

Sea star and sea stacks along Second Beach, Olympic National Park

Mount Rainier landscape alight with wildflowers

MOUNT RAINIER

Towering over the heart of the Cascade Range, Mount Rainier stands as one of the most recognizable features in Washington's diverse landscape. For centuries, this mighty mountain—viewable from nearly every corner of the state—has filled local culture. Native tribes describe the mountain—"Tahoma" to the western tribes—as a mighty source of power and home to gods. Residents throughout Washington see it today as the icon of their Northwest culture and a wonderful wilderness retreat.

From deep old-growth forests in low valley bottoms to the frosty summit of the peak, Mount Rainier boasts an array of secret terrain and ecosystems to explore and enjoy.

Here you'll find wildflower meadows that John Muir called the most superb subalpine gardens that he had ever encountered, more than 100 waterfalls, and nearly 325 lakes.

Year-Round Visitor Centers

- **Henry M. Jackson Memorial Visitor Center**
  At Paradise, 11 miles east of Longmire
- **Longmire Museum**
  On Park Rd. 706, 6 miles from Nisqually Entrance

Seasonal Visitor Centers

- **Ohanapecosh Visitor Center**
  On Wash. 123, inside the park next to the Ohanapecosh area
- **Sunrise Visitor Center**
  On Wash. 410, inside the park, end of White River/Sunrise road

360-569-2211, *www.nps.gov/mora*

▶ The Road to Paradise

The most popular access to the park uses the **Nisqually Entrance** in the park's southwest corner. This route rolls east through the Longmire area before climbing a long, winding road to **Paradise.**

The **Historic Village of Longmire,** nestled at 2,750 feet elevation between **Rampart Ridge** on the north and the **Nisqually River** on the south, cradles the original park headquarters building—still used as the in-park administration hub—the **Longmire Museum,** and the **National Park Inn.**

James Longmire, one of the earliest non-native visitors to the area and the first to build a cabin within what is now the park boundary, discovered mineral hot springs in the meadows and built a hotel and spa to take advantage of those "healing waters."

Later he helped carve the road up the mountain to the broad meadows on the south flank. The awesome splendor of this region earned its names in 1885 from Longmire's daughter-in-law, Martha. On seeing the fields of vibrant wildflowers, she declared, "Oh, it looks just like paradise." The name stuck, and the Paradise meadows today are just as pristine as they were 130 years ago.

1 Kautz Creek Trail The Kautz Creek drainage has been ravaged by floods, decimated by fires, and rearranged by mudslides, so it offers a great lesson in the dynamic nature of a Cascade volcano.

The trail leaves from the north side of the road about 3 miles east of the Nisqually Entrance and weaves up the Kautz Creek Valley. It proceeds through a forest killed by the Kautz Mudflow—a massive debris flow in December 1947 that brought millions of cubic yards of liquid rock and soil down the creek basin, killing or

MOUNT BAKER-SNOQUALMI
CARBON RIVER ROAD
Green Lake
Carbon
9 Tolmie Peak Lookout
Tolmie Peak 5,939 ft
Eunice Lake
Mowich Lake
165
Mowich
Spray Park
8
Mystic Lake
MOUNT RAINIER
MOUNT RAINIER
14,411 ft
GLACIER VIEW WILDERNESS
Lake George
2 Comet Falls
Van Trump Cr.
3 SKYLINE TRAIL
Edith Cr.
Henry M. Jackson Memorial Visitor Center
Paradise Inn
Reflection Lakes
Bench L.
Snow L.
Tatoosh Range
Rampart Ridge
Kautz Cr.
Tahoma Cr.
1 KAUTZ CREEK TRAIL
Longmire Museum
Unicorn Pk. 6,917 ft
706
Nisqually Entrance
Nisqually
52
TATOOSH
GIFFORD
NATIONAL
N
0 miles 4
0 kilometers 6

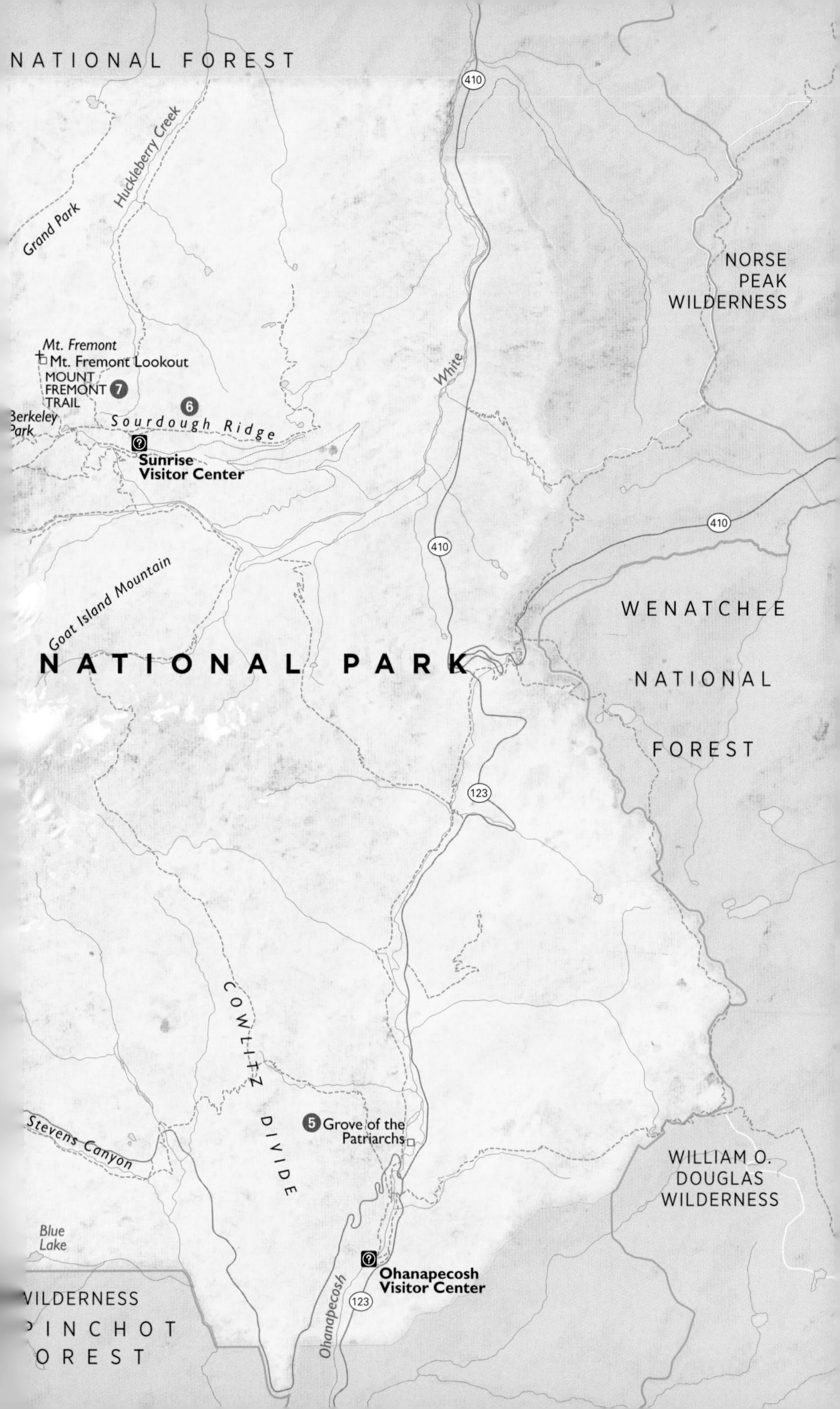

NATIONAL FOREST
410
Huckleberry Creek
Grand Park
NORSE
PEAK
WILDERNESS
Mt. Fremont
Mt. Fremont Lookout
MOUNT
FREMONT
TRAIL
7
6
White
Berkeley
Park
Sourdough Ridge
Sunrise
Visitor Center
410
410
Goat Island Mountain
WENATCHEE
NATIONAL PARK
NATIONAL
FOREST
123
COWLITZ DIVIDE
5
Grove of the
Patriarchs
Stevens Canyon
WILLIAM O.
DOUGLAS
WILDERNESS
Blue
Lake
Ohanapecosh
Visitor Center
123
Ohanapecosh
WILDERNESS
PINCHOT
FOREST

obliterating everything in its path.

This nearly 6-mile one-way route provides proof that a volcano doesn't have to blow its top to unleash destructive power.

2 Comet Falls Many claim this is the most beautiful waterfall in the park, though the competition is fierce. The 300-foot cascade fans out as it crashes down the andesite cliffs, rolls briefly across a rocky meadow, then drops another 20 feet. The two-stage falls provide a show of force and beauty. The trail to this natural wonder climbs the steep valley of the **Van Trump Creek,** offering little along the way other than an experience in the forest primeval, but once you reach the waterfall basin at 1.8 miles the average trail turns exceptional.

Comet Falls

3 Skyline Trail This 5-mile trail leaves in front of the newly renovated **Paradise Inn**—a classic timber-framed lodge—and loops around the broad **Edith Creek Basin.** The pathway leads through alpine flower fields, past a thundering waterfall, and finally up onto the ridge above.

From there you'll ramble along the high ridgeline above the basin before dropping back into the upper meadows past arrays of wildflowers back to the start (stay on the paths, as walking through wildflowers is discouraged and even illegal in some areas of the park, see sidebar opposite).

In this one loop you'll experience the best the Paradise region has to offer in terms of scenic beauty, rugged hiking, and varied terrain and ecosystems. The subalpine zone covers more than 54,000 acres of parkland, providing countless opportunities for viewing flowers.

▶ Stevens Canyon

Stevens Canyon provides access from the park's southeast corner to Paradise. The deep cut of Stevens Canyon separates the wild alpine parklands on the flank of Rainier from the craggy peaks and crystal lakes of the **Tatoosh Range.** Hikers can explore the best of both sides of the canyon, as well as the forest ecosystems of the lower valley.

4 Bench and Snow Lakes While nearby **Reflection Lakes** get all the tourist attention, hikers willing to spend just a little time getting off the road will find these far-more-scenic lakes just minutes away.

In less than a mile (0.8 mile), hikers encounter Bench Lake. Though nestled on a broad shoulder of the ridge—or bench—just above the Stevens Canyon Road, the lake has a backcountry feel, thanks to the wild meadows and forests surrounding the basin, and a great view.

Local Intelligence

The subalpine and alpine meadows that blanket the slopes of Mount Rainier appear tough and resilient, but in actuality they are very fragile and delicate. Because most reside well above the 5,000-foot level, and the annual snowfall at that elevation exceeds 50 feet per year, the vegetation in the meadows enjoys a very short growing season (mid-June through mid-September). That means any plants damaged by wayward hikers take a long time to recover.

For this reason, rangers insist that hikers stay on the trails, especially around the popular **Paradise, Sunrise,** and **Spray Park** areas, where meadows are particularly delicate. Photographers seeking unique shots of wildflowers from within the meadows themselves should ask a park staff member where they may go so that they don't break the law. Options might include north and west of Sunrise in the **Berkeley Park** and **Grand Park** areas.

Snow Lake fills a narrow, usually snow-filled cirque with fabulous views south to **Unicorn Peak.**

5 Grove of the Patriarchs Some of the biggest, oldest trees in the Cascades stand tall here. These silent old men of moss tower overhead, with a few lying down to show just how massive the trunks really are.

The grove resides in a low boggy area across the **Ohanapecosh River,** with the broad, gentle trail starting just 0.25 mile past the park entrance. The trail crosses the burbling river via a stout suspension bridge, which youngsters either love or hate—there's just enough bounce in the bridge to make it fun and exciting.

The grove itself hosts ancient hemlocks, cedars, and Douglas firs that make the rest of the region's forests appear young and tiny. Some of these ancient monoliths measure nearly 40 feet in circumference and tower more than 300 feet tall—and, in some cases, are at least 100 years old.

▶ Sunrise

Perched on the northeastern shoulder of Mount Rainier, Sunrise welcomes the first morning light into the park. While campgrounds and even golf courses once blighted this ridgetop setting, today's visitors find just a couple of rustic CCC structures built in the 1930s and seemingly endless fields of green splashed with vibrantly colored wildflowers.

Positioned just at the timberline, Sunrise offers an array of hiking opportunities, from short, nearly flat routes perfect for families and folks short of time, to long meadow and forest rambles that lead to some of the most picturesque places in a park known for its photogenic wonders.

At 6,400 feet, Sunrise is the highest elevation visitor center and trailhead area in the park, so the road frequently remains closed by snow until late June and the meadows of magenta paintbrush, pearly everlasting, and red mountain heather don't explode until mid- to late July. The colorful displays typically continue through August, providing even late summer visitors the opportunity to experience the vivid color palette of the alpine meadows.

6 Sourdough Ridge The historic structures at Sunrise are surrounded by meadows, and the loop (triangle, actually) route around Sourdough Ridge explores the biggest and most varied meadows in the area.

Starting from the north side of the parking lot, the hard-packed trail climbs a gentle 400 feet to the crest of Sourdough Ridge. During the climb, watch the patches of freshly turned dirt scattered through the meadows. These mounds of soil mark the burrows of hoary marmots—large, brown critters that feed on the abundant vegetation. If you don't see any marmots right away, just listen closely and you'll likely hear their sharp, high-pitched whistles as you walk among their homes.

Follow the ridgetop trail while enjoying the views north all the way to **Glacier Peak** (some 90 miles distant), then turn and descend the third leg of the 1.5-mile triangle back to the trailhead.

The Spray Park trail climbs from forest to subalpine meadow, and finally to alpine meadow. If you want—and you are prepared for it—you can climb up into the true high alpine zone, too.

—ALAN L. BAUER
photographer, naturalist, and author

7 Mount Fremont Trail The era of staffed fire lookouts passed long ago. Today, satellites keep an eye on our wildlands during fire season. But those historic watchtowers still provide a valuable service as recreational destinations (when they are not in use during emergencies).

The stilted cabin of the **Mount Fremont Lookout** stands not on the true summit of Mount Fremont, but on a secondary knob to the north of the peak. This off-the-summit option boasts a great view of Mount Rainier directly from the tower, and the mountain can be appreciated all the way up and back down the trail to the tower.

The positioning of the lookout also provides excellent views to the north. On clear days, Glacier Peak, **Mount Stuart,** and even **Mount Baker** can be seen. If the air is too hazy for those distant views, watch the north side of the ridge—mountain goats frequently rest on the slope as it drops off just past the trail's end.

Along the way, you'll be able to peer down in the wild **Huckleberry Creek Basin,** which is frequented by the White River elk herd as well as some of the region's black bears.

▶ Northwest Corner

The northwest corner of Mount Rainier National Park offers some of the most secret, remote, and pristine wilderness experiences in the park. The best chance for solitude in the park can be found here, on the trails high above the **Carbon River** or beyond the shores of **Mowich Lake.**

This is also one of the best places to encounter shy wildlife. Black bears frequent the berry-rich meadows and mountain goats scamper through the rocky slopes above the subalpine fields.

The **Carbon River Road,** unfortunately, disappeared during the floods of 2006 and again in 2008, forcing visitors to either hike or bike the 5 miles from the park boundary if they want access to those trails along the old road corridor.

Mount Rainier and its reflection

8 Spray Park Alan L. Bauer, a noted northwest photographer, naturalist, and author intimately familiar with Mount Rainier, describes the Spray Park area as the best of the park's fantastic meadows.

"Along the hike you get great views, access to a beautiful waterfall, and gradual transitions through a series of ecosystems," he says. "The trail climbs from forest to subalpine meadow, and finally to alpine meadow. If you want—and you are prepared for it—you can climb up into the true high alpine zone, too."

It's the meadows, especially the transition zone from subalpine (starts just below timberline) to alpine (open fields above timberline), that really make Spray Park special.

The trees fade away as the trail climbs, leaving a path through a world of sparkling blue ponds and emerald green heathers and grasses interrupted by splashes of color from a variety of wildflowers.

The 3-mile walk to Spray Park leads from the shores of Mowich Lake to seemingly endless open meadows of heather and alpine blossoms. (Please respect the plant life and stay on the trails.)

9 Tolmie Peak Lookout Start with a stroll along the shores of Mowich Lake, then climb gently into the adjacent lake basin **(Eunice Lake)** where the first grand views of Tolmie Peak and its lookout tower are found.

The trail climbs steeply from Eunice Lake to the crown of Tolmie Peak, but the constant views of the destination, and the towering hulk of Mount Rainier, make the trip bearable. The summit makes the 3.5-mile trek (one way) totally worthwhile.

A water-carved sculptured trunk along Second Beach

OLYMPIC

Olympic National Park holds many of the world's best remaining old-growth temperate rain forests—those cathedral forests of Sitka spruce, western hemlock, bigleaf maples, and western red cedar fill the river valleys on the west side of the main body of the park. The richness of these valleys exceeds imagination. Moss coats every surface, lichens drape from every limb. Trees grow to more than 300 feet tall and 72 feet or more around the base. The park is truly rife with secrets to be discovered.

Above those majestic emerald valleys stand rugged glacier-covered peaks and jagged rocky ridges. Farther west of the forested valleys runs the coastal strand of Olympic National Park, where you'll find the longest undeveloped stretch of wilderness beach in the lower 48 states. And on the east side of the park are more deep valleys filled with massive Douglas firs and sprawling rhododendron jungles.

Year-Round Visitor Centers

- **Olympic National Park Visitor Center**
  At the park entrance, 3002 Mount Angeles Road, Port Angeles
- **Hurricane Ridge Visitor Center**
  On Hurricane Ridge Road, 17 miles south of Port Angeles
- **Hoh Rain Forest Visitor Center**
  US 101, 31 miles south of Forks

360-565-3130, *www.nps.gov/olym*

▶ Southeast Corner

President Theodore Roosevelt protected Olympic as a national monument in 1909, and his distant cousin President Franklin D. Roosevelt designated it as a national park in 1938. The United Nations recognized the unique nature of the park and designated it as a World Heritage site in 1981.

US 101 runs north parallel to **Hood Canal** and **Olympic,** providing access to the many valleys that radiate out from the park's center. The eastern half of the park receives around 25 to 30 inches of rain annually, less than a quarter of the rainfall on the west side.

As a result, you'll find fewer ferns, less moss, and far more rhododendrons growing on the east side. In fact, some of the rhododendron bushes grow to enormous size, towering 20 to 30 feet over the forest floor.

They also grow in massive jungles, filling entire valleys. Come spring, these jungles turn vibrant pink when the "rhodies," as locals say, explode into bloom.

1 Staircase Rapids Loop This trail provides the rewarding opportunity to explore a "dry-side" river valley. Just inside the park's southeast boundary, this easy route follows the upper **North Fork Skokomish River** upstream from the **Staircase Campground.**

The trail rolls along the cool eaves of an emerald forest and beside the gin-clear waters of the wild river. Rainbow trout hunt the cold depths of the river pools, devouring insects, which live and breed in the waterways. Overhead, kingfishers, Bald Eagles, and Ospreys are frequently seen as they patiently hunt the trout.

In the woods along the riverbanks, black-tailed deer and large Roosevelt elk graze.

All of these critters, and a slew of smaller species, provide ample

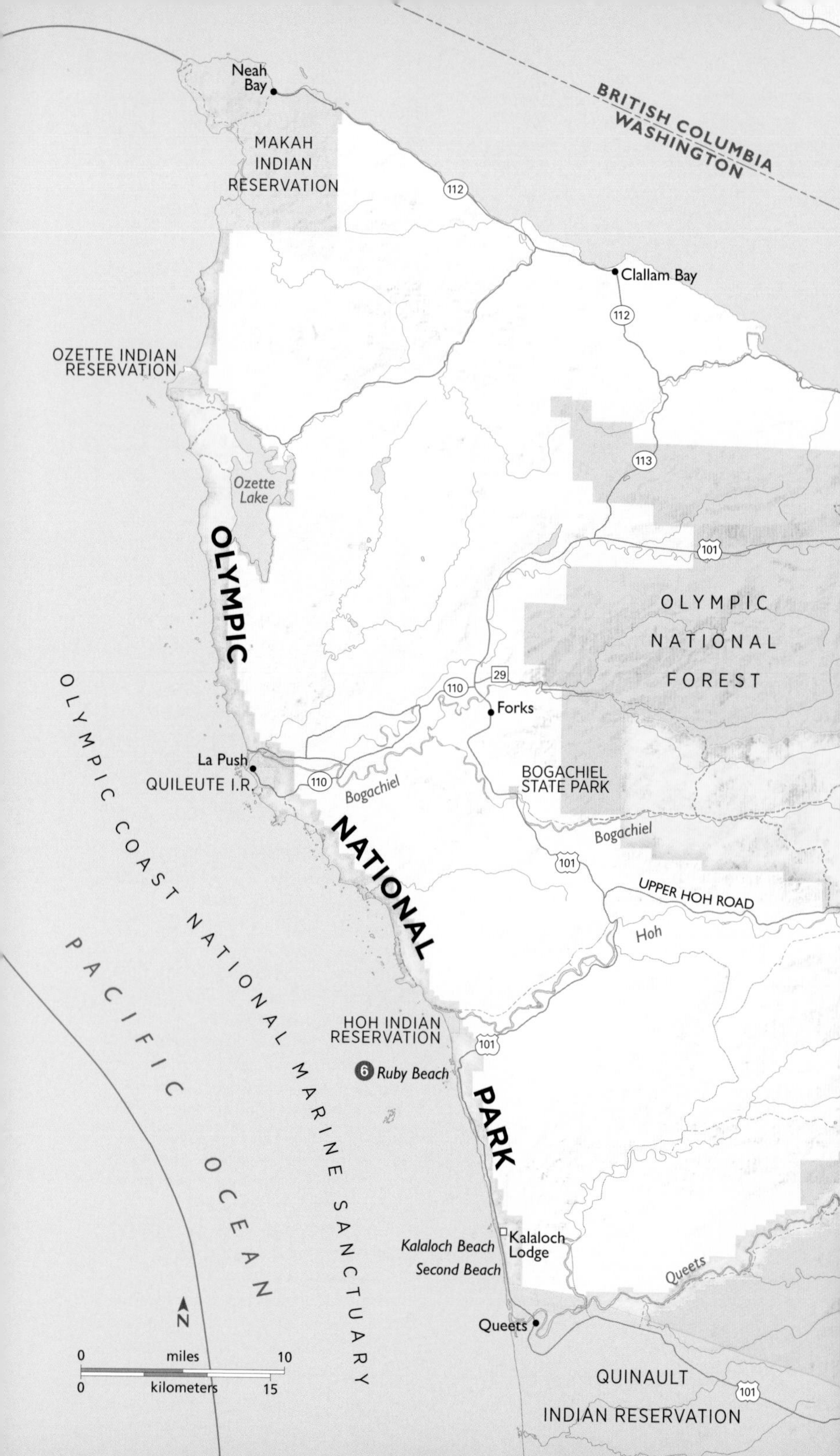
BRITISH COLUMBIA
WASHINGTON
Neah Bay
MAKAH INDIAN RESERVATION
112
Clallam Bay
112
OZETTE INDIAN RESERVATION
113
Ozette Lake
OLYMPIC
101
OLYMPIC NATIONAL FOREST
29
110
Forks
La Push
QUILEUTE I.R.
110
Bogachiel
BOGACHIEL STATE PARK
Bogachiel
NATIONAL
101
UPPER HOH ROAD
Hoh
OLYMPIC COAST NATIONAL MARINE SANCTUARY
PACIFIC OCEAN
HOH INDIAN RESERVATION
101
6 Ruby Beach
PARK
Kalaloch Lodge
Kalaloch Beach
Second Beach
Queets
Queets
N
0 miles 10
0 kilometers 15
QUINAULT INDIAN RESERVATION
101

VANCOUVER ISLAND
14
CANADA
U.S.
Strait of
Juan de Fuca
LOWER ELWHA
KLALLAM
INDIAN RESERVATION
DUNGENESS
N.W.R.
112
112
Port Angeles
Olympic National Park
Visitor Center
Lake
Crescent
101
101
OLYMPIC N.F.
HURRICANE RIDGE
ROAD
KLAHHANE
3 RIDGE
TRAIL
Klahhane Ridge
Sol Duc
Sol Duc Valley 4
Hurricane Hill
5,757 ft
Hurricane Ridge
Visitor Center
Hurricane Ridge
Sol Duc Falls
SOL DUC FALLS
TRAIL
OLYMPIC
N.F.
5 HOH RIVER TRAIL
Hoh
OLYMPIC
Hoh Rain Forest
Visitor Center
Elwha
Dungeness
Mount Olympus
7,965 ft
NATIONAL PARK
Queets
Upper
Lena Lake
Lena
Lake
LENA LAKE
2 TRAIL
HAMMA HAMMA ROAD
N. Fork Skokomish
OLYMPIC
ATIONAL
FOREST
OLYMPIC N.F.
STAIRCASE RAPIDS 1
LOOP
Staircase Campground
Quinault
Lake
Quinault
Lake
Cushman
OLYMPIC NATIONAL FOREST

opportunities for hikers to enjoy a wildlife encounter along this quiet, gentle 3-mile loop.

❷ **Lena Lake Trail** To experience the blooming rhododendron forests, hike the Upper Lena Lake trail in May or early June. The best of the rhodies are found on the trail's lower section.

The path leaves the **Hamma Hamma** road and climbs 1,200 feet through a mix of old-growth and second-growth forest to Lower Lena Lake (3 miles one way).

"I love the climb through the rhody forests into the woodland lake basin," says Robert Moody, senior air quality specialist for Olympic Region Clean Air Agency (ORCAA), which protects the air quality for the Olympic National Park and all the lands surrounding it on the Olympic Peninsula.

The trail starts in the **Olympic National Forest,** as most of the area trails do, and it enters the national park just past Lower Lena Lake. The trail to the upper lake runs another 4 miles into the park, climbing 2,800 feet along the way to the alpine lake above. The entire trail runs 7.3 miles and ascends to 4,500 feet.

Petroglyphs along the park's Pacific coast

The Lena Lake area has a great mix of environments to explore, and enough versatility that it can be a fantastic family hiking destination or a route for hard-core backpackers. It offers something for everyone.

—ROBERT MOODY
senior air quality specialist

▶ Hurricane Ridge Road

To enjoy the high peaks of the Olympics with the least amount of pain, make use of the park's primary roadway: the Hurricane Ridge Road.

Towering over **Port Angeles,** Hurricane Ridge runs parallel to the **Strait of Juan de Fuca,** providing a unique opportunity to enjoy views north and south.

Looking south from the summit of Hurricane Ridge, visitors see the park's central wilderness and the glacier-covered summit of **Mount Olympus.** Turning north provides views across the strait to Victoria, British Columbia, and the interior peaks of Canada's **Vancouver Island.**

Just past the park's visitor center atop Hurricane Ridge, the road ends at the base of **Hurricane Hill.** A short, family-friendly trail leads up the small grade, climbing through brilliant subalpine flower meadows.

Going higher brings better scenery, with magnificent views of the interior Olympics and the valley carved by the mighty **Elwha River** coming into clearer view with each passing footstep.

3 Klahhane Ridge Trail For deeper immersion into the alpine environment, pull off the Hurricane Ridge Road 3 miles below Hurricane Ridge (15 miles from the start of the road in Port Angeles) to find the Klahhane Ridge Trail.

This 5-mile round-trip wild path climbs a series of switchbacks through steep fields of wildflowers before cresting the knife-edged Klahhane Ridge at 6,700 feet. The north face of the ridge drops away in vertical cliffs, while the south slopes down in near-vertical meadows.

Marmots whistle merrily in the meadows, while snowy white mountain goats dance on the cliff faces as you wander past the lupines and other alpine plants. Views north and south are worth the sweat expended to reach the ridge top.

▶ The Rain Forests

The temperate rain forests of the Olympic Peninsula support more biomass per acre of land than any other ecosystem on the planet.

The magnificent old-growth hemlocks, Sitka spruces, and red cedars account for a great deal of that. But the endless layers of moss, lichen, ferns, and other evergreen materials that blanket every surface, usually several feet deep, also make up a significant portion of the biomass total.

All that greenery sprouts from rich soils fed by up to 150 inches of rainfall annually.

Of course, not all living things in the verdant world of the Olympic rain forests grow out of the soil. Vast herds of Roosevelt elk (the largest unmanaged herd in the Pacific Northwest, see sidebar p. 189) call the cathedral

Temperate Hoh Rain Forest

Sol Duc Falls

forests home. If you're traveling here in September, listen for the bugling to locate them, but *beware, they are dangerous, so keep stay your distance.*

Small black-tailed deer also roam these woods, as do mountain lions, which are the one large predator left to hunt the ungulates.

4 Sol Duc Valley To experience the broadest range of beauty found in the rain forests, venture up the Sol Duc Valley from the **Lake Crescent** area of US 101 (which partially circles the park, following the east, north, and west sides).

The **Sol Duc Falls Trail** pierces a magnificent old-growth forest alongside the **Sol Duc River.**

The path leads to one of the most scenic waterfalls in the Olympics—a low, thundering cascade that drops into a narrow gorge. The falls make a great destination for a 1.8-mile round-trip walk.

5 Hoh River Trail The iconic rain forest hike, however, starts just a few miles south on US 101. The Hoh River Trail leads deep into the heart of the ethereal rain forest.

Enjoy a walk of just a few hundred yards, or push up to the very shoulders of **Mount Olympus** (10 miles one way). Regardless of the length of the adventure, the Hoh River Trail

Local Intelligence

President Theodore Roosevelt protected what is now Olympic National Park in 1909 with national monument status primarily because he wanted to ensure the survival of a unique species of elk found primarily in the rain forest valleys on the west side of the park. By 1912, the elk numbers on the Olympic Peninsula had dwindled to fewer than 150 animals. The national monument (and later national park) designation kept hunters from taking those last few animals. Today, the elk thrive and rightfully bear the name of their protector—Roosevelt elk are the largest species of elk, perhaps because of their ready access to rich and plentiful food sources. They graze on the lichens, ferns, and shrubs from the rain forest as well as meadow grasses that blanket the valleys.

provides an unforgettable experience in a valley that defines temperate rain forests. The entire valley plays host to massive old-growth western red cedar, Douglas fir, bigleaf maple, and Sitka spruce.

▶ The Coast

Olympic's coastal strand includes more than 60 miles of wilderness beach, though in truth, it's not exactly what most people think beaches should look like. The Pacific Ocean does roll up on some sandy strips, but most of the park's coastline boasts stretches of rocky strands separated by jagged headlands. Just offshore from these cobblestone beaches rise an array of "sea stacks"—rocky remnants of the former coastline before the tides carved it away. Generally speaking, the north end is rocky and the sea stacks are to the south.

The rocky knobs rising from the surf tend to be popular hangouts for seabirds such as Rhinoceros Auklets, Tufted Puffins, and Brown Pelicans, as well as for marine mammals like seals and sea lions.

Occasionally, black bears will venture out of the coastal forests to wade or swim over to the close-in sea stacks at low tide to hunt for young birds and sea mammals.

❻ **Ruby Beach** Though some of the more remote sections of Olympic provide the best wilderness experiences, they can be hard to reach.

To get a great taste of the park's wild beaches and the powerful Pacific that grinds them down, drop into Ruby Beach in the **Kalaloch Lodge** area off US 101. The lodge provides great overnight accommodations in the main building itself or in a number of small cabins dotting the bluffs above **Kalaloch Beach.**

Ruby Beach has a mix of sand and smooth cobble-like stones, with a heavy layer of driftwood at the foot of the bluffs.

Sea stars

Snow-covered Wizard Island

CRATER LAKE

Imagine a giant thumb pressing down on the top of a 12,000-foot-high volcano, pushing the cone into itself until the top 5,000 feet are gone, leaving a giant basin inside the rim of the collapsed volcano. That's essentially what happened to Mount Mazama in southern Oregon as the force of gravity pushed the mountaintop down into itself. Then, about 7,700 years ago, a final massive eruption—42 times greater than Mount Saint Helens's belch in 1980—emptied the magma chamber, leaving a huge void. The mountain basically imploded, collapsing in on itself to form a vast cliff-lined basin. Over the centuries, winter snow averaging 524 inches per year flowed into the caldera, and with no outlet to drain the water, Crater Lake was born. Today, it averages 1,500 feet deep, with a maximum depth of 1,932 feet—the deepest in the United States. What lies below is a mystery, but aboveground there are a slew of secrets to be found.

Year-Round Visitor Center

- **Steel Visitor Center and Park Headquarters**
  4 miles north of Oreg. 62, south of Rim Visitor Center

Seasonal Visitor Center

- **Rim Visitor Center**
  Off West Rim Drive, Rim Village

541-594-3000, *www.nps.gov/crla*

▶ Wizard Island

Early on, **Mount Mazama** tried to return to its towering height. A cinder cone grew out of red hot cinders ejected from the caldera floor, rising more than 2,000 feet—but then the mountain lost its power.

Scientists say there has been no volcanic activity around Crater Lake for more than 5,000 years.

The cinder cone peak within the mountain stands today as lonely Wizard Island, so named for its resemblance to a sorcerer's hat.

The top of the cinder cone rises 767 feet above Crater Lake's surface. If you want a closer look, the island can be reached by boats operated by park concessionaires.

▶ Mazama Village and Rim Village Area

The road linking two small villages and service centers on the south side of the park provides some of the park's best scenery away from the lake itself.

The 7 miles from Mazama Village to Rim Village exposes you to the region's dry pine forest ecology, with some wonderful wildflower meadows tossed in for good measure.

Before you start your exploration, do take the time to stroll from Rim Village to the **Sinnott Memorial Overlook** for a glance at the color, purity, and depth of Crater Lake.

Dave Grimes, park interpretive ranger, also notes that the Rim Village area makes a great destination for winter recreation enthusiasts, with ranger-led snowshoe trips and opportunities for cross-country skiing and self-guided snowshoeing adventures.

1 Godfrey Glen Step out of the car at Godfrey Glen to walk a gentle 1-mile loop trail through a spectacular stand of old-growth mountain hemlocks and Shasta red fir. The trail skirts alongside beautiful **Annie Creek Canyon** and the tumbling **Duwee Falls.**

Deer, grouse, and rabbits commonly appear here; elk, foxes, porcupines, badgers, and owls also inhabit this emerald forest, although they are

230
N
0 miles 4
0 kilometers 6
ROGUE RIVER-SISKIYOU NATIONAL FOREST
PUMICE DESERT
PACIFIC CREST N.S.T.
CRATER LAKE
Red Cone 7,363 ft
5
Red Cone Spring
4 CLEETWOOD COVE TRAIL
RIM DRIVE
PACIFIC CREST N.S.T.
The Watchman 8,013 ft
Crater Lake
Wizard Island
RIM DRIVE
Rim Village Visitor Center (summer only)
Sinnott Memorial Overlook
RIM DRIVE
62
Steel Visitor Center Park Headquarters
CASTLE CREST WILDFLOWER TRAIL
2
1 GODFREY GLEN TRAIL
Munson Creek
Mazama Village
Duwee Falls
NATIONAL PARK
62
ROGUE RIVER-SISKIYOU NATIONAL FOREST
Annie Creek
PACIFIC CREST N.S.T.
SKY LAKES WILDERNESS
FREMONT-WINEMA NATIONAL FOREST

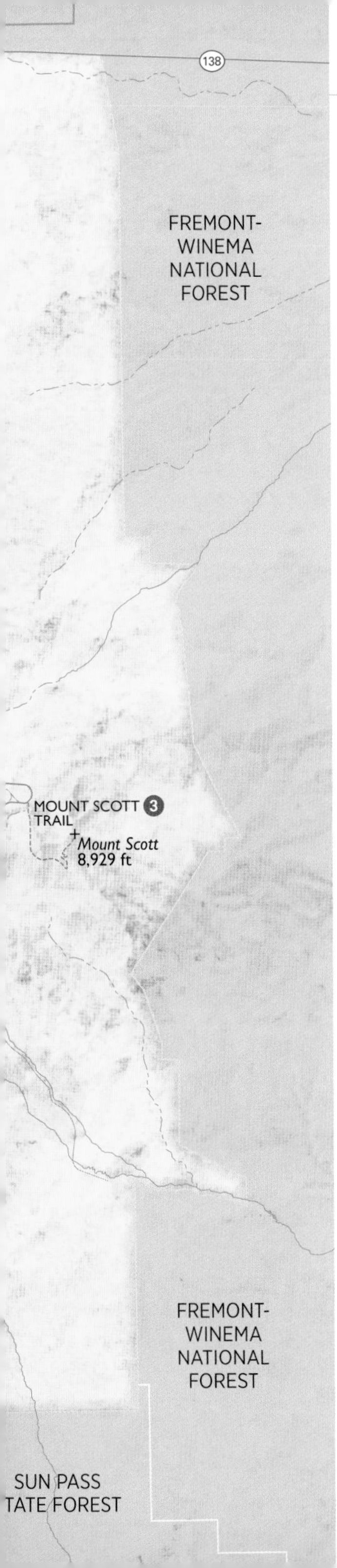

138

FREMONT-WINEMA NATIONAL FOREST

MOUNT SCOTT 3 TRAIL

Mount Scott 8,929 ft

FREMONT-WINEMA NATIONAL FOREST

SUN PASS TATE FOREST

seen less frequently. The trail does roll over a few low rises and ridgelines, but the well-maintained tread makes walking relatively easy.

2 Castle Crest Wildflower Trail
Wildflowers can be found in July and August along this trail near park headquarters, midway between the two villages.

Thriving summer fireweed

The route weaves along a path through a thin subalpine forest and broad wildflower meadows, and alongside **Munson Creek.** The best time to hike this short, exquisite trail is mid- to late summer, when the vast array of wildflower species erupts in a spectrum of colors.

▶ Rim Drive

Because of the park's position high in the Cascade Range, winter comes early and lingers long, meaning most

Wizard Island free of its snowy veil

of the park's roads, such as Rim Drive, aren't free of snow until late June or early July, and they start gathering new snows in late October. *Note: East Rim Dive is not recommended for trailers.*

Rim Drive circles the lake. At least 19 times the road approaches the edge to provide glorious views of the water from a variety of overlooks.

But to truly experience the majesty of the lake's beauty, you should take to your feet and hike up.

3 Mount Scott Trail Views of the full grandeur of Crater Lake require a climb to a high viewpoint, and the Mount Scott Trail provides just such a challenge.

The 8,929-foot mountain to the east of East Rim Drive holds an old fire lookout tower and provides stunning views west across the breadth of the lake.

The 2.5-mile trail climbs steeply at times, but the route pierces fragrant pine forests and wildflower meadows before reaching the summit. Visitors who get an early start will appreciate the morning light as it illuminates all the coves and creases around the lake.

The best secret hike in the park, though, climbs a peak across the lake from Mount Scott. Dave Grimes, interpretive ranger, says: "I think the **Watchman** offers the best of the park in one trail." It is only moderately steep, climbing just 420 feet in 0.8 mile (one way).

4 Cleetwood Cove Trail The Cleetwood Cove Trail goes down 1 mile from the rim to the lakeshore along a modest grade carved into the wooded slopes of the northern edge of the caldera. Descending this switchbacking trail is fairly easy, but the return hike to the trailhead can be a real sweat producer. Warning: Anyone venturing down the trail must be fit enough to come back up under their own power.

The trail ends at a boat dock. A park concessionaire operates a motor launch here that provides tours of the lake—some stop at Wizard Island.

Local Intelligence

The vast depth of Crater Lake is truly impressive, as is the total lake volume—more than 5 trillion gallons of water. It's the quality of that water, though, that truly astounds.

The inky blue liquid is among the clearest lake water on the planet. The test for water clarity involves lowering a black and white disk into the lake and recording the depth at which the disk is no longer visible from the surface. In Crater Lake, a disk was once submerged more than 143 feet before it was lost from sight, and the average clarity of the lake approaches 115 feet. In comparison, Lake Tahoe—another remarkable deep, pristine lake in North America—boasts a clarity level of just 70 feet on average.

▶ Northern Access

The road heading north away from Rim Drive leads through forests of lodgepole pines and open meadows.

Most impressive are the broad fields of feather-light rocks in the **Pumice Desert.** This expanse of volcanic debris is a product of the eruption of 7,700 years ago that blasted pumice across this northern plain, creating a deposit nearly 200 feet thick. The porous rock and sand lack nutrients to support life, so the desert remains mostly barren, with just a few tough grasses sprouting from the field of gray stone.

At the top of Watchman, you'll be directly above Wizard Island, and along the way you can experience a great variety of plant and animal life. It's truly the best place to really take in the full beauty of the park.

—DAVE GRIMES
Crater Lake interpretive ranger

5 Pacific Crest Trail The northern blast zone can be explored on foot by walking west on the Pacific Crest Trail from where it crosses the road, 2 miles north of the Rim Drive junction.

The trail touches on a pumice-rich lava bed before skirting the flank of **Red Cone**—a 7,363-foot cinder cone—where the low, scraggy vegetation along the early section of trail turns into lodgepole pine and full forest. With virtually no elevation gain along the route, you can hike the 3.8 miles to **Red Cone Springs camp** in the morning, eat lunch beside the spring, then walk out refreshed.

Pumice Desert, north of Rim Road Drive

A tagged Northern Spotted Owl among the redwoods

REDWOOD

At least some of what makes Redwood National and State Parks famous can easily be seen from a highway. That may not be entirely a good thing, though. US 101 passes through the northern California park for miles, in places winding among dense groves of tall coast redwoods, the awe-inspiring tree species (the world's tallest) for which the area is named. Many times, a driver pulls over, the family hops out to stare upward and take a few photos, and the trip continues north to Oregon or south to San Francisco.

That hypothetical family may have seen some redwoods, but it certainly did not see the park or its secrets. Redwood National and State Parks—as its name indicates, the park is managed jointly by the National Park Service and California State Parks—is composed of several alluring sections, stretching more than 65 miles along the California coast.

Year-Round Visitor Centers

- **Crescent City Information Center**
  1111 Second Street, Crescent City
- **Thomas H. Kuchel Visitor Center**
  On US 101, Orick

Seasonal Visitor Centers

- **Prairie Creek Visitor Center**
  Off US 101, along Newton B. Drury Scenic Parkway
- **Hiouchi Information Center**
  On US 199, Hiouchi
- **Jedediah Smith Visitor Center**
  On US 199, Redwoods State Park, Hiouchi

707-465-7335, *www.nps.gov/redw*

▶ Southern Park

Entering the park from the south, stop at the **Thomas H. Kuchel Visitor Center** north of US 101 for maps and advice. (There are four other visitor centers, some closed seasonally.) If driving a recreational vehicle or pulling a trailer, ask which park roads are not recommended for large vehicles.

Continue 3.5 miles, turn right on **Bald Hills Road,** and drive 2.5 miles to the **Lady Bird Johnson Grove Trail.** Extremely popular, this hike demands a visit even from those seeking off-the-beaten-path experiences. Short and easy (1 mile), it's also an introduction to old-growth redwood forest. In spring, rhododendrons and azaleas bloom among Douglas fir and tan oak.

❶ Lyons Ranch Trail To reach one of park staffer Debbie Savage's favorite spots, continue on Bald Hills Road another 15 miles.

Stop at the **Redwood Creek Overlook** for a vista of not only the creek watershed, but, on a clear day, the Pacific Ocean 6 miles to the west.

While watching for Roosevelt elk, continue to the start of the Lyons Ranch Trail, in an oak-and-grassland environment different from the rest of the park.

"There's a good view of the ocean and fields of wildflowers in early spring," Savage says. "The 2-mile trail follows an old dirt road that leads to a barn used by sheep ranchers in the early 1900s. It takes some time to drive to the trailhead [for Lyons Ranch], as the road is rough and winding, but the view is worth it."

❷ Newton B. Drury Scenic Parkway Back on US 101, it's about 3 miles north to this 10-mile paved road, which is the best off-highway choice for RVs, and leads to some of the park's most visited attractions. The **Big Tree Wayside** (named for a redwood thought to be more than 1,500 years old) is a must.

Ted Humphry, a park volunteer,

LAKE EARL STATE WILDLIFE AREA
Lake Earl
WALKER ROAD
Smith
197
101
199
Simpson-Reed Grove
8
Middle Fork Smith
SMITH RIVER N.R.A.
TOLOWA DUNES STATE PARK
Jedediah Smith Visitor Center
Hiouchi Information Center
South Fork Smith
Hiouchi
Point St. George
Stout Grove
JEDEDIAH SMITH REDWOODS STATE PARK
SIX RIVERS NATIONAL FOREST
Crescent City
Castle Rock
7
NICKERSON RANCH TRAIL
HOWLAND HILL ROAD
Crescent City Information Center
REDWOOD
East Fork Mill Cr.
West Branch Mill Cr.
6
Enderts Beach
DEL NORTE COAST REDWOODS STATE PARK
COAST RANGE
5
DAMNATION CREEK TRAIL
NATIONAL
False Klamath Cove
Lagoon Creek Picnic Area
False Klamath Rock
4
Hidden Beach
Trees of Mystery
PACIFIC OCEAN
3
Klamath River Overlook
YUROK INDIAN RESERVATION
Klamath
PARK
N
0 miles 4
0 kilometers 6
PRAIRIE CREEK REDWOODS STATE PARK

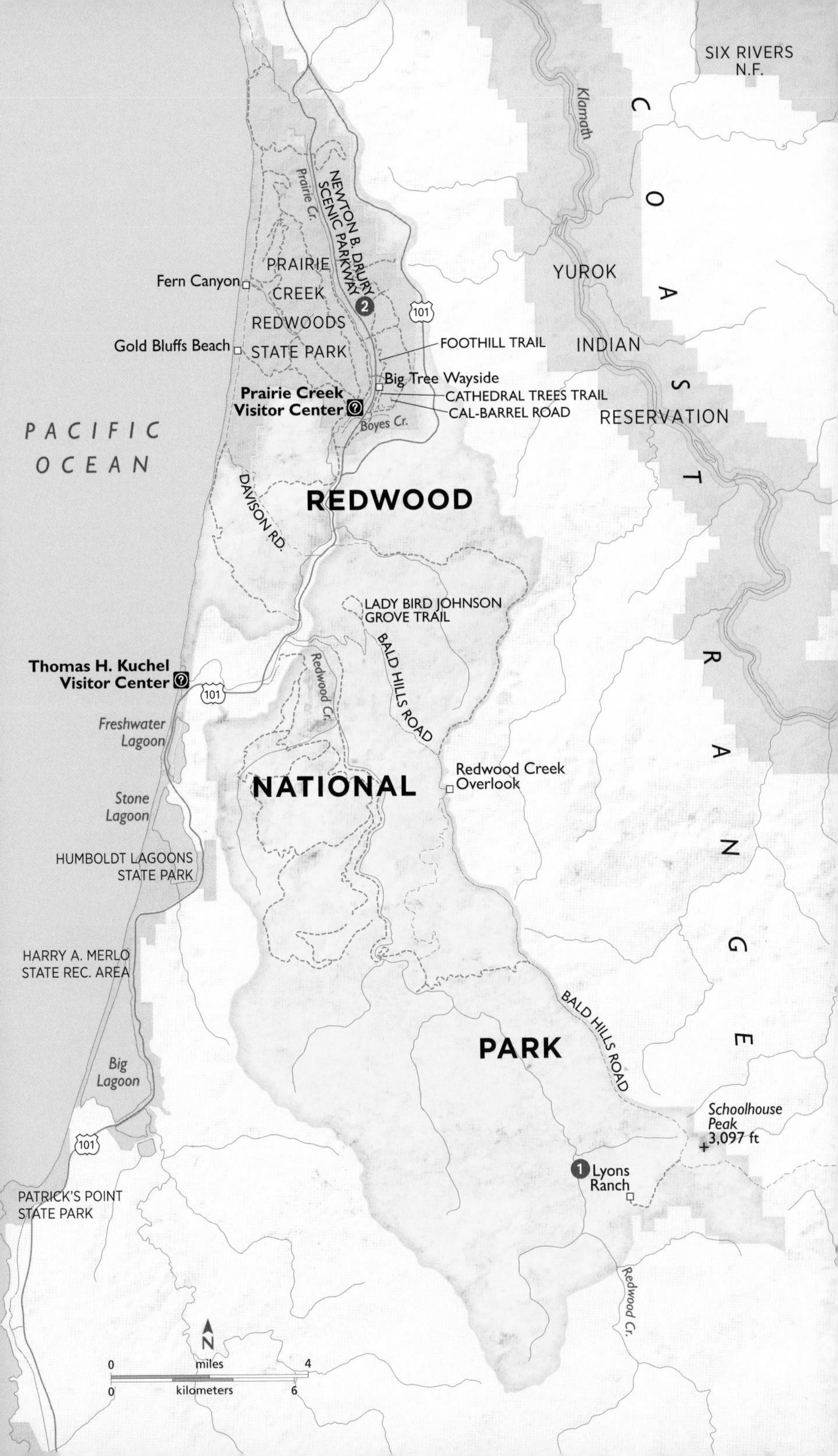

SIX RIVERS N.F.
Klamath
COAST RANGE
YUROK INDIAN RESERVATION
NEWTON B. DRURY SCENIC PARKWAY
Prairie Cr.
PRAIRIE CREEK REDWOODS STATE PARK
Fern Canyon
Gold Bluffs Beach
101
FOOTHILL TRAIL
Big Tree Wayside
CATHEDRAL TREES TRAIL
CAL-BARREL ROAD
Prairie Creek Visitor Center
Boyes Cr.
PACIFIC OCEAN
DAVISON RD.
REDWOOD
LADY BIRD JOHNSON GROVE TRAIL
BALD HILLS ROAD
Thomas H. Kuchel Visitor Center
Redwood Cr.
Freshwater Lagoon
Stone Lagoon
NATIONAL
Redwood Creek Overlook
HUMBOLDT LAGOONS STATE PARK
HARRY A. MERLO STATE REC. AREA
PARK
Big Lagoon
Schoolhouse Peak 3,097 ft
Lyons Ranch
PATRICK'S POINT STATE PARK
N
0 miles 4
0 kilometers 6

enjoys a 2.2-mile loop walk made up of the **Cathedral Trees** and **Foothill Trails.** "Visitors see different redwood forests, from the big valley-floor trees along Foothill, to the smaller redwoods on the Cathedral hillside, to the big bays and maples and alders along Boyes Creek at the transition from forest to prairie."

While you're in this area, don't miss a drive down **Davison Road** (keep your eyes open for elk) to the lovely **Gold Bluffs Beach,** and a take a walk into **Fern Canyon,** where lush green walls rise 50 feet over a small stream.

Also consider the short but very scenic **Cal-Barrel Road,** running east from Drury Scenic Parkway. Winding and unpaved, the road passes among huge redwoods; turnouts offer the chance to park your vehicle and walk among the giant trees for minutes or hours of quiet contemplation.

▶ Northern Park

Aside from the redwoods—certainly worth a trip in themselves—the park includes unspoiled beaches, grassland, beautiful streams, and mixed evergreen forests of Douglas fir, Sitka spruce, and western hemlock.

As staff members like to say, Redwood is "more than tall trees," and the park's "more" includes hiking, beachcombing, and whale-watching, many of which are highlights of the northern part of Redwood.

3 Klamath River Overlook About 3 miles north of the Klamath River bridge on US 101, turn west for the short side trip to this spot, with its viewing platform above the Pacific.

"On a calm summer day you can view the mouth of the Klamath as it meets the ocean," Savage says. "This is a place to watch Bald Eagles, Ospreys, California sea lions swimming in the surf, and gray whales as they migrate up and down the coast between Alaska and Baja California."

4 Hidden Beach Over the next 8 miles of US 101 you'll reach access points for two short hikes recommended by Humphry: "A favorite easy walk is from **Trees of Mystery** or **Lagoon Creek Picnic Area** to Hidden Beach. From the Lagoon Creek approach, you also view the **False Klamath Rock** rookery in spring and summer," hosting seabirds and sea lions.

Hiking in Fern Canyon

Local Intelligence

Time your trip: Many locals believe September and October are the best months to visit **Redwood National and State Parks.** Not only do the summer months have more vacationers, but the coastal areas of the park then are often foggy and chilly (though sites inland a few miles are sunnier). Also, it rains a lot from November through April. May and June, though, are best for seeing wildflowers and blooming shrubs such as rhododendron.

Hidden Beach is a beautiful, isolated small cove with driftwood, a sandy beach, and some tide pools at low tide. I'm often the only one there.

—TED HUMPHRY
Redwood National Park volunteer

5 Damnation Creek Trail Secret recommendations from Humphry include the strenuous 4.2-mile out-and-back Damnation Creek Trail (park at milepost 16 on US 101).

"This hike goes through all the different forest types from deep redwood on the upper trail into Douglas fir and tan oak into Sitka spruce and alder and bay, ending in a very small, private rocky inlet of the Pacific Ocean at the bottom," he says. The trail descends and ascends 1,000 feet between the highway and the ocean.

6 Enderts Beach Road Check the schedule for low tide and visit Enderts Beach, off US 101 just south of **Crescent City.** Explore the rocks of the intertidal zone for a staggering array of sea stars, sea anemones, crabs, chitons, barnacles, and other life-forms in an environment that rivals a rain forest in its diversity.

7 Howland Hill Road East of Crescent City is one of the park's true secret gems: Howland Hill Road, a winding, unpaved route through redwood groves *(not recommended for large vehicles).* For persons with limited mobility, this is an opportunity to drive through a wonderful forest landscape away from the better known park scenic drives.

For hikers, Savage recommends the fairly easy, 1-mile **Nickerson Ranch Trail,** off Howland Hill Road. Aside from the redwoods, she likes this loop "because it follows **Mill Creek,** which provides a sunny corridor lined with a diversity of plants and habitats for a variety of birds."

Continuing east on Howland Hill brings you to **Stout Grove,** arguably the most beautiful grove of redwoods in the park, with a flat, 0.5-mile trail. The open aspect here makes the trees easier to see than at most areas.

8 Simpson-Reed Grove Michael Poole, park staff member, calls the nearby Simpson-Reed Grove "my favorite of all the short redwood walks." It is reached by turning north on Walker Road off US 199 between Crescent City and Hiouchi.

"I like that Simpson-Reed is a more complete-looking old-growth forest," Poole says. "Not only are there redwoods, but I like to tell people to look for the nurse logs [fallen, decaying trunks that serve as habitat for saplings], as well. They are everywhere, with nice big trees growing on them."

The Milky Way from Olmsted Point

YOSEMITE

"Into this one mountain mansion," wrote Yosemite's great bard and advocate John Muir, "nature had gathered her choicest treasures, to draw her lovers into close and confiding communion." In light of the California park's visitation statistics, Muir's eloquence can sound ironic—more than four million visitors a year make the pilgrimage to the park, and the communion can seem too close and confiding. Still, the majesty and ultimate spaciousness of Yosemite override its occasional crowds and protect its secrets. The granite cathedrals still soar above the valley, the Sierra peaks rise even higher, and waterfalls fill the air with the sound of liquid thunder, no matter how many people are there to witness it.

It's easy to avoid too-close communion if you go at the right time. July and August see more than twice as many visitors as the months of May and October—and dawn is almost exclusively yours anywhere in the park.

Year-Round Visitor Center

- **Yosemite Valley Visitor Center**
  Yosemite Village, Arch Rock Entrance

Seasonal Visitor Centers

- **Tuolumne Meadows Visitor Center**
  Tioga Road, Tioga Pass Entrance
- **Wawona Visitor Center**
  Calif. 41, South Entrance off Wawona Road
- **Nature Center at Happy Isles**
  Yosemite Valley, next to the Happy Isles shuttle bus stop

209-372-0200, *www.nps.gov/yose*

▶ Yosemite Valley

Many equate Yosemite Valley with Yosemite National Park, yet the 7-mile-long valley represents just 3 percent of the park's total land area. Still, the valley does pack in the park's most fabled sights and is rightly its center stage. Using the valley's free shuttle service and avoiding popular sights at peak hours during peak months are the best ways to avoid feeling crowded in the valley.

❶ **Valley Floor Loop** The great secret of Yosemite Valley is the hidden-in-plain-sight Valley Floor Loop.

It sounds almost too good to be true: The 13-mile hiking trail (no bikes allowed) circles the valley and links such major sights as **Yosemite Falls, El Capitan,** and **Bridalveil Fall**—yet it sees very little foot traffic.

Using the park shuttle at its two stops along the way—**El Capitan Bridge** and the **Four Mile Trail** trailhead—allows you to hike half the loop or even less. But doing the full distance is surprisingly easy, as the trail is virtually flat, with just a few rises.

As you walk, you can fancy yourself a sojourner in Muir's day, experiencing the beauty of Yosemite in solitary splendor.

"The trail was very popular until 1997," says park ranger Kari Cobb, "when a flood washed away the pavement, and people kind of forgot about it."

Remnants of the pavement remain, but most of the trail is dirt. And although you can hear the sound of cars and shuttles on the valley roads much of the time, you're too enthralled with the woods, meadows, waterfalls, and cliffs to pay the noise much attention.

Start at Yosemite Falls, shuttle stop No. 6; look for the sign for **Upper Yosemite Fall** and **Camp 4;** and proceed walking west. You're quickly in

STANISLAUS NATIONAL FOREST
EMIGRANT WILDERNESS
HOOVER WILDERNESS
SIERRA
Cherry Lake
Lake Eleanor
Hetch Hetchy Reservoir
Grand Canyon of the Tuolumne River
Tuolumne
TUOLUMNE NATIONAL WILD & SCENIC RIVER
YOSEMITE
Tuolumne
Lukens Lake 10
TIOGA RD.
NATIONAL PARK
120
120
120
Tenaya Lake 12
Olmsted Point
Yosemite Valley Visitor Center
SNOW CREEK TRAIL
Tenaya Cr.
Tenaya Canyon
Clouds Rest
1 VALLEY FLOOR LOOP
El Capitan 7,569 ft
Yosemite Falls
Ahwahnee
Mirror Lake 3
Half Dome
Merced
Crane Flat
Ribbon Fall
Pohono Bridge
Yosemite Valley
Glacier Point
Nevada Fall
Vernal Fall
STANISLAUS NATIONAL FOREST
WAWONA TUNNEL
Inspiration Point
2 Tunnel View
Bridalveil Fall
Bridalveil Cr.
Taft Point 8
Sentinel Dome 7
Mt. Starr King 9,092 ft
Arch Rock Entrance
Merced
140
GLACIER POINT ROAD
Mono Meadow 9
MERCED NATIONAL WILD & SCENIC RIVER
South Fork Merced
SIERRA NATIONAL FOREST
CHILNUALNA FALLS ROAD
Chilnualna Fall 6
Wawona Dome
N
Wawona Visitor Center
Wawona Hotel
Wawona
Mariposa Grove Museum
0 miles 10
0 kilometers 15
5 Wawona Meadow
41
Wawona Point 6,810 ft
South Entrance
Tunnel Tree
Grizzly Giant
Mariposa Grove 4

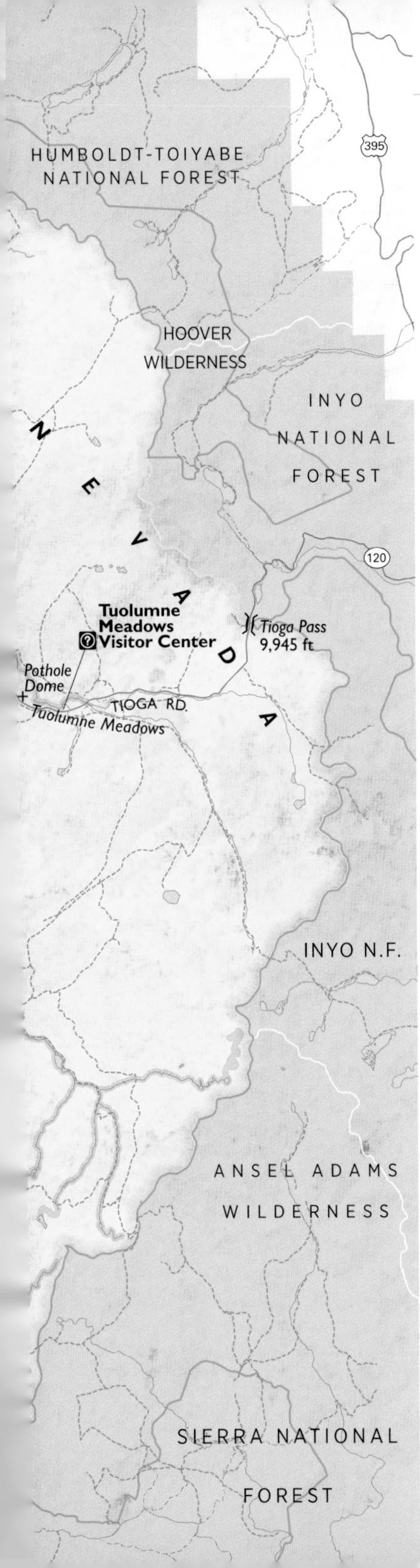

HUMBOLDT-TOIYABE NATIONAL FOREST
395
HOOVER WILDERNESS
INYO NATIONAL FOREST
NEVADA
120
Tuolumne Meadows Visitor Center
Tioga Pass 9,945 ft
Pothole Dome
TIOGA RD.
Tuolumne Meadows
INYO N.F.
ANSEL ADAMS WILDERNESS
SIERRA NATIONAL FOREST

a magic world of boulders and sheer cliffs, and it becomes obvious why the walk-in Camp 4 is known as the climbers' camp.

The trail proceeds west and occasionally crosses the park road, but that's a good thing—it puts you out into lovely **El Capitan Meadow** and skirts the north bank of the **Merced River,** sights that are hidden from the park road by trees. That's the beauty of this hike: You see the whole valley, not just its highlights.

After El Capitan, the trail crosses the Merced River on **Pohono Bridge** and passes by Bridalveil Fall. If Bridalveil Creek is flowing high, you might need to hike up to the road to cross it.

The trail then climbs a bit, opening onto great views of El Capitan Meadow and the monolith itself, as well as **Ribbon Fall** right next door to El Cap. After a long, quiet stretch in the woods, it passes by the backside of lovely **Yosemite Chapel,** where you can cross **Sentinel Bridge** to return to your starting point—or, if you're

A brown bear

Half Dome

staying in **Curry Village** or one of the campgrounds, you can extend your walk another couple of miles.

2 Above Tunnel View Back to the west toward the park entrance, it was the glorious vista from Tunnel View that inspired photographer Ansel Adams—as it has about 50 million other shutterbugs. Visitors stop where the park road emerges from **Wawona Tunnel,** and suddenly they see much of the grandeur of Yosemite Valley—El Capitan, Clouds Rest, Half Dome, Bridalveil Fall, and Cathedral Rocks.

But it's hard to feel like Ansel when you're sharing the view with a few hundred other excited travelers. The solution: Park in (or walk to) the upper parking lot and the trailhead for the route to **Inspiration Point.**

The full hike is 1.2 miles, but you don't have to go far up the steep trail to secure a view all your own, high above the parking lot mob.

3 Mirror Lake and Beyond To the east of Yosemite Village, Mirror Lake is a placid stretch of **Tenaya Creek** that serves as a looking glass for Half Dome. It's not a park secret—the walk up is a very popular paved trail—but doing this 2-mile round-trip hike early in the morning or late in the afternoon means fewer people and prettier light for a beauty shot of Half Dome's reflection.

Take the park shuttle to the trailhead and make the gently climbing walk to the lake, but don't stop there. A dirt (intermittently paved) trail continues east along Tenaya Creek. The secret? Follow it, and very quickly you're in your own world. It's the quietest easy hike in Yosemite Valley.

The trail used to continue around Tenaya Canyon, but a rockfall sealed it off several miles up the path.

If you're feeling ambitious, though, hike as far as the junction with **Snow Creek Trail** (another 1.5 miles, basically flat) and proceed up a few switchbacks on a very steep trail. You soon get a dramatic view of Tenaya Canyon and an angle on **Half Dome** that few people see.

▶ Wawona

The sights around Wawona, near the southern entrance, may not be as fabled as those in the valley (an hour's drive north), but that's precisely why you should allot some time here.

Generally much quieter than Yosemite Valley, its accommodations are likely to be less crowded. Wawona is home to the classic, Victorian-style **Wawona Hotel**—a far less expensive alternative to the park's hostelry, the **Ahwahnee**—a campground, and some rental cabins that are privately owned.

The beauty of Yosemite catches my breath every time I walk out my front door. I can't think of a better place to live and work, This really is a special place that touches a lot of people. It inspires the world.

—DON NEUBACHER
Superintendent, Yosemite National Park

4 Mariposa Grove and Wawona Point You don't have to go to Sequoia National Park to see giant sequoias. Yosemite's Mariposa Grove has some 500 specimens of some of the tallest living things on Earth.

The road (closed in winter) to the grove takes off from the park's southern entrance station. But be warned: The parking lot fills up. Either go early, go late, or take the free shuttle from the **Wawona Store** or the **South Entrance.**

Local Intelligence

Although encounters between bears and humans are much less frequent than they used to be in Yosemite—thanks to visitor education and the strategic placement of food-storage lockers—somewhere between 300 and 500 bears still live in the park and meeting bears is possible.

"We have only black bears; no grizzlies," says Kari Cobb, park ranger. "Black bears are more scavengers than predators." Meaning that Yosemite bears prefer to patrol campgrounds looking for half-open food lockers—they'll enter a site even when people are present—and sniff cars for the presence of food. That includes canned food. The park requires that all food and anything scented (shampoo, bug spray) be stored in lockers at night.

If you encounter a bear, or any animal in the park, Cobb says, most will simply walk away. If you inadvertently find yourself close to a bear, make some noise and perhaps throw a pinecone.

And what if you want to see a bear? "Try any meadow in the park around sunset," says Cobb. Just keep your distance.

A deer in a wildflower field

Then be sure to proceed past the closest trees. One called the **Grizzly Giant** is 0.8 mile, and the **California Tunnel Tree** is nearby.

Keep going another mile to the Upper Grove, where the crowds thin out and you get beyond the reach of the tram tour.

You'll see many more giants as you crest the hill, just before you reach the **Mariposa Grove Museum,** which interprets the life of these amazing trees. More giant sequoias stand on the hill above the museum. If your climbing muscles feel strong, continue by trail to Wawona Point (elevation 6,810 feet) for a dizzying view of Wawona Meadow and **Wawona Dome.** If you return via the **Outer Loop Trail,** you won't have to retrace your steps on the 3-mile hike back down.

5 Wawona Meadow Here's another hidden-in-plain-sight Yosemite walk. The golf course across the road from the Wawona Hotel is obvious, but what isn't obvious is the trail that encircles it and proceeds all the way around Wawona Meadow.

"It's a nice evening stroll with a glass of wine in your hand," says Cobb—although the full loop is 3.5 miles, so you might want to bring a water bottle as well.

Early on you get some nice views across the golf course to the hotel, but soon you leave civilization behind and it becomes a solitary walk in the woods—just you, scads of birds, and the odd mule deer.

Occasionally the trees open up to reveal the wildflower-strewn meadow, especially at the far end of the loop, where you'll be glad you decided to go all the way.

6 Chilnualna Fall The full hike to Chilnualna Fall is a challenging one—4.1 miles one way, 2,400 feet of gain. But don't write this one off due to lack of time or ambition; a mini version of the hike is less than 0.5-mile round-trip.

The road to the trailhead, **Chilnualna Falls Road,** is just off Wawona Road north of the hotel. It leads 2 winding miles through a residential section of Wawona.

The hike up takes only about 15 minutes, yet you still get the rush of standing face-to-face with a roaring cascade that would be a major attraction if it were in Yosemite Valley. In Wawona, the secret is all yours.

▶ Glacier Point Road

Glacier Point, at the end of Glacier Point Road (closed in winter), is one of Yosemite's must-see wonders—the overlook is perched 3,000 sheer feet above the floor of Yosemite Valley and the views down and across are amazing.

You get a great look at both **Upper** and **Lower Yosemite Falls, Vernal** and **Nevada Falls, Half Dome,** and **High Sierra peaks** in the distance.

If you just hop out of your car, have a look from the nearest viewpoint, and be on your way, you might miss the actual Glacier Point. It requires a short walk downhill past the geology exhibit to another viewing platform, from which you can see a distinctive overhanging slab.

Though it gives most people shudders to imagine walking out on this overhang, many famous old photos depict people posing on it, including a trio of can-can dancers.

Once you've had your fill, head back on Glacier Point Road and stop at some of the other, equally compelling attractions along the way. You'll find far less company at each of them.

7 Sentinel Dome Most of us won't reach the top of Half Dome, but the 1.1-mile hike to the apex of Sentinel Dome serves up a stellar view for somewhat less effort.

You see the backside of the dome as you approach, and it looks steep, but the trail winds around the huge granite mound to a much easier approach.

The slope is still somewhat challenging, but remember, this is Yosemite granite; the traction is superb. And so is the view from the top—the valley, Half Dome, Upper Yosemite Fall (which you can hear)—from a somewhat higher perspective than Glacier Point.

8 Taft Point and the Fissures The trail to Taft Point departs from the same trailhead as the Sentinel Dome trail, but the view and the experience are entirely different. The 1.1-mile trail winds through some forest and meadows, then drops a few hundred feet until you're on the west edge of a steep side canyon whose granite

Vernal Fall

Local Intelligence

Photography has a long history in Yosemite, dating back to the images of Carleton Watkins in the 1860s—and later Albert Bierstadt and Eadweard Muybridge—that helped publicize Yosemite and stimulate the movement for its protection.

Ansel Adams, of course, created iconic images of the park in the 20th century. He showed them in the same gallery in **Yosemite Valley** that continues to bear his name. Every special-edition Ansel Adams print sold there is produced by photographer Alan Ross, who was an assistant to Adams from 1974 to 1979. Today Ross leads photography workshops in the park and creates images of his own.

Ross admires Adams's work for its unpretentiousness. "Every single image is from the heart," he says. "He wasn't trying to impose any meaning in the photograph other than the photograph itself."

Ross's advice to Yosemite photographers: "Stop and smell the roses. Sit down and enjoy the spot. The best way to capture majesty is to soak it up for a bit. Let your feelings guide you."

Some of the places Ross likes to capture majesty are **Yosemite Valley View, Tenaya Canyon,** and the **Merced River** at **Happy Isles.**

rim is cleaved by deep, sheer fractures that are just a few feet wide—the Fissures—yet plunge 2,000 feet straight down.

Taft Point itself is something of a Glacier Point for El Capitan fans—it looks directly across the valley to the face of the great monolith. You can also see El Capitan Meadow and the Merced River snaking through it.

Dogwood tree above the Merced River

9 Mono Meadow This meadow, off Glacier Point Road, is a small, secluded glen reached by a 1-mile downhill walk. Much of it is boggy—enjoy it from the perimeter and from the trail—but it's full of wildflowers, bird life, and serenity. It also affords a superb view of **Mount Starr King** (9,092 feet) to the northeast.

▶ Tioga Road

Tioga Road is the main artery through Yosemite's high country, climbing from 6,200 feet at its west end, **Crane Flat,** to 9,945 feet at **Tioga Pass** before it exits the park. The road typically closes in November and opens in late May.

Many visitors simply make the drive, stop at a few scenic viewpoints, and move on, while others use its trailheads for backpacking trips into the high country. But a number of overlooked short hikes branch off from Tioga Road for a quick but fine taste of the high country.

⑩ **Lukens Lake** Even though you know you're hiking to a lake, the sight of Lukens is a pleasant surprise after a 0.8-mile approach that ascends a slight forested rise, then leads to a creek at the edge of a long meadow, bright with wildflowers in summer, with the lake shimmering at the far end.

Stay to the left and follow the trail to the far end of the lake—a fine spot to picnic and watch birds.

⑪ **Olmsted Point** A large turnout and an obvious view of Yosemite high country make Olmsted Point a popular stop on Tioga Road. But be sure to take the stone steps down and the 0.2-mile trail across solid granite to reach the real viewpoint.

From here you look down on **Tenaya Canyon** across miles of mostly bare granite. The most prominent rise on the near horizon is Half Dome, which looks very different from this eastern perspective compared to the familiar views from Yosemite Valley and Glacier Point.

⑫ **Tenaya Lake** "No one walks to the opposite side of Tenaya Lake," says Kari Cobb. "It's a shame. It's a great loop trail with great views."

Tenaya is very much a high country lake at 8,149 feet, surrounded by granite domes and lodgepole pine forest. A flat, 2.5-mile trail circles it and leads to those terrific views, many of them reflected in the lake's deep blue (and very chilly) water.

Fall foliage illuminates the Merced River

Giant Forest in Sequoia National Park

SEQUOIA

"Sequoias," wrote John Muir, "towering serene through the long centuries, preaching God's forestry fresh from heaven." The Scottish-American naturalist was one of the primary forces behind this California park's creation in 1890. A week after its designation, Congress summarily tripled the preserve's size. Over the years, Sequoia has expanded into one of the nation's largest parks, and it lies side by side with Kings Canyon National Park.

The Giant Forest area and its leafy legends—like the General Sherman Tree—get plenty of visitors, especially with recent enhancements to the road network. The rest of Sequoia remains refreshingly devoid of apparent human impact, in particular a vast backcountry that includes Kern Canyon and 14,494-foot Mount Whitney. While it might take a backpack and good pair of hiking boots to explore Sequoia's secrets, there are plenty of secluded spots near the park's heart.

Year-Round Visitor Center

- **Foothills Visitor Center**
  On Generals Highway, 1 mile north of Ash Mountain Entrance

Seasonal Visitor Centers

- **Lodgepole Visitor Center**
  On Generals Highway, 2 miles north of the General Sherman Tree
- **Mineral King Ranger Station**
  On Mineral King Road, 28 miles from Three Rivers

559-565-3341, *www.nps.gov/seki*

▶ Giant Forest

Generals Highway meanders through Sequoia's western regions between the **Foothills Visitor Center** and the **Grant Grove** section of **Kings Canyon National Park.**

Along the way are Giant Forest's celebrated sequoias. Start your visit at the Giant Forest Museum for an excellent introduction to the park's natural and human history.

❶ **General Sherman Tree** From the museum you can drive, hop the shuttle, or hike (roughly 2 miles) to the General Sherman Tree. At 275 feet, the tree has an estimated volume of more than 52,000 cubic feet, making it the largest living thing on Earth—and the most photographed plant in the park. Nearby **Congress Trail** can be crowded. But Giant Forest is laced with other less trafficked routes.

"There's a maze of trails that connect in different ways in the Giant Forest," says Becky Satnat, a ranger at Sequoia and Kings Canyon National Parks for 22 years. "Any trails in the middle of the grove are good for avoiding the crowds." To explore these routes, she suggests purchasing a detailed trail map of Giant Forest (available at the museum and visitor centers).

❷ **Trail of the Sequoias** Satnat says the most challenging (and rewarding) secret hike is Trail of the Sequoias, a 5-mile loop that starts beneath the **Chief Sequoyah Tree.**

The path climbs over several ridges and down into secluded **Log Meadow,** coined for the hollowed-out sequoia cabin built by pioneer rancher Hale Tharp in the 1860s, the oldest European structure in the park. From there, the trail loops around to **Crescent** and **Circle Meadows,** with plenty of giants (like **Chimney Tree** and the **Pillars of Hercules**) along the way; it takes about four hours to complete the circuit back to the General Sherman parking lot.

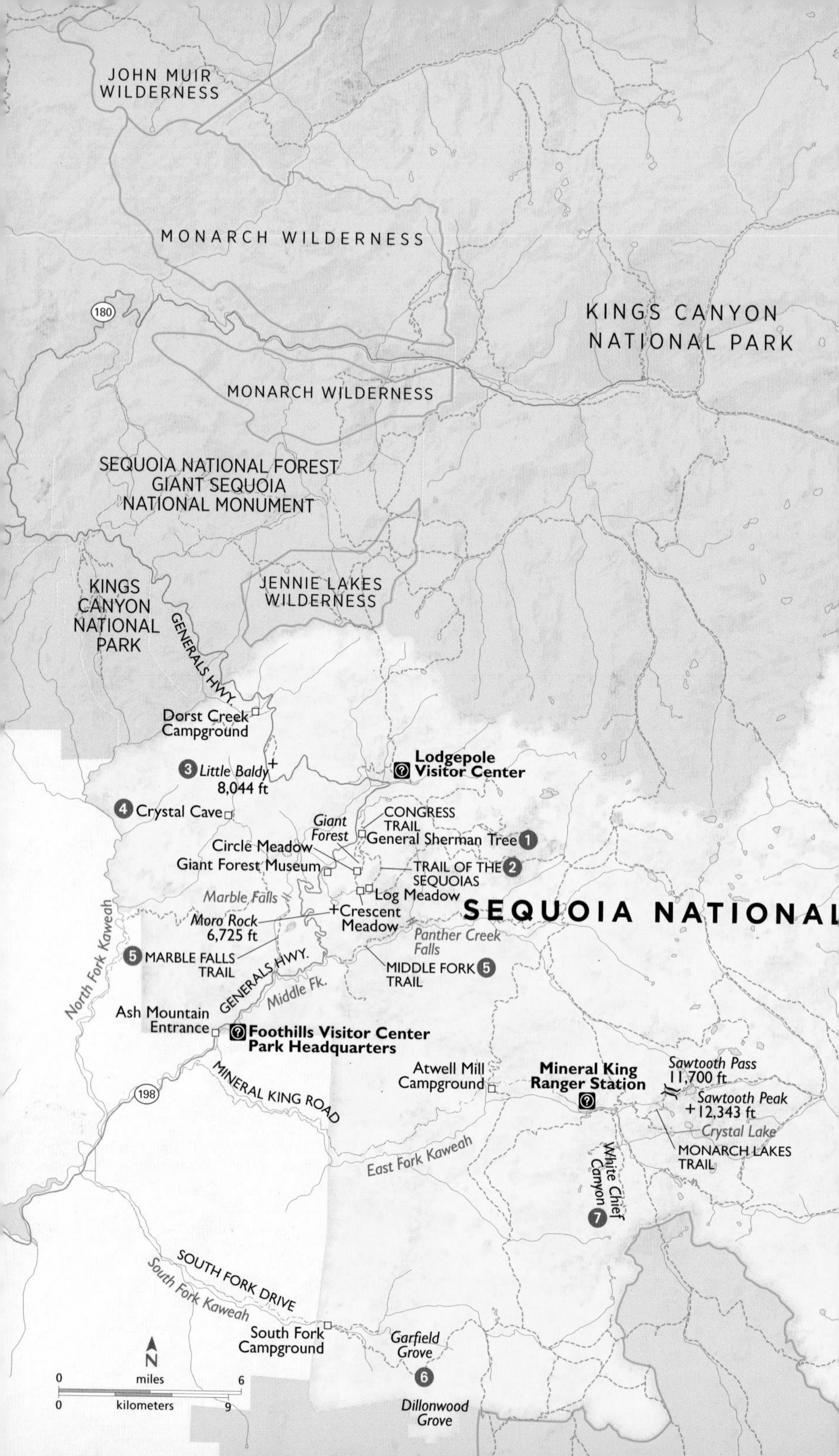

JOHN MUIR WILDERNESS
MONARCH WILDERNESS
180
KINGS CANYON NATIONAL PARK
MONARCH WILDERNESS
SEQUOIA NATIONAL FOREST
GIANT SEQUOIA NATIONAL MONUMENT
KINGS CANYON NATIONAL PARK
JENNIE LAKES WILDERNESS
GENERALS HWY.
Dorst Creek Campground
3 Little Baldy 8,044 ft
Lodgepole Visitor Center
4 Crystal Cave
CONGRESS TRAIL
Giant Forest
General Sherman Tree 1
Circle Meadow
Giant Forest Museum
TRAIL OF THE SEQUOIAS 2
Marble Falls
Log Meadow
SEQUOIA NATIONAL
Moro Rock 6,725 ft
Crescent Meadow
Panther Creek Falls
North Fork Kaweah
5 MARBLE FALLS TRAIL
GENERALS HWY.
MIDDLE FORK 5 TRAIL
Middle Fk.
Ash Mountain Entrance
Foothills Visitor Center Park Headquarters
198
MINERAL KING ROAD
Atwell Mill Campground
Mineral King Ranger Station
Sawtooth Pass 11,700 ft
Sawtooth Peak 12,343 ft
Crystal Lake
MONARCH LAKES TRAIL
East Fork Kaweah
White Chief Canyon 7
SOUTH FORK DRIVE
South Fork Kaweah
South Fork Campground
Garfield Grove
6
Dillonwood Grove
N
0 miles 6
0 kilometers 9

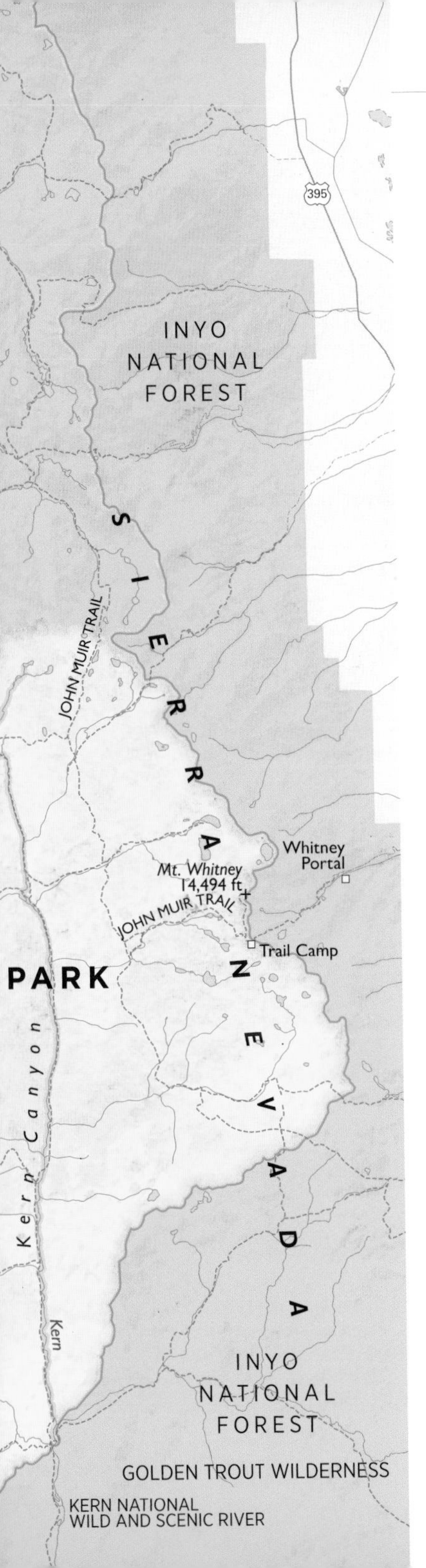

3 Little Baldy Although **Moro Rock** is a popular summit in the Giant Forest area, in summer, the steep trail morphs into a highway of camera-clad hikers. An alternative to Moro Rock is a granite dome called Little Baldy, about a mile east of **Dorst Creek Campground.**

"[Little Baldy] is a little gem, and it's not too far from the road," says Erika Jostad, park ranger.

The total round-trip distance is 3.6 miles with some elevation gain, so plan about 90 minutes for the hike.

▶ The Foothills

The far western part of Sequoia National Park offers a contrast in landscape and temperament to the redwood belt and the High Sierra.

Little Baldy has a terrific view toward the west, and also to the east, so it's one of those 360-degree-around kind of places.

—ERIKA JOSTAD
Sequoia National Park ranger

Ranging between 500 and 5,000 feet in elevation, the region is clad in oaks and chaparral vegetation, and it is perforated by valleys and caves. Foothills Visitor Center near the **Ash Mountain Entrance** offers an overview of the park's diverse biosphere.

Unlike higher elevations of Sequoia that are often snowed in, the foothills area is open year-round. Summer temperatures can hit triple digits, but during the other seasons the hiking weather is sublime.

"This area is characterized by bands of limestone and marble," says Jostad. "The marble is that same [geological] feature that **Crystal Cave** is in, the lower end of it. So this is where a lot of our cave features are.

"But you also get unique vegetation. In the springtime you might see yucca blooming. The buckeye trees are there, which have nice blossoms. It's also a great place for spring wildflowers. And really, spring starts in February down in the foothills."

4 Crystal Cave One of the park's major landmarks, Crystal Cave perches on the upper edge of the foothills. The 45-minute daily tours (between Memorial Day and Labor Day) are a park staple.

Less known are tours by the Sequoia Natural History Association *(www.sequoiahistory.org):* the historical candlelight walk, the junior cave adventure for kids, and the four- to six-hour cave tour that involves belly-crawling through muck, mud, and tight places.

5 Middle Fork and Marble Falls Trails Satnat recommends a couple of day hikes in the area. Middle Fork Trail leads 3 miles up **Kaweah River** to **Panther Creek Falls.** "People can just walk on it as long as they want and then come back," Jostad explains. "But it does continue many miles into the Sequoia backcountry."

Mountaineer's route up Mount Whitney

Even tougher is Marble Falls Trail (3.9 miles) to the cascade of the same name. Both trails are easily doable in a single day for anyone in good physical condition. Bring water.

▶ South Fork

Another lush foothill area is South Fork in Sequoia's southwest corner. Exit the park via the Ash Mountain Entrance, drive 6 miles south along Calif. 198, and then 13 miles east along South Fork Drive.

6 Garfield and Dillonwood Groves Just inside the national park boundary on the South Fork Drive is a small campground, the jumping-off point for hikes to secluded Garfield and Dillonwood Groves, home to giant sequoias, including **King Arthur Tree,** the tenth largest tree in the world by volume.

Added in 2001 via private donation, Dillonwood is the latest addition to Sequoia National Park.

"Garfield is a pretty good-sized giant sequoia grove," says Jostad. "It's a very nice place to visit in the spring and fall. In the spring, for instance, you get a lot of wildflowers in that area. Getting into Dillonwood is a lot more challenging."

▶ Mineral King

The Mineral King area in south-central Sequoia became part of the national park less than four decades ago. The moment you first lay eyes upon this striking highland valley, you wonder what took so long.

Mountains climb up from the meadow-strewn valley, carved

Local Intelligence

At 14,494 feet, Mount Whitney is the highest mountain in the lower 48 states. The western slope lies inside **Sequoia National Park,** the eastern slope in **Inyo National Forest.** Despite its height and intimidating façade, Whitney is comparatively easier to scale than other ultrahigh mountains (but still very difficult).

"I've climbed Mount Whitney more times than I'd like to admit," says Erika Jostad, the ranger who oversaw the far eastern sector of Sequoia National Park for 18 years.

The mountain is most often conquered from **Whitney Portal,** near the town of **Lone Pine** in the **Owens Valley** east of the national park. "It's about 11 miles from Whitney Portal up to the summit," says Jostad. "And it's extremely strenuous. The elevation changes a lot and you should adequately acclimate yourself to the altitude before attempting the climb. The trail starts at 8,361 feet, which is high to begin with for most people. And then you're talking about adding 6,130 more feet on top of that."

The United States Forest Service offers an excellent online guide to climbing Mount Whitney from the eastern side, including checklists for planning and equipment.

by bygone glaciers and the East Fork Kaweah River. The vegetation is an eclectic blend of sequoia, pine, and fir trees, with alpine plants at higher elevations. Giant sequoias cluster on either side of the river at **Atwell Mill Campground** and are easy to reach from the main road.

"Mineral King wasn't even added to the park until 1978," says Satnat, "because Walt Disney wanted to build a ski resort there."

An epic environmental battle that raged for nearly a decade thwarted Disney and kept the valley pristine—not the first time that mankind tried to conquer the valley.

"The name Mineral King comes from an 1870s mining boom," Satnat explains. "It was mostly silver, but other minerals, too. There's still a lot of old mines up that way."

"It's unique in the Sierra," adds Jostad. "A true alpine valley. A lot of rock types that you don't see elsewhere in the park and different plant associations. It's the old rock of the Sierra Nevada before it was transitioned into granite or metamorphic rock. It's also got marble outcrops and caves. And it's got its mining history."

The only road into Mineral King is a steep 25-mile drive from Calif. 198, which starts outside the Ash Mountain Entrance. *Note: No RVs or oversize vehicles permitted.* Its proximity to the **John Muir Trail** and Mount Whitney make the valley a prime starting point for backpacking.

But there are plenty of day hikes to lakes and overlooks above the valley. In fact, the trail density is the highest in the park—11 different routes start from Mineral King.

7 White Chief Canyon Jostad likes the hike up to **White Chief Canyon.** "White Chief was one of the mines, so you see some of the mining history that was there," she observes. "It's also possible to get up close and personal with the marble, and you see polished marble in the streambed." The round-trip is about 8 miles, with an elevation gain of almost 1,800 feet.

Full moon rising over Zabriskie Point

DEATH VALLEY

Death Valley, which spans California and Nevada, is desert and mountain laid bare and dissected. You wouldn't think such a barren place would have secrets—but you would be wrong. Extremes and oddities are everywhere. A shimmering salt pan of a desert floor. The lowest and hottest place in North America. Mountains largely bereft of trees, but presenting geology lessons written in stony hues of red, blue, green, and yellow. Sand dunes, volcanic craters, and critters that live nowhere else on Earth. The most improbably sited castle you'll ever see.

Much of Death Valley can seem ferocious and forsaken, but the National Park Service has done a brilliant job of making the park highly visitable. During the park's most pleasant months, fall through spring, short walks can take you beyond Death Valley's intimidating veneer. It's then that a park labeled death truly comes to life.

Year-Round Visitor Centers

- **Furnace Creek Visitor Center**
  On Calif. 190, Furnace Creek resort area
- **Scotty's Castle Visitor Center and Museum**
  On Nev. 267, north end of park

760-786-3200, *www.nps.gov/deva*

▶ Badwater and the Valley Floor

Badwater is the lowest place in North America—a puddle of foul-tasting water beside **Badwater Road,** 282 feet below sea level, that takes two minutes to see, and that's exactly how long most visitors spend there.

But **Badwater Basin—**that vast, cracked, parched-looking, bright white salt flat that extends clear across the valley floor to the base of the **Panamint Range,** distills everything that is wonderful about Death Valley.

Walk out on that extraordinary valley floor until you can no longer read the SEA LEVEL sign tucked into a palisade of the **Black Mountains** above Badwater and can barely see the parked cars.

Enjoy a surface that is both crisp and pliant, like strolling on chocolate-chip cookies. Observe the geometric patterns of the floor plates, lifted by expanding salt crystals.

"There might be water out there," says Alan Van Valkenberg, Death Valley interpretive ranger. "That alone is kind of fascinating."

So is the sense of solitude—but you're not alone. "There's life, too: microscopic extremophiles growing under the salt," Van Valkenberg adds.

❶ **Devils Golf Course** A few miles up the road from Badwater, the valley floor gets even stranger. Trying to hit a seven iron out of the extensive rough that is ironically named Devils Golf Course would be hellish; not that there's a green anywhere near.

Here crystallized minerals reacting with groundwater have lifted themselves into tightly packed ridges and globules up to 2 feet high. You can walk out as far as you wish—most of the ridges will support your weight, though the going is clumsy, a bit like walking across crunchy broken glass.

▶ Black Mountains

The rugged range that rises above Death Valley's eastern flank holds the park's most fabled drive-up viewpoints, **Zabriskie Point** and **Dantes View**, both off Calif. 190.

The point looks out over barren badlands that glow in early morning light, making it a popular place to gather for sunrise.

Dantes View stares nearly 6,000 feet straight down onto Badwater. Once you've taken in these views, get out and hike the short trail to Zabriskie Point.

Death Valley is known for its extremes: hottest, driest, lowest. But Death Valley is so much more than that. It is full of surprises, with changing colors, layers of rock that twist and turn, and life where nothing should survive. Death Valley must be seen in every season to truly grasp its majesty, its beauty, and its awe-inspiring wonder.

—SARAH CRAIGHEAD
Superintendent
Death Valley National Park

2 Artists Drive This one-way scenic loop off Badwater Road climbs steeply into the mountains south of Zabriskie Point, giving you an up close look at side canyons whose minerals shine in shades of ocher, red, and tan.

But don't just drive; get out and walk. You can park at the second dip (the dips are obvious) and walk a mile or so up an unnamed, unsigned canyon—you're likely to have it to

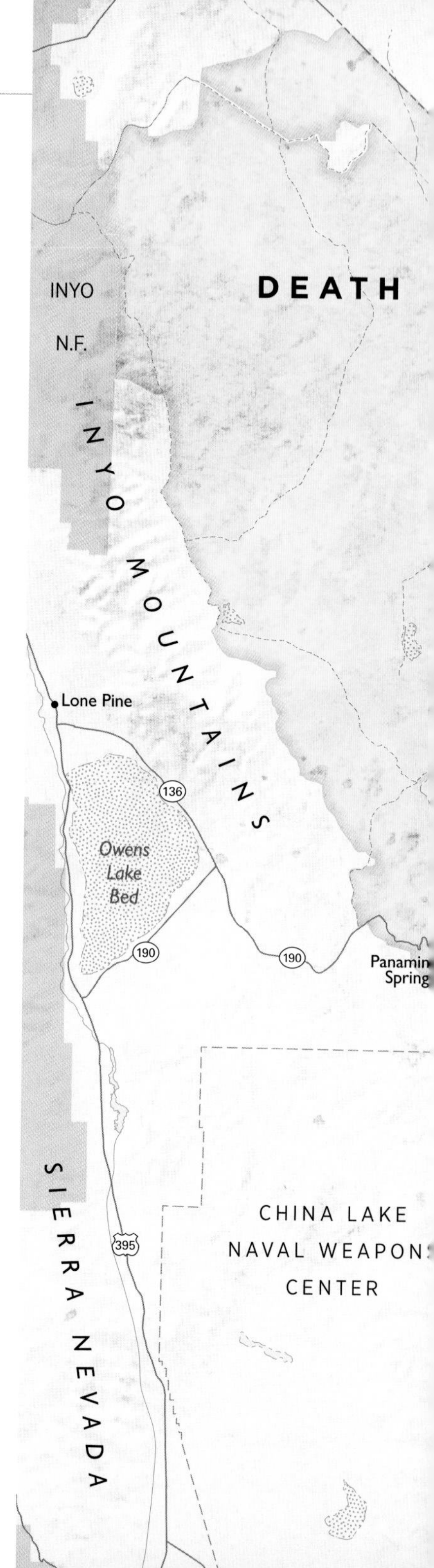

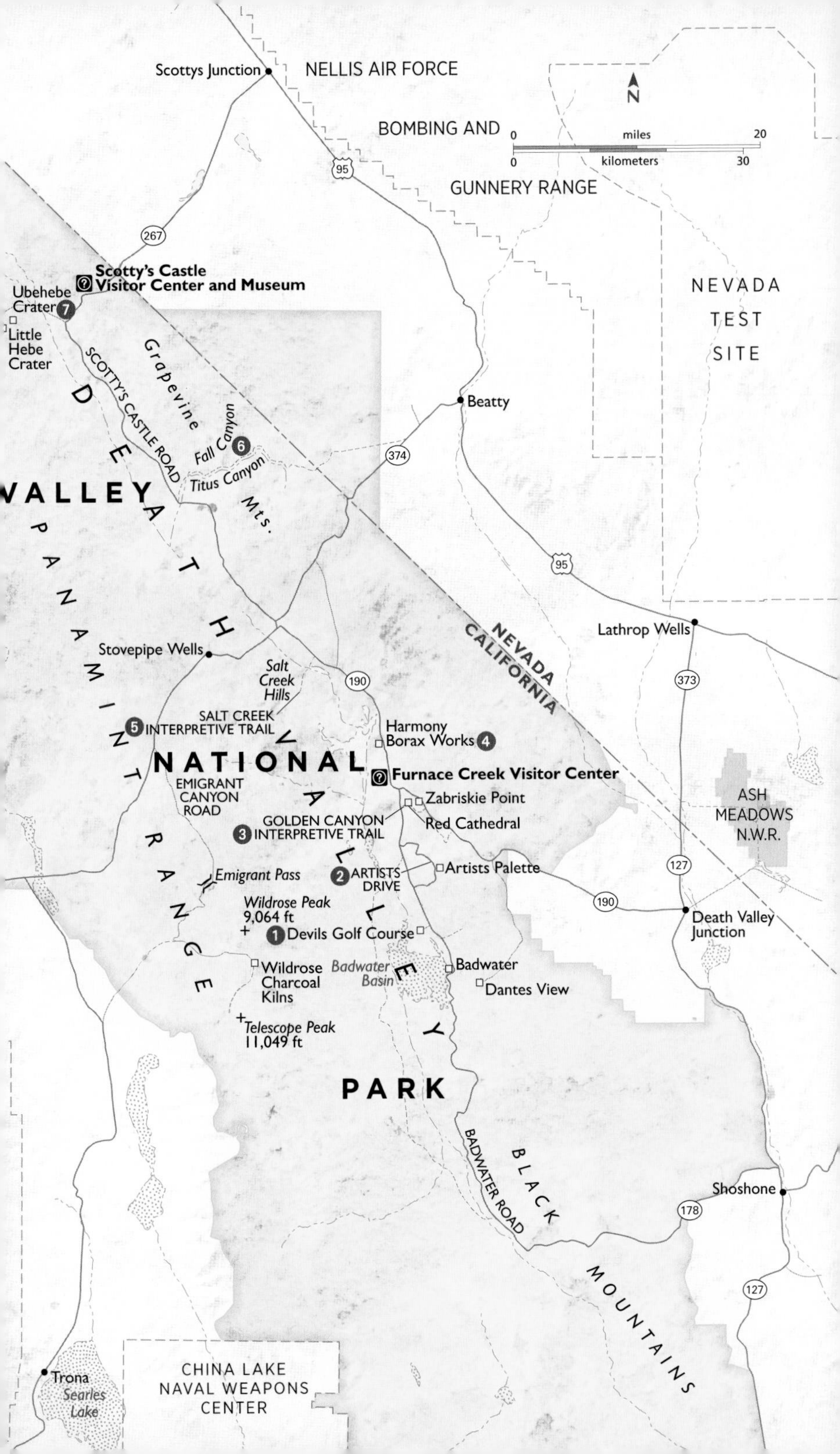
Scottys Junction
NELLIS AIR FORCE
BOMBING AND
GUNNERY RANGE
N
0 miles 20
0 kilometers 30
95
267
Scotty's Castle
Visitor Center and Museum
Ubehebe
Crater
7
Little
Hebe
Crater
SCOTTY'S CASTLE ROAD
Grapevine
Mts.
Fall Canyon
6
Titus Canyon
NEVADA
TEST
SITE
Beatty
374
VALLEY
DEATH
PANAMINT RANGE
95
NEVADA
CALIFORNIA
Lathrop Wells
Stovepipe Wells
Salt
Creek
Hills
190
373
SALT CREEK
5 INTERPRETIVE TRAIL
Harmony
Borax Works 4
NATIONAL
Furnace Creek Visitor Center
EMIGRANT
CANYON
ROAD
Zabriskie Point
Red Cathedral
GOLDEN CANYON
3 INTERPRETIVE TRAIL
ASH
MEADOWS
N.W.R.
Emigrant Pass
2 ARTISTS
DRIVE
Artists Palette
127
190
Wildrose Peak
9,064 ft
1 Devils Golf Course
Death Valley
Junction
VALLEY
Wildrose
Charcoal
Kilns
Badwater
Basin
Badwater
Dantes View
Telescope Peak
11,049 ft
PARK
BADWATER ROAD
BLACK
MOUNTAINS
Shoshone
178
127
Trona
Searles
Lake
CHINA LAKE
NAVAL WEAPONS
CENTER

Local Intelligence

What keeps a park naturalist in love with Death Valley for 21 years? "It's akin to the prospectors of the old days," says Alan Van Valkenberg, a ranger who has served that long at the park. "The freedom to explore."

While most national parks admonish visitors to stick to established footpaths, Death Valley permits cross-country walking. "You think, 'Hey, it's a national park and I'm supposed to stay on trails,'" says Van Valkenberg, "but once you get past that, you realize you can wander anywhere your feet will carry you. That's pretty liberating. You never run out of discoveries."

Van Valkenberg also encourages prepared explorers to hike by night, when a bright moon or a star-filled sky provides ample illumination in light-colored open spaces. "Under a full moon you can see all the colors—the reds, yellows, oranges, and purples," he says.

yourself—until it narrows to about 15 feet and becomes impassable without rock-climbing gear.

At the apex of Artists Drive is **Artists Palette,** where an easy walk starts from a parking area and leads up a wash whose bordering rock faces are painted in reddish shades as well as in lavender and blue.

3 Golden Canyon Here is one of the park's interpretive nature walks—a brochure available at the trailhead off **Badwater Road** explains the canyon's geological phenomena at ten stops along the way.

It's a popular walk. Its secret, though, lies beyond stop No. 10, well past the point most people turn around. It's a 400-foot, red fluted wall known as the **Red Cathedral,** 1.25 miles from the trailhead.

Do this walk in late afternoon, when the low rays of the sun set the towering wall glowing with a brilliant red.

▶ Furnace Creek Area

Furnace Creek is the heart of the park, site of park headquarters, a visitor center, the country's lowest golf course, three campgrounds, and two inns—**Furnace Creek Ranch** and **Furnace Creek Inn.**

Even if you're not staying in Furnace Creek, take the time to park at the ranch and check out the **Borax Museum** in the oldest structure in Death Valley.

It explains the history of borax mining and displays some nifty rock specimens. It also helps answer the inevitable question: Why in the world would pioneers endure the hardships of living here?

4 Harmony Borax Works With a bit of borax lore under your belt, you'll appreciate the short walk around the well-preserved ruins of Harmony Borax Works, just north of Furnace Creek. Check out the adobe masonry that surrounds the borax-refining machinery, and the big-wheeled 20-mule team wagon dozing in the sun just below the plant.

5 Salt Creek A boardwalk nature trail along Salt Creek is a perfect platform for viewing one of the park's rarest denizens, the Salt Creek pupfish. The tadpole-size critters are especially active in spring—mating season—darting about in the clear saline water.

For a sense of solitude, take a short

off-trail walk from the end of the boardwalk into the Salt Creek Hills—dry-mud mounds that give way to small dry-mud canyons.

▶ Scotty's Castle

Scotty's Castle is hardly a secret—the ornate villa is the park's most popular attraction—but there's an alternative tour of the castle that's worth sticking around for after the main tour.

The hour-long **Underground Tour** literally plumbs the subterranean world beneath the home, whose owner, Albert Johnson, was a civil engineer with a penchant for technology. The tour starts in a basement and proceeds through a system of tunnels.

You see such innovations for the period—1930s and '40s—as hollow insulation tiles, massive nickel-iron batteries for storing electricity generated by a Pelton wheel, and (outside) a solar water heater.

❻ Titus and Fall Canyons Walking up either of these side-by-side canyons off **Scotty's Castle Road** gets you quickly into a spectacular, steep-sided defile carved into the **Grapevine Mountains.**

Each walk is lined with steep walls of twisted, metamorphosed marble and dolomite. Titus is easier going because you're walking up a road, but you might meet vehicles coming toward you on the one-way passage.

On the other hand, you reach narrow sections just 15 feet wide in less than a mile. Because it follows a road, this is the rare trail in the park that you can take dogs on. "But keep them on a leash," says Van Valkenberg. "There are bighorn sheep up there."

A signed trail at the mouth of Titus Canyon leads over to Fall Canyon, whose floor is coarse sand—slower going, but you're almost guaranteed solitude for whatever portion of the 3.5-mile hike you opt for.

Early morning is the best time to hike either canyon.

❼ Ubehebe Crater Just west of Scotty's Castle is a little slice of Mars known as Ubehebe Crater, a maw of a volcanic crater a half-mile wide and 600 feet deep.

Geologists once assumed that the crater was thousands of years old, but they now estimate that the blast could have occurred as recently as 800 years ago.

To best appreciate the crater and the alien landscape that surrounds it, follow the 1.5-mile (round-trip), signed trail that leads above Ubehebe's west rim and climbs to **Little Hebe Crater.**

You get great views of both craters and two other smaller ones as well as of some dramatic gullies carved into the gray, cinder-strewn landscape.

Aerial view of Ubehebe Crater

Namesake Joshua trees

JOSHUA TREE

To the untrained eye, Joshua Tree National Park in California looks like a vast expanse of desert wilderness littered with gigantic piles of rusty brown rocks and punctuated by scraggly trees. Ironically, to the trained eye of a desert aficionado, it looks the same way. Desert lovers hold deep affection for Joshua Tree's spaciousness, its amazing rocks—fabled among rock climbers—and its signature Joshua tree, but they also understand that secrets lurk behind the scenes, particularly evidence of human residents. Curious travelers willing to go afoot in Joshua Tree receive all sorts of rewards—bighorn sheep and desert tortoises; weathered remains of the mines and abodes of dreamers and desperadoes; pictographs and bedrock mortars left by Native Americans; and countless members of the yucca family, which put Mormon pioneers in mind of prophets with upraised arms.

Year-Round Visitor Centers

- **Oasis Visitor Center**
  At Twentynine Palms, Oasis of Mara
- **Joshua Tree Visitor Center**
  6554 Park Boulevard, Joshua Tree Village
- **Cottonwood Visitor Center**
  At Cottonwood Spring, 8 miles north of I-10

Seasonal Visitor Center

- **Black Rock Nature Center**
  At Black Rock Campground, Yucca Valley

760-367-5500, *www.nps.gov/jotr*

▶ Hidden Valley

Hidden Valley is about as close as Joshua Tree comes to a hub, yet many visitors miss the rock-ringed enclave for which it's named. This is what climbers call "Real Hidden Valley," adjacent to Hidden Valley picnic area and across the street from the campground.

"It encapsulates what the park is all about," says Joe Zarki, chief of interpretation—meaning Hidden Valley combines natural and human history with the presence of rock climbers.

A marked, 1-mile nature trail slithers through a portal of gigantic boulders, loops among huge rock formations, and leads to a secluded natural arena that was once lush with native bunchgrass—and hence a favorite spot for cattle rustlers to graze their contraband.

Watch for climbers challenging cracks and faces on formations such as **Sports Challenge** and **Gateway Rock.** A branch trail on the east side leads to an impressive spire called **Hidden Tower,** a popular climbing spot because it harbors near-vertical routes not as difficult as they look.

❶ Desert Queen Ranch Scads of dreamers—not to be confused with Native Americans—ambled through Joshua Tree in the 19th and 20th centuries, but rancher Bill Keys stands out as Edison of the Mojave Desert, the rare man to stake a claim, eke out a living, and even raise a family there.

Keys worked his Desert Queen Ranch from 1917 until his death in 1969. The well-preserved cattle ranch is open only to ranger-led tours (call the park for reservations), and it's worth it to make arrangements to visit.

The 1916–17 family home is still lovely. A windmill towers over orchards, gardens, and all manner of carts, gizmos, trucks, and gold-mining machinery. Watch for bighorn sheep on nearby rocky promontories.

❷ Barker Dam and Petroglyphs

Keys's stamp is on another Hidden Valley site called Barker Dam. Keys fortified and extended a mortared-stone barrier to catch winter rain that would pour through a usually dry wash.

It worked—it supplied much of the water for his ranch, cattle, and **Desert Queen Mine—**and still does. Hence the improbable sight of a lake (if there's been sufficient winter rain) in the heart of the bone-dry park.

The trail departs from a parking area just east of Hidden Valley. On the return part of the 1.3-mile loop, look for an alcove with the most vivid pictographs in the Mojave. Native? Yes, but enhanced (read: vandalized) by a Disney film crew in the early '60s for that epic *Chico, the Misunderstood Coyote.*

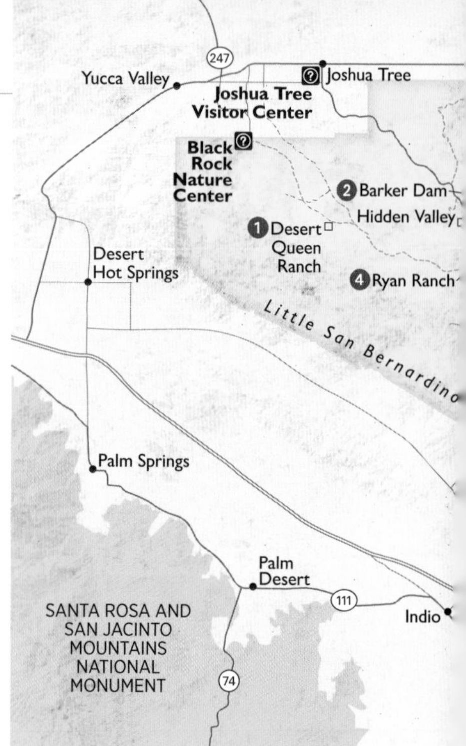

Barker Dam

❸ Wall Street Mill

A separate trail leads 1.1 miles from the Barker Dam parking area to yet another Keys site.

Wall Street Mill was a stamp mill for processing ore from Desert Queen Mine. The mill itself is one of the best preserved of its ilk in the desert, as is a windmill en route, while some old utility trucks lie decaying in the desert sand. Zarki, however, suggests another reason to make this easy hike. "It's the place where Keys got into a gunfight with his neighbor Worth Bagley. It was a law-of-the-desert kind of thing; Keys felt he should be able to cross Bagley's property to get to his."

A stone marker beside the trail reads: HERE IS WHERE WORTH BAGLEY BIT THE DUST AT THE HAND OF W.F. KEYS. MAY 11, 1943.

Keys ended up serving five years in prison. The intercession of a part-time desert rat named Erle Stanley Gardner—yes, the author of the Perry Mason mysteries—got him a hearing and eventually a pardon.

▶ Park Boulevard East of Hidden Valley

Park Boulevard east of Hidden Valley climbs **Sheep Pass** between two mountainous regions of the park. **Jumbo Rocks** is the most popular stop along the way—particularly for the short hike to **Skull Rock—**but lesser known sites are also worthwhile.

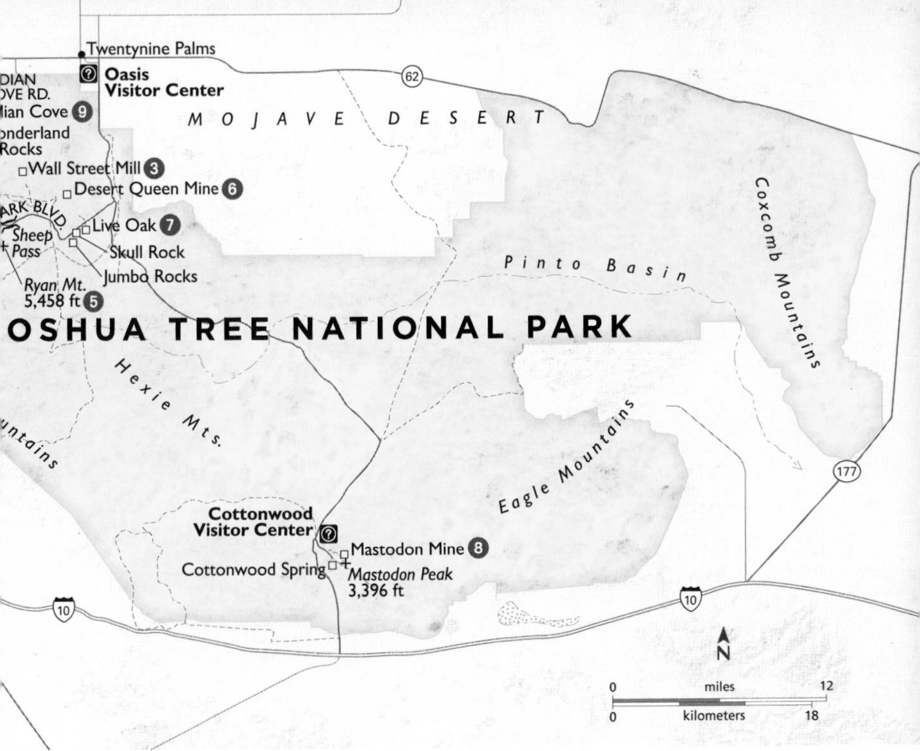

> *The park holds lots of secrets, lots of discoveries to be made. The real secret is to get out and see. You don't have to stay on the trail. If you want to go somewhere, just get out of the car and go.*
>
> —JEFF OHLFS
> *Joshua Tree National Park chief ranger*

4 Ryan Ranch Ryan Mountain was named for homesteaders Jep and Tom Ryan. What's left of their cattle ranch lies just to the west of there; a half-mile trail leads to it from Park Boulevard.

The Ryans sited their home here for its water, which they pumped 3.5 miles cross-desert to their gold mine. Remains of gorgeous rust-colored adobe masonry only hint at what a fine stand this ranch was in its time.

5 Ryan Mountain If you're up for a bit of elevation gain, the 1.5-mile hike to the top of Ryan Mountain (5,458 feet) delivers the best view of the heart of the park.

It's also an outstanding piece of trail building—lots of stone steps assure firm footing for the 1,100-foot ascent. Do it early in the morning and you'll have shade most of the way up.

From the top you can see all of the west side of the park and beyond to **Mount San Jacinto,** the **Wonderland of Rocks** to the north, and vast **Pinto Basin** to the east.

From the same trailhead parking area, a short trail leads to the **Indian Cave**—a natural rock lean-to on which you can see the effects of years of campfire smoke.

Wildflowers in the Live Oak area

6 Desert Queen Mine A smooth dirt road leads north from Park Boulevard to the trailhead for Desert Queen Mine, where you can see the ghostly remnants of tailings, cyanide tanks, machinery, and shafts that composed the most productive gold mine in Joshua Tree. It produced 3,845 ounces of gold from 1894 to 1961. A 0.25-mile walk leads to an overlook directly above the ruins.

7 Live Oak You might think Live Oak is simply a name for a picnic area—not a secret. Wrong. Drive west on the dirt road past the main picnic area until it ends, then follow a short trail down to, yes, a towering live oak—a tree you'd expect to see on the coast or in the central valley of California, but not in this world of cactus, mesquite, and Joshua trees. How does it survive? "Deep roots," answers Zarki.

▶ Cottonwood Spring

The entire Cottonwood Spring area, 7 miles north of the park's southern entrance, is something of a secret. Most park visitors stick to the north, or whiz by Cottonwood if they enter from the south.

The spring itself waters a desert oasis shaded by native desert fan palms towering 75 feet above it. It's a pleasant, restful spot just a short walk from the trailhead, filled with the sound of birdsong.

Nearby are some bedrock mortars—smooth cavities in stone left by native Cahuilla women who crushed and ground seeds and piñon nuts with stone pestles.

8 Mastodon Mine If you've done some exploring in Joshua Tree, you might think, "Why visit another mine?" But the point of seeing

Mastodon Mine is the walk, because in the Cottonwood area you're in the Colorado Desert, entirely different from the Mojave Desert of the northern part of the park.

Instead of Joshua trees you'll encounter palo verde trees and tall, spindly ocotillo, which burst into red blossoms March through June. The 2.3-mile loop trail leads to **Mastodon Peak** and great views, then passes by mining ruins and the Winona stamp mill on the way back to Cottonwood.

▶ Indian Cove

You don't just happen upon Indian Cove, a popular camping area at the northern end of the Wonderland of Rocks. It's not on the way to anywhere else in the park, but rather secretly accessed from Indian Cove Road 7 miles west of the town of **Twentynine Palms.**

9 Indian Cove Nature Trail Off by itself at the far west end of Indian Cove Campground is the Indian Cove Nature Trail, which leads into the secret world of a desert wash—"a corridor of biodiversity," as one interpretive sign puts it. Among the highlights along the 0.5-mile walk are flowery desert willows and desert almonds, whose fruit natives dried for food. In spring and fall, keep an eye out for desert tortoises.

Cholla Cactus Garden

Local Intelligence

Over the centuries Joshua Tree National Park's human denizens included Native Americans, miners, and cattle ranchers.

"I have a deep appreciation and respect for their way of life," says Jeff Ohlfs, the park's chief ranger, who has lived here for 21 years. "They knew how to survive off the land. Chester Pinkham [a miner] saw more of this park than anyone who's ever worked here, and he traversed it all by mule."

Although the native presence dates back at least 5,000 years, traces of their lives aren't widely evident. "That's because they were nomadic," explains Ohlfs. "There are no pueblos or Ancestral Puebloan ruins here."

More recent human arrivals, however, left plenty behind. Miners recorded thousands of claims in the area. Not all were worked, but many were, accounting for the abundance of mining ruins. Cattle ranchers went where the water was, staking claims at many watering holes and seeps. Of the settlers, prospectors get Ohlfs's vote as the toughest. Their creature comforts? Only a bedroll. "But that's just how they lived. They knew nothing else," he observes.

Santa Cruz Island

CHANNEL ISLANDS

Discovering the Channel Islands is like tumbling through a time warp into a California everyone assumed had long ago vanished. While mainland southern California has burgeoned, with more than 20 million people filling every beach and crowding into every canyon, the islands have been idling in the Santa Barbara Channel, as close as 17 miles to the mainland, but rarely visited. When the National Park Service took over their management in 1980, they found a reasonably intact mirror of old mainland California, plus a few surprises.

Years of private ownership created some ecological problems on the islands, but the Park Service has worked diligently to eradicate invasive animal and plant species and to restore the islands to what they truly are: a wild slice of southern California, a place of solitude and beauty. The entire park is one of the great secrets of our National Park System.

▶ Santa Cruz Island

Santa Cruz is the largest of the Channel Islands and by far the most visited. Don't let that put you off—there's never a sense of crowding on any of the Channel Islands.

As with all the islands except **Santa Rosa,** the only way to visit Santa Cruz is by boat with the park's concessionaire, Island Packers *(www.islandpackers.com).*

The island is famous for its sea caves—some of the world's largest—which make it a world-class destination for sea kayaking.

Some come to snorkel and dive in the chilly (55°F to 68°F) water or to sun on the beach near the landing site. But most visitors simply come to walk and enjoy the island's serenity.

Year-Round Visitor Centers

- **Robert J. Lagomarsino Visitor Center**
  1901 Spinnaker Drive, Ventura
- **Outdoor Santa Barbara Visitor Center**
  113 Harbor Way, 4th Floor, Santa Barbara
- **Anacapa Visitor Center**
  On East Anacapa

805-658-5730, *www.nps.gov/chis*

❶ Cavern Point and Potato Harbor Once you've landed on Santa Cruz, received an orientation from a park ranger, and taken in the visitor center, you'll want to make the 1-mile walk to Cavern Point.

As you ascend the hill above **Scorpion landing,** the view just keeps getting better as you near the point, from which you can see migrating gray whales in season (December to April).

Most people stop there and loop down to the campground to return, but the 2-mile coastal-bluff hike on the **North Bluff Trail** from Cavern Point to Potato Harbor is even more spectacular—vast ocean and mainland views from 350 feet above the water surface. Try it out.

Notice occasional piles of seashell fragments? "Those are shell middens," explains Bill Faulkner, a park ranger. "They're everywhere on the island. They indicate where native Chumash people camped thousands of years ago."

❷ Scorpion Canyon If you follow the basic, signed **Scorpion Canyon Loop Trail,** you'll have a 4.5-mile walk in the interior of the island, but you might miss the chance of seeing one of the world's rarest bird species, the Island Scrub-jay—a

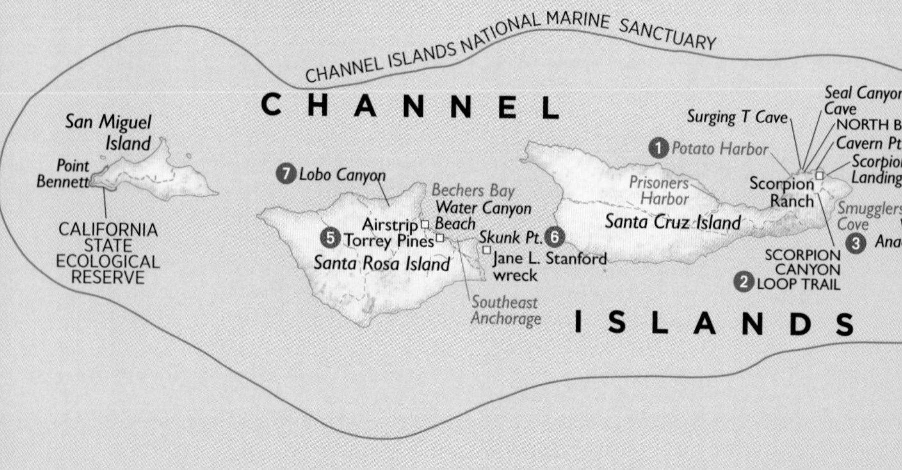

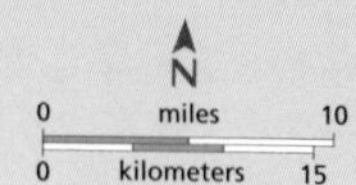

type of jay that lives only on Santa Cruz Island. To see (or hear) it, walk through the upper campground, but continue straight (west) up a rocky dry wash. Look for small groves of oaks and endemic ironwoods, where the jays are most likely to be spotted—or their screeches heard.

Speaking of rare species, you may also see the endemic island fox in the park campgrounds on the way to or from Scorpion Canyon.

"They're cute, but *don't* feed them," warns Faulkner. "We don't want them to get habituated to human food."

3 Smugglers Cove The 7.5-mile round-trip hike to Smugglers Cove is one few visitors make. It crosses the island south on an old ranch road from **Scorpion Ranch,** climbs high enough to yield good views of **Anacapa Island,** passes a historic grove of cypress trees (a nice spot for a picnic), and lands you at a secluded beach.

"It's at the mouth of an incredible little valley," says Yvonne Menard, chief of interpretation. "Ranchers here had groves of olive trees, and you'll see their adobe ranch buildings from the 1880s."

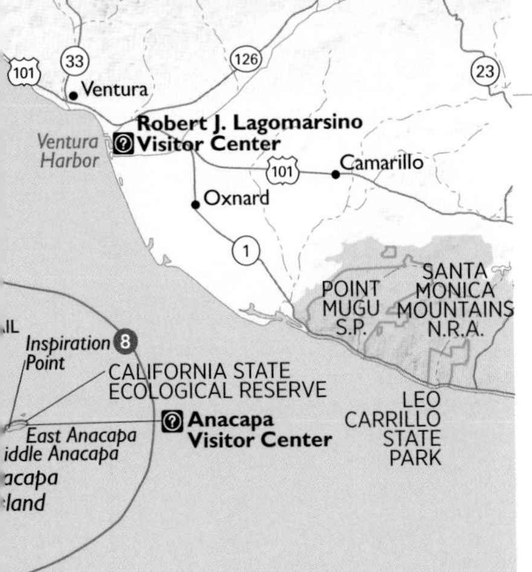

4 The Sea Caves The north coast of Santa Cruz Island is riddled with sea caves, many of them huge—of the 100-some caves, 72 are more than 200 feet long.

Exploring them by kayak is thrilling, though best done with a guide who can read the tides and swell and know which caves are safe to enter. The park website has a list of authorized outfitters.

Not that the paddling is difficult. "It takes no skill," says Eric Little, kayak guide for Santa Barbara-based Aquasports. "I take people out who have never seen the ocean before."

A typical trip is a half day—an early boat out to Scorpion, a safety briefing, and a few hours of exhilarating paddling. Harbor seals may accompany you as you traverse the cliffs.

The experience inside the caves is as much auditory as visual—the sound of surge, swash, and blowholes. A helmet and headlamp are musts to avoid contact with barnacle-encrusted walls and ceilings. Some caves are so narrow that you have to back in. One called **Seal Canyon Cave** is about 6 feet wide, 10 feet high, but goes back at least 600 feet.

An endangered island fox

▶ Santa Rosa Island

The second largest of the Channel Islands, Santa Rosa offers one thing none of the others do—an airstrip. You can go either by boat with Island Packers or by plane from the town of Camarillo with Channel Island Aviation. Some visitors fly in to surf, fish, and hike and fly right back, though there's plenty on the island to justify more than a day trip.

5 Torrey Pines A grove of Torrey pines on a bluff above **Bechers Bay** is one of those Channel Islands time-warp experiences. These leftovers from the Pleistocene age occur only here and on the California mainland around La Jolla.

❻ **Water Canyon Beach and Skunk Point** Water Canyon Beach is probably Santa Rosa's most obvious feature—2 miles of white-sand beach arcing southeast from the landing pier. But don't just walk the beach; keep going to **Southeast Anchorage** and beyond to Skunk Point.

You'll see tide pools, blowholes, coastal cliffs with views of Santa Cruz Island, and the offshore wreck of the four-masted lumber schooner *Jane L. Stanford.* (Note that access to Skunk Point is restricted to the area below the main high tide. To protect nesting Snowy Plovers, you can't visit the back beaches and sand dunes from March 15 to September 15.)

❼ **Lobo Canyon** Lobo Canyon is a sandstone cliff cut by a perpetual stream of water and equally perpetual wind that would be right at home in a place like Utah.

It runs 2.5 miles from an old ranch road down to the ocean, and it takes a side turn into a true slot canyon. Its walls are lined in smooth faces of purple and yellow sandstone, and toyon and wild cherry trees spring from the banks of the stream.

It's an 8-mile round-trip from the campground to the start of Lobo Canyon, but the Park Service often provides lifts to the entrance and guided hikes for overnighters.

▶ Anacapa

Anacapa, composed of three small islands, is the closest of the Channel Islands to the mainland, making it ideal for a quick day trip.

❽ **Inspiration Point** This is the must-see place on East Anacapa. In the clear water, bat rays dart amid a forest of giant kelp. Unsurprisingly, it invites diving and snorkeling. "The diving is amazing," says Faulkner. "The giant kelp is like the rain forest of the marine environment."

Anacapa is also home to a working lighthouse, whose horn sounds every 18 seconds. And watch for Bald Eagles, which have returned to the island after a 60-year absence.

A hidden cove near the East Point of Santa Rosa Island

Local Intelligence

"In the Channel Islands, a lot of work goes into restoration and recovery of the native and endemic plants and animals that call these islands home," says Bill Faulkner, interpretive ranger.

Faulkner cites examples of recent park projects that have helped island natives resurge: eradication of rats on Anacapa that benefited nesting seabirds; and removal or eradication of sheep, cattle, elk, Golden Eagles, and feral pigs from Santa Cruz and Santa Rosa, resulting in saving the endemic island fox and the return of nesting Bald Eagles. The outlawing of the pesticide DDT helped bring back the Brown Pelican, which breeds on West Anacapa and Santa Barbara Islands, from near extinction.

Now the park is focusing on restoring native vegetation. "A lot of seabirds rely on native plant species," reports Laurie Harvey, park biologist. "The more intact the ecosystem, the better for key species like the Xantus's Murrelet, Ashy Storm-petrel, and Cassin's Auklet."

The islands are often called North America's Galápagos. The mixing of warm and cool waters here creates rich biodiversity, from microplankton to the largest species of all, the blue whale.

—DEREK LOHUIS
Channel Islands National Park ranger

▶ San Miguel Island

A warning: San Miguel, 58 miles from **Ventura Harbor,** is only for the determined and hardy.

First, it's a four-hour boat trip just to get there with Island Packers, which generally makes runs to the island eight times per year: two day trips and six three-night camping trips, so planning is required. Second, be prepared: The island is frequently hammered by fierce 30-knot winds.

It's all worth it, though, for the 16-mile round-trip guided hike to **Point Bennett** to view one of North America's prime wildlife spectacles—some 30,000 seals and sea lions hauled out on the point's beaches.

On the way you'll see the caliche forest—strange sand castings that amount to a petrified forest of ancient vegetation.

▶ Santa Barbara Island

The smallest and most southerly of the Channel Islands, Santa Barbara has great snorkeling at its **Landing Cove—** where sea lions cooperatively congregate for photographers—and 5 miles of hiking trails. Be sure to make the 4-mile round-trip hike to Arch Point to view the sea lion rookery.

Island Packers runs trips to Santa Barbara throughout the summer and fall. The boat schedule generally requires a three-day stay at the island's fine little campground—call ahead for reservations.

Lava flowing from Pu'u 'Ō'ō

HAWAI'I VOLCANOES

The awesome power of nature is nowhere more evident than in the eruption of a volcano, and Hawai'i Volcanoes National Park encompasses two of the most active volcanoes in the world—Kīlauea and Mauna Loa. Both mountains—and the entire Big Island of Hawai'i—sit atop the "hot spot" in the 3,600-mile-long Hawaiian Island-Emperor Seamount chain that over many eons has created the entire Hawaiian archipelago, and is responsible for the flow of bright red magma that has been issuing from rifts on the sides of Kīlauea and Mauna Loa for thousands of years.

Encompassing more than 333,000 acres, Hawai'i Volcanoes extends from the island's edge on the Pacific Ocean to the summit of Mauna Loa, 13,677 feet in the air—a home for the hottest secrets of any park.

Year-Round Visitor Center

- **Kīlauea Visitor Center**
  On Hawaii 11, Crater Rim Drive, between mile marker 28 and 29, southwest of Hilo

  808-985-6000, *www.nps.gov/havo*

▶ Kīlauea Visitor Center and Jaggar Museum

Visitors can get a good sense of the park in as little as three hours by visiting the Kīlauea Visitor Center and Jaggar Museum, then driving along **Chain of Craters Road** directly down to the Pacific.

But spending a day or more walking the park's more than 150 miles of trails, or camping in any of several designated areas, allows a much deeper appreciation of Hawai'i Volcanoes' many geologic subtleties, its rare wildlife, and the ancient Hawaiian culture that still holds this land sacred.

The Kīlauea Visitor Center is the place to start, just inside the park's main entrance. Here, rangers answer questions about what to see and do, a bookstore sells maps, videos, and souvenirs, and informative displays provide a history and lay of the land.

Less than 3 miles from the visitor center on **Crater Rim Drive** is **Jaggar Museum** and an overlook that provides the closest view of **Kīlauea Caldera,** which is considered the summit of the Kīlauea Volcano. There's an easy nature trail that connects the visitor center and Jaggar Museum. It leads past several steam vents and provides views into the crater.

The last summit eruption was on March 19, 2008, when rocks and lava blew from the **Halema'uma'u Crater** and covered 65 acres, creating a vent and a boiling lava lake. Though vents in the caldera are continuously issuing steam that can be seen from a distance any time of day, the secret is that it is at night (the park is open 24 hours a day, year-round) that the lava lake inside Halema'uma'u Crater gives off an eerie red glow to the sky.

▶ Chain of Craters Road

The main route from the park entrance to the sea is Chain of Craters Road, a 36-mile round-trip that leads along the **East Rift of Kīlauea** before dropping to the coast.

The road descends 3,700 feet in 20 miles and ends where a 2003 lava flow crossed it. Along the way, signs are posted showing a history of recent eruptions—1969, 1972, 1979—and overlooks where you can view the devastation.

About halfway down, a turn in the

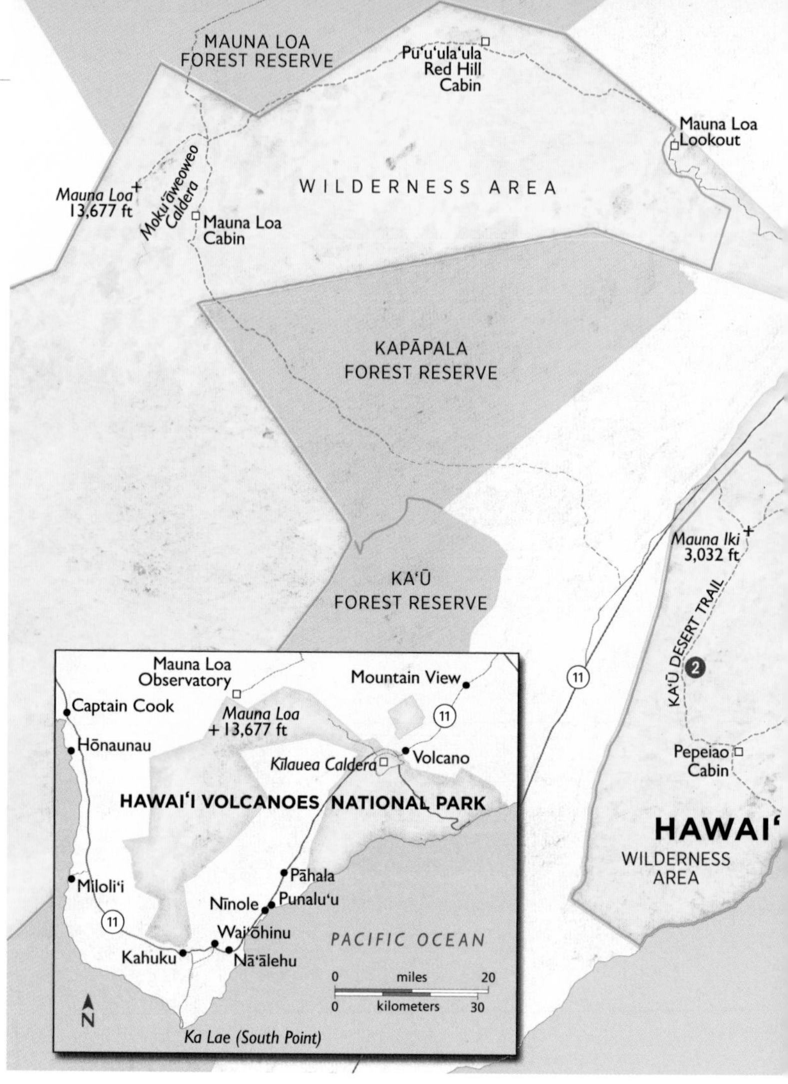

road opens onto a vast panoramic view of the ocean. From there, Chain of Craters Road descends quickly to sea level, ending at **Hōlei Sea Arch.** Take the short walk to the cliff's edge to view the arch and the sheer drop-off to the crashing waves.

❶ Thurston Lava Tube and Kīlauea Iki Two of the most popular day hikes start just off Chain of Craters Road—Kīlauea Iki and Thurston Lava Tube.

Of the two, the Thurston Lava Tube is easier and more family friendly. Named after one of the park's greatest advocates, Lorrin Thurston, this 0.33-mile walk leads through a lush fern forest and a massive lava tube.

A more engaging adventure is Kīlauea Iki, a moderate-to-challenging 4-mile hike (two to three hours) that starts in a rain forest on the crater rim and descends 400 feet to the crater floor. As you pass through the foliage on your way down, keep an eye to the tree canopy where you might spot a brilliant crimson 'Apapane bird, whose only known habitat is in Hawai'i, or to the sky, where White-tailed Tropicbirds and Hawaiian Hawks often soar.

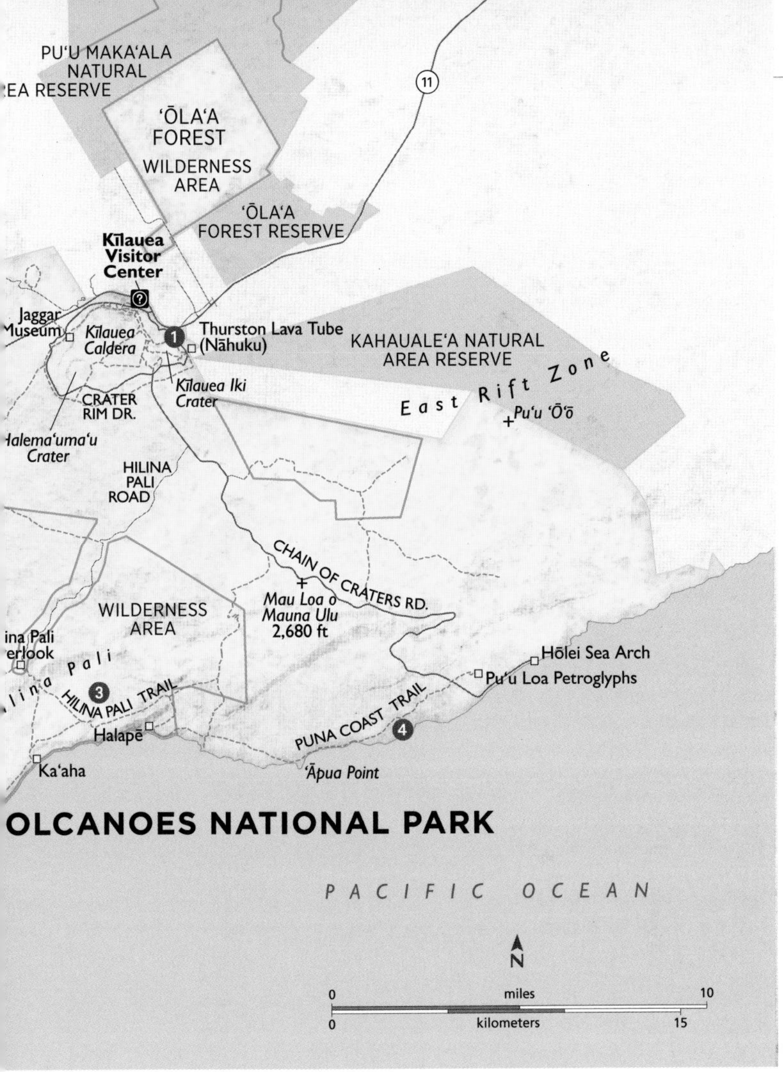

Once on the crater floor, you'll walk across the site of the last major eruption of Kīlauea Iki (1959), when lava spewed from a vent in the crater wall for five weeks, with one geyser of lava reaching 1,900 feet in the air—a record for the highest lava fountain ever measured in Hawai'i.

2 Ka'ū Desert Trail You'll definitely want to take the turn off Chain of Craters Road onto the 11-mile, one-lane Hilina Pali Road that leads to **Hilina Pali Overlook.**

The views from this vantage point are expansive—extending over the 2,000-foot cliff and down to the vast Pacific. But don't just point your camera, shoot, and leave.

Jim Gale, chief of interpretation, suggests jumping on the Ka'ū Desert Trail that starts here for a unique hike. This less traveled, 4.8-mile trek skirts the rim of **Hilina Pali** offering panoramic ocean views as it makes its way to rustic **Pepeiao Cabin,** where an overnight permit is required to stay.

The trail is distinctive for the wide, black *pāhoehoe* lava flows through which it crosses. "It is a transition area," Gale says, "where water comes splashing in heavy rains, creating erosion gullies and flowing rivers. The plants, ash, and lava terrain here are remarkable, as are the panoramic views of the ash dunes near the coast."

The Ka'ū Desert Trail turns uphill from Pepeiao Cabin for a very remote, 7.3-mile hike through 1920 and 1971 lava flows to Mauna Iki, where the unusual lava phenomenon called "Pele's hair" is found.

"Pele's hair is volcanic glass tinsel," Gale says, "formed when particles of molten lava are thrown into the air and spun by the wind into long, hairlike strands. It is one of the most fragile features in the park."

▶ Coastal Trails

There are more than 32 miles of Pacific coastline in Hawai'i Volcanoes National Park, and more than 20 miles of trails on or near the water.

They can be reached from several points, including Hilina Pali Overlook; the **Mau Loa o Mauna Ulu** area of the Chain of Craters Road; and the Pu'u Loa parking area, off the same road.

❸ **Hilina Pali Trail** Extending from Hilina Pali Overlook, the 3.8-mile Hilina Pali Trail is highly recommended by Gale. It leads down the mountainside via a switchback stone walkway built in the 1930s to **Ka'aha.** Once at the base of the *pali,* the terrain flattens out and traverses a region used by the War Department for bombing practice during World

The face of the park changes with every major eruption. Hawai'i Volcanoes National Park is a walk through geologic time. It is very dynamic, very alive.

—JIM GALE
Hawai'i Volcanoes National Park chief of interpretation

Local Intelligence

National parks can be spiritual places, but not many have their own resident goddess. Count Hawai'i Volcanoes National Park as an exception. Here, Pele, Hawai'i's powerful fire goddess, is said to live in **Halema'uma'u Crater,** near the park's main entrance. In ancient Hawai'i, people displayed great respect for their deities, calling on them to bless food crops and bring success in fishing, good tidings for family, or strength in battle.

Today, "We look at Pele as a grandmother figure," explains Danny Akaka, one of Hawai'i's most respected elders and cultural ambassadors. "She takes care of our land. When we go visit Tutu Pele, we take an offering and lay it on the edge of the crater in respect. We want our children to grow up with a strong connection to our cultural past."

Most often, the offering is an open *maile* lei—made from the vines and leaves of Hawai'i's maile plant. Akaka explains: "It represents an umbilical cord that connects us to the spiritual side."

Aerial shot of the park coastline

War II. Occasionally, unexploded ordinance is still found. Once at Ka'aha, broad coastal views reveal numerous sea arches in an area Gale describes as "pristine."

From Ka'aha, you can continue along the Hilina Pali Trail on a 6-mile trek across a magnificent tabletop bluff and then back down to the ocean at **Halapē,** a favored destination of hearty wilderness hikers. Though the hike to Halapē can be grueling, the payoff is a secret sandy beach where you can pitch a tent under palm trees next to the ocean.

4 Puna Coast Trail The Puna Coast Trail between the Halapē campsite and the Pu'u Loa trailhead is just over 11 miles long and can be hot many months of the year.

The hike leads past **'Āpua Point,** where the ocean is also accessible (albeit dangerous riptides are common), and through vast lava fields.

Across Chain of Craters Road from the Puna Coast Trailhead is the more popular **Pu'u Loa Petroglyph Trail,** a 1.4-mile round-trip to an area where thousands of ancient Hawaiian rock carvings can be seen.

▶ Mauna Loa Summit

The higher elevations of Hawai'i Volcanoes National Park are far less user-friendly than other areas of the park and, according to Gale, should only be attempted by experienced hikers in extremely good physical condition.

"It's more mountaineering than hiking," he says. "Conditions can change rapidly near the summit, and you have to be ready to bivouac overnight in freezing temperatures. Blizzards, high winds, and whiteouts are not uncommon any time of year."

For those who attain the 13,677-foot-high summit, however, the reward is views sweeping across the island to sister volcano Mauna Kea (a few feet taller at 13,769 in elevation), down to the **Kailua-Kona Coast** and the Pacific Ocean, and into **Moku'āweoweo Caldera.**

The Mauna Loa Trail begins at the Mauna Loa Lookout, at an elevation of 6,662 feet. Gale describes the terrain as a series of "fissures leading through the rift zone and false summits before the top. It is a rigorous but rewarding experience."

Milky Way over Haleakalā Crater

HALEAKALĀ

Covering 33,450 acres—8,260 of which are inaccessible wilderness—and named for the dormant volcano Haleakalā (meaning "house of the sun") that dominates Maui's skyline, Haleakalā National Park has two access points. The more popular leads to the crater rim (9,740 feet) from the tourism-heavy side of the island between Wailea and Kahului; the other is from Kīpahulu, on the remote eastern shore near the town of Hāna.

There are no highways or trails connecting the upper and lower parts of the park. Although more than one million people visit the summit of Haleakalā each year, many in organized tour groups to watch sunrise, the park is beautiful throughout the entire day, and sunrise from the summit is a very different experience than sunset from the beaches. If you seek a more in-depth exploration of the secrets of Haleakalā, embark on any of the web of hiking trails that start near the visitor centers.

Year-Round Visitor Centers

- **Park Headquarters Visitor Center**
  On Hawaii 378, park summit entrance
- **Haleakalā Visitor Center**
  11 miles south (uphill) of Park Headquarters
- **Kīpahulu Visitor Center**
  On Hawaii 31

808-572-4400, *www.nps.gov/hale*

▶ Park Headquarters Visitor Center

Park Headquarters Visitor Center is the place most people start their visit. Interpretive guides are available here to answer questions, make suggestions, and help you get your bearings.

❶ **Hosmer Grove Loop** This is an easy but rewarding hike that starts 1 mile below the Park Headquarters Visitor Center.

Next to the drive-in campground, a short trail leads through *ōhia' a lenua* trees and native shrubland. In addition to viewing the unique flora of the park at this elevation (7,000 feet), Hosmer Grove is an exceptionally good area for bird-watching, with several native forest birds—including Hawai'i's endangered honeycreepers—regularly spotted. At night, the Hawaiian hoary bat sometimes makes an appearance.

❷ **Halemau'u Trail** An area that offers both easy and more moderate hiking options is the Halemau'u Trail, which begins at the 8,000-foot level (3.5 miles upslope from the Park Headquarters Visitor Center) and leads 1.1 miles through native shrubland to the rim of **Ko'olau Gap.**

Here, the cliffs drop off 1,000 feet and you are treated to extraordinary views across the upper reaches of the park. If you are looking for a short walking experience, this is a good one.

Pressing forward from the rim, though, a longer and less traveled trail descends 1,400 feet down a sometimes steep (and narrow) series of switchbacks to the valley floor.

The views along this portion of the trail are remarkable, revealing the valley that shows various shades of muted rust and brown, is punctuated by lava flows and lava cones, and is in many places covered in cinder ash.

At the 3.7-mile mark of this trail, you'll run across **Hōlua Cabin** and campsite for overnight stays (with permit). Less than a mile beyond the cabin, a cursory jaunt off the Halemau'u Trail, is the 1-mile **Silversword Loop** that leads through an area displaying one of the greatest concentrations of *'āhinahina* (silversword plants) in the park. A mature 'āhinahina can stand 8 feet tall, with misty silver fingers emanating from a spiny center stalk.

The Halemau'u Trail is one of the park's primary hiking arteries. It extends 10.3 miles from the trailhead to the **Palikū Cabin** and the **Kaupō Trail.** The trail also branches off to **Keonehe'ehe'e** (Sliding Sands) **Trail.** An 11.2-mile day hike follows Halemau'u Trail out and back to the Haleakalā Visitor Center via Keonehe'ehe'e.

▶ Haleakalā Visitor Center

Haleakalā National Park preserves the volcanic landscape of the upper slopes of the mountain and protects the unique and fragile ecosystems that include many rare and endangered plants and forest birds. But it is not the jungle-covered Hawai'i portrayed in Hollywood movies. Instead, you'll get a glimpse into the geologic history of the island chain and its fiery volcanic past.

Start at the Haleakalā Visitor Center and hike from there. Trails range from ten-minute strolls to overnight trips. Three rustic cabins are available by reservation.

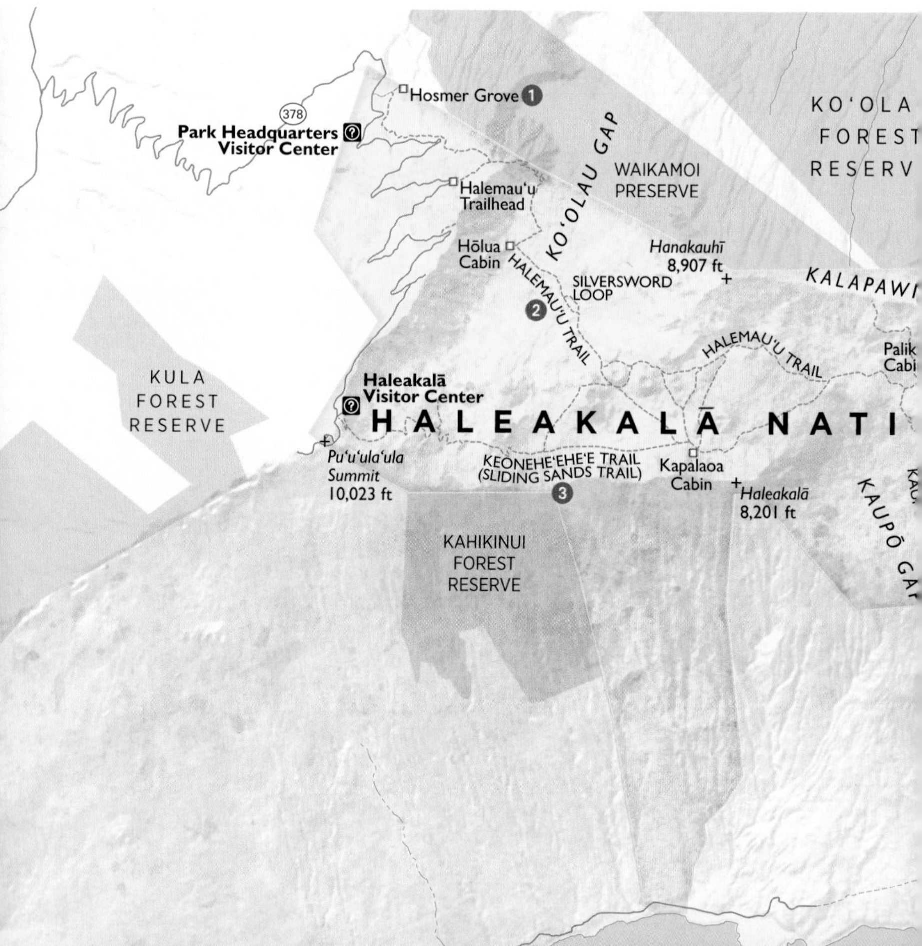

3 Keonehe'ehe'e Trail The Keonehe'ehe'e Trail sets out from the visitor center and descends 2,500 feet through a cinder desert to the crater floor and a vast wilderness area. The trail's Hawaiian name, Keonehe'ehe'e, refers to how a *he'e*—or octopus—moves across the reef. In the soft cinders, hikers experience a trail that slides octopus-like underfoot. The footing is safe, but it adds to the challenge of hiking back up the steep trail to the visitor center.

The first portions of the Keonehe'ehe'e Trail are beautifully desolate, with little shrubbery and no trees or greenery of any sort. But the red-hued cinder ash is otherworldly, particularly as you pass the frequent *pu'u* (cinder cones) along the way.

Kapalaoa Cabin is found 5.6 miles from the trailhead, and Palikū Cabin is 9.3 miles from the trailhead. Both require permits for overnight stays.

4 Kaupō Trail One of the less traveled and most spectacular trails in the upper regions of the park is the Kaupō Trail.

Considered one of the premier hikes in Hawai'i, the upper trailhead is found near Palikū Cabin. Park Superintendent Sarah Creachbaum calls this area "one of the most beautiful places on the planet. We get

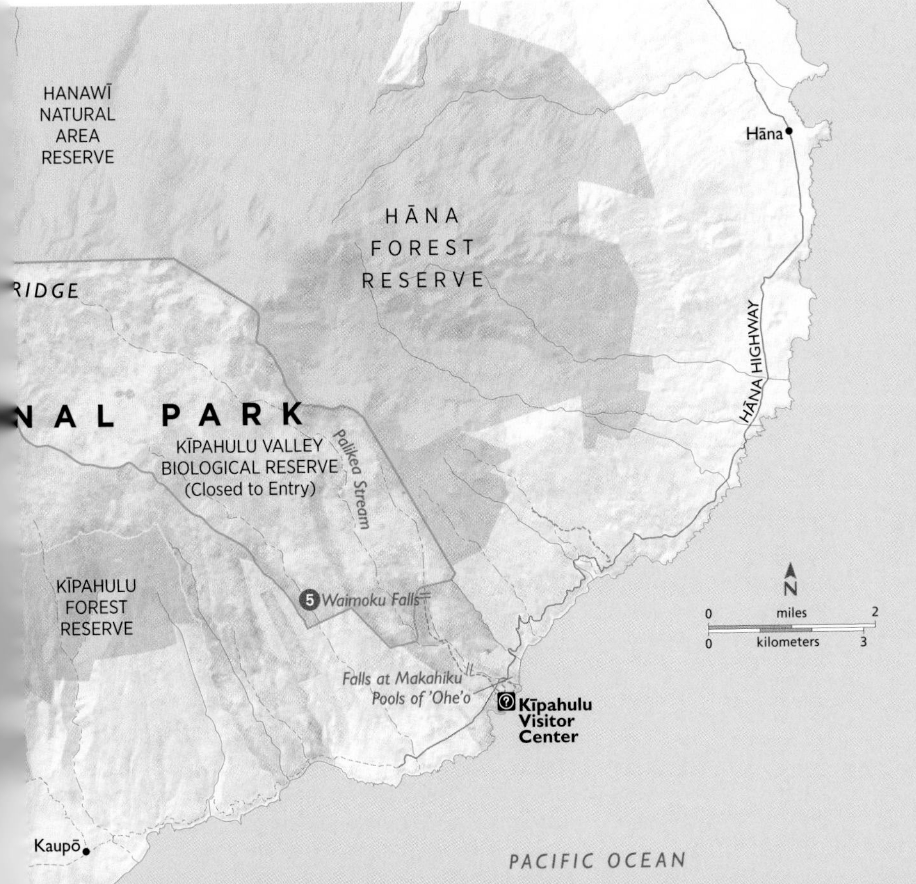

A boardwalk through a bamboo forest at Haleakalā

only 30 inches of rain per year at the summit near the visitor center," she says, "but just above the *pali* (cliff) in this part of the park is a big bog that gets more than 420 inches per year," creating lush scenery with frequent waterfalls visible from the trail.

Many hikers find hiking up the rugged and steep Kaupō Trail from the ocean easier than hiking downhill from the cabin. The trail traverses the outer wall of the verdant pali, with broad views toward the **Big Island of Hawai'i** and down toward the southeastern shore of **Maui.**

The trail actually goes beyond park boundaries through privately owned lands. The property owners have granted hikers permission to pass through provided they stay on the designated trails.

Local Intelligence

Haleakalā figures prominently in Hawaiian mythology. One of the most widely told stories recalls an achievement of Maui, an ancient Polynesian sailor and navigator with many feats and tales to his credit. One of his accomplishments, it has been told for generations, was to slow the sun as it crossed the sky.

Throughout Polynesia, this tale is most prominent in **Hawai'i** and **Aotearoa** (New Zealand), the two portions of the "Polynesian Triangle" farthest from the Equator, which share seasonal changes in day length—important knowledge for island mariners.

Beyond the scenery, our greatest resources are people and their traditional knowledge. When I hear a storyteller share an adventure of Maui, I get a glimpse into [secret] knowledge I can't get from a book.

—JEFF BAGSHAW
Haleakalā National Park ranger

▶ Kīpahulu

The other park entrance is via Kīpahulu. To get to the Kīpahulu Visitor Center, you need to take one of the most dramatic drives in the Hawaiian Islands, the **Hāna Highway,** a 68-mile route along the scenic east coast of Maui.

With 620 hairpin curves, 59 bridges, and numerous turnouts to get the cameras out for photography, it often takes more than 2.5 hours to get to the town of **Hāna** from **Kahului.**

Another 30 minutes (12 miles) past Hāna is the Kīpahulu Visitor Center and the coastal area of Haleakalā National Park. Far different than the more barren upper reaches, at Kīpahulu the terrain is green with rain forest vegetation and where waterfalls are common.

Hāna and Kīpahulu were once densely populated and farmed. The Kīpahulu portion of the park was added not only to preserve scenery, but also to allow a glimpse into traditional Hawaiian lifestyles. Walter Pu, park guide, says that for him, "Kīpahulu is living the past, sustaining the future."

5 Waimoku Falls Stop first at the visitor center to enjoy cultural demonstrations and get hiking advice. Short trails branch out from there to the coast and upslope to view Waimoku Falls (2 miles one way) and **Falls at Makahiku** (1 mile one way).

While many are tempted to swim in the **Pools of 'Ohe'o,** wise visitors will just take pictures while keeping their feet dry.

Visitors who disregard the warning signs can easily slip on the smooth rocks or be swept out to sea without a moment's notice by "freshets"—flash floods that come without warning.

And even clear, calm, fresh waters can be home to parasites such as *giardia* and *spirulosis* in modern Hawai'i. A spontaneous swim can lead to months of medical care.

'Ohe'o Gulch, aka Seven Sacred Pools

"When in need of peace, calm, and tranquillity, it's the comforting hidden solitude and stunning beauty of our priceless treasures—our national parks—that bring me back to life."

—SUE VENTO
NATIONAL PARK TRUST LEADERSHIP COUNCIL

[4]

MORE PARK SECRETS

Bleached caribou antler on tundra, Gates of the Arctic National Park

CONGAREE

CEDAR CREEK

Located just 20 miles from South Carolina's capital, Congaree National Park encompasses 27,000 acres of old-growth bottomland hardwood forest, the largest such expanse remaining in the southeastern United States. With an average canopy height of over 100 feet, the trees form one of the tallest temperate deciduous forests in the world.

Trails are concentrated in the park's western portion, leaving the rest of the floodplain forest untouched. The secret? "Most people don't think to see the park by water," says Lindsay Compton, interpretive park ranger.

Entering at the Cedar Creek canoe access, committed paddlers can take a two-day trek following the creek through the center of the park to the **Congaree River,** which forms the southern boundary. Trees overhang the narrow, black-water creek, while alligators bask in the sunshine on the broad river.

"It's going into one of the densest parts of the park that's never been logged," Compton says. "It gives people a good idea as to why this area was preserved—there's really not much else like it in the state."

803-776-4396, *www.nps.gov/cong*

DRY TORTUGAS

CORAL REEFS

Some of North America's most pristine coral reefs cluster around the low-lying islands of the Dry Tortugas. Ships, carrying everything from Spanish explorers to coffee and tobacco, used to get tangled in the seven sand and coral islands about 70 nautical miles from Key West, Florida, so it's no surprise that this park is both naturally beautiful and historically significant. Visits often start at **Fort Jefferson,** one of the Americas' largest masonry-built forts.

Snorkelers at Dry Tortugas, which is only accessible by boat or seaplane (look for the namesake sea turtles on the journey there), need only wade into the water to see purple sea fans and brain coral along with bluehead wrasse and rainbow parrotfish.

Less known is that this is also one of the country's best places to see wild conch. The giant-shelled mollusk's populations have shrunk, but here they still crawl among the sea grasses.

305-242-7700, *www.nps.gov/drto*

VIRGIN ISLANDS

REEF BAY TRAIL

Protecting over 7,000 acres, Virgin Islands National Park comprises almost two-thirds of the island of **St. John,** the smallest of the United States Virgin Islands. Within the park, archaeological sites dating from as early as 840 B.C. to Columbus's arrival in 1493 can be found on almost every beach and bay.

Discover ancient petroglyphs—rock carvings—on the Reef Bay Trail. Located on an old carriage road, the trail descends through St. John's thickly forested steep slopes to the coast. About 2 miles along the trail, an offshoot leads to petroglyphs that are "a well-kept secret and a special experience for folks," says Superintendent Mark Hardgrove.

The island's early inhabitants, the Taino Indians, carved the geometric symbols into a 70-foot-tall rock face. A quiet waterfall usually flows over the carvings into a large pool at the base of the cliff. It sometimes dries up in winter—splash water from the pool onto the carvings to make them pop for photos.

340-776-6201, *www.nps.gov/viis*

MAMMOTH CAVE

VIOLET CITY LANTERN TOUR

Under the hills of Kentucky, the world's longest known cave system twists and turns for more than 390 miles. Curious tourists have wandered Mammoth Cave's tunnels for about 200 years, but spelunkers still discover and chart new limestone caverns and passageways today.

The only way to descend into the labyrinth is on a ranger-led tour, which typically follows electrically lit passageways. For a different perspective, take this relatively secret excursion: Grab a kerosene lamp as tourists did two centuries ago for the Violet City Lantern Tour.

The soft light casts monster-size shadows, and without the usual illumination to see, your other senses heighten—listen for water cascading through the caverns, feel the ancient cave walls, and smell the fresh cave air.

270-758-2180, *www.nps.gov/maca*

CUYAHOGA VALLEY
SUSTAINABLE FARMS

Named for an American Indian word meaning "crooked river," the water that flows between Cleveland and Akron in Ohio forms the core of one of America's most eclectic national parks. Here you can hike through a rocky gorge, but also attend a concert; ride a scenic railroad, then refine your golf swing; or explore beaver habitat in the morning, then admire art at an old, repurposed gas station in the afternoon.

For a lesser known experience, tour the dozen farms affiliated with Cuyahoga Valley. These aren't historical sites focused on blacksmith demonstrations and old-fashioned agriculture (though you'll find that too, at the independently operated **Hale Farm and Village** inside the park). Instead, they're small, privately run sustainable farms dedicated to preserving the Midwest's agricultural landscape and lifestyle.

Drop by **Sarah's Vineyard,** for example, any time during regular hours, but be sure to call ahead before visiting the other farms.

330-657-2752, *www.nps.gov/cuva*

ISLE ROYALE
PASSAGE ISLAND

Located in the northwestern portion of Lake Superior 56 miles from Michigan's Upper Peninsula, Isle Royale National Park preserves the largest island in the world's largest freshwater lake, as well as more than 450 surrounding islands. For more than 50 years, Isle Royale's isolation has made it the perfect place for scientists to study its wolves and their predator-prey relationship with moose—and a secret spot for you to explore.

Experience the farthest boundaries of the park on Passage Island, located about 3.5 miles off the northeast end of the main island. Visitors can reach here via their own boats or the excursion boat M.V. *Sandy,* operated by the Rock Harbor Lodge.

"Most people only know about Passage Island because there is a lighthouse there, but it is so much more," says Liz Valencia, the park's chief of interpretation and cultural resources. "There are no moose there, so the vegetation is different than on the main island. In the summer, it has an almost jungle-like quality."

906-482-0984, *www.nps.gov/isro*

VOYAGEURS

CHAIN OF LAKES

Named for the French Canadian traders who transported furs in birch-bark canoes, Voyageurs National Park protects more than 200,000 acres along Minnesota's Canadian border. Moose, timber wolves, black bears, and white-tailed deer roam the park's boreal forest and exposed Precambrian rocks that are more than two billion years old.

Avoid the crowds on the larger waterways and take the 2-mile **Locator Lake Trail** to the Chain of Lakes, a set of four inland bodies of water on the **Kabetogama Peninsula.** Canoes stored at the head of Locator Lake can be rented for $10 a day, and campsites at each lake allow you to explore for days.

"I liked the anticipation of wondering what the next lake might look like, and looking for bear or moose," says Kathleen Przybylski, a former park staffer who paddled the length of the chain. "It's a more wilderness type of experience, feeling like you're the only ones out there. There's a good chance you will be the only people on the lake."

218-283-6600, *www.nps.gov/voya*

HOT SPRINGS

TAKING THE WATERS

In the 19th century, a steaming pocket of central Arkansas evolved from a rugged settlement to a glamorous destination for soothing hot water treatments said to cure all sorts of ills. Along **Bathhouse Row,** which is the heart of the park, you can still walk through rooms filled with stained glass and statues and take a dip in traditional baths or at a modern-day spa.

But why stop with just soaking? Come armed with a jug so you can "quaff the elixir," as visitors used to say when they tipped their heads back and gulped the springs' bounty. Rangers won't speak to the water's curative power, but they will certify that it's safe to drink at designated fountains.

So go ahead and take home your share of the 700,000 gallons collected from the springs daily. The water comes out hot—the springs average 143°F—but some say it's delicious when chilled.

501-620-6715, *www.nps.gov/hosp*

GUADALUPE MOUNTAINS

PERMIAN REEF TRAIL

For proof that landscapes can change drastically over time, consider the Guadalupe Mountains. Millions of years ago they were part of a tropical reef, populated by sponges, algae, and other ocean creatures.

When the water receded, natural forces buried the reef, then pushed it skyward and sculpted the limestone peaks now in the park. The highest part of the more-than-40-mile range is preserved in this West Texas area, where more than 80 miles of trails weave through rocky cliffs, oak and maple forests, and desert scrub.

Many come to admire the park's gorgeous canyons and vistas—**McKittrick Canyon** is popular, with fall colors that rival New England's. But to best appreciate how the landscape came to be, hike the Permian Reef Trail, a secret spot that draws geologists from across the world.

The 8.4-mile path climbs 2,000 feet alongside cacti and canyon views. From boulders to rock walls, the limestone along the way is etched with the remains of sponges, cephalopods, and other ancient ocean life.

915-828-3251, *www.nps.gov/gumo*

CARLSBAD CAVERNS

YUCCA CANYON TRAIL

Located in southeastern New Mexico's Guadalupe Mountains, Carlsbad Caverns National Park is mostly known for the 117 caves that lie beneath its rocky slopes and canyons. Aboveground, however, holds wonders as well—250 million years ago the mountains were a reef that edged an inland sea, and the rocks are studded with the preserved bodies of sponges, algae, and nautilus.

"People come here to visit the caves, but most people forget the fact that there's over 46,000 acres here, and most of that is wilderness," says Paula Bauer, management assistant. "There's marvelous hiking here."

Bauer recommends the Yucca Canyon Trail, which runs along the southwestern corner of the park. Accessible by road for high-clearance vehicles, the trail climbs a side canyon, then levels out on top of an escarpment that offers a dizzying view of the vast **Permian Basin,** all that remains of the inland sea.

Near the end of the 7.7-mile trail, hikers are rewarded with a secret—a stand of ponderosa pines, which is an unusual sight in Carlsbad. Explains Bauer: "They're a holdover from when this wasn't a desert."

575-785-2232, *www.nps.gov/cave*

SAGUARO

RINCON MOUNTAINS

With arms reaching upward and a tall, majestic silhouette, it's no wonder the saguaro cactus has become an icon of the Southwest. The plant can grow up to 50 feet tall and weigh as much as 16,000 pounds—and has so captured our imaginations that we protect part of its habitat in Saguaro National Park near Tucson in Arizona.

Just west of the city, the park's **Tucson Mountain District** is widely known for hillsides dotted with the statuesque cacti. Many people, however, overlook the park's eastern unit, which not only includes saguaros, but also features the moister, cooler ecosystems of the Rincon Mountains.

Says Natalie Rose, park ranger: "Once you get past a certain elevation here, you lose the saguaros and the cacti, and you start seeing a whole different level of nature."

Rincon Mountain District: 520-733-5153,
Tucson Mountain District: 520-733-5158, *www.nps.gov/sagu*

GREAT SAND DUNES

CASTLE CREEK PICNIC AREA

Climbing up to 750 feet and softly waving in the shadow of the Sangre de Cristo Mountains, Colorado's Great Sand Dunes are spectacular on their own. This park, however, also includes 13,000-foot mountain peaks, fragrant piñon-juniper woodlands, open grasslands, alpine tundra, and **Medano Creek,** which generates waves up to a foot high—a rare phenomenon called "surge flow."

You'll certainly want hiking gear, but here's the secret: Pack as if you were visiting a ski lodge and water resort, too. You can sail down the dunes on slick-bottomed sleds or snowboards, and, in spring and early summer, kids can use inner tubes to bob in Medano Creek's unusual waves. For both activities, head to the Castle Creek Picnic Area. You'll have snowcapped mountains in the background, swimmers splashing in the creek below, and the wind in your face as you career down a dune. See the park website for information about creek flows, road conditions, and weather alerts.

719-378-6399, *www.nps.gov/grsa*

BLACK CANYON OF THE GUNNISON

PAINTED WALL

Deeper than it is wide in some places, the Black Canyon rises more than 2,700 feet above the Gunnison River in Colorado. This plunging, rocky scar is many times steeper than the Grand Canyon and is so forbidding that only the most determined hikers reach the bottom.

But from its rim, you see rare Precambrian rock—at nearly two billion years old, this type of stone normally remains locked up beneath the Earth's surface and rarely sees the light of day. Drive along the South Rim to get a good view of Painted Wall—the highest cliff in Colorado—and divine its secrets.

"It looks like somebody hand-painted it," says Sandy Snell-Dobert, ranger. "There are streaks of pink in the shape of serpents or dragons going across the dark rock background."

970-641-2337, *www.nps.gov/blca*

GREAT BASIN

BRISTLECONE PINE GROVE

No water drains to an ocean in the Great Basin, a vast area that stretches from the tall Sierra Nevada range in California to Utah's Wasatch Range. Located in eastern Nevada, Great Basin National Park protects a diverse landscape of high-altitude desert valleys, salt flats, and rolling ridges crowned by 13,063-foot **Wheeler Peak.**

Most visitors come for the famed **Lehman Caves,** but for a secret treat, stay aboveground and take the **Wheeler Peak Scenic Drive** to the campground at the mountain's base. Then follow the **Bristlecone and Glacier Trail** 1.4 miles to a grove of magnificent bristlecone pines perched on the slopes of Wheeler Peak. Through the trees, hikers can glimpse magnificent views of the Snake Valley spread out below. Above the grove the trail ends at one of Nevada's few glaciers, a mass of boulders and ice steadily inching its way down the peak.

"Those trees are 5,000 years old," says Superintendent Andy Ferguson of the bristlecone pines. "They don't fall down, they just weather away. People who go to the grove often all say they have the same feeling—that it's a spiritual visit."

775-234-7331, *www.nps.gov/grba*

KINGS CANYON

CALIF. 180

Adjoining and mutually operated with Sequoia National Park (see pp. 212–217), Kings Canyon is often overlooked in favor of its more famous partner. But its glacier-carved canyons and rugged mountains in the southern **Sierra Nevada** offer an equally stunning landscape in central California.

The vast majority of the park is designated wilderness, but visitors can follow Calif. 180 into the eponymous Kings Canyon to its end in the park. "It's the largest canyon in the park into which you can drive," says Becky Satnat, park ranger. The road, open only in summer, runs along the rushing white water of the **South Fork Kings River,** hemmed in by narrow canyon walls. Near its end the canyon widens and travelers can see peaks in the distance.

Concludes Satnat about this secret: "People think a dead-end road is boring, but it ends in an absolutely gorgeous place."

559-565-3341, *www.nps.gov/seki*

LASSEN VOLCANIC

DEVILS KITCHEN

The largest hydrothermal area west of Yellowstone, this northeastern California park is sprinkled with seething steam vents, bubbling mudpots, and boiling pools. Lassen Peak blew its top in 1915—the last eruption in the lower 48 before Mount Saint Helens exploded in 1980. While the mountain that dominates Lassen Volcanic National Park has quieted down, it's still considered an active volcano.

Bumpass Hell Trail, with its convenient location and boardwalk past hissing volcanic phenomena, is understandably a visitor hot spot. But travelers often overlook the fascinating sulfur-scented secret known as Devils Kitchen.

Tucked into the **Warner Valley**'s upper reaches, this trail isn't all boardwalks, so in some places you'll find yourself stepping on the hard-packed crusty ground, with steam thumping below the surface, mud boiling around you, and the aroma of questionable cooking wafting through the air. Just don't stray from the established trail. *Be warned: One wrong step and your foot could sink through thin crust and plunge into scalding mud.*

530-595-4480, *www.nps.gov/lavo*

NORTH CASCADES

UPPER STEHEKIN VALLEY

Less than three hours from Seattle, Washington's North Cascades National Park preserves a wide array of biodiversity, from its western temperate rain forest to its eastern dry ponderosa pine ecosystem. More than 300 glaciers can be found in the park's jagged, comparatively young mountains, with dramatic landscapes spread over 9,000 feet of vertical relief.

Experienced backcountry travelers in search of secret solitude can take the **Bridge Creek Trail** into the Upper Stehekin Valley, in the park's southern section. The narrow, forested area is surrounded by 7,000- to 9,000-foot glaciated peaks, crowned by 9,220-foot **Goode Mountain.** A side trip along the **Goode Ridge Trail** takes hikers into a spectacular horseshoe surrounded by giant ridges that reveal the park's mountainous grandeur.

"Most people don't visit the valley," says Charles Beall, chief of interpretation and education for the park. "It's not supereasy to get to, but once you're there, it's easy to feel like you're all alone."

360-854-7200, *www.nps.gov/noca*

GLACIER BAY

BEARDSLEE ISLANDS

Just over 200 years ago, Glacier Bay was almost completely covered by ice. Since then, the receding glaciers have revealed a dynamic landscape of rugged mountains and temperate rain forest along Alaska's **Inside Passage.** Marine life is the highlight: harbor porpoises, Steller sea lions, and humpback, minke, and killer whales abound in the park's waters.

The vast majority of Glacier Bay National Park and Preserve's visitors arrive on cruise ships, and few venture into the many small inlets and coves. For a semi-secret adventure, rent a kayak in **Bartlett Cove** and explore the Beardslee Islands, a complex of about two dozen small islands in the lower part of the bay. Take care not to get stranded by tides that can rise and fall up to 25 feet—at low tide, some of the areas of the Beardslees are very shallow or exposed mudflat.

"Anyone seeking a short adventure can pick their own island, pitch a tent, and experience the sights and sounds of Glacier Bay's wilderness firsthand," says Tom VandenBerg, supervisory park ranger. "Bald Eagles, black bears, harbor seals, and humpback whales are all common in this beautiful area."

907-697-2230, *www.nps.gov/glba*

WRANGELL-ST. ELIAS

KENNECOTT

At more than 13 million acres, Wrangell-St. Elias in southeastern Alaska is the United States' largest national park. Here, four major mountain ranges come together, combining volcanoes, coastal mountains, and more than 150 glaciers into a protected place bigger in area than Switzerland. This is Alaska wilderness so untamed that experienced hikers often set off to make their own trails.

While many visitors are drawn to Wrangell-St. Elias to escape the daily grind of the lower 48 states, it is little known that the park ties its history to American industry. Now a scenic cluster of red and white buildings, the mill town of Kennecott supported the world's most productive copper mine a century ago.

Hoping to supply copper for everything from electrical wires to cars, the wealthy Morgan and Guggenheim families invested in the mine despite its location on a remote, snow-covered mountain. It was a Warren Buffett-style move: When the vein ran out in 1938, the mine had made $100 million in profits and enriched the heritage of this monumental park.

907-822-7250, *www.nps.gov/wrst*

KENAI FJORDS

NORTHWESTERN FJORD

With over half of the park covered in ice, Kenai Fjords National Park offers some of the starkest scenery in southern Alaska. The **Harding Icefield** and its nearly 40 outflowing glaciers envelop more than 700 square miles of the **Kenai Mountains.** The deep coastal fjords carved by the glaciers form rare estuary ecosystems found in only six locations in the world.

Skip the crowds in **Aialik Bay** and kayak through Northwestern Fjord, which is less exposed to the Gulf of Alaska than many of the park's other bays and fjords. Northwestern's brilliant greenish blue color, caused by glacial melt, "looks very inviting," says Kristy Sholly, the park's chief of interpretation.

For often solitary wildlife-watching, paddle to **Northwestern Glacier** at the head of the fjord. Harbor seals hang out here, and the fjord's steep sides make excellent nesting areas for seabirds such as Pigeon Guillemots and the rare Kittlitz's Murrelet. *Attention kayakers: Hire a guide to get through strong tides.*

907-422-0500, *www.nps.gov/kefj*

KATMAI

BROOKS CAMP

With 2,200 brown bears and 15 volcanoes—some steaming—Katmai is like Alaska in concentrate. Here you'll find the **Valley of Ten Thousand Smokes,** named for its landscape of once fuming fumaroles, and you might be able to snap that iconic photo of a bear catching salmon in a waterfall.

For a relaxing trip, proceed to Brooks Camp—the square-mile area where as many as 100 bears can roam during peak activity periods. The secret to seeing furry wildlife is patience; stay for at least two days, says ranger Roy Wood. "Allow yourself to fall into the rhythm of bears and the slower-paced life," he advises. The bears, which come to stuff themselves with salmon, sometimes doze on paths—one once dug a "bed" by the visitor center and took a nap. The rangers function as "bear traffic control," closing trails and bridges to avoid close human encounters with animals that can weigh up to 900 pounds.

907-246-3305, *www.nps.gov/katm*

LAKE CLARK

TLIKAKILA RIVER

Inaccessible by any road, Lake Clark National Park and Preserve protects 4 million acres of dynamic wilderness in south-central Alaska, including two active volcanoes: **Mount Iliamna** and **Mount Redoubt.** The **Chigmit Mountains** strike through the park's center, bridging the **Aleutian Range** to the south and the **Alaska Range** to the north.

Most visitors stick to the coastal areas along the **Cook Inlet** for bear viewing, but a few strike inland to brave the Class II and III rapids on the broad Tlikakila River. Originating in **Lake Clark Pass** and fed by a series of glaciers, the brown, fast-moving river runs through the center of the park and offers thrilling rafting and kayaking during multiday trips. King, coho, and sockeye salmon forge upstream through the sixth largest lake in Alaska to spawn in summer. The river certainly can be called secret: "Tlikakila usually doesn't get anyone on it, maybe only once a year," reports chief ranger Rich Richotte.

907-781-2218, *www.nps.gov/lacl*

DENALI

TATTLER CREEK

Only a single road cuts through Denali National Park and Preserve's 6 million acres, leading from taiga forest to alpine tundra shadowed by 20,320-foot **Mount McKinley,** the tallest peak in North America. The Athabascan native people named the mountain "Denali," meaning "high one." (Indeed, those trying to spot the summit from a distance often look too low in the sky.) The park in central Alaska was established to protect such wildlife as caribou, grizzly bears, and wolves—not to mention a rich secret history.

Experienced hikers can strike out from the park road near mile 37 (follow bear safety protocols, please) and climb up Tattler Creek to locate the "dance floor"—a spot where tracks of hadrosaurs and theropods can be seen on a rock outcrop. Since 2005, thousands of those kinds of dinosaur tracks and fossils have been discovered. "We're well known for our current large mammals, but we also have a rich prehistoric history," says Kris Fister, the park's public affairs officer. "We have this picture of the ecosystem 65 to 71 million years ago."

907-683-9532, *www.nps.gov/dena*

GATES OF THE ARCTIC

AGIAK LAKE

Located entirely north of the Arctic Circle, Gates of the Arctic National Park and Preserve sets aside some of Alaska's most pristine wilderness, and it can't help being secret. The mountains of the **Brooks Range** soar to the north, while millions of ponds dot valleys where waterfowl like swans, geese, cranes, loons, gyrfalcons, Short-eared Owls, and montane shorebirds nest in endless summer sunlight.

Upon first arrival, visitors may feel that no humans have ever set foot in Gates of the Arctic: There are no roads, no trails, and no campsites. Thousands of archaeological sites, however, testify to the people who have lived and traveled in the area for over 13,000 years. For example, take a floatplane to Agiak Lake to explore hundreds of rock cairns that line the valley for nearly a mile. These guided caribou into the lake, where Nunamiut Inuit hunters in kayaks hunted them with lances.

907-692-6922, *www.nps.gov/gaar*

KOBUK VALLEY

KOBUK RIVER

Bracketed by the **Baird Mountains** to the north and the **Kobuk Sand Dunes** to the south, Kobuk Valley National Park protects 1.7 million acres well above the Arctic Circle in Alaska. The broad Kobuk River Valley presents a stunning landscape of open woodland and thick tundra. The largest caribou herd in the state, in excess of 300,000 animals, travels through the park during its yearly migrations in late May and early September.

With no trails, no roads, and no ranger stations in the park, "even the easiest thing here is hard-core," says Linda Jeschke, park ranger. For hardy paddlers with their own boats and backcountry survival skills, she recommends a seven-day trip down the Kobuk River between the villages of **Ambler** and **Kiana.**

"In that time you may not see another human being," Jeschke says. The slow and easy river, edged in spruce forest, winds through the park for 61 miles. Near **Kavet Creek,** a 2- to 3-mile trek from the river brings hikers to a mostly secret spot: the 100-foot-high **Great Kobuk Sand Dunes,** the largest active dune field in arctic North America.

907-442-3890, *www.nps.gov/kova*

NATIONAL PARK OF AMERICAN SAMOA

HOMESTAY PROGRAM

Traveling thousands of miles to a place where the coconut tree has its own creation myth comes with many rewards: The National Park of American Samoa is a paradise of deep blue waters, secluded beaches, rain forest–covered volcanic islands, and reefs of colorful fish and intricate corals.

These three islands in the southwestern Pacific Ocean are also a cultural park preserving the *fa'asamoa*—the Samoan way. Soak up a secret hospitality by signing up for the park's homestay program, in which you room with the locals. Getting to Samoan hosts can be an adventure itself—you might ride alongside gasoline and groceries on a supply barge or travel in a fisherman's scow.

Once arrived, you may have the opportunity to learn to climb a coconut tree, spear an octopus, or weave leaves into mats. On Sundays, chances are foods such as banana and breadfruit will be prepared in an oven of heated rocks, an *umu*. At the visit's conclusion, ranger Joe Leleua playfully warns, "They're going to make you dance."

684-633-7082, *www.nps.gov/npsa*

Solomon Bay, Virgin Islands National Park

NATIONAL
GEOGRAPHIC
GUIDE TO THE
National Parks
of Canada

Small glacier near Mount Caubvick/Mont D'Iberville

TORNGAT MOUNTAINS

NEWFOUNDLAND & LABRADOR

ESTABLISHED 2005

9,700 sq km/2,400,000 acres

The region of Torngait, or "a place of spirits," was named after Torngarsoak, the most powerful spirit in Inuit mythology. Like the spirits, the land tends to be harsh. But the stark beauty of the region is tempered by the hospitality of the people and the unique opportunity to participate in traditional practices firsthand.

Coming to a sharp point at the northeasternmost edge of continental Canada, Torngat Mountains National Park covers a wedge of land between northern Quebec and the Labrador Sea. Rising from a rugged and barren coastline, this mountain range at the tip of Labrador is home to the highest peaks on mainland Canada east of the Rockies (the highest being Mount Caubvick at 1,652 m/5,420 ft). Massive, glacier-carved fjords, some more than 1 km (0.6 mi) high, saw-tooth the coast. Vast, exposed mountainsides put their underlying geologic formations on swirling display.

As you travel through this country, a couple of the most striking elements against the green velvet landscape are the surreal, luminescent blue icebergs that stud the dark waters and *nanuk*—the polar bears that wander the shores.

Torngat Mountains is the first national park in Labrador and the newest national park in Canada. The park is on the migratory path of the George River caribou herd, once the world's largest, but now numbering fewer than 100,000. The mountains are also home to wolves, arctic foxes, peregrine falcons, and the world's only tundra-dwelling black bears.

The park is above 55 degrees latitude and the tree line. Although Inuit no longer live here year-round, they still use the region for traditional food gathering. An all-Inuit cooperative management board, the first in the Parks Canada system, provides advice and guidance for the management of the park.

How to Get There

There are no roads to the Torngat Mountains. Access is through charter air flight or boat. Charter flights to Saglek Bay in Labrador may be arranged through Air Inuit *(www.airinuit.com)*, usually departing from Kuujjuaq in Nunavik (northern Quebec); Air Labrador *(www.airlabrador.com)*; or Innu Mikun *(www.provincialairlines.ca)*, departing from Goose Bay, Labrador.

Charter flights land on an airstrip near a military radar station, just south of where Torngat Mountains Base Camp and Research Station is located. The final leg from the airstrip to base camp requires a boat trip or a helicopter ride. The Labrador Inuit Development Corporation (709-922-2143) has a weekly return charter flight from Goose Bay to Saglek, departing every Saturday during the summer operating season.

Expedition Cruise ships travel to the park and into some of the fjords. For an updated list of cruise companies, check the Cruise Newfoundland and Labrador website *(www.cruisetheedge.com)*.

Those who seek to arrange their own travel into the park should contact Parks Canada to secure permits and arrange orientation sessions (888-922-1290).

When to Go

The summer season is short and the mildest weather occurs from mid-July to mid-August. For spring conditions, March and April can be good times to travel.

Mean average temperatures in the park range from 4°C (39°F) in the summer to minus 16.5°C (2°F) in the winter.

Climatic conditions, influenced heavily by latitude, altitude, and coastal currents, can change rapidly. Heavy wind, fog, and strong rain can sweep in, grounding planes and boats.

How to Visit

Last year about 450 visitors set foot in the Torngats, about one-third of whom travelled through on cruise ships, zipping ashore on zodiacs for day excursions. The number of visitors who came for a more immersive stay in base camp—including scientific researchers—numbered fewer than a hundred. Seven self-supported groups made their way into the park last year.

Because of its remote location, it's time-consuming and expensive to travel to the Torngats. A trip of at least four days makes sense to get a meaningful visit of the park.

TORNGAT EXPERIENCE

Torngat Safaris, officially launched in 2010, is a joint cooperation between the Labrador Inuit Development Corporation, Parks Canada, and Inuit-owned Cruise North Expeditions *(www.cruisenorthexpeditions.com)*. They offer four-night and seven-night stays.

The base for these organized expeditions is kANGIDLUASUk (St.

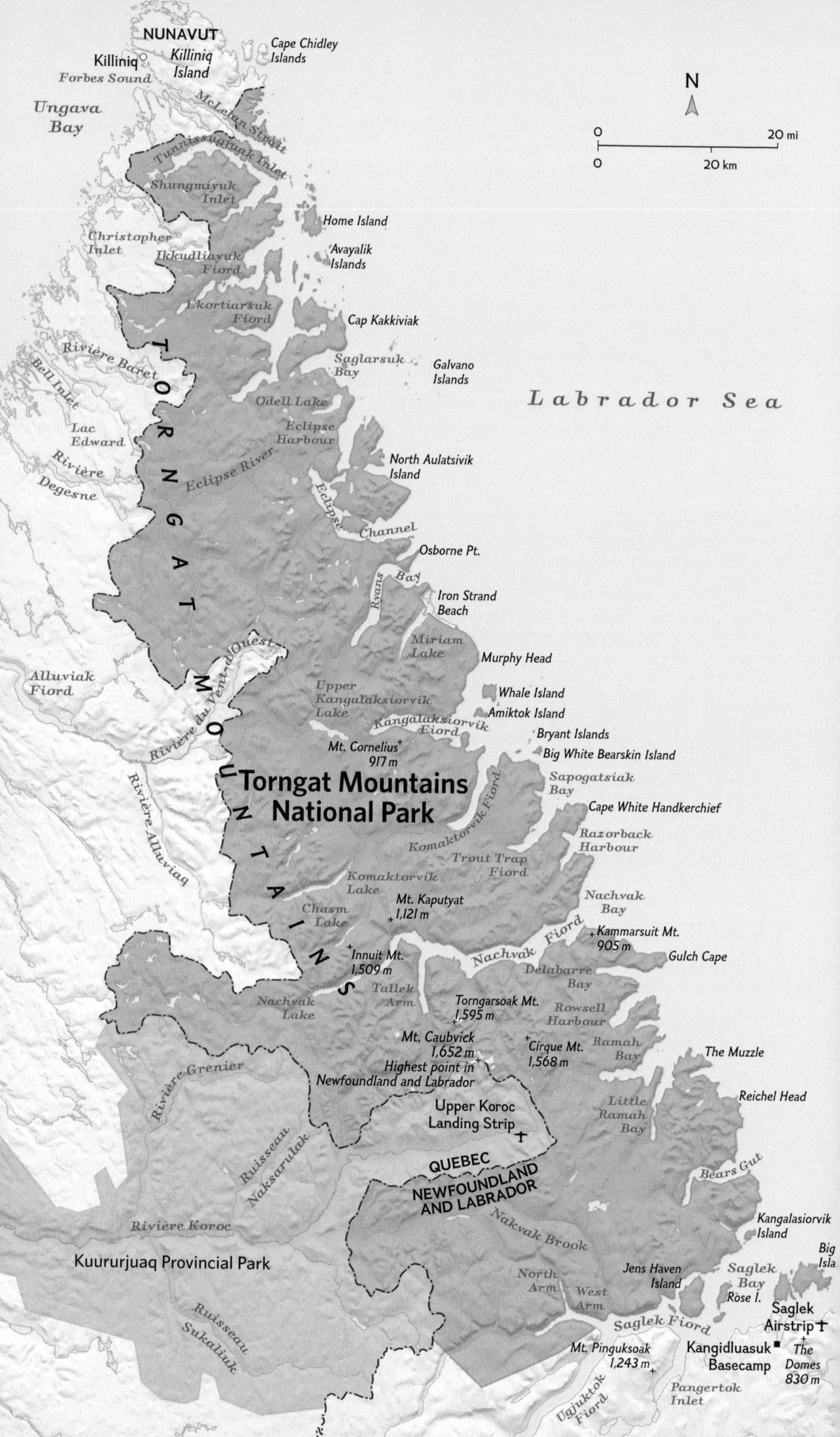

NUNAVUT
Killiniq
Killiniq Island
Cape Chidley Islands
Forbes Sound
Ungava Bay
McLelan Strait
Tunnissugjuak Inlet
Shungmiyuk Inlet
N
0
20 mi
0
20 km
Home Island
Christopher Inlet
Avayalik Islands
Ikkudliayuk Fiord
Ekortiarsuk Fiord
Cap Kakkiviak
Rivière Baret
Bell Inlet
Saglarsuk Bay
Galvano Islands
TORNGAT MOUNTAINS
Labrador Sea
Odell Lake
Lac Edward
Eclipse Harbour
Rivière Degesne
Eclipse River
North Aulatsivik Island
Eclipse Channel
Osborne Pt.
Ryans Bay
Iron Strand Beach
Miriam Lake
Murphy Head
Rivière du Vent-d'Ouest
Alluviak Fiord
Upper Kangalaksiorvik Lake
Whale Island
Amiktok Island
Kangalaksiorvik Fiord
Bryant Islands
Mt. Cornelius 917 m
Big White Bearskin Island
Rivière Alluviaq
Torngat Mountains National Park
Sapogatsiak Bay
Cape White Handkerchief
Komaktorvik Fiord
Razorback Harbour
Trout Trap Fiord
Komaktorvik Lake
Nachvak Bay
Chasm Lake
Mt. Kaputyat 1,121 m
Kammarsuit Mt. 905 m
Innuit Mt. 1,509 m
Nachvak Fiord
Gulch Cape
Delabarre Bay
Tallek Arm
Nachvak Lake
Torngarsoak Mt. 1,595 m
Rowsell Harbour
Mt. Caubvick 1,652 m
Highest point in Newfoundland and Labrador
Cirque Mt. 1,568 m
Ramah Bay
The Muzzle
Rivière Grenier
Upper Koroc Landing Strip
Reichel Head
Little Ramah Bay
Ruisseau Naksarulak
QUEBEC
NEWFOUNDLAND AND LABRADOR
Bears Gut
Rivière Koroc
Nakvak Brook
Kangalasiorvik Island
Kuururjuaq Provincial Park
Big Isla
North Arm
Jens Haven Island
Saglek Bay
West Arm
Rose I.
Saglek Airstrip
Ruisseau Sukaliuk
Saglek Fiord
Mt. Pinguksoak 1,243 m
Kangidluasuk Basecamp
The Domes 830 m
Ugjuktok Fiord
Pangertok Inlet

John's Harbour) in Sallik (Saglek) Bay, just outside the southern end of Torngat Mountains National Park. The base camp is an assembly of semipermanent wall tents, housing kitchen and mess areas, parks offices, and supply depots. Among them are rows of tents for short-term guests and staff. Torngat Safari guests stay in heated wall tents and sleep on cots. There is plenty of opportunity for interaction with the base camp Inuit staff and visiting researchers over meals in the mess tent and during evening presentations.

Fresh drinking and washing water comes straight from the stream beside the camp, but they also just recently installed flush toilets and hot showers. More permanent structures have been constructed to support the work of visiting research scientists. The other notable physical feature of the camp is the 10,000-volt electric fence that surrounds it, keeping out nearby polar bears.

Polar bear safety is of paramount concern in the park. Parks Canada recommends that visitors hiking in the park, especially those on overnight trips, engage the services of experienced Inuit polar bear guards. In the event this is not possible, visitors should have portable electric fences, appropriate bear deterrents, and/or a trained bear dog.

After settling into camp on your first day, part of the orientation will be a bear safety talk followed by a video—the first of its kind—that accumulates polar bear knowledge from Inuit elders. Inuit bear guards (allowed to carry firearms in the park) will accompany any foray outside the base camp and they soon become fixtures of the landscape, often distant figures in high-visibility vests or silhouettes on the horizon. It's common practice for Inuit to periodically turn around and survey the land behind them to make sure they're not being stalked. Along with the awe-inspiring scale of the Torngats, being in the midst of an apex predator is part of the experience, putting humans into their proper perspective.

INUIT GIFT

Torngat Mountains isn't just about grand landscapes. In fact, the park itself was a gift from the Inuit people to Canada, and interaction with the Inuit guides—most of whom have lived off this land for generations—can easily be the richest part of your visit here.

This isn't just their homeland in the conceptual sense. As you glide along the banks of a fjord, your Inuit guide might point to the spot where his mother was born. Or he may spot wildlife off in the distance, a polar bear perhaps or caribou, that would otherwise have gone unnoticed. He might even kneel down by evidence of habitation by the Inuit, or by their predecessors the Dorset and Thule, such as a Ramah chert shard tool nestled in the tundra or the faint remains of a tent ring.

As seminomadic subsistence hunters, the Inuit were inextricably tied to the land, and an intimate

Artifact from a Thule sod house, Nachvak Fjord

Southwest Arm, Saglek Fjord

Arctic hare

knowledge of the habits of wildlife is still of great importance. Experiencing traditional Inuit harvesting practices can be as hands-on as rolling up sleeves and helping to dress and skin a caribou or just simply observing. Others may prefer to fish for arctic char, wander in the tidal zone picking mussels, or pluck berries. It's also possible to join the guides on their hunt for caribou and seal.

Excursions from base camp are usually made on working longliners with all-Inuit crew. A typical outing might be to **Sallikuluk** (Rose Island), where there are more than a dozen archaeological sites, dating back 5,000 years. You can stand on the edge of sod-house excavations, in some cases numbering as many as 14 dwellings in one place. Besides traditional stone burial sites scattered over the island, one mass burial site houses repatriated ancestral remains.

Helicopters are best for hitting remote points north including **Nachvak Fjord,** 70 km (43 mi) as the crow flies from base camp, with its archaeological sites and broad inland valleys.

Another outing could be to the north arm of **Sallik (Saglek) Fjord,** about three hours by boat from base camp. Along the way, crumbling cliffs of gneiss—shot through with striations—tower along the shore. Some of the rock in this area is 3.9 billion years old, putting it among the oldest on the planet. At the end of the inlet, you can go ashore for a meal of freshly caught arctic char and *panitsiaks* (bannock) baked over a beach fire. This is a good place for overnight excursions in the park.

NORTHERN LIGHTS

Wherever one stays in the park, there's the opportunity to view *atsanik*—the **northern lights.** On a good night, swaths of green light might arc across the night sky before seemingly turning to liquid and dripping down in molten tendrils. If you haven't already felt that spirits inhabit the park, that sight alone will convince you otherwise.

TORNGAT MOUNTAINS NATIONAL PARK

(Parc national des Monts-Torngat)

INFORMATION & ACTIVITIES

VISITOR & INFORMATION CENTRE

Parks Canada has a visitor reception and orientation tent at the **Torngat Mountains Base Camp and Research Station** in St. John's Harbour in Saglek Bay. Available from late July to the end of August. For information call (709) 922-1290 or (888) 922-1290.

SEASONS & ACCESSIBILITY

Park open year-round; visits recommended in March and April and from early July to September. No road access or facilities. Landing permits required for aircraft or helicopters. Access to Inuit lands on the coast at Iron Strand Beach requires permission from the Nunatsiavut Government; call (709) 922-2942.

HEADQUARTERS

Box 471, Nain, NL A0P 1L0. Phone (709) 922-1290 or (888) 922-1290. torngats.info@pc.gc.ca; www.parkscanada.gc.ca/torngat.

FRIENDS OF TORNGAT MOUNTAINS

Torngat Arts and Crafts, P.O. Box 269, Nain, NL A0P 1L0. Phone (709) 922-1659. torngatartscrafts@gmail.com.

ENTRANCE FEE

No entry fee.

PETS

Pets must be under control at all times.

ACCESSIBLE SERVICES

None.

THINGS TO DO

Hiking, mountain climbing, backcountry skiing, sailing or motorboat tours along the coast, and fishing in the park can be arranged.

Tour company licensed to operate in Torngat National Park: **Cruise North Expeditions** 111 Peter St., #200, Toronto, ON M5V 2H1. (416) 789-3725 or (888) 263-3220. www.cruisenorthexpeditions.ca.

SPECIAL ADVISORIES

- All visitors must register before entering and leaving Torngat Mountains National Park either by phone, fax, or in person at the administration office in Nain.
- Travel with experienced Inuit polar bear guards is recommended.
- The weather is highly variable. In summer, temperatures can drop from mild during the day to below freezing at night. Dress appropriately.
- Do not plan on using wood for cooking. Build only small fires in emergencies, and ensure they are extinguished when you are done.
- Do not remove artifacts or disturb features at archaeological sites.

CAMPGROUNDS

No designated campsites or facilities. Visitors may camp anywhere in the park except at archaeological sites.

HOTELS, MOTELS, & INNS

(unless otherwise noted, rates are for a 2-person double, high season, in Canadian dollars)

<u>*Outside the park:*</u>

Atsanik Lodge Sand Banks Rd., Nain, NL A0P 1L0. (709) 922-2910. $150-$165.

Auberge Kuujjuaq Inn Kuujjuaq, QC J0M 1C0. (819) 964-2903. reservationskuujjuaqinn@tamaani.ca. $275.

For more accommodations contact the Fédération des coopératives du Nouveau-Québec (FCNQ), (514) 457-3249 or (866) 336-2667, www.fcnq.ca.

NATIONAL MARINE CONSERVATION AREA

SAGUENAY-ST. LAWRENCE
QUEBEC

This 1,245 sq km (481 sq mi) marine park near the village of Tadoussac at the confluence of the Saguenay and St. Lawrence Rivers offers jaw-dropping scenery and whale-watching opportunities from land, boat, and kayak. It was created in 1998 to protect and showcase part of the St. Lawrence Estuary and the Saguenay Fjord.

Kayaking along the Saguenay River

Jointly managed by the provincial and federal governments, this stunning park features one of the southernmost fjords in the world. Measuring 276 m (905 ft) deep in some places, the fjord is home to more than ten species of marine mammals including seals, seabirds, blue whales, and about a thousand endangered St. Lawrence belugas.

The marine park's headquarters (418-235-4703, *www.parcmarin.qc.ca*) are located in the pretty village of **Tadoussac** *(www.tadoussac.com)*, a few hours north of Quebec City along Hwy. 138 and a ferry ride from Baie-Sainte-Catherine. French explorer Jacques Cartier came here in 1535. Pierre Chauvin built the first trading post in 1599, and explorer Samuel de Champlain arrived in 1603. Fur traders and the area's First Nations people traded at Tadoussac. Visitors can find accommodations in local hotels and B&Bs, as well as at Camping Tadoussac and Camping du Domaine des Dunes *(www.domaine desdunes.com)*.

From Tadoussac, go to the **Marine Environment Discovery Centre** in Les Escoumins, about 30 km (19 mi) from Tadoussac, to participate in a dive without getting wet. Sit in a theatre and watch a giant screen as biologist-divers equipped with a camera go live beneath the St. Lawrence River. You may see sea stars and other marine life. Visitors can talk to divers underwater through a real-time two-way video link and follow along on the dive. The centre also has a permanent exhibit about the rich marine life that makes the St. Lawrence so attractive for whales.

WHALE-WATCHING: One of the highlights for visitors to the park is being able to see whales. The sociable and highly vocal beluga is often called "sea canary" because its calls are reminiscent of singing. It also emits ultrasonic sounds for echolocation. The returning echo allows it to locate prey, find holes in the ice, and avoid obstacles. Whale-watching boats and Zodiacs operate from May to October, departing from Tadoussac or Baie-Sainte-Catherine. It can get chilly on the water, so wear long pants and bring a hooded windbreaker, sweater, gloves, and a hat.

Whale-watching companies include: Croisières Otis *(www.otisexcursions.com)*, Croisières Groupe Dufour *(www.dufour.ca)*, Croisières 2001 *(www.quebecweb.com/croisieres2001)*, and Croisières AML *(www.croisieresaml.com)*. Some of these companies also offer tours of the Saguenay Fjord.

Regulations adopted in 2002 require that motorized boats and kayaks stay at least 400 m (1,312 ft) from beluga and blue whales and impose speed limits and flyover height restrictions.

The marine park covers a portion of the St. Lawrence Estuary and Saguenay Fjord, but visitors can whale-watch and experience the park from interpretation and observation points set up on dry land along the park's boundary. Each site focuses on a particular theme related to the marine environment.

MARINE OBSERVATION: At **Cap de Bon-Désir,** 25 km (15.5 mi) east of Tadoussac, fresh water from the St. Lawrence River mixes with salt water from the Gulf of St. Lawrence. This makes the St. Lawrence Estuary a rich environment for marine life and Cap de Bon-Désir a good spot to learn about the evolution of navigation on the St. Lawrence and the diversity of marine life. Visitors can whale-watch from land at the end of a 500-m (1,640 ft) trail and also participate in interpretive activities.

Pointe-Noire sits across from Tadoussac, at the confluence of the Saguenay Fjord and the St. Lawrence Estuary. An exhibit at this interpretation and observation centre explains riptide zones and the formation of plumes. A panoramic trail leads to a lookout. The site also has alignment beacons that guard the mouth of the Saguenay River.

Baie Sainte-Marguerite, 30 km (19 mi) from Tadoussac, is another good spot for beluga-watching. The whales sometimes stay there for hours. An interactive exhibit at the

A child examines the living treasure at a tide pool.

Sea anemones

Beluga Discovery Centre shares information with visitors about the habitat in which belugas live.

These and a number of other sites link together to form the Saguenay-St. Lawrence Discovery Network (call 888-773-8888 for a brochure). Other sites focus on the area's history. The **Centre d'interprétation Archéo Topo** *(www.archeotopo.com)* in Bergeronnes, for example, looks at the park's archaeology and paleohistory. At **Saint-Fulgence,** the fjord's rocky cliffs disappear, only to be replaced by large marshes. There is a 605-m (1,985 ft) spit. The spit and marsh are a unique feature of the fjord. The **Centre d'interprétation sur les battures et de réhabilitation des oiseaux** looks at the plants and birds that make their home in the Saguenay's tidal flats.

KAYAKING: Novice kayakers can try half-day excursions in the sheltered waters of **Baie Éternité,** on the south side of the Saguenay River. More experienced paddlers could opt for the 72-km (45 mi) scenic route from **Sainte-Rose-du-Nord** to Tadoussac at the mouth of the St. Lawrence River. Mer & Monde Écotours *(www.mer-et-monde.qc.ca)* in Tadoussac and Azimut Aventure *(www.azimutaventure)* in Baie-Sainte-Catherine offer guided sea-kayaking tours in the Saguenay Fjord and out onto the St. Lawrence Estuary. **Saguenay-St. Lawrence Marine Park,** 182, rue de l'Église, Tadoussac, phone (418) 235-4703.

Beluga whale

FATHOM FIVE
TOBERMORY, ONTARIO

Fathom Five plucked its moniker from Shakespeare's *The Tempest:* "Full fathom five thy father lies; Of his bones are coral made; Those are pearls that were his eyes: Nothing of him that doth fade." A fitting namesake considering the purpose of the park is preservation.

A diver explores an historic shipwreck in Fathom Five National Marine Park.

Largely underwater, Fathom Five (114 sq km/28,170 acres) was established in 1972 to protect the many shipwrecks that litter its shoals. In 1987, the park was transferred to the federal government to become Canada's first national marine conservation area. It is also the sister park to Bruce Peninsula National Park (see pp. 122–127).

The water clarity here, caused by a natural absence of silt and algae, makes for first-rate scuba-diving. Visitors can dive the coastal caves or snorkel the skeletal remains of 19th-century schooners that carried supplies between the villages on Georgian Bay. If you prefer to stay dry, book a cruise with the Blue Heron Company or rent a canoe or kayak from a local outfitter.

BOAT CRUISES: The Blue Heron Company (855-596-2999, *www.blueheronco.com*) is open from early May to early October.

There is a ticket kiosk on the east side of **Little Tub Harbour,** but the main parking lot and central ticketing location are at 7425 Hwy. 6 across from the Tobermory Community Centre. You'll find a good range of transportation services, tailored to all schedules. There are five different options for exploring Fathom Five. Departure times are date-dependent, so check the website for current information.

Hop on a Zodiac boat and zip over to **Flowerpot Island**. The 15-minute option goes straight there, while a longer 25-minute tour passes over two shipwrecks—the *Sweepstakes*

◗ NATIONAL MARINE CONSERVATION AREA

Dolomite rock formations on Flowerpot Island

schooner and the *City of Grand Rapids* steamer—before heading to the island. If you'd like more time to observe the wrecks, sign up for a two-hour tour aboard the *Great Blue Heron*. This glass-bottom boat offers eerie, incredible views of the shipwrecks in **Big Tub Harbour** before it completes a circle around the islands.

The *Blue Heron V* allows for the same glass-bottom view of the harbour floor but skips the smaller islands in favour of a long look at Flowerpot Island. You also have the option to disembark at **Beachy Cove** and explore the island's hiking trails and lighthouse, but you must make this decision when you buy your ticket.

During peak season (June–early Sept.), you can sign up for a two-hour sunset cruise along the northern coast of the Bruce Peninsula all the way to Cave Point. Departure times vary, so be sure to call ahead for information.

(Note that while the larger tour boats accommodate strollers and wheelchairs, the Zodiac boats do not, so plan accordingly.)

DIVING: Some of the most incredible sights (and interesting stories) in Fathom Five lie below the waves. Not only is the park home to submerged cliffs, overhangs, forests, and underwater waterfalls, it also acts as the final resting place for more than 20 different shipwrecks. The frigid freshwater temperature here (even during summer it can drop to a mere 4°C/39°F 30 m/98 ft down) and the absence of marine ecosystems help preserve the remains, another part of the reason Tobermory is known as the scuba-diving capital of Canada.

All divers must register and obtain dive tags at the visitor centre on Chi sin tib dek Rd. before the first dive of each season. Book lessons and rentals in Tobermory. Centrally located in Little Tub Harbour, Divers Den (519-596-2363, *www.diversden.ca*) offers everything from basic open water training to advanced technical certifications including night diving and peak performance buoyancy up to the Divemaster level. It operates from mid-May through October but is open year-round to answer questions and accept bookings.

Walk-on scuba charters make regular departures for popular sites including the ***W.L. Wetmore*** (a storm-wrecked ship off **Russel Island** that's suitable for divers and snorkellers) and the caves at the **Grotto** along the Georgian Bay shoreline. Phone ahead as schedules vary from spring to fall. If you want to visit a combination of dive sites not included in the standard schedule, ask about tailoring a tour. Dive boats can be booked for full and half days.

Be sure to ask your guide for the history of the wrecks you're diving. The ***Avalon,*** at the mouth of **Hay Bay,** was a floating restaurant until it was stranded in 1980 and eventually burned by vandals. The ***Arabia,*** a barque that foundered off **Echo Island** in the 1800s, lay undiscovered for almost a hundred years. It wasn't until the 1970s, when fishermen in the area noticed their catches coming up with bellies full of corn scavenged from the supplies aboard the ship, that people realized the massive wreck sat 34 m (110 ft) down.

G & S Watersports (519-596-2200, *www.gswatersports.net*), located in Little Tub Harbour, also provides diving services.

PADDLING: You can explore the waters of Fathom Five by kayak or canoe. Check Thorncrest Outfitters (888-345-2925, *www.thorncrestoutfitters.com*) for reasonably priced rentals from mid-June to mid-September. The Tobermory store is located on Hwy. 6, just across the road from the turnoff to Little Tub Harbour. Note that you must arrange any necessary park permits on your own as they are not included in rental fees.

Kayaking is an ideal way to discover the endless coves of Fathom Five's many islands and inlets. First-timers can book a tour of the Tub. This full-day paddle is the perfect introduction to sea kayaking on Georgian Bay and comes complete with certified guides, safety gear, and lunch. More experienced paddlers can head all the way out to Flowerpot Island for an overnight camping trip. If you intend to do this, be sure to book well in advance (the island's six sites start to fill up as soon as registration opens in early May), and remember to take extra food and water as weather conditions on the bay can delay departures.

Beachy Cove, on the south side of the island, hosts the only docks on Flowerpot. Campsites are a short walk east on the **Loop Trail.** From here, continue northeast along the trail, past the towering sea stacks that give the island its name. Just beyond the second flowerpot is a large cave with an observation deck. Farther along the path is the stunning **Castle Bluff** light station. The light itself is automated now, but volunteers with Friends of Fathom Five offer tours of the original keeper's house.

During the summer, the island is also staffed with Parks Canada employees who can answer your questions about Fathom Five and Bruce Peninsula.

Flowerpot is the only island with trails and camping, although day use is permitted on all the others. Though the marine park is one of the most ecologically healthy places on the Great Lakes, the food web is in a period of change. A long legacy of invasive species and overfishing, compounded with more recent climate change and coastal development stresses, is transforming the ecosystem. Currently, invasive mussel species are depleting many of the nutrients native species rely on, but natural populations (including lake trout, cisco, and sturgeon) are making a slow, steady comeback.

Fathom Five Parks Canada Visitor Centre, Chi sin tib dek Road, Tobermory, phone (519) 596-2233 ext. 0.

Moonrise over snow-blanketed mountains

SIRMILIK

NUNAVUT
ESTABLISHED 2001
22,200 sq km/5,485,739 acres

Sirmilik National Park is home not only to breathtaking views of the sea, mountains, and broad valley vistas, but also to an amazing variety of marine and avian wildlife. One of Canada's most accessible high Arctic parks, Sirmilik is truly a jewel in Canada's celebrated national parks network. Bylot Island offers stunning sights: deep, navy blue waters setting off the glistening white glaciers and icebergs that rise out of them, tinged with turquoise. Visitors may also catch sight of some of the hundreds of narwhals and seals that inhabit the park.

For thousands of years, right up to the present, the rich diversity of Arctic wildlife in the park supported the nomadic Inuit people. For centuries, they centred their existence around the demands of the land and its weather: Their survival depended on it. When the wind blew and the temperature plummeted, they stopped and found shelter, and continued only when the weather eased. Their culture and history is still well documented today for visitors to Sirmilik National Park.

Sirmilik, pronounced Siir-mi-lick, means "place of glaciers" in Inuktitut. The park covers much of the north tip of Baffin Island, and is bordered by the communities of Arctic Bay and Pond Inlet. Established as a national park as the result of the Nunavut Land Claim Agreement in February 2001, Sirmilik is still a fairly unknown expanse of land. The park encompasses the Bylot Island Bird Sanctuary, jointly managed by Parks Canada and the Canadian Wildlife Service, where greater snow goose research has been conducted for more than three decades. Bylot Island is the nesting site for more than 40 species of migratory birds.

How to Get There

From Iqaluit, travel to Pond Inlet (one of the two gateway communities into Sirmilik National Park) is possible in six or seven days with either First Air or Canadian Northern airlines. First Air also offers flights that will take you to the other, smaller gateway community of Arctic Bay. Air travel between Arctic Bay and Pond Inlet is possible only via Iqaluit, although spring travel by snow machine and summer travel by boat can also get you from one to the other.

From Pond Inlet or Arctic Bay, hire a snow machine for transport, or engage an outfitter or guide to lead you into Sirmilik National Park, preferably in spring when the ice is still safe to traverse. You can also ski across the ice of Eclipse Sound—approximately 25 km (16 mi) from Pond Inlet—in spring to get to the park. Floe edge tours from the sea ice are also available in the spring.

If travelling with the comfort of modern conveniences appeals to you, you can visit the park in summer as a passenger on one of the many expedition cruise ships that spend up to two days sailing the sounds and inlets around Sirmilik. Depending on the itinerary of the cruises, passengers may be able to go ashore for some exploration within the park. In summer, you can also hire a kayak guide to lead you on a trip into the waters of the park.

When to Go

Sirmilik is in the high Arctic wilderness, so the best time to go is in spring or summer, which in this region means May through September when the sun is shining for the better part of 24 hours. July is ice breakup month and the park is not accessible, as the ice will no longer support ski or snow machine travel. Boats and ships can't travel the waters around this time either, because of the hazards posed by the breaking ice. August to mid-September is the best season for boating and hiking in the park. From late September to late March, Sirmilik's weather turns harsh and stormy. The dark season, during which the sun is hardly in evidence at all, lasts for two solid months around the time of the winter solstice.

How to Visit

Sirmilik offers a variety of activities for hardy travellers eager to learn about the park's geology and wildlife. If you're willing to put forth some effort, you can get a close-up look at glaciers, icebergs, and the marine life residing off the floe edge. The park's population of Arctic seabirds make it a wonderful destination for the avid bird-watcher. If you're feeling adventurous, you can dive under the sea ice for intimate encounters with the marine life living in the waters, including narwhal and beluga whales and walruses. Summer is the best time to meet Inuit residents and learn about their culture, ancient and modern. Watch craftsmen at work, and take in Inuit art and performances in either Pond Inlet or Arctic Bay.

To ensure your safety on kayak, boat, ski, or hiking expeditions, rely on the skills of outfitters and guides to arrange your visit into the park. As in all national parks in Nunavut, Sirmilik expeditions are backcountry adventures and are generally not suitable excursions for small children or elderly travellers. As this is still a relatively new park, it doesn't yet have established routes for you to follow through the park. However, by the same token, Sirmilik offers you the opportunity to blaze your own trails, depending on what you wish to see and how skilled a hiker you are. Make sure you bring a good camera with you: The beauty and awesome vastness of Sirmilik National Park afford visitors a wealth of photo opportunities.

HIKING & PADDLING

One of the most frequently hiked areas of the park is the **Mala River Valley** on the **Borden Peninsula.** Some camping and hiking around **Pond Inlet** is possible, though these excursions won't necessarily take you into the park. Exploring the area around Pond Inlet will give you the opportunity to examine the remnants of sod huts built in past centuries by the North Baffin Inuit, which are a testament to their resilient culture.

Outfitters will take you into Sirmilik to explore the cultural sites protected within the park's boundaries. A single row of ten sod houses built at the foot of the mountains along the north coast of Borden Peninsula is one of the most important and evocative cultural

Black-legged kittiwake gull rookery on a cliff

sites along this coast. These durable Thule-era houses are constructed of stone, whalebone, and sod.

BYLOT ISLAND & BORDEN PENINSULA

Guided kayak trips of various lengths and to various parts of the park can be arranged. Floe edge excursions near **Bylot Island** will give you close-up encounters with marine mammals and can be booked in the spring. You can also arrange to partake in diving expeditions, guided by outfitters, and based out of **Arctic Bay.** Only the most experienced skiers and climbers should attempt spring glacier crossings on Bylot Island.

Many of Bylot Island's 16 alpine glaciers are visible from the waters of **Eclipse Sound** and from **Navy Board Inlet. Oliver Sound**'s deep waters, glaciers, and sheer cliffs shelter a rich variety of sea life from the inclement weather of North Baffin Island. The sprawling Borden Peninsula is also within park boundaries. Partially covered with glaciers, its tortuous geological formations are composed of red sandstone that's layered, striped, and folded with shades of ochre and magenta. These cliffs are home to thousands of nesting seabirds. Colonies of murres, kittiwakes, and fulmars come here to prey on fish from Lancaster Sound to feed their nestlings. The **Baillarge Bay bird sanctuary,** a small crescent of cliffs that is habitat for seabirds, is also protected as part of the park.

Sirmilik National Park's high concentration of seabirds and other Arctic life like narwhals, seals, and polar bears is a result of the rich, highly productive waters of **Lancaster Sound,** just north of Bylot Island and the Borden Peninsula. The waters of the sound are capable of supporting a hugely diverse array of life, and Parks Canada is studying the feasibility of creating a national marine protected area in Lancaster Sound to extend the park's protection to this rare Arctic marine ecosystem.

There's a healthy polar bear population in this park, especially along the Lancaster Sound area, so if you're planning to traverse parts of the

SIRMILIK NATIONAL PARK

(Parc national Sirmilik)

INFORMATION & ACTIVITIES

VISITOR CENTRE

Nattinnak Visitor Centre Phone (867) 899-8225. **Sirmilik Park Office** phone (867) 899-8092

SEASONS & ACCESSIBILITY

Park office open year-round. The park is inaccessible during ice breakup in mid-June to late July and when the ice freezes in mid-October to early November. Travel to the park is not advisable November to February. Access is by boat from late July to September or by snow machine from late September to early July from **Pond Inlet** or **Arctic Bay.** Contact Nattinnak Visitor Centre to make arrangements with outfitters. Endless daylight May–August; no daylight in December and January. Late March–early June is the best time of year for winter activities.

HEADQUARTERS

P.O. Box 300, Pond Inlet, NU X0A 0S0. Phone (867) 899-8092. www.parkscanada.gc.ca/sirmilik.

ENTRANCE FEES

The daily backcountry excursion fee per person is $25, or $147 for a season's pass. For large commercial groups the fee is $12 per person for short stays on shore (such as a cruise ship visit).

PETS

Pets are not recommended as they can attract polar bears. If a pet is taken into the park it must be leashed at all times.

ACCESSIBLE SERVICES

None.

THINGS TO DO

Skiing, mountaineering, and winter camping. Windslab is the common form of snow; deep powder rare. In late July to early September, sea kayaking and boating in **Oliver Sound** south of Pond Inlet; **Lancaster Sound** between Devon Island and Sirmilik; **Eclipse Sound** waterway to Bylot Island, **Navy Board Inlet,** and **Borden Peninsula.**

SPECIAL ADVISORIES

- Before visiting, contact the park to book an appointment for mandatory registration and pre-trip orientation, during which you will need to provide park staff with a detailed itinerary of your planned trip and arrange a post-trip deregistration.
- Weather may delay flights to the North.
- Allow for flexibility in scheduling.
- Talk to park staff to identify areas with thinner ice. Sea ice close to river mouths is generally thin. Do not approach areas with deep snow and water on top, as this indicates open water beneath. Avoid travelling through bays and inlets with

Iceberg on Pond Inlet dwarfs human visitor.

landscape on foot, it is very advisable to travel with a qualified guide who knows the region and can provide you the necessary gear for a safe trek.

INUIT COMMUNITIES

Hotel accommodations are available in the local communities, or you can also arrange a home stay with an Inuit family. If you'd rather brave the elements, Arctic camping is possible at **Salmon River** just outside Pond Inlet. If you do plan to camp narrow channels, as they often have strong currents in spring.

- Boaters should be prepared for strong winds, floating ice, and strong tides.
- No campfires allowed. Campers are advised to bring white gas and portable stoves.
- Visitors must be prepared for whiteouts, avalanches, and extreme weather. Travel in groups of at least four is advised. Individuals must have training in glacier travel and crevasse rescue.
- Avoid polar bears, which are most active along the coast of the Borden Peninsula and along the north, west, and east coasts of Bylot Island. Avoid females and cubs in March and April and from July to October.

CAMPGROUNDS

No designated campgrounds. Select campsites in durable locations where signs of your occupation will be minimized. Avoid camping in steep terrain or near potential wildlife habitat, such as sedge meadows. Do not dig trenches around tents or build rock windbreaks. Camping near floe edge can be dangerous.

HOTELS, MOTELS, & INNS

(unless otherwise noted, rates are for a 2-person double, high season, in Canadian dollars)

Pond Inlet, NU X0A 0S0:

The Sauniq Hotel Box 370. www.pondinlethotel.com. (867) 899-6500. $225 per person.

Arctic Bay, NU X0A 0A0:

Tangmaarvik Inn P.O. Box 130. (867) 439-8005. $215 per person.

LICENSED TOUR OPERATORS

Tour companies licensed to operate in Sirmilik National Park:

Adventure Canada 14 Front St. South, Mississauga, ON L5H 2C4. (800) 363-7566. info@adventurecanada.com; www.adventurecanada.com.

Arctic Kingdom Marine Expeditions Inc. 3335 Yonge St., Suite 402, Toronto, ON M4N 2M1. (888) 737-6818. adventures@arctickingdom.com; www.arctickingdom.com.

Black Feather Wilderness Adventure Company 250 McNaughts Rd., Parry Sound, ON P2A 2W9. (888) 849-7668. info@wildernessadventure.com; www.blackfeather.com.

Cruise North Expeditions Inc. 111 Peter St., Suite 200, Toronto, ON M5V 2H1. (416) 789-3752. info@cruisenorthexpeditions.com; www.cruisenorthexpeditions.com.

Polar Sea Adventures (tour and equipment rentals) P.O. Box 549, Pond Inlet, NU X0A 0S0. (867) 899-8870. info@polarsea.ca; www.polarseaadventures.

Quark Expeditions 93 Pilgrim Park, Waterbury, VT 05676. (203) 803-2888. enquiry@quarkexpeditions.com; www.quarkexpeditions.com.

Whitney & Smith Legendary Expeditions P.O. Box 8576, Canmore, AB T1W 2V3. (800) 713-6660. info@legendaryex.com; www.legendaryex.com.

in Sirmilik, be sure to confirm with an outfitter what equipment and supplies you should bring with you. If you're eager to immerse yourself in local culture, some outfitters can arrange a visit with the Inuit at their outpost camps. This may give you a chance for a taste of local cuisine too: Recently harvested local food is sometimes offered as part of this experience. Near the communities of Arctic Bay and Pond Inlet, there are opportunities to fish for arctic char or to pick berries in the late summer.

Community visitor centres provide a rich offering of local art, including hand carvings, dolls (Pond Inlet is known for dolls that reflect the culture and customs), fabric painting, hats, jewellery, and items crafted from narwhal tusks. These unique pieces are also available for purchase at the local co-op store. This is a wonderful opportunity to come away from your trip with a locally made item that evokes the culture and traditions of the people of Sirmilik.

Reversing Falls, at the mouth of Ford Lake, with 8-m (26 ft) tides surging in and out.

UKKUSIKSALIK

NUNAVUT
ESTABLISHED 2003
20,000 sq km/4,942,108 acres

Ukkusiksalik National Park surrounds the inland sea of Wager Bay and is Nunavut's only unglaciated national park. The park has extraordinarily rich concentrations of marine wildlife, and the Inuit came to harvest it hundreds of years ago and remain on the land today. In the wake of centuries of human activity, Ukkusiksalik has become the site of more than 500 documented archaeological sites that date back more than a thousand years.

Ukkusiksalik National Park was signed into existence on August 23, 2003, by an agreement between the government of Canada and the Kivaaliq Inuit Association. Since then, final park boundaries have been established and the park is expected to be gazetted in the Canadian Parliament as a fully established national park in 2011.

Ukkusiksalik (pronounced Oo-koo-sick-sa-lick) is the Inuktitut word meaning "place where there is stone to carve pots and oil lamps." Given the size of Wager Bay, and the fact that the park completely encompasses this large body of water, the best way to see it is by boat.

There's a great deal to see and do in Ukkusiksalik. Venturing into

Wager Bay places you in the territory of the explorers who once sought the Northwest Passage—the first "Qablunaat" (white man) sailed into Wager Bay in 1742 hoping it was the long-sought-after passage. Wager Bay has been called an inland sea, and visiting it by boat will help visitors understand how the early explorers might have mistaken it for a passage to the Pacific.

This history of exploration, the archaeological record of the Inuit on the land, and the more recent presence of the Hudson's Bay Company's trading post in Ukkusiksalik make this park an exciting destination for the history buff. The historic Hudson's Bay Company buildings date from the 1920s and are where Iqungajuk, the only Inuk Hudson's Bay post manager, lived and worked. The site is located on Ford Lake and can be accessed through the reversing tidal falls.

There are numerous archaeological sites scattered around the shoreline of Wager Bay. Inuksuit—stone cairns used by the Inuit people—are plentiful across the landscape. An Inuksuit could be used to mark a trail, or served as a cache to store meat from the harvest and protect it from carnivorous wildlife like wolverines or foxes. Some trails of caribou herds are marked with these Inuit cairns, which could also serve as hunters' blinds for when the caribou passed by.

Ukkusiksalik is located on a continental flyway, and visitors will encounter a great number of migratory birds nesting in or passing through its sprawling landscape. These include species like predator hawks and peregrine falcons. The peregrine falcon, while rare in other parts of the continent, is quite plentiful in the park.

The park is also well populated with polar bears. Any travel to Ukkusiksalik is best done in the company of guides and outfitters who are trained and equipped to deal with the hazards of polar bear country. But the beauty of this park, with its rolling ochre and grey hills, its waterfalls and rare tidal reversing falls, will make travel to Ukkusiksalik well worth your while.

How to Get There

Fly from Winnipeg, or Yellowknife via Edmonton, to Rankin Inlet to get to the central Arctic (called the Kivalliq Region), where Rankin is the hub community. Charter flights can access the park from Baker Lake or Rankin Inlet. Check with Ukkusiksalik park staff about the status of airstrip conditions prior to chartering an aircraft, because the runways are remote and often unmaintained. Access to Ukkusiksalik National Park can also be achieved by contracting a licensed outfitter and chartering a boat from Repulse Bay (the closest community to the park) or from Rankin Inlet and other communities in the Kivalliq Region.

Spring snow-machine access is also possible in April and May using licensed outfitters. Make sure you factor the time needed to cover the distances to Ukkusiksalik by land or by water into your travel time, and always allow an additional couple of days in case weather intervenes.

When to Go

July and August are the best months to see the park. While it may be possible to fly into the park by charter earlier or later in the spring and summer season, July is when the area is awash in wildflowers. You can see the fall colours beginning to

form on the tundra, along with ripening berries, in August. Travelling to the park in April by airplane or snow machine is also possible, since the sun will be high in the sky and you'll have 16 hours a day of bright sunlight glinting off the snow.

How to Visit

If **Sila Lodge** (Wagner Bay) is operating, the staff there can arrange guided hikes and guided boat trips. If the lodge is not operating, however, visitors will need to seek tour operators and guides to facilitate onshore excursions from a base camp, and use a chartered boat to explore the park. For more information on Sila Lodge, contact the park office. A few intrepid visitors have explored small parts of the park via kayak, but the presence of polar bears in the water and along the shores of Wager Bay make this a highly inadvisable approach.

Park staff are located year-round at the administration and operations centre and office in **Repulse Bay** and are available to discuss your trip throughout the planning stages.

Once the park is gazetted (in 2011), registration, orientation, and a post-trip debrief will be mandatory. Before the park is gazetted, it is recommended that you receive an orientation before entering the park so that staff can monitor your trip and assist if you have any problems. Government of Nunavut Territorial regulations remain in force until ownership of the lands that make up Ukkusiksalik is officially transferred to Parks Canada.

WILDLIFE

A trip to Ukkusiksalik centres upon life on the inland sea—**Wager Bay.**

Top: A visitor at Thule site near Brown River. Middle left: Astarte fritillary. Middle right: Arctic ground squirrel. Bottom: Aurora borealis near Wager Bay.

UKKUSIKSALIK NATIONAL PARK

(Parc national Ukkusiksalik)

INFORMATION & ACTIVITIES

HEADQUARTERS

P.O. Box 220, Repulse Bay, NU X0C 0H0. Phone (867) 462-4500. ukkusiksalik .info@ pc.gc.ca; www.parkscanada.gc.ca/ ukkusiksalik.

Field Unit Office Box 278, Iqaluit, NU, X0A 0H0. Phone (867) 975-4673.

SEASONS & ACCESSIBILITY

Park open year-round; park office open weekdays. Park accessible by boat in July and August from **Rankin Inlet, Repulse Bay, Chesterfield Inlet, Baker Lake,** or **Coral Harbour,** or a charter flight from Baker Lake or Rankin Inlet. Travel restricted or impossible during ice breakup in May and June. Travel to the park not recommended in fall and winter. Flights and charters to Repulse Bay, Chesterfield Inlet, Baker Lake, and Coral Harbour available from Winnipeg via Rankin Inlet, or from Ottawa via Iqaluit, or Edmonton via Yellowknife. Kenn Borek Air provides Twin Otter aircraft. Call (867) 252-3845. Charters into the park must be by Single Otter if the runway is suitable. Contact the park office for information about current air companies flying charters in the area.

ENTRANCE FEES

None until the park is gazetted.

PETS

All pets must be on a leash.

ACCESSIBLE SERVICES

None.

THINGS TO DO

Once the park is gazetted, contact Repulse Bay office for mandatory registration, pre-trip orientation, and post-trip deregistration. At the orientation, visitors must provide park staff with a detailed itinerary of the trip, including side trips. The park is mostly navigable by water. Boating and paddling in **Wager Bay,** hiking with experienced guides and outfitters, and wildlife viewing (polar bears, seals, beluga whales, narwhals). Archaeological sites can be seen throughout the park, including an ancient gymnasium-like structure, food caches, and tent circles. To find outfitters contact Nunavut Tourism office in Kivalliq (866-686-2888) or Parks Canada office in Repulse Bay.

TOUR COMPANIES

There are currently no tour companies licensed to operate in Ukkusiksalik; however, once the park is gazetted, business licences and guide permits will apply. There are currently tour companies operating in the area that visitors can approach to access the park:

Adventure Canada Lochburn Landing
14 Front St. South, Mississauga, ON L5H

Boating from place to place around the shore offers visitors the quickest and best way to access the myriad smaller bays along the coast of Wager Bay. One of these excursions can expose visitors to several of the park's most exciting features, such as the archaeological sites, fabulous views, and hilltop and river valley hikes. Moreover, from the boat you'll get a good look at some of the marine life and wildlife that inhabit the park, too.

Ukkusiksalik National Park is first and foremost about Arctic wildlife. Visitors to the park may see caribou wandering by, alone or in groups. In the waters, whales and fish abound; the sky is filled with a huge range of bird species. Sik-sik (ground squirrel) will sit on their haunches and chatter at you. You may see a fox or a wolf, but you're almost guaranteed to catch sight of a polar bear and probably more than once, sometimes at a distance, but perhaps much closer.

You may see polar bears with their cubs, harvesting seals,

2C4. (800) 363-7566. info@adventure canada.com; www.adventurecanada.com.
Arctic Odysseys 3409 E. Madison, Seattle, WA 98112. (206) 325-1977. www .arcticodysseys.com.
Canadian Arctic Holidays 151 Basswood, Aylmer, QC J0X 1N0. (877) 272-7426. canadianarctic@serioussports.com.
Grand Nord/Grand Large (GNGL) 15, rue Richelieu, 75005, Paris, France. +33 40 46 05 14.

SPECIAL ADVISORIES

- Exercise polar bear safety procedures.
- Twenty-four-hour daylight in summer.
- Tides and currents may affect boating. Boating only possible between July and September. Consult the Canadian Ice Service on the Environment Canada website for sea ice conditions.
- If travelling in the spring, talk to park staff to identify areas with thinner ice. Do not approach areas with deep snow with water on top, as this indicates open water beneath. Avoid travelling through bays and inlets with narrow channels, as they often have strong currents in spring.
- Be able to recognize and prevent the onset of hypothermia.
- Water should be fine filtered and treated or boiled before drinking.
- Be cautious crossing rivers and streams and do not cross during episodes of high water—wait for water levels to drop.
- Visitors should be experienced in recognizing avalanche hazards, route-finding skills, and self-rescue techniques.
- Visitors must be self-sufficient and able to handle medical or wildlife-related emergencies.
- In case of emergency call Jasper National Park Emergency Dispatch (780) 852-3100.

CAMPGROUNDS

No designated campgrounds. Visitors must stay in hard-sided accommodations or camp with bear fencing or overnight in closed boats. Campsites and food containers should be bear-proof. Camping near floe edge can be dangerous.

HOTELS, MOTELS, & INNS

(unless otherwise noted, rates are for a 2-person double, high season, in Canadian dollars)

Baker Lake, NU X0C 0A0:
The Iglu Hotel (867) 793-2801. www .bakerlakehotel.com. $215 per person.

Rankin Inlet, NU X0C 0G0:
The Turaarvik Hotel (867) 645-4955. www.rankininlethotel.com. $205-$245.
Nanuq Lodge P.O. Box 630. (867) 645-2650. www.nanuqlodge.com. $200.

scrounging along the coastline looking for fish or a whale carcass, or feeding on seaweed. Because the polar bear population is so high, it is important for visitors to travel with licensed tour operators once the park is gazetted and guides who are familiar with polar bear behaviour and know how to keep bears at a safe distance from humans. Contact park staff for the latest information on the companies providing services to the park.

Barren-ground caribou at Ford Lake

NATIONAL MARINE CONSERVATION AREA

LAKE SUPERIOR
ONTARIO

To understand the evolution of the Lake Superior National Marine Conservation Area, it helps to know that when the Welland Canal that links Lake Erie and Lake Ontario was built in the mid-1800s, bypassing Niagara Falls and allowing large boats to move from the St. Lawrence River into the upper Great Lakes, it inadvertently also allowed lamprey eels to bypass the falls for the first time.

A foggy morning in Lake Superior National Marine Conservation Area

By the mid-20th century, the voracious eels had severely reduced the lake's once teeming population of trout. Meanwhile, many of the 800 rivers and streams that flow into Lake Superior had become polluted and a daily rain of particulate poisons was settling on the lake from the air.

Although its ecology has drastically altered from what it was before the construction of the canal, Lake Superior is the cleanest of the Great Lakes.

The Ojibwe name for Lake Superior is Gichigami, meaning "big water." The size, power, and unpredictability have led many to think of Lake Superior as an "inland sea."

During the late 1990s, concerned shore dwellers and conservationists began promoting the idea of some form of protection for the lake and its islands. In 2007, after years of consultation between the federal government, regional First Nations, and stakeholders, a 10,000 sq km (2.5 million acres) section of the lake and its bed, stretching from

Thunder Cape in the west to past the town of Terrace Bay in the east and south to the U.S. border, was established as a national marine conservation area.

While the designation protects an enormous range of mammals, birds, and some 70 species of fish, it also preserves historic remnants such as shipwrecks, lighthouses, and ancient pictographs. In addition, it promotes the preservation and awareness of First Nations culture, past and present.

Unlike Canada's national parks, which permit no industrial activity within their borders, the mandate for Lake Superior support sustainable activities vital to the economy of the area such as shipping and commercial and sport fishing. At the same time, it prohibits waste dumping, mining, and oil and gas exploration, as well as any other industrial activity that might harm the area's ecology.

ON WATER & ON LAND: The best way to appreciate the waters and islands of Lake Superior is by boat, say on a fishing or kayaking venture out of one of the public boat launches on beaches in communities along the North Shore. There are areas in which the lake is so clear that boaters can see bottom and sometimes the wrecks of some 17 old vessels more than 20 m (66 ft) down. At Silver Islet, the shaft of the 19th-century silver mine, once the richest on Earth, is clearly visible in the lake bed.

The marine conservation area offers unparalleled waters for trout, whitefish, lake herring, and walleye. The waters surrounding the many islands near Rossport and Terrace Bay offer unique routes for kayakers.

Outfitters in the northern coastal towns offer tours and supplies. Camping sites, while rare to preserve the ecosystems, are available on the islands.

As an extension of its ecological and cultural aims, the marine conservation area supports the participation of local residents in stewardship and conservation initiatives and encourages their collaboration in directing the future of this vast and invaluable marine and boreal resource.

The headquarters for **Lake Superior National Marine Conservation Area** is located in Nipigon, Ontario. Call (807) 887-5467 for more information.

Kayaking through a rock arch in Lake Superior

Preserving Starry Skies

Diamond dust. It looks as if the mighty hands of the gods spread a broad arc of diamond dust across the heavens. The sharp, cold glitter of thousands of distant stars encircles the sky with a ghostly embrace of ancient light. This is the Milky Way, our home galaxy. But only if you are lucky enough to be somewhere free of light pollution will you see its majestic splendour.

Comet Lulin as it passed near Saturn, in the early hours of February 24, 2009

When was the last time a view of the night sky sent shivers up your spine? Most North Americans live in urban areas where there is so much artificial light at night that the stars are only a faint memory. From cities and towns we see only a handful of the brightest stars. The rest are lost in an expanding glow of artificial light that is enveloping the world. Globally, more than 1.3 billion people—one fifth of the world's population—can no longer see the Milky Way with unaided eyes.

In the face of swelling populations and spreading urbanization, what can be done to save some of the night? The Royal Astronomical Society of Canada has initiated a Dark Sky Preserve (DSP) program *(www.rasc.ca/lpa/darksky.shtml)*. Working with partners like Parks Canada, the program has been remarkably successful in establishing areas where nature's night environment is protected and preserved for the benefit of all species, including humans.

"Parks Canada supports the DSP program," says Jonathan Sheppard, of Kejimkujik National Park and National Historic Site, "because it fits our mandate of protection, education, outreach, and visitor experience: protecting nocturnal ecology, implementing an energy-saving dark-sky-compliant lighting strategy for our facilities, teaching about astronomy and light control, working with astronomy partners, and creating new, engaging programs for visitors."

DSPs protect the night sky by controlling the number, placement, and design of lighting fixtures. No excess light spills over where it is not needed. Eliminating light pollution ensures visitors can appreciate the night while also providing plants and animals with the most natural habitat possible.

Every species on Earth is connected and interdependent. Can we afford to ignore half of the systems that sustain us? Life's systems have evolved, and continue to need, to experience the day-night cycle. It is necessary for our health and well-being.

Light pollution affects humans and wildlife, interfering with the growth, behaviour, and survival of nocturnal species everywhere. Many species need the day-night cycle to synchronize their biological rhythms. Some adapt behaviour in response to changing nighttime light levels from the lunar cycle. But light levels at night in urban and suburban areas are brighter than full moonlight.

Parks Canada is charged with protecting and presenting Canada's natural and cultural heritage, and fostering understanding, appreciation, and enjoyment of that heritage into the future. People come to Canada's national parks for recreation and to reconnect with nature. DSPs enable us to fully experience nature's diurnal cycle. We can see the stars and feel night's whispering magic. DSPs will become increasingly important as society becomes more urbanized with more people living in a 24-hour artificial day.

By lighting up the night we have divorced ourselves from our evolutionary history and cultural heritage. We have disconnected ourselves from Earth's life-sustaining natural systems. We are losing touch with our place in the universe.

We must dim the lights!

Parks Canada's Dark Sky Preserves are leading the way, becoming "dark beacons" of hope for the future of our natural environment. Come see the stars!

— MARY LOU WHITEHORNE, *President*
The Royal Astronomical Society of Canada

RASC Dark Sky Reserves/Preserves

The Royal Astronomical Society of Canada has certified 11 Dark Sky Preserves in Canada to date. Seven* of these are part of the Parks Canada system. More are planned.

- Torrance Barrens Dark Sky Reserve, ON—1999
- Cypress Hills National Park Dark Sky Preserve, AB—2005*
- Beaver Hills Dark Sky Preserve, AB—2006
- Point Pelee National Park Dark Sky Preserve, ON—2006*
- Gordon's Park Dark Sky Preserve, Manitoulin Island, ON—2008
- Kouchibouguac National Park Dark Sky Preserve, NB—2009*
- Bruce Peninsula National Park and Five Fathoms National Marine Park Dark Sky Preserve, ON—2009*
- Mount Carleton Provincial Park Dark Sky Preserve, NB—2009
- Grasslands National Park Dark Sky Preserve, SK—2009*
- Kejimkujik National Park and National Historic Site Dark Sky Preserve, NS—2010*
- Jasper National Park Dark Sky Preserve, AB—2011*

A view of Death Lake and the surrounding forests and cliffs

NAHANNI

NORTHWEST TERRITORIES
ESTABLISHED 1972
over 30,000 sq km/413,000 acres

In the summer of 1928, American adventurer Fenley Hunter paddled up the South Nahanni River hoping to find a huge waterfall that seemed largely the stuff of Dene legend at the time. Hunter thought he would never make it. Halfway upstream he wrote: "The Nahanni is unknown and will remain so until another age brings a change in the conformation of these mountains. It is an impossible stream, and a stiff rapid is met on average every mile, and they seem countless."

The subsequent decades have proved Hunter wrong. Multiday canoeing, kayaking, and rafting trips on the South Nahanni, and to a lesser extent on the Flat and Little Nahanni Rivers, are now the main attractions in Nahanni National Park Reserve. The park is more than 30,000 sq km of wilderness that rolls out of the ice fields, mountains, alpine tundra, and boreal forest along the Continental Divide separating the Yukon and Northwest Territories.

For experienced paddlers, the South Nahanni is what Everest is to mountaineers—remote, breathtaking, and mystical. The river may not be the most difficult in the world, but neither is it for the faint of heart. It plunges through a series of four spectacular canyons, churning up rapids, boils, and whirlpools with sinister names such as Hell's Gate, or misleading ones like Tricky Current and Lafferty's Riffle, which can be equally challenging. Here, grizzly bears, black bears, moose, mountain caribou, trumpeter swans, and upland sandpipers are among the 42 species of mammals and 180 species of birds found in the park.

Nahanni is rich with legends of lost gold, murder, and headless men, along with airier lore of tropical gardens and Dene spirits that dwell in the vents of the river valley's tufa mounds and hot springs. Undisturbed by roads or seismic lines, Nahanni was, along with Yellowstone, one of the first parks to be listed as a World Heritage site.

While river trips are recommended only for skilled paddlers or those travelling with licensed outfitters, visitors of all ages can fly into Virginia Falls, which is twice the height of Niagara.

How to Get There

You can get to Nahanni by flying to Fort Simpson via Yellowknife, and then to the river by floatplane from Fort Simpson. Alternatively, you can make the 18-hour, 1,470-km (913 mi) drive from Edmonton to Fort Simpson in two days along the Mackenzie Highway. For those driving north from Edmonton looking for a hotel, High Level in Alberta is the best stopover. Twin Falls Park, 72 km (45 mi) north of the Alberta/Northwest Territories border, offers good camping.

Note: One can drive to Fort Simpson via the Alaska and Liard Highways.

When to Go

The South Nahanni is in a serious spring flood up until early June and sometimes later. The risk of severe weather toward the end of August makes it unwise to go any later, so the best time is between June and August.

How to Visit

Take a day trip from Fort Simpson, Fort Liard, and Muncho Lake in northern British Columbia; trips involve a 90-minute to two-hour flight to **Virginia Falls** and the surrounding area. Air charter service information can be found at www.pc.gc.ca/pn-np/nt/nahanni/visit/visit3.aspx#air.

A Parks Canada interpreter is usually on hand at Virginia Falls to give visitors a briefing about the area and what they can see. You can then take a very easy 30-minute hike to the **Virginia Falls viewpoint,** which offers a breathtaking view of **Sluicebox Rapids** and the waterfall. The more demanding portage trail around the falls takes about an hour. Pack a rain jacket or an extra sweater if you choose to do this. While it might be sweltering at the top of the falls, the temperature drops by at least 10 or 15 degrees down below in the mist.

You can also plan canoe, kayak, and raft trips—they'll take from eight days to three weeks. Parks Canada highly recommends that people go with a registered, licensed outfitter (see p. 308). Starting points are the **Moose Ponds** (21 days), **Island Lakes** (14–18 days), **Rabbitkettle Lake** (10–14 days), and **Virginia Falls** (7–10 days). The ending points are **Blackstone Territorial Park** for campers and **Lindberg Landing** (250-233-2344) for those who want a cozy cabin. (Deregistration takes place at the Nahanni National Park Reserve Office in Nahanni Butte.)Both are located on the **Liard River** near the confluence of the South Nahanni.

If you wish to paddle on your own, Nahanni River Adventures

(a licensed outfitter) has a guide *(www.nahanni.com/rentals/selfguided.html)* which you should bring along with your 1:250,000 topographical maps.

Advanced reservations and permits are required. Visitors must register and check out at the beginning and end of their trip.

CHALLENGING WHITEWATER ROUTES

Apart from the Moose Ponds route, which has about 50 km (31 mi) of very challenging, continuous white water, experienced paddlers have little to be concerned about until they get to Virginia Falls. Immediately downstream of the falls, however, is some challenging white water: **Canyon Rapids** followed by **Figure Eight Rapid** (Hell's Gate), **Wrigley Whirlpool, George's Riffle,** and then **Lafferty's Riffle.** Spray covers are recommended. Difficulty of these rapids depends entirely on river water levels.

HIKES & HIGHLIGHTS ALONG THE NAHANNI

The **Cirque of the Unclimbables** was so named by Arnold Wexler and a small group of American rock climbers in 1958. When they encountered this cluster of jagged peaks and sheer rock walls, they were haunted by what they saw before them. It looked like the craggy spires of Yosemite, which Ansel Adams had made famous during his mountain photography expeditions in the 1920s.

When Wexler and his colleagues got over the shocking head-on view of the 2,740-m-high (9,000 ft) fins of wind and ice-polished granite standing tall and angular and facing one another in a half circle, the adjoin-

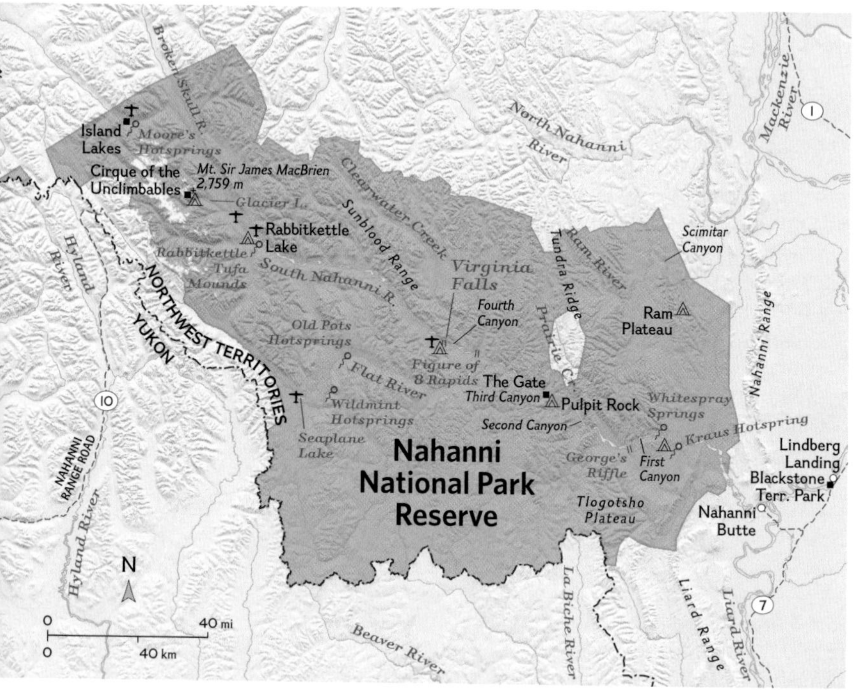

ing mountains suddenly looked small and terribly ordinary. Turning toward his partners, Wexler declared most of the peaks "unclimbable."

Most trips into the Unclimbables begin at **Glacier Lake,** a designated landing spot in the park. It is also possible (but not easy) to get to the Unclimbables from **Brintnell Creek** along the South Nahanni, an easy day's paddle from Island Lakes. The trail from here is at best indistinct.

From Brintnell Creek, hike upstream for 1 km (0.6 mi) until you get to a snye (a side channel) coming off the South Nahanni. Watch out for a heavily blazed pine tree. The trail eventually makes an abrupt left turn. Follow the trail over rolling hills until it nears Brintnell Creek, then follow the north bank of the creek west to Glacier Lake. Count on losing the trail a number of times along the way. Allow a day to get to Glacier Lake, and another half day to get to the **Fairy Meadows,** which is located at the foot of the Unclimbables.

Continue along to **Rabbitkettle Lake** (Gahn Hthah Mie) and its famous tufa hot springs, the largest in Canada. Some of these terraced mounds of calcium carbonate precipitate are 27 m (89 ft) high and 70 m (230 ft) in diameter. Yambadezha, "protector of the people," is said to inhabit one of the vents. It is this spirit, so the Dene legend goes, that went down to Nahanni Butte and drove away two giant beavers that would drown boaters with a slap of their enormous tails.

From the campground at Rabbitkettle, one can hike to the **Secret Lakes**—a series of small, deep lakes nestled in the sides of the mountain valley. There are two 10-km (6 mi) routes in the area; ask the staff based at Rabbitkettle for advice. Note that Rabbitkettle is a hot spot for grizzly bears and black bears, so tread cautiously.

Kayaking on the South Nahanni River

Downriver the **Sunblood Mountains** trailhead (8 km/5 mi one way) is located across the river from the Virginia Falls Campground. To get there safely, paddle upstream a few hundred metres and cross the river to the sign that marks the beginning of the trail. Follow this trail to an open scree ridge and continue to the peak of Sunblood. Start early, bring water, and enjoy the spectacular views of the river and waterfalls below.

Marengo Falls (4 km/2.5 mi one way): There are two ways to get to this small waterfall that drops 30 m (98 ft) over a series of limestone ledges. Parks Canada interpreters will be happy to point you to the two routes from **Virginia Falls.** All you'll need is a GPS or map and compass.

THE THIRD CANYON

In **Third Canyon,** the river takes a sharp turn before cutting a narrow, steep-sided slit through rock streaked red with iron, known as **The Gate.** Passing through this peaceful stretch of water in 1927, author/adventurer Raymond Patterson wrote, "The whole thing was like a great gateway through which I glided silently, midget like.

NAHANNI NATIONAL PARK RESERVE

(Réserve de parc national Nahanni)

INFORMATION & ACTIVITIES

VISITOR CENTRE

Nahanni National Park Reserve office Fort Simpson. Phone (867) 695-3151. Open daily June to October; weekdays rest of year. **Nahanni Butte** (867) 602-2024. Duty officer on call 24 hours a day, June–Sept. (867) 695-3732.

SEASONS & ACCESSIBILITY

Park open year-round, peak season May to August. No roads lead to the park; accessible by chartered floatplane from licensed company. Park permits required for landing at Virginia Falls and Rabbitkettle Lake. Floatplanes accessible from Fort Simpson, Fort Liard, and Yellowknife, NT; Fort Nelson and Muncho Lake, BC; and Watson Lake, YT. Licensed charter companies: Simpson Air, Ltd. (867) 695-2505; South Nahanni Airways (867) 695-2007; Wolverine Air (867) 695-2263; Air Tindi (867) 669-8200; Alpine Aviation (Yukon) Ltd. (867) 668-7725; Kluane Airways/Inconnu Lodge (250) 860-4187; Liard Tours/Northern Rockies Lodge (250) 776-3482.

HEADQUARTERS

10002 100 St., P.O. Box 348, Fort Simpson, NT X0E 0N0. Phone (867) 695-3151. www.parkscanada.gc.ca/nahanni.

ENTRANCE FEES

Backcountry excursion and camping permits are $25 per person per day, $147 per person per year. Reservation requests, member list form, and emergency contact and equipment list forms must be provided to park office.

PETS

Pets permitted but not recommended; must be on a leash at all times.

ACCESSIBLE SERVICES

None.

THINGS TO DO

Most visitors start their trips from **Virginia Falls** (typically 7–10 days) or **Rabbitkettle Lake** (10–14 days). Other starting locations include **Island Lakes** (14–18 days; flat, with Class II rapids), the **Little Nahanni River** (6–7 days to paddle to Rabbitkettle Lake and join South Nahanni; Class II–IV rapids), or **The Moose Ponds** (outside park boundary; 21 days; Class II–IV white water). Alternate routes include **Seaplane Lake/Flat River** (4-5 days; Class II-V rapids) and **Glacier Lake.** Permits required. River guide pamphlets available for $5. Reservations must be confirmed with park office.

Canoeing in the **South Nahanni River** between June and September.

Hiking in the **Cirque of the Unclimbables; Glacier Lake** (accessed from South Nahanni River north of park boundary); **Secret Lakes** (6–10 km/4–6 mi, one way); **Sunblood Mountain** (8 km/5 mi,

I have seen many beautiful places in my lifetime, but never anything of this kind."

Just past **Big Bend,** where the **Funeral Range** ends and the **Headless Range** begins, is where the headless bodies of the McLeod brothers, Willie and Frank, were found after they went missing in 1903 searching for an Indian tale of gold piled high in the region. A note carved in a sled runner that read, "We have found a prospect," resulted in a mini gold rush and murderous incidents that are why the Nahanni has been called the "Valley of the Vanishing Men."

Prairie Creek (4 km/2.5 mi one way) is a large alluvial fan that can't be missed. Stay left of Prairie Creek's channels when you begin the hike; when Prairie Creek exits the mountains, climb over a saddle to the west of the gap, to get to a floodplain flanked by the vertical canyon walls.

The dry gravel fan of **Dry Canyon Creek** (10 km/6 mi one way) is at the one way); **Marengo Falls** (4 km/2.5 mi, one way); **Scow Creek/Headless Range** (8 km/5 mi, one way); **Prairie Creek** (4 km/2.5 mi, one way); **Sheaf Creek-Tlogotsho Plateau** (10 km/6 mi, one way); **Dry Canyon Creek** (10 km/6 mi, one way); **Ram Creek** (15 km/9 mi, one way); **Lafferty Creek** (10 km/6 mi, one way).

Fishing permitted in all park waters at any time of year with five fish limit for daily catch-and-possession. Fishing permits are $34 per year.

Licensed river outfitters include: Black Feather—The Wilderness Adventure Company (705) 746-1372 or (888) 737-6818; Nahanni River Adventures (867) 668-3056; Nahanni Wilderness Adventures (403) 678-3374.

SPECIAL ADVISORIES

- Open fires for cooking or heat not permitted. Fire-box and fire-pan rentals available at Deh Cho Hardware, Fort Simpson. Phone (867) 695-2320.
- Campsites forbidden near staff cabins.
- Solid experience in white-water paddling or rafting, self-rescue skills, and knowledge of travelling and camping in remote wilderness environments recommended.
- Consult park map for boundaries.

CAMPGROUNDS

Virginia Falls Campground by reservation. Maximum group size 12 people, 2-night stay, $25 per person per day or $147 per person per year. Collection box at kiosk at Virginia Falls. Travel time to campsite is 2 to 3 days paddling time if starting from Rabbitkettle Lake; 6 to 7 days if starting from Island Lakes; 10 days if starting from the Mooseponds. Travel time depends on weather conditions and off-river hiking time. Canoe racks, food caches, and composting toilets available. Use caution when approaching portage landing. **Rabbitkettle Lake** campgrounds are off the shores of the lake 300 m (984 ft) north of staff cabin, and on an island in the South Nahanni River across from portage landing. Both campgrounds have food caches and outhouses. No camping permitted at portage landing. **The Gate (Pulpit Rock)** is a designated campsite. Composting toilet available. **Kraus Hotsprings** former homestead of Mary and Gus Kraus. Hot springs along river's edge. Check-in station, food cache, and outhouse available. Use of soap prohibited.

HOTELS, MOTELS, & INNS

(unless otherwise noted, rates are for a 2-person double, high season, in Canadian dollars)

Outside the park:

Fort Simpson, NT XOE ONO:

Deh Cho Suites 10509 Antoine Drive, Box 60. (867) 695-2309 or (877) 695-2309. $175-$195.

Maroda Motel 9802 100th St. (867) 695-2602. $115-$170.

Nahanni Inn Box 258. (867) 695-2201. $115-$170.

Nahanni Butte, NT XOE ONO:

Nahanni Butte Inn and General Store Box 149. (867) 602-2002.

far eastern end of **Deadmen Valley.** Hike along gravel beds of the steep-walled canyon. Several draws and ridges to the east will take you to the **Nahanni Plateau.** Note that the canyon can flood in a thunderstorm.

OTHER RIVERS

Lafferty Creek (10 km/6 mi one way) joins the South Nahanni near the bottom of First Canyon at km 260. Some boulder walking and scrambling will be necessary to get through.

Kraus Hotsprings, located a kilometre downstream of Lafferty Creek at the end of a long rapid (Lafferty's Riffle), is the site of an old homestead. Here, weary paddlers can soak their bones in one of the warm springs percolating from the gravel.

The **Flat River** and **Little Nahanni River** both flow from the Yukon Divide and provide alternative and somewhat more challenging ways of exploring Nahanni National Park.

A watery playground, the Gulf Islands offer a wealth of ecological and cultural attractions.

GULF ISLANDS

BRITISH COLUMBIA

ESTABLISHED 2003

62 sq km/15,321 acres (36 sq km/8,896 acres on land and water; 26 sq km/ 6,425 acres of adjacent marine area)

Nurtured by a unique Mediterranean climate, Gulf Islands National Park Reserve supports a stunning diversity of rare bird-, plant, and marine life spread across 15 islands and innumerable islets and reefs in the northern reaches of the inland Salish Sea.

There's no gate or interpretive centre at this national park reserve: Much of the nearly 36-sq-km park is spread over 699 sq km (270 sq mi) of sheltered ocean separating mainland Vancouver from the city of Victoria on Vancouver Island, and some of it is under water. Much of the park is located on the bigger southern Gulf Islands, including Saturna, North and South Pender, and Mayne.

The abundant marine life, climate, and physical beauty of this archipelago—protected in the rain shadow of two mountain chains—have attracted people for more than 5,000 years. First were the Coast Salish, thriving on the bountiful shellfish, plants, and game; Spanish explorers followed, adding their names on waterways and islands. The British joined the Hawaiians and other Europeans as pioneer farmers, clearing great swaths of the forest to plant apple orchards and graze sheep.

The latest wave of settlers—mostly artists, seasonal cottagers, and retirees—have created enormous new development pressures across the southern Gulf Islands in the later part of the 20th century and into the 21st, threatening the endangered ecosystems found only in this microclimate, including the multitude of rare life-forms associated with the meadows and rocky outcrops occupied by the Garry oak, British Columbia's only native oak. The demand for waterfront property has also threatened the last critical habitats for fish, seals, sea lions, and killer whales.

In 2003, Canada's federal government gathered together a patchwork of existing ecological reserves, provincial parks, and newly acquired lands under the banner of a national park reserve. The park reserve remains a work in progress, with new acquisitions ongoing.

How to Get There

There is regular car/passenger ferry service (BC Ferries) to the larger southern Gulf Islands throughout the year from Swartz Bay (near Victoria) and the Tsawwassen ferry terminal accessible from Vancouver. The rest of the parklands and marine protected waters open to the public are only reachable via private means—passenger ferry, water taxi, boat, or even kayak.

When to Go

The dry, warm season between June and early October is the best time for most activities in the park. Services and some park access are limited in the winter.

How to Visit

In the absence of visitor centres, the Parks Canada website provides maps and information about hiking routes, boating, and other activities.

If you have only one day, take a car ferry to Saturna Island, the biggest and least developed of the southern Gulf Islands with national park land on them. Home to about one-third of the park's total land area, it offers short trails, day-use areas, and some of the most commanding views in the region. Accommodations are limited; book ahead if you want to stay overnight, especially in summer. There are no reservable campsites on Saturna Island.

For a very popular but no less spectacular view of the park, spend a second day exploring Sidney Spit on Sidney Island, wandering the beautiful sandy beaches, forests, and meadows.

Note: There are no garbage cans throughout the park: Pack out what you pack in. Bring your own drinking water, too, as it is in short supply during summer across the Gulf Islands.

Bald eagle *(Haliaeetus leucocephalus)*

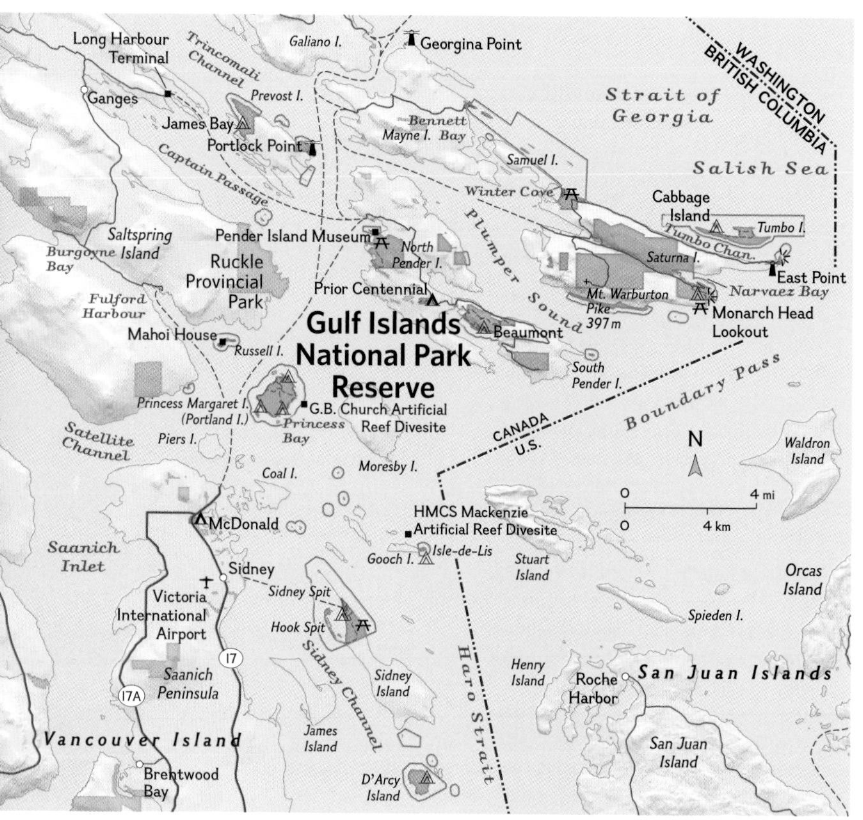

SATURNA ISLAND

a full day

Largely undeveloped and home to just 350 people, **Saturna Island** provides visitors with a glimpse of what the Gulf Islands were like a hundred years ago.

To stand atop **Mount Warburton Pike**—at 397 m (1,303 ft) the second highest peak in the park—take East Point Road from the ferry terminal for about 2 km (1.25 mi), turning right onto Harris Road for about five minutes; a left turn onto Staples Road, a steep winding gravel route, will take you to the top, named for a British explorer and author who bought several large parcels on the island in the 1880s to farm sheep.

On a clear day you can see from Victoria's Oak Bay to the Olympic Mountains and the San Juan Islands in the east. Directly across Plumper Sound is **South Pender Island.** From this vantage point falcons, eagles, and feral goats are common sights—the latter have roamed wild on Saturna Island for more than a century, descendants of livestock kept by early settlers.

Now backtrack to the junction of East Point Road and Narvaez Bay Road, turn right, and follow Narvaez Bay Road to its end, where there is parking for a short trail down to stunning Narvaez Bay, named for Spanish explorer José María Narváez, who captained the naval schooner *Santa Saturnina* (thus the island's name) through these waters in 1791.

One of the most beautiful little bays in the park, **Narvaez Bay** penetrates for almost 2 km (1.25 mi) into the island's southeast shore. Walk down the former driveway past the bike rack for about 1 km (0.5 mi), through to the field at the bottom—turn left and walk down to the campsites and the bay. Narvaez Bay is remote and secluded, except for the odd sailboat that anchors in its protected clear green waters. Be cautious on the cliff edges and rocky promontories, particularly if it is wet.

The easiest way to get to the **Monarch Head lookout** at the head of the bay is to walk about 40 m (130 ft) up Narvaez Bay Road from the parking lot and take the trail on the left (two large rocks mark the trail). Follow the trail until it comes out into a small clearing, then follow the signs up another little logging road; the route is steep, but it only takes about ten minutes to hike up to the lookout. From atop the bluff, watch for killer whales and porpoises in **Boundary Pass,** amid the busy shipping lane and boat traffic using the nearby international border.

Exploration of the western Saturna parklands begins with a hike to **Boat Passage** in **Winter Cove,** a picturesque, sheltered spot that is a popular day-use area, especially with private boaters. From Narvaez Bay Road, turn right on East Point Road, then left on Winter Cove Road, then take the first right, which will take you into the national park at Winter Cove. Here a gravel-groomed trail (about 1.6 km/1 mi round-trip) loops through Douglas-fir and red alder forests to the water. If possible, time your visit close to low tide: That's when the currents pushing between the point and Samuel Island create fast-flowing rapids.

To get back to the parking lot, follow the loop trail that parallels the shoreline around two saltwater lagoons and follow the boardwalks back to the trailhead.

As dusk falls, kayaks lie at rest on the southwest side of Princess Margaret Island. Sea kayaking is one of the best ways to explore the Gulf Islands, offering an intimate experience with nature.

East Point, on the far eastern tip of the island, is home to an automated light station and restored fog alarm/heritage centre. It also offers close proximity to an offshore marine oasis that regularly attracts killer whales, sea lions, and seals.

Follow East Point Road for 10 km (6.2 mi) (it eventually becomes Tumbo Island Road), much of it with ocean views, to the road's terminus. Walk through an open grassy field to the restored **1938 Saturna fog alarm building**—the island's most photographed building. A local historical group hosts a heritage centre here, detailing local island history and the nautical feats of the Spanish explorers who "discovered" the island.

A five-minute walk takes you to the tip of East Point, where on a clear day, spectral Mount Baker rises in the northeast—an active volcano almost 3,353 m (11,000 ft) high in Washington's nearby North Cascades—looming above all else. Arrive at low tide, when the flow of water rushing through **Tumbo Channel** is at its greatest—and behold the water accelerating to up to 14 knots—so fast that it is audible.

The unusual concentration of marine life here is the result of the upwelling and collision of nutrient-rich currents: Just offshore, the waters of Boundary Pass, the Strait of Georgia, and Washington's Puget Sound collide. The aptly named **Boiling Reef,** situated in the midst of this aquatic chaos, is a resting place for seabirds and a haul-out for seals (year-round) and sea lions (fall to spring). Resident and transient killer whales, which patrol these waters between spring and fall, often appear along the cliff immediately below the light station, seemingly so close one could jump on their backs as they swim by.

Across the water from the point is **Tumbo Island,** now a park property. Bring binoculars, and look upon one of the best examples of pristine Garry oak grassland meadow, an ecosystem endemic to this region; this is what a Garry oak ecosystem would have looked like 150 years ago.

SIDNEY & HOOK SPITS

1 to 2 days

At the northern end of Sidney Island, in Haro Strait, you will find Sidney Spit along with the hook spit, the main attractions of this 4 sq km (990 acres) chunk of park reserve.

Through time Sidney Island has been used by humans for First Nations clam harvesting, as a brick factory, then later a provincial and now federal park. Most of the island is still in private hands.

A private 12-m (40 ft) passenger ferry travels the 3.7 km (2 nautical mi) between the town of Sidney on Vancouver Island and Sidney Island from May to September (call for times; Alpine–Sidney–Spit Ferry 250-474-5145). There is pay parking at the Sidney Pier Hotel or Port Sidney Marina, from which you can walk in two minutes to Beacon Pier dock; remember to pack snacks and water.

The ferry lands at a day-use area situated at the base of **Sidney Spit—**a thin, white arm of sand that reaches more than 2 km (1.2 mi) into Haro Strait; you can walk its entire length, right to the light beacon at the point.

Hook Spit—a second spit that is equally long—is located to the west, curling into a hook creating a lagoon. This inner lagoon is closed to boating in order to protect the sensitive eelgrass beds, which provide important bird and fish habitat. Hiking is permitted on the outside of Hook

Spit, provided visitors stay out of the vegetated area and walk along the beach. The inner lagoon side of the spit is a special preservation area; there is no access.

Because the lagoon is situated on the Pacific flyway, migratory birds use it as a stopover for their spring and fall migrations; in all, at least 150 species of resident and migratory birds can be seen here—including bald eagle, great blue heron, purple martin, and multiple species of grebe and cormorant.

To explore the spit, take the 2-km (1.2 mi) loop trail (about 40 minutes to complete) that can be picked up directly from the day-use area at the ferry dock and follow it through Douglas-fir and arbutus forests heavily thinned by the island's very large population of fallow non-native deer. These small, reddish-coloured deer (the males often display impressive palmated antlers) were likely brought to the island in the early 1900s, where they have thrived ever since without predators. Each winter since 2005, the park closes for several months to facilitate a First Nations hunt for the invasive deer on Sidney Island.

Follow the trail along the eastern edge of the island; a staircase leads down to a beautiful eastward view facing the United States at **East Beach.** Continue on the trail; at the campground the route loops back across toward the lagoon, where you will approach a large clearing. It is a gathering point for large herds of deer. (Remember: It is a federal offence to disturb the deer.) The trail passes an old ranger station and returns to the ferry dock.

Pink seablushes and purple camas carpet a meadow.

Steller sea lions

GULF ISLANDS NATIONAL PARK RESERVE
(RÉSERVE DE PARC NATIONAL DES ÎLES-GULF)

INFORMATION & ACTIVITIES
HEADQUARTERS
Sidney Operations Centre 2220 Harbour Rd., Sidney, BC V8L 2P6. Phone (250) 654-4000 or (866) 944-1744. www.parkscanada.gc.ca/gulf.

SEASONS & ACCESSIBILITY
Sidney Operations Centre open weekdays, year-round.

ENTRANCE FEES
No entry fee.

THINGS TO DO
Kayaking, powerboating, and whale-watching. Road cycling, hiking, beach walking.

You can picnic in **Winter Cove** or **East Point** on Saturna Island, **Sidney Spit** on Sidney Island, or **Roesland** on North Pender Island.

Interpretive programs offered on Saturna, Mayne, Sidney, Russell, and Pender Islands from June to early September. Naturalist presentations are given on some ferry rides.

SPECIAL ADVISORIES
- Bring water supplies and containers for packing out garbage.
- No bike lanes or paved shoulders for cyclists on Saturna, Mayne, and Pender Islands. Cycling on park trails not allowed.
- Visitors should remain on designated hiking trails.
- Consult the Canadian Hydrographic Service website *(www.charts.gc.ca)* for tide timetables before visiting tide pools.

CAMPGROUNDS
Backcountry campgrounds with tent pads or tent platforms and pit or composting toilets are available on **Cabbage Island;** at **Narvaez Bay** on Saturna Island; **D'Arcy Island; Isle-de-Lis; Portland Island; James Bay** (Prevost Island), accessible by water only; and **Beaumont** (South Pender). Camping at **Sidney Spit** is accessible by seasonal foot passenger ferry from **Sidney** (Vancouver Island). For schedule and fee information call (250) 654-4000. **Beaumont, Cabbage Island, Narvaez Bay** campgrounds and **Sidney Spit** open mid-May to late September. **D'Arcy Island, Isle-de-Lis,** and **James Bay** campgrounds open June to late September. For group camping reservations, contact the park office at (866) 944-1744.

Mooring buoys at **Sidney Spit, Beaumont,** and **Cabbage Island** are $10 per night, 14-day maximum stay. Vehicle accessible camping is available at **McDonald Campground** (mid-May–early Oct.) on Vancouver Island and at **Prior Centennial Campground** (May–early Oct.) on Pender Island; reservations can be made by contacting the Parks Canada Reservation System at (877) 737-3783 or www.pccamping.ca.

Camping fees are $14 per party or $5 per person in backcountry campsites. Call park office for special rates and group campsite reservations. Visit park website for updated fees.

HOTELS, MOTELS, & INNS
(unless otherwise noted, rates are for a 2-person double, high season, in Canadian dollars)

Outside the park:
Saturna Island, BC V0N 2Y0:
Saturna Lodge 130 Payne Rd. (250) 539-2254. innkeeper@saturna.ca; www.saturna.ca. $120–$170.

Sidney, BC:
Beacon Inn at Sidney 9724 Third St., Sidney by the Sea, V8L 3A2. (250) 655-3288 or (877) 420-5499. info@beaconinns.com; www.thebeaconinn.com. $150–$260.
Cedarwood Inn & Suites 9522 Lochside Dr., V8L 1N8. (250) 656-5551 or (877) 656-5551. info@thecedarwood.ca; http://thecedarwood.ca. $125–$425.
Sidney Waterfront Inn & Spa 9775 First St., V8L 3E1. (250) 656-1131 or (888) 656-1131. stay@sidneywaterfrontinn.com; www.sidneywaterfrontinn.com. $135–$314.

NATIONAL MARINE CONSERVATION AREA

GWAII HAANAS
BRITISH COLUMBIA

Setting a global precedent, Gwaii Haanas National Park Reserve, National Marine Conservation Area Reserve, and Haida Heritage Site is the first protected area to extend from the seafloor to the mountaintops. It is a victory recognizing that for the Haida, the land, sea, and people are interconnected and inseparable.

A colourful sunflower star lurks in the shallows of an inlet.

Gwaii Haanas extends approximately 10 km (6.2 mi) offshore and encompasses 3,400 sq km (1,313 sq mi) of the Hecate Strait and Queen Charlotte Shelf. It is the first national marine conservation area reserve established under Canada's National Marine Areas Conservation Act. The designation aims to protect the ecological and cultural resources of the area so that ecologically sustainable use can continue. The area supports the Haida's traditional harvest of marine resources as well as commercial fisheries that include herring roe, halibut, salmon, rockfish, geoduck clam, and red sea urchin.

These nutrient-rich waters support some of the most abundant, diverse, and colourful intertidal communities found in any temperate waters. From ocean abyss to continental slope to shallow shelf to rugged islands, this marine area is one of biological richness and is home to more than 3,500 marine species, including species at risk, and 20 species of whales, dolphins, and porpoises. Above the waters, the area provides nesting for more than 370,000 pairs of seabirds.

As a protected region, safeguarded from large-scale fishing and petroleum interests, Gwaii Haanas offers visitors an unparalleled opportunity to appreciate and enjoy the beauty and abundance of the oceans.

DIVING: This rich and colourful underwater world teems with kelp forests, sea stars, anemones, sea urchins, and a vast array of fish species and offers spectacular diving opportunities. The best diving is in spring when the area boasts crystal clear waters; in the summer, warm waters create algae blooms that can compromise visibility. Because of the remoteness and logistical difficulty in transporting tanks and refilling them, it is easiest to join a guided dive trip. Diving in Gwaii Haanas is not for beginners—divers should be experienced cold-water dry suit divers and should bring their own suits. (Note: The closest hyperbaric chamber is in Vancouver, which could take several hours to reach even by air.) One local dive operator is **Moresby Explorers** (800-806-7633, *http://divegwaiihaanas.com*).

SNORKELLING: While diving might be reserved for only the experienced, snorkelling offers a way for everyone to enjoy the underwater beauty of Gwaii Haanas. The thermal springs at **Hot Spring Island** make the underwater plant life extra colourful and **Burnaby Narrows** offers unparalleled snorkelling in an incredibly rich area of biodiversity.

KAYAKING: There are several ways to enjoy kayaking in Gwaii Haanas. Kayakers who are experienced and self-reliant and have the gift of time may choose to spend days or weeks exploring the park. Those less experienced but still ambitious may choose a guided kayaking trip. Even novice kayakers may still have the chance to paddle in paradise, as many of the sailing tour operators carry kayaks with them on their voyages.

BOATING & SAILING: There are 11 buoys spread throughout the marine park—they range from large can buoys that can accommodate several vessels to smaller buoys suitable for only one boat. In some places, boats may need to anchor without buoys. The general anchoring policy for the park is that a vessel is permitted to stay in any one place for up to three nights, but after that it must move locations, weather permitting.

SALTWATER FISHING: The Haida people have since time immemorial used these waters to harvest food and continue this practice today. A licence is required for all saltwater fishing in Gwaii Haanas and these can be obtained online from Fisheries & Oceans Canada (*www.pac.dfo-mpo.gc.ca/fm-gp/rec/licence-permis/index-eng.htm*) or at local retail outlets. Freshwater fishing within the park is prohibited. In addition, there are some areas within Gwaii Haanas Marine Area that are closed to all fishing or have fishing restrictions.

MARINE MAMMAL-WATCHING: Marine mammals inspire awe, spark our imaginations, and fill our hearts. It can be hard to control excitement but please use caution in areas of marine mammal activity, show courtesy by slowing your speed, and keep a distance of at least 100 m (330 ft). It is never safe to swim with or feed the marine life.

At the southern tip of Gwaii Haanas near **Cape St. James** is a

Dusk over the islands

large sea lion rookery with a large breeding colony of Steller sea lions. There are also several other haul-outs in Gwaii Haanas, one located near **Cumshewa Head.** Sea lions are particularly vulnerable during the breeding and pupping season (May–July). Female sea lions (cows) give birth high on the rocks to protect their young from being swept away by waves and drowning. Use caution and leave at the first sign of agitation. Any disturbance that causes the mother to change spots risks her pup falling into a crack in the rocks or into the ocean and drowning.

More than 20 species of whales, dolphins, and porpoises can be seen in the Gwaii Haanas Marine Conservation Area, including orcas (killer whales), humpbacks, minkes, and grey whales. Humpback whales, known for their acrobatics, arrive each April to feed on herring. They have spent the winter in either Mexico or Hawaii and pass through on their migration. Grey whales also pass through each spring on their way to their summer feeding grounds in the Bering Sea. Large aggregations of a hundred or more whales can often be found just north of Tanu feeding in the plankton-rich outflow waters.

There are some guidelines to keep in mind when encountering these majestic sea creatures: Travel parallel to whales and dolphins and never travel through them with the intent of having them ride your bow. When approaching, do so from the side instead of from the front or behind.

In the spring, thousands of dolphins, killer whales, salmon, and halibut can be found in the nutrient-rich waters near Hot Spring Island.

Gwaii Haanas National Marine Conservation Reserve: Gwaii Haanas National Park Reserve and Haida Heritage Site, Queen Charlotte, BC V0T 1S0. Phone (250) 559-8818. gwaiihaanasmarine@pc.gc.ca.

AUTHORS' SECRETS

Each of the authors have hundreds of secrets that haven't been included in this book. Here are the single ones they've chosen to share.

GREAT SMOKY MOUNTAINS

Before the picnickers arrive (around 10 a.m.), I like to hike the Metcalf Bottoms Trail up to the one-room Little Greenbrier Schoolhouse. The 0.7-mile trail though the woods retraces the route the children living in Metcalf Bottoms in the late 1800s and early 1900s would have followed to get to school.

—MARYELLEN DUCKETT
POWELL, TENNESSEE

JOSHUA TREE

There's a remote, off-trail spot in Joshua Tree National Park where a reclusive Swedish prospector named Samuelson spent his idle hours carving screeds into granite boulders. The craftsmanship is remarkable, even if the spelling isn't—chiseling block letters into hard granite is unthinkably difficult. Some of them are diatribes, while others are gentle thoughts like "Study nature, you can't go wrong." I like to go out there just to sit quietly and tap into the silence and solace he found amid that jumble of mute boulders and Joshua trees reaching toward the deep blue sky.

—ROBERT EARLE HOWELLS
CULVER CITY, CALIFORNIA

HAWAI'I VOLCANOES

Most people visit Hawai'i Volcanoes National Park during the day, but my "secret" time to go is at night, when the crowds have dissipated and the red glow of molten lava illuminates the sky. This is when I can feel the full Hawaiian spirituality of the park.

—GEORGE FULLER
KAMUELA, HAWAI'I

ARCHES

Exploring Fiery Furnace's maze of sandstone fins with a compass, a climbing harness, and a length of rope is my escape. Each time, it feels like a page out of Jules Verne's A Journey to the Center of the Earth, *leading to a new personal discovery.*

—CHARLES KULANDER
MOAB, UTAH

WRANGELL-ST. ELIAS

My "secret spot" is Icy Bay in Wrangell–St. Elias National Park in Alaska. Imagine Yosemite Valley as a seawater-and-glacier-filled fjord and you've got some idea what Icy Bay is like. Thousand-foot waterfalls plunging down sheer granite cliffs. Glaciers tumbling down to the edge of the bay, cotton candy blue icebergs, islands with glacial ponds where you can swim on sunny summer days, and wildlife galore—whales and dolphins, Bald Eagles, grizzly bears. I'm not worried about giving the secret away, because Icy Bay is nearly impossible to reach. You've got to fly in by bush- or floatplane, explore the bay by kayak, camping as you go. Not a single road—or anything man-made—within miles. John Muir would have been blown away.

—JOE YOGERST
SAN DIEGO, CALIFORNIA

MOUNT RAINIER

The crystal clear Ohanapecosh River flows through the heart of the popular Ohanapecosh Campground. Most campers appreciate its stunning beauty but fail to realize it holds a treasure: Native cutthroat and rainbow trout hide in plain sight within those waters. Try fly-fishing for these feisty fish to truly experience the river.

—DAN A. NELSON
PUYALLUP, WASHINGTON

OLYMPIC

I love exploring the tide pools of Olympic National Park. They can be subtle—just small basins of saltwater tucked into the rugged coast—but peer into them and you'll find miniature worlds filled with sea urchins, sea stars, and other creatures.

—RACHAEL JACKSON
WASHINGTON, D.C.

YELLOWSTONE

Solitude is the key to understanding Yellowstone. One of my favorite activities is an evening visit to wildlife-rich Hayden Valley. I park the car and hike west, away from the road. Among the rolling, grass-covered hills are many good vantage points to sit quietly and watch for wildlife.

—JEREMY SCHMIDT
WILSON, WYOMING

BIG BEND

Visiting remote Big Bend might be a onetime experience, so here's my advice: Make your trip in spring after an especially wet winter (check with park rangers for conditions). If your timing's right, you'll enjoy one of North America's most spectacular wildflower shows.

—MEL WHITE
LITTLE ROCK, ARKANSAS

GREAT BASIN

I doubt if most people realize there's a six-story arch in Great Basin National Park, near the far southeastern corner of the park. Lexington Arch is unusual in that it's made of limestone, not sandstone. Park rangers theorize that the arch was once the doorway to a massive, now vanished cave.

—KAREN CARMICHAEL
WASHINGTON, D.C.

ILLUSTRATIONS CREDITS

Front Cover: (UP), Wayne Boland/Getty Images; (LO Left to Right), Dave G. Houser/Corbis; Tim Fitzharris/Minden Pictures/Corbis; David Tipling/Getty Images; Jeff Foott/Discovery Channel Images/Getty Images; Spine, Eric Foltz/iStockphoto; Back Cover (Left to Right): Saravanan Suriyanarayanan/National Geographic My Shot; Ian Shive/TandemStock.com; Eric Foltz/iStockphoto; Michael Melford/National Geographic Stock; 2-3, Michael Melford/National Geographic Stock; 4, Carr Clifton/Minden Pictures/National Geographic Stock; 7, www.brianruebphotography.com/Getty Images; 10, Chris Murray Photography; 12-3, Laurie Chamberlain/Corbis; 15, Michael Melford/National Geographic Stock; 16, Ron and Patty Thomas/Getty Images; 18, Michael Melford/National Geographic Stock; 19, Carr Clifton/Minden Pictures/National Geographic Stock; 20-1, StockStudios/iStockphoto; 24, Wildnerdpix/Shutterstock; 25, Jeffrey M. Frank/Shutterstock; 26, Norman Tomalin/Alamy; 28-9, Dean Pennala/Shutterstock; 32, Edward Kennair Jr./National Geographic My Shot; 35, Michael Melford/National Geographic Stock; 36-7, Paul Marcellini/Tom Stack Assoc/Alamy; 38, Ian Shive/Aurora Photos; 40, Tania Thomson/Shutterstock; 41, Masa Ushioda/www.coolwaterphoto.com; 42-3, Matt Propert, NGS; 46-7, Phil Schermeister; 49, Vicki Beaver/Alamy; 50, Carr Clifton/Minden Pictures/National Geographic Stock; 52-3, Phil Schermeister; 57, Kerrick James Photog/Getty Images; 58-9, Ian Shive/TandemStock.com; 61, Darlene Cutshall/Shutterstock; 62, Yva Momatiuk & John Eastcott/Minden Pictures/National Geographic Stock; 63, Sharon Day/Shutterstock; 64-5, Glenda Wilburn/National Geographic My Shot; 67, Mike Buchheit/Shutterstock; 68-9, Bill Hatcher/National Geographic Stock; 70, Alexey Stiop/Shutterstock; 71, Natalia Bratslavsky/iStockphoto; 73, Motmot/Shutterstock; 74-5, Phil Schermeister; 77, Raymond Gehman/National Geographic Stock; 78, Carr Clifton/Minden Pictures/National Geographic Stock; 80, Peter Wey/iStockphoto; 81, magmarcz/Shutterstock; 82-3, Marc Adamus; 84, Alaskaphoto/Shutterstock; 87, Bennett Barthelemy/TandemStock.com; 89, Adrian Baras/Shutterstock; 90-1, Tim Fitzharris/Minden Pictures/National Geographic Stock; 92, Tim Fitzharris/Minden Pictures/National Geographic Stock; 95, Peter Wey/Shutterstock; 96, Mike Norton/Shutterstock; 98-9, George H. H. Huey; 103, Phil Schermeister; 104-5, Kipp Schoen/iStockphoto; 107, Jeff Ross/National Geographic My Shot; 108, Justin Reznick/iStockphoto; 111, SCPhotos/Alamy; 112-3, Mike Norton/Shutterstock; 114, Ralf Broskvar/Shutterstock; 116, Kushch Dmitry/Shutterstock; 117, Tim Fitzharris/Minden Pictures/National Geographic Stock; 118, Morey Milbradt/Alamy; 119, Geir Olav Lyngfjell/Shutterstock; 120-1, Tim Fitzharris/Minden Pictures/National Geographic Stock; 123, Sergio Ballivian/TandemStock.com; 125, Bob Pool/Getty Images; 127, David Muench/Muench Photography Inc.; 128-9, Tom Bean/Alamy; 131, Paul E. Tessier/Getty Images; 132-3, Paul E. Tessier/iStockphoto; 134-5, Phil Schermeister; 138, Jeff Stenstrom/National Geographic My Shot; 139, Annie Griffiths/National Geographic Stock; 140-1, Danita Delimont/Gallo Images/Getty Images; 142, Michael Melford/National Geographic Stock; 144, Willard Clay/Getty Images; 146-7, Carr Clifton/Minden Pictures/National Geographic Stock; 150, Daniel M. Silva/Shutterstock; 151, Jim Laybourn/National Geographic My Shot; 152, Alexey Kamenskiy/Shutterstock; 153, Rick Laverty/Shutterstock; 154, Boyd Taylor/National Geographic My Shot; 155, Michael Melford/National Geographic Stock; 156-7, Ted Wood/Aurora Photos; 159, Ken Canning/iStockphoto; 160, Ashok Rodrigues/iStockphoto; 162, Carey Plemmons/National Geographic My Shot; 163, Jeffrey T. Kreulen/Shutterstock; 164-5, Steven Gnam/TandemStock.com; 167, Skip Brown/National Geographic Stock; 168, Michael Melford/National Geographic Stock; 169, Prisma Bildagentur AG/Alamy; 170, studioworxx/iStockphoto; 172, Tomas Kaspar/age fotostock; 174-5, Jeffrey Murray/Aurora Photos; 178, Michael J. Thompson/Shutterstock; 181, Mark R./Shutterstock; 182-3, Ian Shive/TandemStock.com; 186, Carr Clifton/Minden Pictures/National Geographic Stock; 187, Radoslaw Lecyk/Shutterstock; 188, Galyna Andrushko/Shutterstock; 189, Melissa Farlow/National Geographic Stock; 190-1, Christian Heeb/LAIF/Redux Pictures; 193, Nancy Nehring/iStockphoto; 194, Mike Norton/Shutterstock; 195, Curved Light USA/Alamy; 196-7, Michael Nichols, NGP; 200, Kevin Schafer/Corbis; 202-3, Shawn Reeder; 205, Richard Nowitz/National Geographic Stock; 206, Shawn Reeder; 208, Heather Ferguson/National Geographic My Shot; 209, Kristine Brodfuehrer/iStockphoto; 210, Steven Castro/Shutterstock; 211, Artifan/Shutterstock; 212-3, Tim Fitzharris; 216, Kyle Sparks/Aurora Photos; 218-9, Tim Fitzharris/Minden Pictures/National Geographic Stock; 223, Michael Melford/National Geographic Stock; 224-5, Phil Schermeister; 226, Tom Grubbe/Getty Images; 228, Eric Foltz/iStockphoto; 229, Eric Foltz/iStockphoto; 230-1, Marc Muench/Muench Photography Inc.; 233, Ian Shive/TandemStock.com; 234, Ian Shive/TandemStock.com; 236-7, Frans Lanting/National Geographic Stock; 241, Frans Lanting/National Geographic Stock; 242-3, Wally Pacholka; 246, Dan Barnes/iStockphoto; 247, Ron Niebrugge/Alamy; 248, Michael Melford/National Geographic Stock; 263, Jason Patrick Ross/Shutterstock; 264-5, Carr Clifton/Minden Pictures/National Geographic Stock; 266, Heiko Wittenborn/Parks Canada; 269, Heiko Wittenborn/Parks Canada; 270 (LE & RT), Heiko Wittenborn/Parks Canada; 272 & 273, Marc Loiselle/Parks Canada; 274 (UP), Louis Falardeau/Parks Canada; 274 (LO), Nelson Boisvert/Parks Canada; 275, John Butterill/Parks Canada; 276, Don Wilkes/Parks Canada; 278, Paul Nicklen/National Geographic Stock; 281, Gordon Wiltsie/National Geographic Stock; 282, Lee Narraway/Parks Canada; 284, Lee Narraway/Parks Canada; 287 (All), Lee Narraway/Parks Canada; 289, Lee Narraway/Parks Canada; 290 & 291, GaryandJoanieMcGuffin.com; 292, Steve Irvine/National Geographic My Shot; 294, Raymond Gehman/National Geographic Stock; 297, D. Harvey/Parks Canada; 300, Josh McCulloch/Parks Canada; 301, naturediver/Shutterstock; 303, Chris Cheadle/Parks Canada; 305 (UP), Emily Gonzales/Parks Canada; 305 (LO), Christian J. Stewart/Parks Canada; 307, Mark Hiebert/Parks Canada; 309, Chris Cheadle/Parks Canada.

Acknowledgments

We are indebted to the many individuals within the National Park Service and the in the individual parks that have helped us prepare this book. We are also especially grateful to the National Park Trust and its staff for all their assistance.

INDEX

Boldface indicates illustrations.

Secrets of the National Parks

Mel White, Robert Earl Howells, Dan A. Nelson, Jeremy Schmidt, Joe Yogerst, Charles Kulander, Maryellen Duckett, George Fuller, Rachael Jackson, Karen Carmichael, *Authors*

Published by the National Geographic Society

John M. Fahey, *Chairman of the Board and Chief Executive Officer*
Timothy T. Kelly, *President*
Declan Moore, *Executive Vice President; President, Publishing and Travel*
Melina Gerosa Bellows, *Executive Vice President; Chief Creative Officer, Books, Kids, and Family*
Lynn Cutter, *Executive Vice President, Travel*
Keith Bellows, *Senior Vice President and Editor in Chief, National Geographic Travel Media*

Prepared by the Book Division

Hector Sierra, *Senior Vice President and General Manager*
Janet Goldstein, *Senior Vice President and Editorial Director*
Jonathan Halling, *Design Director, Books and Children's Publishing*
Marianne R. Koszorus, *Design Director, Books*
Barbara A. Noe, *Senior Editor, National Geographic Travel Books*
R. Gary Colbert, *Production Director*
Jennifer A. Thornton, *Director of Managing Editorial*
Susan S. Blair, *Director of Photography*
Meredith C. Wilcox, *Director, Administration and Rights Clearance*

Staff for This Book

Caroline Hickey, *Project Editor*
Media Development Group, *Text Editors*
Sanaa Akkach, *Art Director*
Matt Propert, *Illustrations Editor*
Linda Makarov, *Designer*
Carl Mehler, *Director of Maps*
XNR Productions, Michael McNey, *Map Research and Production*
Sarah Alban, Anne Alexander, Danielle Fisher, Margaret Krauss, Jane Plegge, Nicholas Rosenbach, *Contributors*
Michael O'Connor, *Associate Managing Editor*
Judith Klein, *Production Editor*
Michael Horenstein, *Production Manager*
Galen Young, *Rights Clearance Specialist*
Katie Olsen, *Production Design Assistant*

Manufacturing and Quality Management

Phillip L. Schlosser, *Senior Vice President*
Chris Brown, *Vice President, NG Book Manufacturing*
George Bounelis, *Vice President, Production Services*
Nicole Elliott, *Manager*
Rachel Faulise, *Manager*
Robert L. Barr, *Manager*

CELEBRATING 125 YEARS

The National Geographic Society is one of the world's largest nonprofit scientific and educational organizations. Founded in 1888 to "increase and diffuse geographic knowledge," the Society works to inspire people to care about the planet. National Geographic reflects the world through its magazines, television programs, films, music and radio, books, DVDs, maps, exhibitions, live events, school publishing programs, interactive media and merchandise. *National Geographic* magazine, the Society's official journal, published in English and 33 local-language editions, is read by more than 60 million people each month. The National Geographic Channel reaches 435 million households in 37 languages in 173 countries. National Geographic Digital Media receives more than 19 million visitors a month. National Geographic has funded more than 10,000 scientific research, conservation and exploration projects and supports an education program promoting geography literacy. For more information, visit www.nationalgeographic.com.

For more information, please call 1-800-NGS LINE (647-5463) or write to the following address:

National Geographic Society
1145 17th Street N.W.
Washington, D.C. 20036-4688 U.S.A.

For information about special discounts for bulk purchases, please contact National Geographic Books Special Sales: ngspecsales@ngs.org

For rights or permissions inquiries, please contact National Geographic Books Subsidiary Rights: ngbookrights@ngs.org

Library of Congress Control Number: 2012953600

ISBN: 978-1-4262-1015-0 (trade)
ISBN: 978-1-4262-1106-5 (regular)
ISBN: 978-1-4262-1107-2 (deluxe)

Printed in the United States of America

13/QGT-LPH/1

The information in this book has been carefully checked and to the best of our knowledge is accurate. However, details are subject to change, and the National Geographic Society cannot be responsible for such changes, or for errors or omissions.